Learning And Mastering Tableau For Work In 2023

Learning And Mastering Tableau For Work In 2023
First Edition

The information contained in this book is for general information and educational purposes only. While every effort has been made to ensure the accuracy of the information and data, errors may exist and the information may not be complete or current. No representation is made as to the accuracy or completeness of the information, and the information is provided "as is" without warranty of any kind, either express or implied. The user of this information is solely responsible for verifying the accuracy of the information and using it at their own risk. The publisher and authors of this book shall not be liable for any errors or omissions, or for any actions taken in reliance on the information contained herein.

Contents

Chapter 1
Introduction And Fundamentals Of Tableau

Introduction

Tableau is a data visualization and business intelligence tool that allows users to connect to, visualize, and analyze data using a variety of charts, graphs, people with little or no technical background to create professional-quality data visualizations.

With Tableau Desktop, you can:

- Connect to a wide range of data sources, including Excel, CSV, and databases like MySQL, Oracle, and SQL Server.
- Clean and prepare your data using features like data blending, calculation fields, and data hierarchies.
- Create a variety of charts and graphs, including bar charts, line graphs, scatter plots, and pie charts.
- Use interactive filters, parameters, and dashboard actions to explore and analyze your data in more depth.
- Customize the look and feel of your dashboards and reports using themes, colors, and layout options.
- Publish and share your dashboards and reports with colleagues, clients, and stakeholders using Tableau Server or Tableau Online.

Overall, Tableau Desktop is a powerful and flexible tool for exploring and understanding your data, and can be used by anyone from data analysts and business intelligence professionals to students and researchers.

Get the sample data

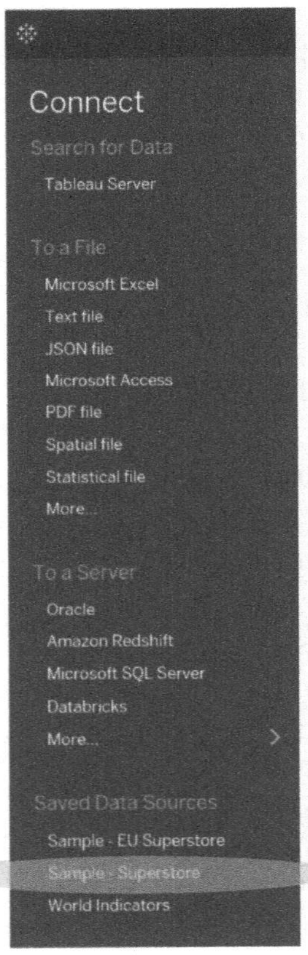

With this book, we aim introduce and master Tableau in order excel in whichever work capacity you find yourself. All the examples and visualizations used in the ensuing chapters refer to the Sample - Superstore data provided by Tableau.

Upon open of Tableau, you will find on the bottom lefthand side the option to open a Saved Data Source.

- Sample – EU Superstore
- Sample – Superstore
- World Indicators

We will be using the second saved data source; "Sample – Superstore" throughout this book. It is highly recommended that you also use this dataset as you follow along. Tableau, being a BI tool, is best learnt by actually **DOING**, testing, playing around and being curious as there are various ways to get a desired result.

Connect to your data

The first step is to connect to the data you want to explore.

We will be using the sample data previously mentioned. But in real case scenarios; this is the point where you choose the source of your data which could be anything from an Excel spreadsheet to a data hosted on a server or in the cloud. We will go further into details on how to connect to a data source further down in the book.

Start Page

The start page in Tableau Desktop is a central location from which you can do one of three things:

1. Connect to your data
2. Open your most recently used workbooks, and
3. Discover and explore content produced by the Tableau community.[4]

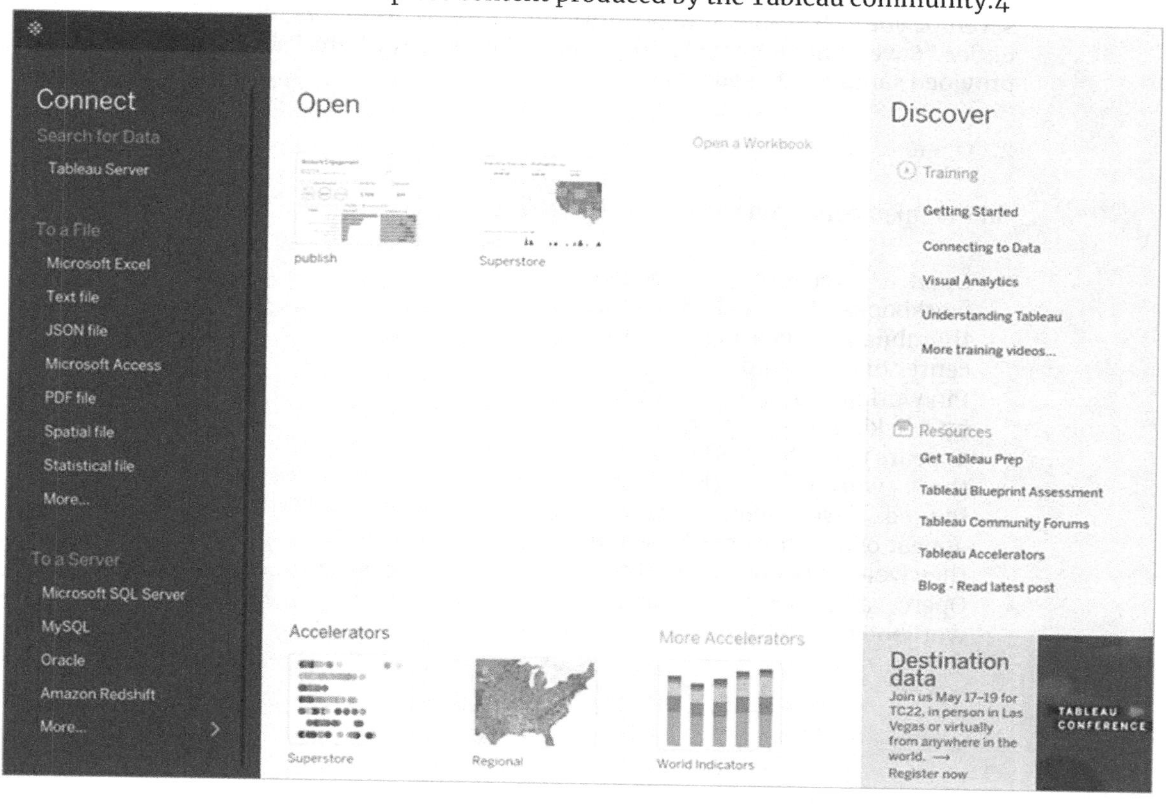

1. Connect

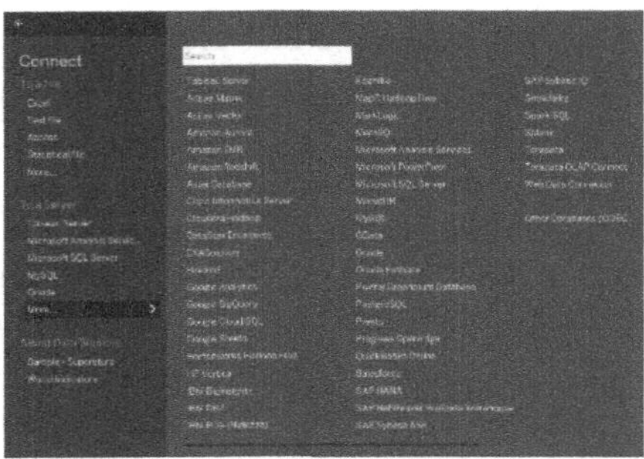

Connect as the name implies serves to connect you to a data source. This source can be from a "static" file or a server.

There are various types of files you can connect to, from Microsoft Excel files, text files, Access files, Tableau extract files, to statistical files, such as SAS, SPSS and R.

When connecting to a Server, you have a multitude of options; connecting to data stored in databases like Microsoft SQL Server or Oracle. You will find the full list of servers when clicking on the "More..." link as pictured above.

You can also connect to and open data sources that you have previously saved to your My Tableau Repository directory. This will be displayed under "Saved Data Sources". This is also the section where Tableau has provided sample data sources.

2. Open

On the Open pane, you can:

- Open recently opened workbooks by click on the thumbnail appearing in the center of the "window".
- Pin workbooks to the start page by clicking the pin icon that appears in the top-left corner of the workbook thumbnail. Pinned workbooks always appear on the start page, even if they weren't opened recently.
- Open and explore sample workbooks.

3. Discover

The third section is the discover pane. It provides you with various links, tips and resources to help on your learning journey. You have the option to see popular views in Tableau Public, read blog posts and news about Tableau as well as find training videos and tutorials to help you get started.

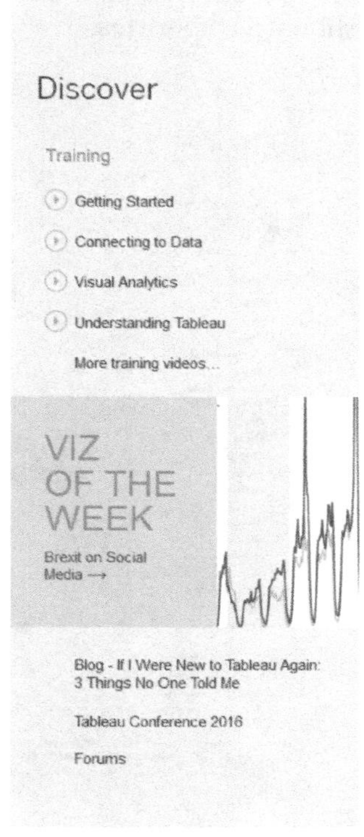

The Tableau Workspace

The Tableau workspace consists of menus, a toolbar, the Data pane, cards and shelves, and one or more sheets. Sheets can be worksheets, dashboards or stories.

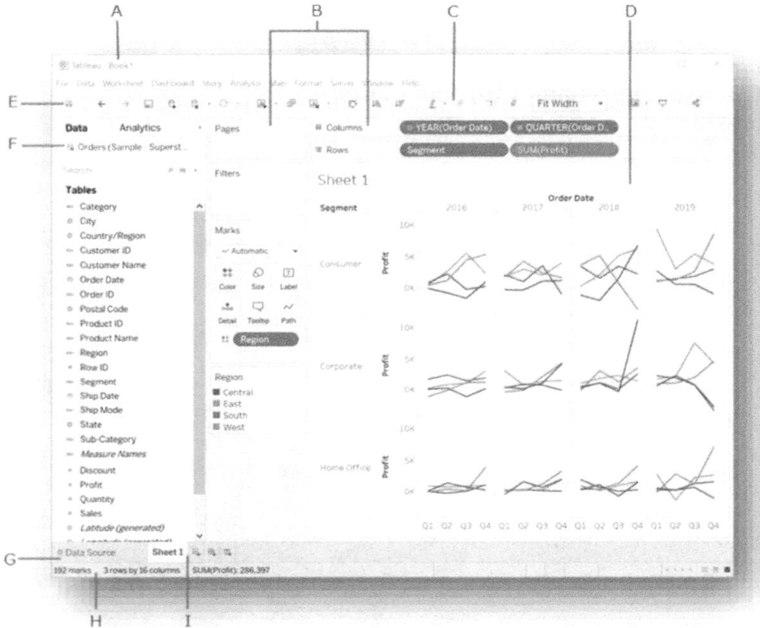

A. Workbook name. A workbook contains sheets. A sheet can be a worksheet, a dashboard, or a story.

B. Cards and shelves - Drag fields to the cards and shelves in the workspace to add data to your view.

C. Toolbar – Use the toolbar to access commands and analysis and navigation tools.

D. View - This is the canvas in the workspace where you create a visualization (also referred to as a "viz").

E. Click this icon to go to the Start page, where you can connect to data.

F. Side Bar - In a worksheet, the side bar area contains the **Data pane** and the **Analytics pane**.

G. Click this tab to go to the Data Source page and view your data.

H. Status bar - Displays information about the current view.

I. Sheet tabs - Tabs represent each sheet in your workbook. This can include worksheets, dashboards and stories.

Data Source Page

If you want to make changes to the Tableau data source, you can do that by going to the data source page. Tableau takes you to the data source page after you establish the initial connection to your data. You can also access the data source page by clicking the Data Source tab from any location in the workbook.

Although the look of the page and the options available vary depending on the type of data that you are connected to, the data source page generally consists of four main areas: left pane, canvas, data grid, and metadata grid.

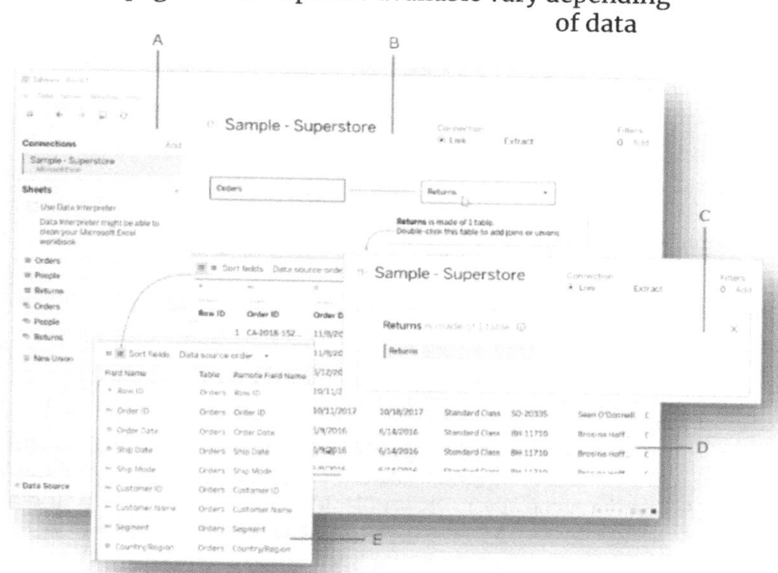

- The left pane [A] displays the connected data source and other details about your data. You can also use the left pane to add more connections to the data source.
- The canvas [B] opens with the logical layer, where you can create relationships between logical tables.
- The physical layer [C] can be accessed by double-clicking a table in the logical layer. This is also where you can add joins and unions between tables.
- The data grid [D] displays the first 1,000 rows of the data contained in the Tableau data source. You can also use the data grid to make general modifications to the Tableau data source like sorting or hiding fields; renaming fields or resetting field names; creating calculations; changing the column or row sort; or adding aliases.
- The Metadata grid [E] displays the fields in your data source as rows so that you can quickly examine the structure of your Tableau data

source and perform routine management tasks, such as renaming fields or hiding multiple fields at once.

Status Bar Information

The status bar is located at the bottom of the Tableau workspace. It displays descriptions of menu items as well as information about the current view. For example, the status bar below shows that the view has 143 marks shown in 3 rows and 12 columns. It also shows that the SUM(Sales) for all the marks in the view is $2,297,201.

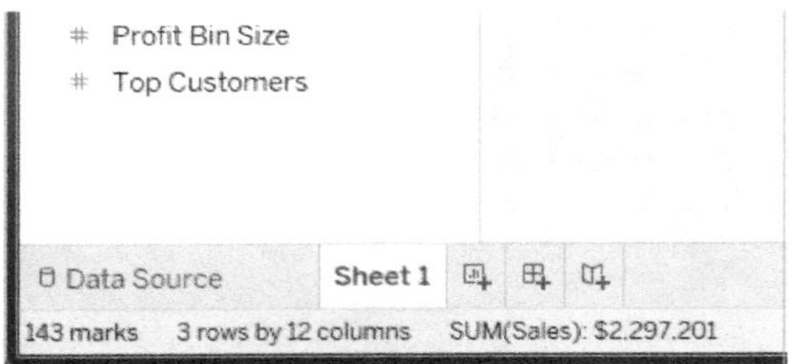

You can hide the status bar by selecting **Window** > **Show Status Bar**.

Areas of the Data pane

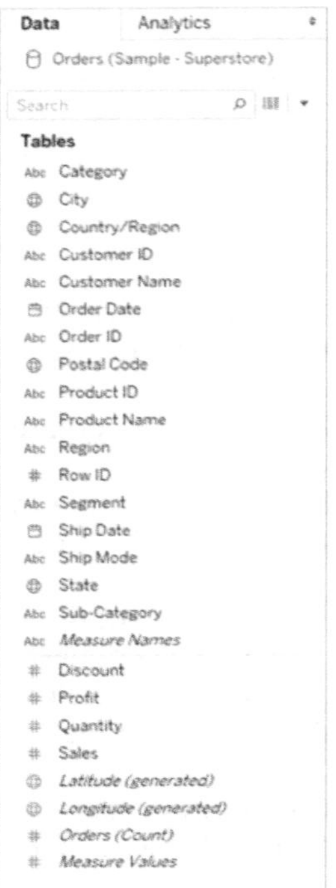

After you connect to your data and set up the data source with Tableau, the data source connections and fields appear on the left side of the workbook in the Data pane.

You build visualizations by adding fields from the Data pane to the view.

Fields can be organized by table (**Group by Data Source Table**) or folder (**Group by Folder**). Dimensions are displayed above the grey line, and measures below the grey line for each table or folder. In some cases, a table or folder might contain only dimensions, or only measures to start with.

- Calculated fields are listed with their originating field, if all of their input fields come from the same table.

- Sets are listed with the table with their originating field.

- Parameters are global to the workbook and are displayed in the Parameters area.

- Fields that don't belong to a specific table are displayed in the general area below the tables. These include: aggregated calculations, calculations that use fields from multiple tables, Measure Names and Measure Values.

Below the data source connections in the **Data** pane are the fields that are available in the currently selected data source. You can toggle between the **Data** and **Analytics** panes in a worksheet.

The Data pane includes:

- **Dimension fields** – Fields that contain qualitative values (such as names, dates or geographical data). You can use dimensions to categorize, segment, and reveal the details in your data. Dimensions affect the level of detail in the view. Examples of dimensions include dates, customer names and customer segments.

- **Measure fields** – Fields that contain numeric, quantitative values can be measured. You can apply calculations to them and aggregate them. When you drag a measure into the view, Tableau applies an aggregation to that measure (by default). Examples of measures: sales, profit, number of employees, temperature, frequency.

- **Calculated fields** – If your underlying data doesn't include all of the fields you need to answer your questions, you can create new fields in Tableau using calculations and then save them as part of your data source. These fields are called calculated fields.

- **Sets** – Subsets of data that you define. Sets are custom fields based on existing dimensions and criteria that you specify.

- **Parameters** – Values that can be used as placeholders in formulas, or replace constant values in calculated fields and filters.

By default the field names defined in the data source are displayed in the Data pane. You can rename fields and member names, create hierarchies and organize the fields into groups and folders.

Chapter 2
Building Your First Visual Element In Tableau

Build the view

A **view** is a visualization or viz that you create in Tableau. A viz might be a chart, a graph, a map, a plot or even a text table.

Every view that you build in Tableau should start with a question. What do you want to know?

Every time you drag a field into the view or onto a shelf, you are asking a question about the data. The question will vary depending on where you drag various fields, the types of fields, and the order in which you drag fields into the view.

For every question you ask, the view changes to represent the answer visually - with marks (shapes, text, hierarchies, table structures, axes, color).

Different ways to start building a view

When you build a view, you add fields from the **Data** pane. You can do this in different ways;

- Drag fields from the **Data** pane and drop them onto the cards and shelves that are part of every Tableau worksheet.
- Double-click one or more fields in the **Data** pane.
- Select one or more fields in the **Data** pane and then choose a chart type from **Show Me**, which identifies the chart types that are appropriate for the fields you selected.

- Drop a field on the **Drop field here** grid, to start creating a view from a tabular perspective.

As you start exploring data in Tableau, you will find there are many ways to build a view. Tableau is extremely flexible, and also very forgiving. As you build a view, if you ever take a path that isn't answering your question, you can always undo to a previous point in your exploration.

- To undo or redo, click undo ← or redo → on the toolbar.

You can undo all the way back to the last time you opened the workbook. You can undo or redo an unlimited number of times.

Build a view from scratch

The following steps will show how to build a basic view that shows year-by-year profit. Now, this is going to be a "do as I do" exercise. Don't worry if you don't understand all of it straight away. We will go over all the concepts at a later stage.

The most important thing at this point is that we want to hit the ground running by having a view created right off the bat and making you do the tableau manipulations to get you going.

1. From the **Dimensions** area in the **Data** pane, drag the **Order Date** field to the **Columns** shelf. You might need to expand the Order hierarchy to see Order Date.
When you drag a field over a shelf, a plus sign indicates that the shelf can accept the field.

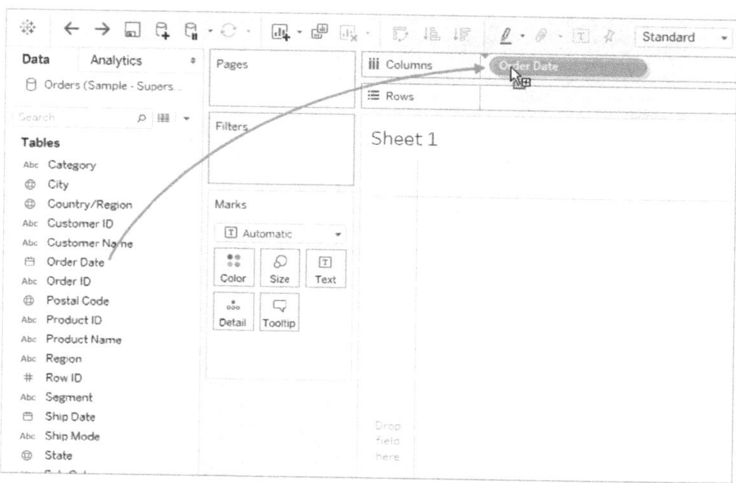

The resulting table has four columns and one row. Each column header represents a member of the Order Date field (the default date level is YEAR). Each cell contains an 'Abc' label, which indicates that the current mark type for this view is text.

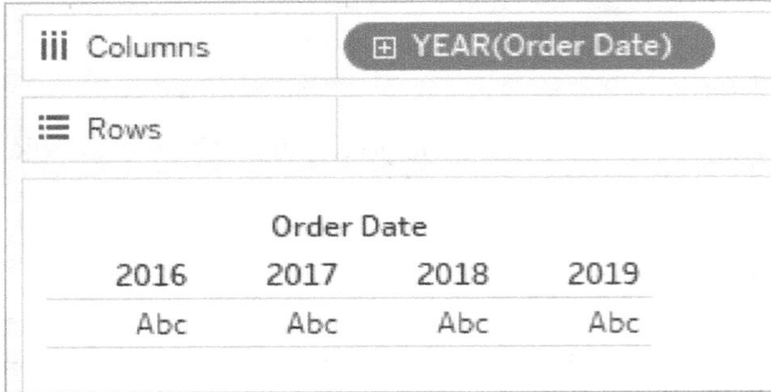

The default date level is determined by the highest level that contains more than one distinct value (for example, multiple years and multiple months). That means that if [Order Date] contained data for only one year but had multiple months, the default level would be month. You can change the date level using the field menu.

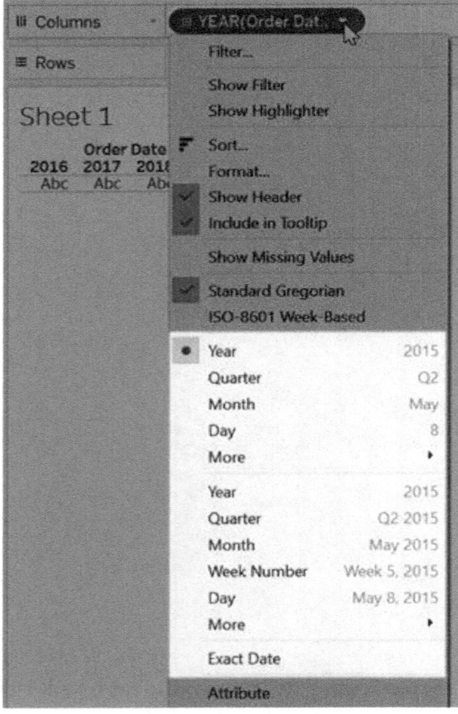

2. From the **Data** pane, drag the **Profit** field to the **Rows** shelf.

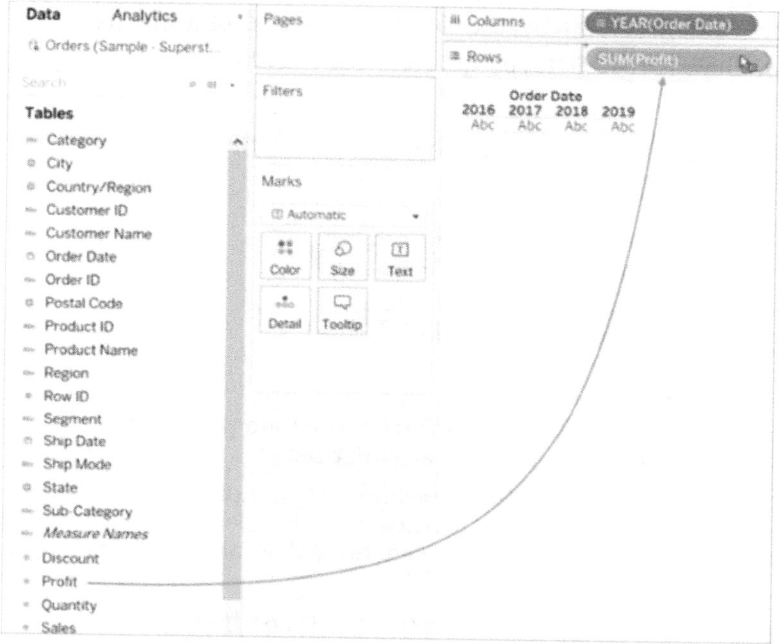

Tableau transforms the table into a line chart and creates a vertical axis (along the left side) for the measure.

A line chart is a great way to compare data over time and identify trends effectively.

This line chart shows profit over time. Each point along the line shows the sum of profit for the corresponding year.

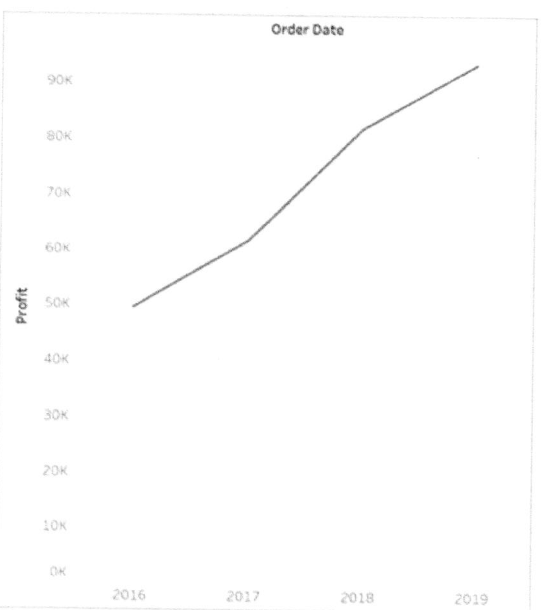

The next step is to drill a little deeper into the time dimension.

Drill into the data

You can modify the view to show quarters in addition to years. As you drill down into the hierarchy, the view changes to become a nested table.

You can show **[Order Date]** by quarters using either of the following methods:

- Click the plus button ⊞ on the left side of the field **YEAR(Order Date)** field on Columns.

- Drag the Order Date field (again) from the Data pane and drop it on the Columns shelf to the right of Year(Order Date).

The new dimension divides the view into separate panes for each year. Each pane, in turn, has columns for quarters. This view is called a **nested table** because it displays multiple headers, with quarters nested within years.

Increase the level of detail with small multiples

You can modify the nested table view to add customer segment. This will create a small multiples view.

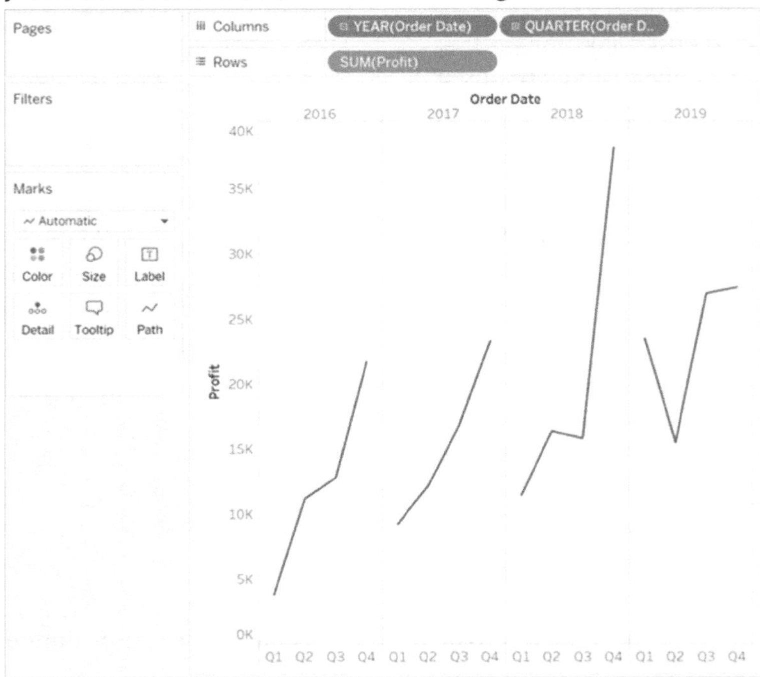

Drag the **Segment** dimension from the **Data** pane. Drop it just to the left of **SUM(Profit)** on Rows.

The field is added to the Rows shelf and row headers are created. Each header represents a member of the Segment field.

You could achieve the same result by dropping **Segment** just to the left of the Profit axis in the view (show below). Tableau often supports multiple ways to add fields to the view.

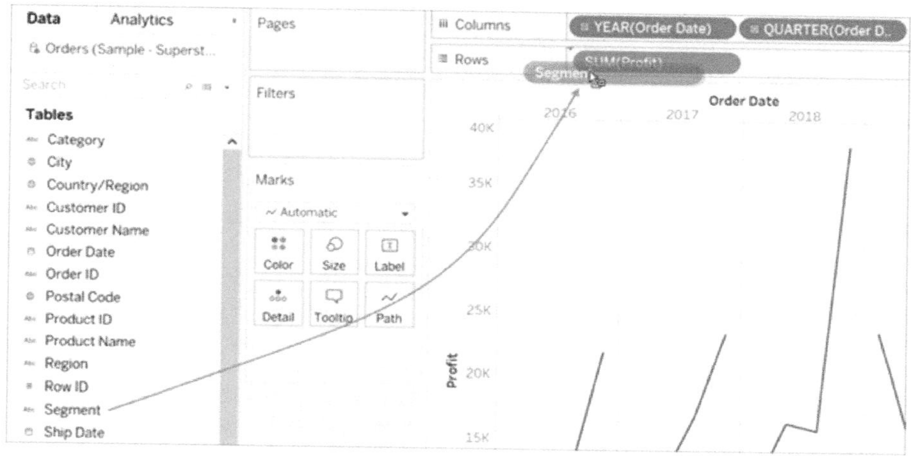

Note: Tableau does not allow you to place a dimension to the right of a measure on either the Rows or Columns shelves because that visual structure would not make sense in the view.

The new dimension divides the view into 12 panes, one for each combination of year and segment. This view is a more complex example of a nested table. Any view that contains this sort of grid of individual charts is referred to as a small multiples view.

At this point you probably don't want to make the view any more granular; in fact, you may want to simplify the view by removing (that is, filtering) some data.

Filter the view to focus your exploration

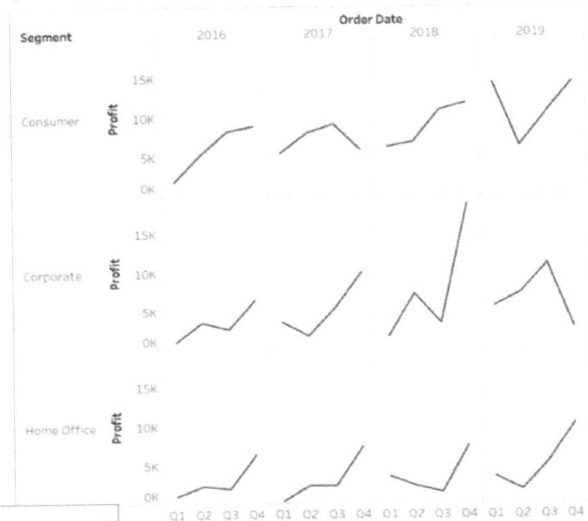

You can decide to focus your exploration by only showing a subset of the data, such as modifying the view to show only data for orders in 2012 and 2013.

1. Drag the **Order Date** measure from the **Data** pane and drop it on the **Filters** shelf.

Filter Field [Order Date]

How do you want to filter on [Order Date]?

Relative Date
Range of Dates
Years
Quarters
Months
Days
Week numbers
Weekdays
Month / Year
Month / Day / Year
Individual Dates
Count
Count (Distinct)
Minimum
Maximum
Attribute

Next > Cancel

2. In the Filter Field dialog box, choose the date level you want to filter on – **Years**. Then click **Next**.
3. In the next pane, clear any two years that you do not want to include in the view.
4. When you are finished, click **OK**.

The view updates to only show data rows where Order Date is 2018 or 2019. Tableau can now allocate more space to the data that interests you.

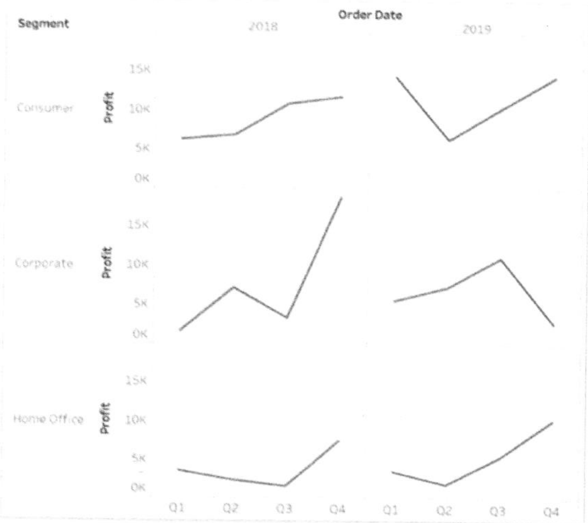

Next, you will increase the detail in your data exploration by dragging a field to Color on the Marks card.

Use the Marks card to add depth to your analysis

You can modify the view to color the marks based on the region.

5. Drag the **Region** dimension from the **Data** pane and drop it on **Color**.

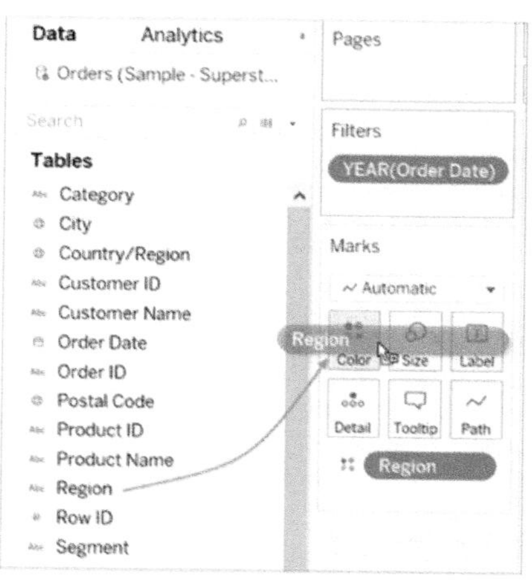

Placing a dimension on **Color** separates the marks according to the members in the dimension, and assigns a unique color to each member. The color legend displays each member name and its associated color.

Each pane now has four lines, one for each region. The viz is now showing profit data summarized the Region level of detail.

This view now shows profit for each customer segment and region for 2012 and 2013.

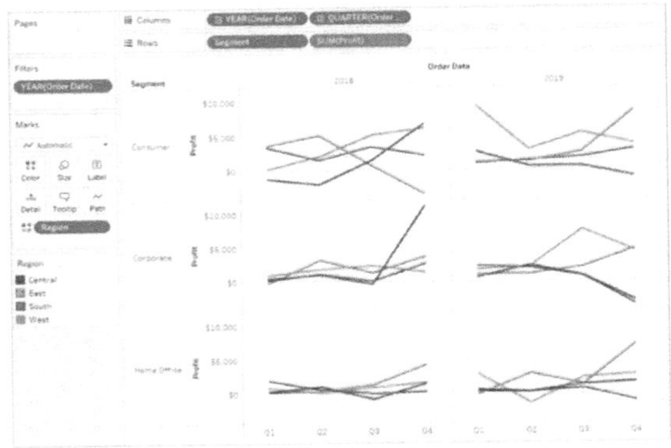

Chapter 3
Tableau Elements

The View area

Data views are displayed in a table on every worksheet. A table is a collection of rows and columns, and consists of the following components: Headers, Axes, Panes, Cells and Marks. In addition to these, you can choose to show or hide Titles, Captions, Field Labels and Legends.

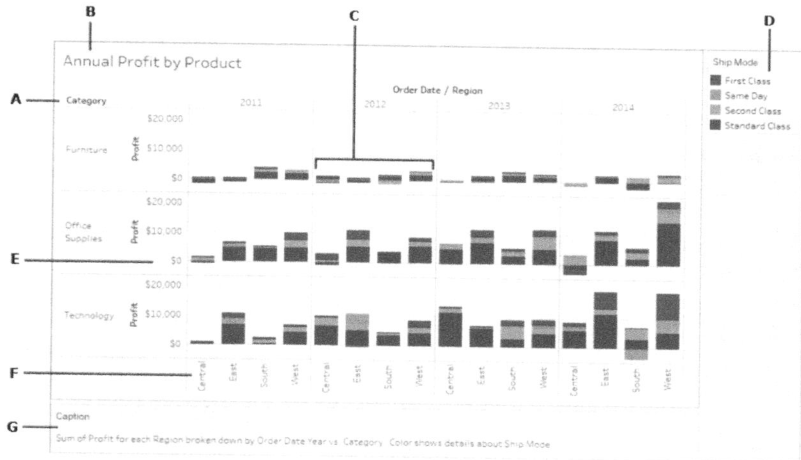

A. Field Labels - The label of a discrete field added to the row or column shelf that describes the members of that field. For example, Category is a discrete field that contains three members; Furniture, Office Supplies and Technology.

B. Titles - The name that you give your worksheet, dashboard, or story. Titles display automatically for worksheets and stories and you can turn them on to display them in your dashboards.

C. Marks - The data that represents the intersection of the fields (dimensions and measures) included in your view. Marks can be represented using lines, bars, shapes, maps and so on.

D. Legends - A key that describes how the data is encoded in your view. For example if you use shapes or colors in your view, the legend describes what each shape or color represents.

E. Axes - Created when you add a measure (fields that contain quantitative, numerical information) to the view. By default, Tableau generates a continuous axis for this data.

F. Headers - The member name of a field.

G. Captions - Text that describes the data in the view. Captions can be automatically generated and can be toggled on and off.

Headers

Headers are created when you place a dimension or discrete field on the **Rows** shelf or the **Columns** shelves. The headers show the member names of each field on the shelves. For example, in the view below the column headers show the members of the **Order Date** field and the row headers show the members of the **Sub-Category** field.

You can show and hide row and column headers at anytime.

Sheet 1

	Order Date			
Sub-Category	2012	2013	2014	2015
Accessories	$25,014	$40,524	$41,896	$59,946
Appliances	$15,314	$23,241	$26,050	$42,927
Art	$6,058	$6,237	$5,910	$8,914
Binders	$43,488	$37,453	$49,485	$72,986
Bookcases	$20,037	$38,544	$26,275	$30,024
Chairs	$77,242	$71,735	$83,919	$95,554
Copiers	$10,850	$26,179	$49,599	$62,899
Envelopes	$3,856	$4,512	$4,730	$3,379
Fasteners	$661	$545	$960	$858
Furnishings	$13,826	$21,090	$27,874	$28,915
Labels	$2,841	$2,956	$2,827	$3,861
Machines	$62,023	$27,764	$55,907	$43,545
Paper	$14,835	$15,288	$20,638	$27,718
Phones	$77,391	$68,314	$78,660	$105,643
Storage	$50,329	$45,048	$58,632	$69,834
Supplies	$14,394	$1,952	$14,278	$16,049
Tables	$46,088	$39,150	$60,833	$60,894

To hide headers:

- Right-click (control-click on Mac) the headers in the view and select **Show Header**.

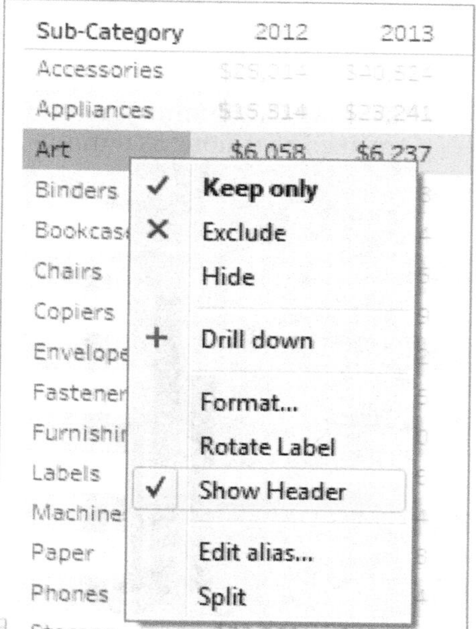

To show headers:

- Select the field in the view whose headers you want to show and select **Show Header** on the field menu.

Hiding headers can be useful when you are working with multiple measures.

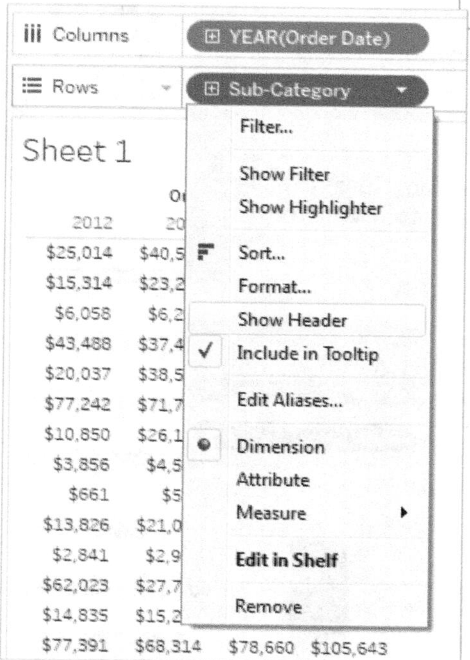

Axes

Axes are created when you place a measure or continuous field on the **Rows** or **Columns** shelves. By default, the values of the measure field are displayed along a continuous axis.

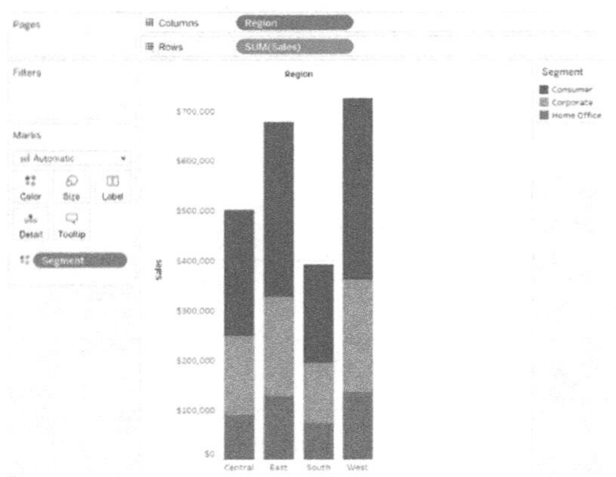

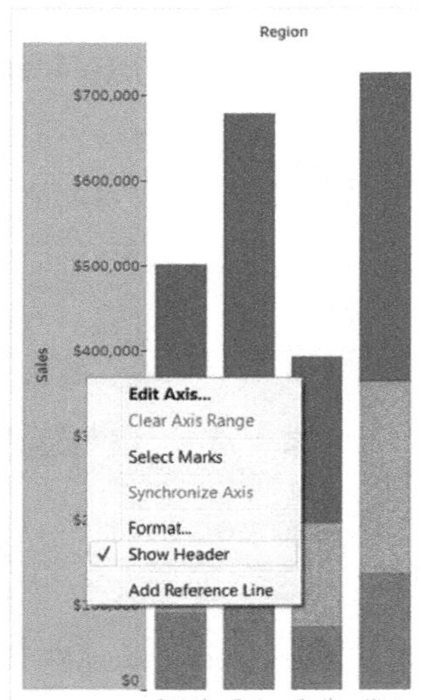

You can show and hide axes at any time.

To hide axes:

- Right-click (control-click on Mac) the axis in the view and select **Show Header** to clear the check mark next to this option.

To show axes:

- Right-click (control-click on Mac) the measure in the view whose axis you want to show and select **Show Header** on the field menu.

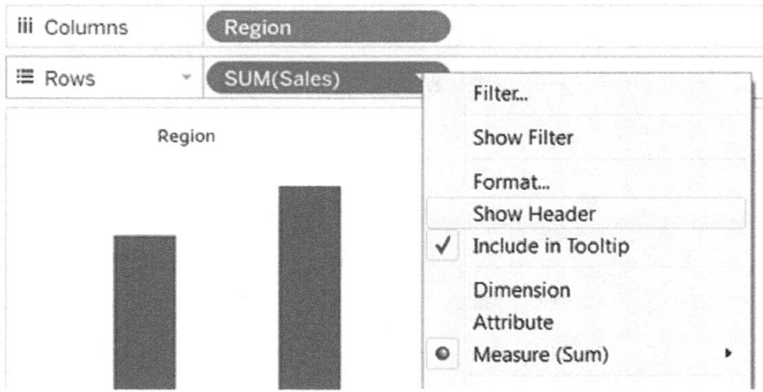

Panes

A pane is defined by the intersection of fields on the rows and columns shelves.

In a table calculation, this is seen as one or more cells that belong to the same field, which are computed down or across according to the calculation, as in the example below:

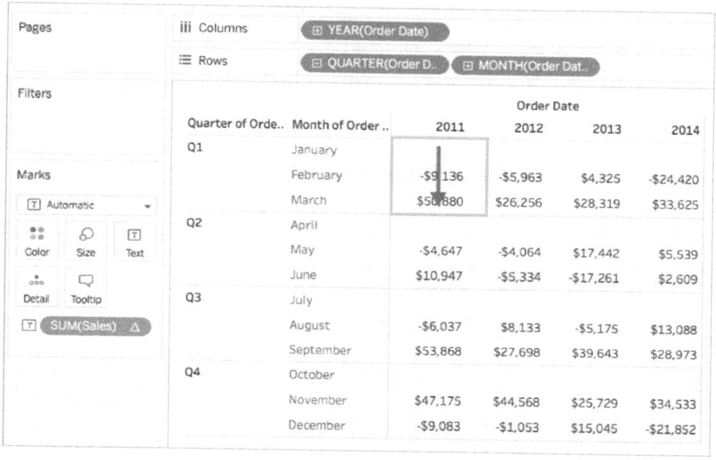

Pages | Columns: YEAR(Order Date) | Rows: QUARTER(Order D.. MONTH(Order Dat..
Filters
Marks: Automatic | Color | Size | Text | Detail | Tooltip | SUM(Sales) Δ

Quarter of Orde..	Month of Order ..	Order Date 2011	2012	2013	2014
Q1	January				
	February	-$9,136	-$5,963	$4,325	-$24,420
	March	$50,880	$26,256	$28,319	$33,625
Q2	April				
	May	-$4,647	-$4,064	$17,442	$5,539
	June	$10,947	-$5,334	-$17,261	$2,609
Q3	July				
	August	-$6,037	$8,133	-$5,175	$13,088
	September	$53,868	$27,698	$39,643	$28,973
Q4	October				
	November	$47,175	$44,568	$25,729	$34,533
	December	-$9,083	-$1,053	$15,045	-$21,852

Cells

Cells are the basic components of any table you can create in Tableau, defined by the intersection of a row and a column. For example, in a text table, a cell is where the text is displayed, as shown in the view.

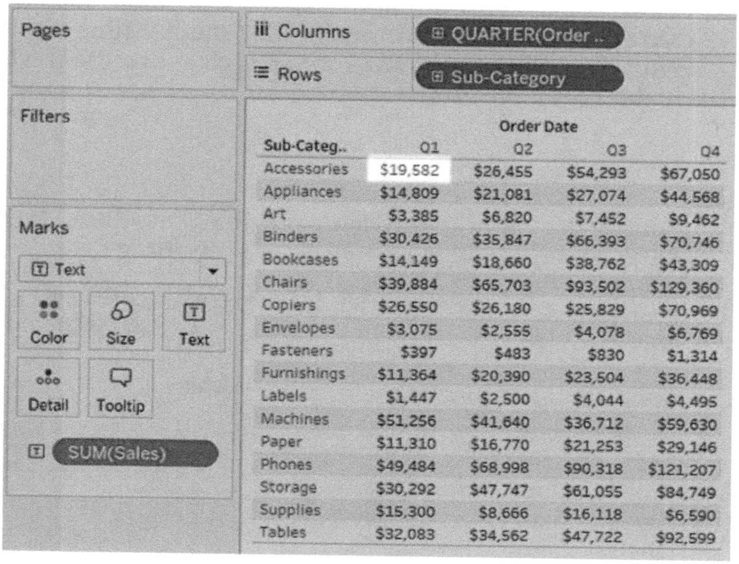

Pages | Columns: QUARTER(Order .. | Rows: Sub-Category
Filters
Marks: Text | Color | Size | Text | Detail | Tooltip | SUM(Sales)

Sub-Categ..	Order Date Q1	Q2	Q3	Q4
Accessories	$19,582	$26,455	$54,293	$67,050
Appliances	$14,809	$21,081	$27,074	$44,568
Art	$3,385	$6,820	$7,452	$9,462
Binders	$30,426	$35,847	$66,393	$70,746
Bookcases	$14,149	$18,660	$38,762	$43,309
Chairs	$39,884	$65,703	$93,502	$129,360
Copiers	$26,550	$26,180	$25,829	$70,969
Envelopes	$3,075	$2,555	$4,078	$6,769
Fasteners	$397	$483	$830	$1,314
Furnishings	$11,364	$20,390	$23,504	$36,448
Labels	$1,447	$2,500	$4,044	$4,495
Machines	$51,256	$41,640	$36,712	$59,630
Paper	$11,310	$16,770	$21,253	$29,146
Phones	$49,484	$68,998	$90,318	$121,207
Storage	$30,292	$47,747	$61,055	$84,749
Supplies	$15,300	$8,666	$16,118	$6,590
Tables	$32,083	$34,562	$47,722	$92,599

Marks

When you drag fields to the view, the data are displayed using marks. Each mark represents the intersection of all of the dimensions in the view.

Columns: YEAR(Order Date)
Rows: Region

	Order Date			
Region	**2011**	**2012**	**2013**	**2014**
Central	Abc	Abc	Abc	Abc
East	Abc	Abc	Abc	Abc
South	Abc	Abc	Abc	Abc
West	Abc	Abc	Abc	Abc

For example, in a view with **Region** and **Year** dimensions, there is a mark for every combination of those two dimensions (East 2011, East 2012, West 2011, West 2012, etc.). In this case, the mark type is set to Text, so the **Abc** represents the location where the value for the text mark will appear – once a measure such as **Sales** is added to the view.

Marks can be displayed in many different ways including lines, shapes, bars, maps and so on. You can show additional information about the data using mark properties such as color, size, shape, labels, etc. The type of mark you use and the mark properties are controlled by the Marks card. Drag fields to the Marks card to show more data. For example, the same view above is shown again below but this time with **Profit** on Color. With this additional information, it is clear that the West region had the highest profit in 2014.

Control the marks in the view using the Marks card. Use the drop-down menu to specify the type of mark to show. Drag fields to the Marks card and use the drop-down controls to add more information to the view and control the color, shape, size, labels and number of marks in the view.

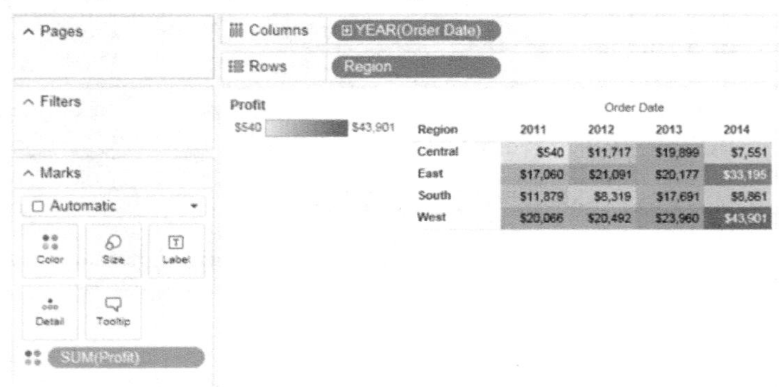

Tooltips

Tooltips are additional data details that display when you hover over one or more marks in the view. When you select one or more marks and hover, tooltips also include options to filter marks (exclude or keep only), display marks that have the same values, create groups, create sets or display the underlying data.

Tooltip command buttons for exploring data in a viz

The top of the tooltip lists commands for filtering data, creating a group, sorting the selection and view the underlying data. For example, you can use the tooltip to quickly remove an outlier in a scatter plot. Each of the commands are described below.

To see tooltip commands, hover over a mark and then keep the cursor still. The

- **Keep Only** - creates a filter that removes all other data.
- **Exclude** - creates a filter that removes the selected data.
- **Group Members** - creates a group based on the selection. If the selection contains multiple dimensions, you can group on one dimension or all dimensions.
- **Create Set** (Tableau Desktop only) - creates a new set containing the selected members. You can create a new set or add members to an existing set.

- **View Data** - opens a window displaying the data. You can view the summarised data or the underlying data.

These commands are visible by default. You can disable the commands in the **Edit Tooltip** dialog box by deselecting **Include command buttons**. Doing so will also hide the aggregation summary if multiple marks are selected.

Disable tooltip commands

If you don't want users to be able to access tooltip commands, you can disable them.

1. Click Tooltip on the Marks card or select **Worksheet** >**Tooltip**.

2. In the Edit Tooltip dialog box, clear the **Include command buttons** check box.

Tooltip settings apply to the active worksheet and can be different for each sheet in the workbook.

Titles

You can show titles on any worksheet, dashboard or story. For worksheets and stories, a title is displayed by default, but you can remove it. For dashboards, you can add a title. By default, the title is the name of the sheet, but you can edit the title to change the text and include dynamic values such as page number and sheet name.

Show and hide titles in worksheets

Titles are shown by default for worksheets and are included as part of the worksheet, shown at the top of the view. You can move the title to the sides or the bottom of the view. However, when you move the title from the top of the view, it becomes a **Title** card and displays like any other card in the view.

Note: If you move a title from the top position and then hide it; when you show the title again, it appears back at the top of the worksheet in its default position.

To show or hide titles in a worksheet

- From the toolbar menu, click **Worksheet** > **Show Title.**

- On the toolbar, click the drop-down arrow on the **Show/Hide Cards** button and select **Title** from the context menu.

Toggle the check mark on or off to show or hide the title.

Show and hide titles in dashboards

You can turn on titles for dashboards. The title appears as part of the dashboard.

To show or hide titles on a dashboard, from the toolbar menu, select **Dashboard** > **Show Title**.

When you add worksheets to the dashboard, the title of the worksheet automatically shows, even if you turned off the title on the worksheet itself. To turn off the title for the worksheet on the dashboard, do the following steps:

1. In the dashboard, select the worksheet to highlight it.

2. In the top right corner of the highlighted worksheet, click the drop-down arrow and select **Title** in the context menu to clear the check mark.

Captions

All views can have a caption that is either automatically generated or manually created. The caption is displayed on the Caption card.

To show a caption in a worksheet, select it on the **Show/Hide Cards** toolbar menu or select **Worksheet** > **Show Caption**.

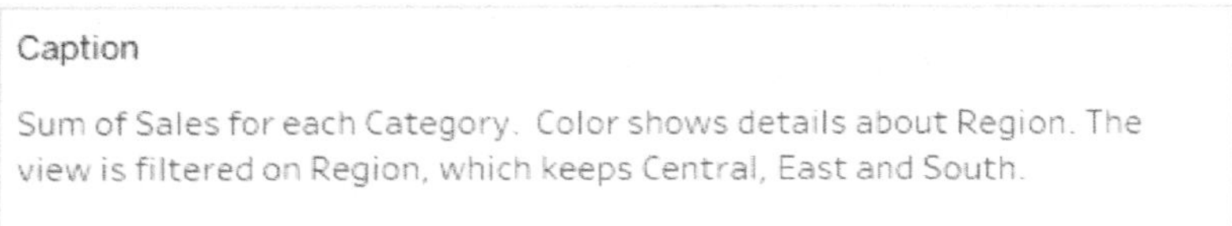

The caption is automatically generated by default.

To edit the caption, double-click the Caption area in the view. In the **Edit Caption** dialog box, you can use change the font, size, color, and alignment and style.

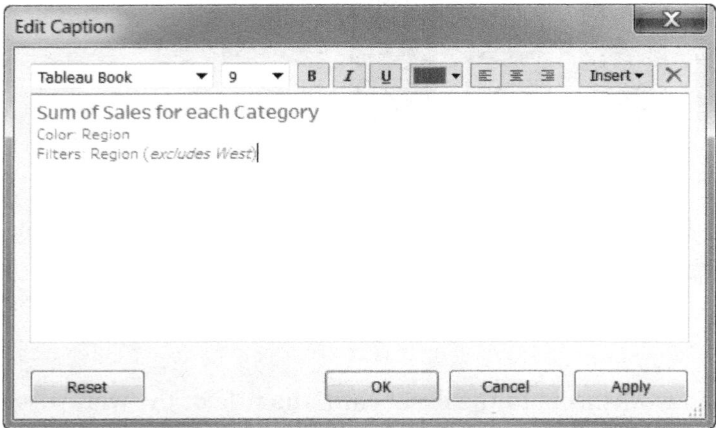

Click the **Insert** menu to add automatic text such as page number, sheet name, and field and parameter values.

The caption can optionally be included when printing, printing to PDF and publishing to Tableau Server. When you export the view as an image to another application like Microsoft PowerPoint, you can optionally include the caption.

Field Labels

Placing discrete fields on the rows and column shelves creates headers in the view that display the members of the field. For example, if you place a field containing products on the rows shelf, each product name is shown as row headers.

In addition to showing these headers, you can show field labels, which are labels for the headers. In this example, the rows are labeled **Category**, to indicate that the discrete category names are members of the **Category** field.

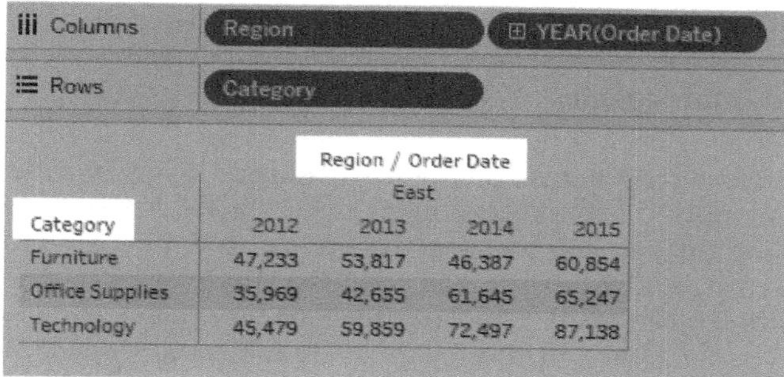

Legends

When you add fields to Color, Size and Shape on the Marks card, a legend displays to indicate how the view is encoded with relation to your data.

Color Legend

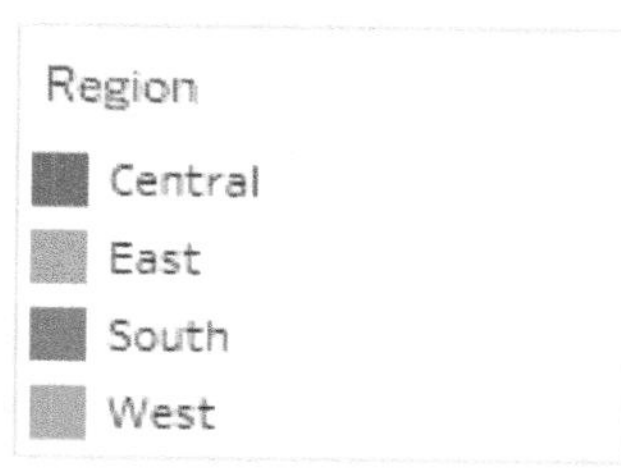

Size Legend

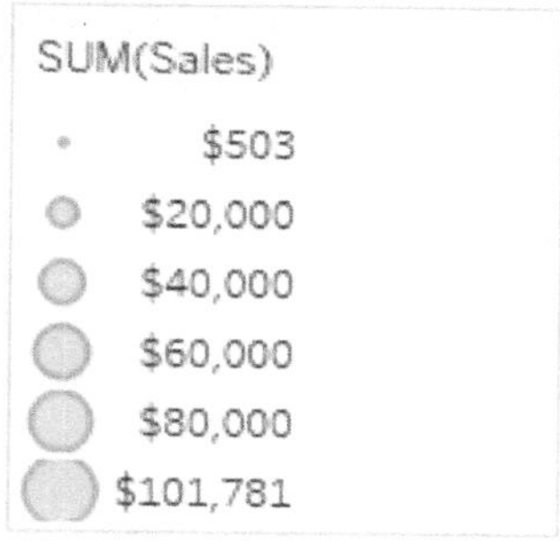

Shape Legend

Category
Furniture
Office Supplies
Technology

Not only do legends help you understand encodings, you can also use legends to sort, filter and highlight specific sets of data.

Measure values and color legends

If you include the **Measure Values** and **Measure names** fields in your views, you can create either a single combined color legend or separate color legends for your measures. If you drag the **Measure Values** field to Color on the Marks card, by default Tableau creates a single color legend that applies one color palette to all marks in the view.

Workbooks and Sheets

Tableau uses a workbook and sheet file structure, much like Microsoft Excel. A workbook contains sheets. A sheet can be a worksheet, a dashboard, or a story.

- A **worksheet** contains a single view along with shelves, cards, legends, and the Data and Analytics panes in its side bar.

- A **dashboard** is a collection of views from multiple worksheets. The Dashboard and Layout panes are available in its side bar.

- A **story** contains a sequence of worksheets or dashboards that work together to convey information. The Story and Layout panes are available in its side bar.

Create new worksheets, dashboards, or stories

There are several ways to create new sheets in a workbook, dashboard, or a story. You can create as many sheets in a workbook as you want.

To create a new worksheet, dashboard, or story, click the **New Worksheet**, **New Dashboard,** or **New Story** button at the bottom of the workbook.

To rename a new worksheet, dashboard, or story, right-click (Ctrl-click on a Mac) the tab and then select the **Rename** command.

More ways to create new worksheets

Create a new worksheet by doing one of the following:

- Select **Worksheet** > **New Worksheet**.
- Right-click any open tab in the workbook, and select **New Worksheet** from the menu.
- On the toolbar, click the drop-down arrow on the **New Worksheet** button and then select **New Worksheet**.
- Press Ctrl + M on your keyboard (Command-M on a Mac).

More ways to create new dashboards

Create a new dashboard by doing one of the following:

- Select **Dashboard** > **New Dashboard**.
- Click the **New Dashboard** button at the bottom of the workbook.

- Right-click on any open tab in the workbook, and select **New Dashboard** from the menu.

- On the toolbar, click the drop-down arrow on the New Worksheet button and then select **New Dashboard**.

More ways to create new stories

Create a new story by doing one of the following:

- Select **Story** > **New Story**.
- Click the **New Story** button at the bottom of the workbook.

- Right-click on any open tab in the workbook, and select **New Story** from the menu.
- On the toolbar, click the drop-down arrow on the **New Worksheet** button and then select **New Story**.

Undo, redo, or clear sheets

Every Tableau workbook contains a history of steps you have performed on the worksheets, dashboards, and stories in that workbook for the current work session.

To move backward through the history, click **Undo** on the toolbar or press Ctrl + s on your keyboard (Command-s on a Mac).

To move forward through the history, click **Redo** on the toolbar or press Ctrl + Y (Command-Y on a Mac) on your keyboard.

To remove all fields, formatting, sizing, axis ranges, filters, sorts, and context filters in the sheet, click **Clear Sheet** on the toolbar.

To clear specific aspects of the view, use the Clear Sheet drop-down menu.

Duplicate a sheet

When you want to use an existing sheet as a jumping off point for more exploration, you can duplicate that sheet. The duplicated sheet contains all of the same fields and settings as a starting point for new analysis.

Duplicate creates a new version of a worksheet, dashboard, or story you can modify without effecting the original sheet.

To duplicate the active sheet, right-click the sheet tab (control-click on Mac) and select **Duplicate**.

Note: When you duplicate a dashboard, a new version of the dashboard is created, but it still references the original worksheets that were used to create the dashboard.

Navigate and Organize Sheets

There are three ways to navigate and view the sheets in a workbook:

- Tabs at the bottom of the workbook
- In the filmstrip view
- In the sheet sorter view

The tabs are useful when you want to quickly navigate between a small number of sheets. If your workbook has a large number of sheets, you can use the sheet sorter to easily navigate them all.

You can also drag and drop to do the following:

- Reorder the sheets
- Create new sheets
- Duplicate or delete existing sheets from any of the views

Navigate with sheet tabs

Each sheet is represented as a tab along the bottom of the workbook. Select any tab to open the corresponding worksheet.

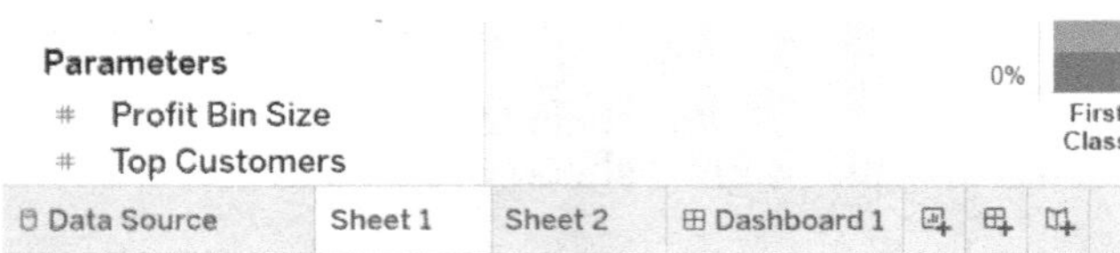

In the bottom right corner of the application window, there are several controls that you can use to advance through each sheet or quickly jump to the first or last sheet in the workbook. These controls are only available when there are too many sheet tabs to show across the bottom of the application window.

You can also navigate between sheets using the window menu or move through the multiple worksheets by pressing the left or right arrow keys on your keyboard.

To navigate through multiple worksheets, first select a worksheet tab at the bottom of the workbook.

Show thumbnails with the filmstrip

Similar to the sheet tabs, the filmstrip displays along the bottom of the workbook. However, instead of just sheet names, the filmstrip also shows a thumbnail image of each sheet. The filmstrip is useful when you are using Tableau to present your analysis and works well when you are working in Presentation mode.

Open the filmstrip by clicking the **Filmstrip** button on the status bar (bottom right corner) of the workbook. Just as for the tabs, select the thumbnail image for the sheet you want to open. You can right-click the images to specify commands that apply to each sheet.

Sheet commands

Use sheet commands to manage and organize your worksheets. For example you can create new sheets, duplicate sheets, copy formatting, apply color, or delete the sheet entirely.

You can access sheet commands on the right-click menu (Control-click on a Mac) in the worksheet, sheet sorter, or the filmstrip view. To apply commands to multiple sheets at once, press the Ctrl key (Shift key on a Mac), and then select the sheets.

To make it easier to identify and group sheets, you can assign a color to sheets. You can select from seven different colors. Selecting **None** clears the color.

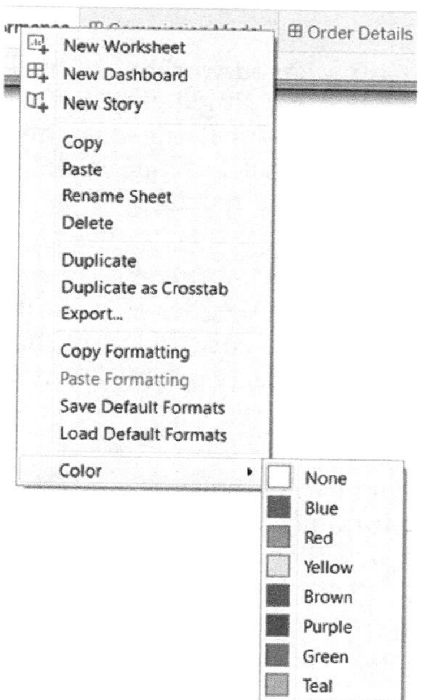

To assign a color to sheets, select one or more sheets, right-click the sheets (Control-click on the Mac), select **Color**, and then pick a color.

The color strip appears on the bottom of the tab or sheet.

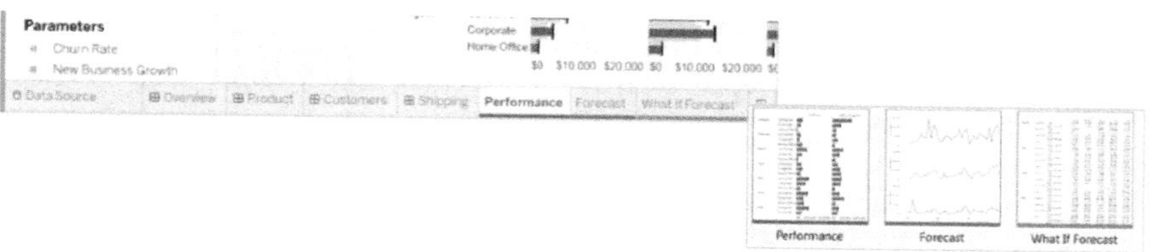

Tableau File Types and Folders

You can save your work using several different Tableau specific file types: workbooks, bookmarks, packaged data files, data extracts, and data connection files. Each of these file types is described below.

- **Workbooks (.twb)** – Tableau workbook files have the .twb file extension. Workbooks hold one or more worksheets, plus zero or more dashboards and stories.

- **Bookmarks (.tbm)** – Tableau bookmark files have the .tbm file extension. Bookmarks contain a single worksheet and are an easy way to quickly share your work.

- **Packaged Workbooks (.twbx)** – Tableau packaged workbooks have the .twbx file extension. A packaged workbook is a single zip file that contains a workbook along with any supporting local file data and background images. This format is the best way to package your work for sharing with others who don't have access to the original data.

- **Extract (.hyper or .tde)** – Depending on the version the extract was created in, Tableau extract files can have either the .hyper or .tde file extension. Extract files are a local copy of a subset or entire data set that you can use to share data with others, when you need to work offline, and improve performance.

- **Data Source (.tds)** – Tableau data source files have the .tds file extension. Data source files are shortcuts for quickly connecting to the original data that you use often. Data source files do not contain the actual data, but rather, the information necessary to connect to the actual data, as well as any modifications you've made on top of the actual data such as changing default properties, creating calculated fields, adding groups, and so on.

Packaged Data Source (.tdsx) – Tableau packaged data source files have the .tdsx file extension. A packaged data source is a zip file that contains the data source file (.tds) described above, as well as any local file data such as extract files (.hyper or .tde), text files, Excel files, Access files, and local cube files. Use this format to create a single file that you can then share with others who may not have access to the original data stored locally on your computer.

These files can be saved in the associated folders in the My Tableau Repository directory, which is automatically created in your My

Documents folder when you install Tableau. Your work files can also be saved in other locations, such as your desktop or a network directory.

Fields in the Calculation editor

Fields in the calculation editor are color coded by field type.

VISUAL CUE	DESCRIPTION
[ORANGE]	The field is a dimension, set or measure.
[Parameters].[PURPLE]	The field is a parameter. Tableau appends [Parameters] to avoid ambiguity when a parameter has the same name as another field
[ORANGE].[ORANGE]	The field is from a secondary data source.
BLUE()	The field is a calculation function.

Chapter 4
Data Analysis

Plan the Data Source

At the center of Tableau is your data. How successful you are with exploring data, answering questions, and building visualizations for yourself or others to consume all depend on the underlying data.

If your goal is to do some quick exploration or ad-hoc analysis, you might be able to hop in, connect to some data, drag and drop a bit to build some vizzes, and hop out with the information you need. But if your goal is to create an analysis or data source that will be used more than once, it's best to think through and plan your data source.

Tableau data sources

A Tableau data source is the link between your source data and Tableau. It is essentially the sum of your data (either as a live connection or an extract), the connection information, the names of tables or sheets containing data, and the customizations that you make on top of data to work with it in Tableau. Those customizations include things like how the data is combined and metadata such as calculations, renamed fields and default formatting.

A Tableau *data source* may contain multiple *data connections* to different databases or files. Connection information includes where the data is located, such as a file name and path or a network location, and details on how to connect to your data, such as database server name and server sign-in information.

Tableau data sources can remain embedded in the workbook where they were originally created, or they can be published separately. Published Data Sources allow for centralization and scaling of curated data sources.

Considerations for a Tableau data source

Before anything else, make sure you're clear on the purpose of the data source. If you're creating a catch-all data source for a wide variety of users with broad questions, you'd go about it differently than if you were constructing a niche data source optimized for performance. It's important to know your goal from the outset.

With that goal in mind, there are several items to consider and plan before you build a data source in Tableau:

- Location and access
- Shape and cleanliness
- The data model and combining data
- Metadata and customization
- Scalability, security and discoverability
- Performance and freshness

Location and access

The location of your data can be as simple as a single excel file on your computer or a Google sheet you've created, or as complex as multiple databases using various technologies. Access can also involve specific drivers or connectors for a database or login information for a database server.

Questions to consider:

- Do the correct Tableau users have access and permissions to the data and to Tableau?
- What user account should be used to log into the database?
- Will user filtering or row level security be needed?
- Is the source data on premises or in the cloud?
  - This may have implications if the data is published to Tableau Online.

- Are there **Supported Connectors**?

- Are there any limitations for that database (does it support all the functionality you hope to use)?

Shape and cleanliness

Your organization may already have well-structured data that you can connect to or ETL processes you can leverage, or you may need to use Tableau Prep Builder to perform cleaning and shaping operations to get your data into a useful format.

Questions to consider:

- Is the data well-structured for use with Tableau?

- Should **Tableau Prep Builder** and Tableau Prep Conductor be used to clean and **automate** data prep flows?

- What calculations or manipulations would be best done natively in Tableau?

- Is any of this data unnecessary? Is any data missing?

- What is the best way to combine each table of data?

Combine Data

If your data comes from one table, you can **connect to your data** to create the data source, drag the table onto the canvas and then start building your view. But if your data is spread across multiple tables – or across multiple databases – you'll need to combine it. Combining data happens on the Data Source Page.

Methods of combining data

Relationships are the default way to combine data in Tableau. Relationships are a dynamic, flexible way to combine data from multiple tables for analysis. If necessary, tables can also be joined or unioned. Data sources can also be blended. Let's take a look the options for how data can be combined in Tableau and some of the situations when each method is useful.

Relationships	Establish the potential for joins between two tables based on related fields. Does not merge data together to create a new, fixed table. During analysis, queries the relevant tables automatically using the contextually-appropriate joins to generate a custom table of data for that analysis. Maintains the appropriate level of detail, does not lose data, keeps appropriate aggregations and handles nulls.
Joins	Merge two tables of data based on a join clause and join type to form a new, fixed table of data. Often used to add new columns of data across the same basic row structure. May cause data loss with some join types if fields are not present in all tables. May cause data duplication if tables are at different levels of detail.
Unions	Merge two or more tables of data to form a new, fixed table of data. Used to append (add new rows of) data across the same basic column structure.
Blends	Work across two or more separate Tableau data sources. Data remains separate. Tableau queries the data sources independently and visualizes the results together in the view, based on the linking fields established for that sheet. Mimics the behavior of a left join and may filter data from secondary data sources.

Relationships

Relating is a method for working with data from multiple tables based on shared fields – columns – between those tables. Establishing a relationship informs Tableau how rows can be connected across tables. Tableau holds that information but does not immediately bring the rows together. Instead, when a visualization is created, the fields involved in the analysis are traced back through the relationship and the appropriate data is returned from its original table.

Because the data is never fully brought together into a single table outside the context of a visualization, relationships are useful when the data is at different levels of detail or granularity. For example, if you need to work with data about daily rainfall in one table but hourly temperatures in another.

Tableau supports relationships between tables in the same database and between tables in different databases.

Join

Although the default method for combing data in Tableau Desktop is relating, there are cases when you may want to join tables. Joining is a method for combining tables related by common fields. The result of combining data using a join is a table that extends horizontally by adding columns of data.

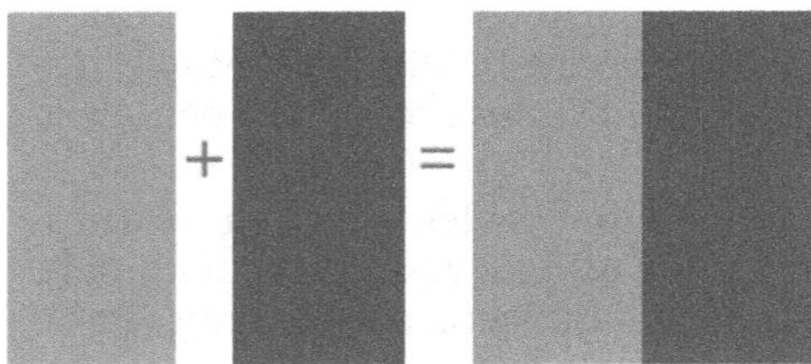

Join Types

Name	# of Siblings
Taylor	2
Alex	3
Shannon	0
Tracy	1

Name	Eye Color
Taylor	Blue
Alex	Brown
Morgan	Brown

Inner Join

Name	# of Siblings	Eye Color
Taylor	2	Blue
Alex	3	Brown

Left Join

Name	# of Siblings	Eye Color
Taylor	2	Blue
Alex	3	Brown
Shannon	0	*null*
Tracy	1	*null*

Right Join

Name	Eye Color	# of Siblings
Taylor	Blue	2
Alex	Brown	3
Morgan	Brown	*null*

Outer Join

Name	# of Siblings	Eye Color
Taylor	2	Blue
Alex	3	Brown
Shannon	0	*null*
Tracy	1	*null*
Morgan	*null*	Brown

Data blending

When you use data blending to combine your data, you combine data in what is called a primary data source with common fields from one or more secondary data sources.

Data blending is useful when you need to change how the data source is configured on a sheet-by-sheet basis, when you want to combine databases that don't allow relationships or joins such as cube data sources or Published Data Sources.

The result of combining data using data blending is a virtual table that extends horizontally by adding columns of data. The data from each data source will be aggregated to a common level before being displayed together in the visualization.

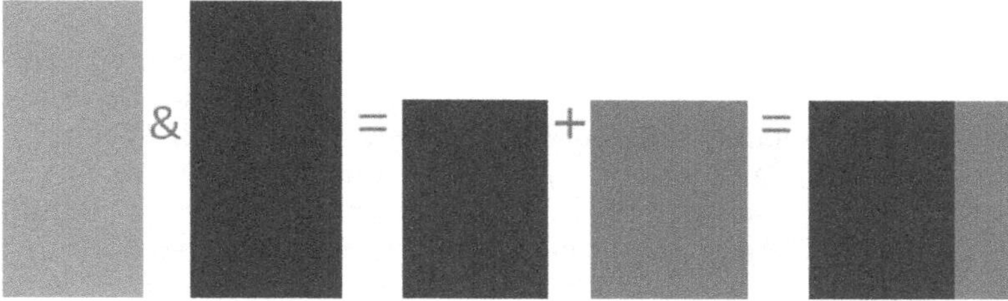

Union

Unioning is a method for appending values (rows) to tables. You can union tables if they have the same columns. The result of combining data using a union is a virtual table that has the same columns but extends vertically by adding rows of data.

You can union tables in one of two ways: manually or using wildcard search.

Structure Data for Analysis

There are certain concepts that are fundamental to understanding data prep and how to structure data for analysis. Data can be generated, captured and stored in a variety of formats, but when it comes to analysis, not all data formats are created equal.

Data preparation is the process of getting well formatted data into a single table or multiple related tables so it can be analyzed in Tableau. This includes both the structure, i.e. rows and columns, as well as aspects of data cleanliness, such correct data types and correct data values.

How structure impacts analysis

The structure of your data may not be something you can control. The rest of this topic assumes you have access to the raw data and the tools needed to shape it, such as Tableau Prep Builder. However, there may be situations when you can't pivot or aggregate your data as desired. It is often still possible to perform the analysis but you may need to change your calculations or how you approach the data. But if you can optimize the data structure it will likely make your analysis much easier.

Data Structure

Tableau Desktop works best with data that is in tables formatted like a spreadsheet. That is, data stored in rows and columns, with column headers in the first row. So what should be a row or column?

What is a row?

A row, or record, can be anything from information around a transaction at a retail store, to weather measurements at a specific location, or stats about a social media post.

It's important to know what a record (row) in the data represents. This is the *granularity* of the data.

Here, each record is a day

Date	Max TemperatureF	Mean TemperatureF	Min TemperatureF
1/1/2015	42	34	26
1/2/2015	42	37	32
1/3/2015	41	38	35
1/4/2015	51	45	38
1/5/2015	54	52	49
1/6/2015	54	49	43
1/7/2015	46	44	42
1/8/2015	46	41	35
1/9/2015	50	44	38
1/10/2015	46	45	43

Here, each record is a month

Date	Max TemperatureF	Mean TemperatureF	Min TemperatureF
January	63	45	26
February	62	49	33
March	69	51	31
April	77	52	37
May	82	59	43
June	92	68	49
July	95	71	54
August	92	69	54
September	81	61	45
October	74	58	45
November	60	44	25

Tip: A best practice is to have a unique identifier, a value that identifies each row as a unique piece of data. Think of it like the social security number or URL of each record. In Superstore, that would be Row ID. Note that not all data sets have a UID but it can't hurt to have one.

Try to make sure you can answer the question "What does a row in the data set represent?". This is the same as answering "What does the TableName(Count) field represent?". If you can't articulate that, the data might be structured poorly for analysis.

What is a field or column?

A *column* of data in a table comes into Tableau Desktop as a *field* in the data pane, but they are essentially interchangeable terms. A field of data should contain items that can be grouped into a larger relationship. The items themselves are called *values* or *members.*

What values are allowed in a given field are determined by the *domain* of the field. For example, a column for "grocery store departments" might contain the members "deli", "bakery", "produce", etc., but it wouldn't include "bread" or "salami" because those are items, not departments. Phrased another way, the domain of the department field is limited to just the possible grocery store departments.

Additionally, a well-structured data set would have a column for "Sales" and a column for "Profit", not a single column for "Money", because profit is a separate concept from sales.

- The domain of the Sales field would be values ≥ 0, since sales cannot be negative.

- The domain of the Profit field, however, would be all values, since profit can be negative.

Note: *Domain* can also mean the values present in the data. If the column "grocery store department" erroneously contained "salami", by this definition, that value would be in the domain of the column. The definitions are slightly contradictory. One is the values that could or should be there, the other is values that actually are there

Categorizing fields

Each column in the data table comes into Tableau Desktop as a field, which appears in the **Data** pane. Fields in Tableau Desktop must be either a dimension or measure and either discrete or continuous (color coded: blue fields are discrete and green fields are continuous).

Probably the most important, fundamental concept to understanding Tableau is the difference between discrete versus continuous fields.

- *Dimensions* are qualitative, meaning they can't be measured but are instead described. Dimensions are often things like city or country, eye color, category, team name, etc. Dimensions are usually discrete.

- *Measures* are quantitative, meaning they can be measured and recorded with numbers. Measures can be things like sales, height, clicks, etc. In Tableau Desktop, measures are automatically aggregated; the default aggregation is SUM. Measures are usually continuous.

- *Discrete* means individually separate or distinct. Toyota is distinct from Mazda. In Tableau Desktop, discrete values come into the view as a label and they create panes.

- *Continuous* means forming an unbroken, continuous whole. 7 is followed by 8 and then it's the same distance to 9, and 7.5 would fall midway between 7 and 8. In Tableau Desktop, continuous values come into the view as an axis.

- Dimensions are usually discrete, and measures are usually continuous. However, this is not always the case. Dates can be either discrete or continuous.

  - Dates are dimensions and automatically come into the view as discrete (aka date parts, such as "August", which considers the month of August without considering other information like the year). A trend line applied to a timeline with discrete dates will be broken into multiple trend lines, one per pane.

  - We can chose to use continuous dates if preferred (aka date truncations, such as "August 2017", which is different than "August 2018"). A trend line applied to a timeline with continuous dates will have a single trend line for the entire date axis.

Binning & Histograms

A field like age or salary is considered continuous. There is a relationship between the age 34 and 35, and 34 is as far from 35 as 35 is from 36. However, once we're past age 10 or so, we usually stop saying things like we're "9 and a half" or "7 and ¾". We're already binning our age to neat year-sized increments. Someone who is 12,850 days old is older than someone who is 12,790 days old, but we draw a line and say they're both 35. Similarly, age groupings are often used in place of actual ages. Child prices for cinema tickets might be for kids 12 and under, or a survey may ask you to select your age group, such as 20-24, 25-30, etc.

Histograms are used to visualize the distribution of numerical data using binning. A histogram is like a bar chart, but rather than being discrete categories per bar, the rectangles making up the histogram span a *bin* of a continuous axis, such as range of the number of blossoms (0-4, 5-9, 10-14, etc.). The height of the rectangles is determined by frequency or count of those values. Here, the y-axis is the count of plants that fall into each bin. Seven plants have 0-4 blossoms, two plants have 5-9 blossoms and 43 plants have 20-24 blossoms.

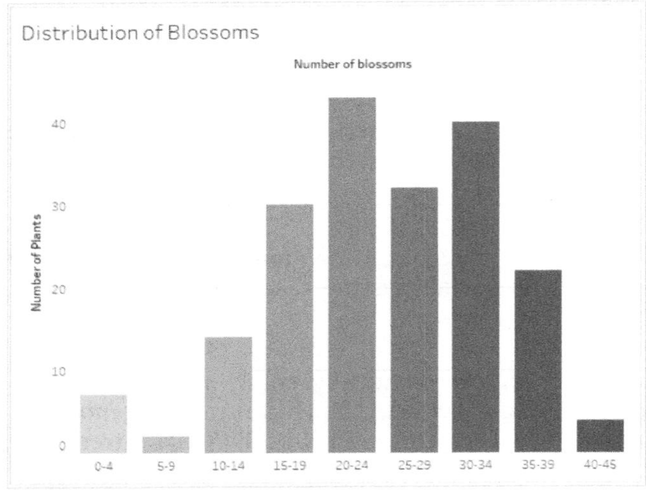

Data Types

Databases, unlike spreadsheets, usually enforce strict rules on data types. Data types classify the data in a given field and provide information about how the data should be formatted, interpreted and what operations can be done to that data. For example, numerical fields can have mathematical operations applied to them and geographic fields can be mapped.

Tableau Desktop assigns whether a field is a dimension or measure, but fields have other characteristics that depend on their data type.

ICON	DATA TYPE
Abc	Text (string) values
(calendar icon)	Date values
(calendar with clock icon)	Date & Time values
#	Numerical values
T|F	Boolean operators (relational only)
(globe icon)	Geographic values (used with maps)

Some functions require specific data types. For example, you cannot use CONTAINS with a numerical field. Type functions are used to change the data type of a field. For example, DATEPARSE can take a text date in a specific format and make it a date, thus enabling things like automatic drill down in the view.

Create a Data Source or Add a New Connection with Clipboard Data

Sometimes you want to pull in data from an outside source for some quick analysis. Rather than create a whole data source and then connect in Tableau, you can copy and paste the data directly into your workbook. Tableau automatically creates a data source that you can begin analyzing.

When you paste data on the data source page, Tableau creates a new connection in the existing data source.

When you paste data on the sheet, Tableau creates a new data source that you can begin analyzing. When you paste the data as a data source, the data source is saved as a text file to your Tableau Repository when you save the workbook.

You can copy and paste data from a variety of office applications including Microsoft Excel and Microsoft Word. You can also copy and paste HTML tables from web pages. Tables that are copied as comma separated values or tab delimited can be pasted into Tableau.

Note: Not all applications use these formats when copying.

1. Select the data you want and copy it to the clipboard.

2. Open Tableau Desktop and do one of the following:

1. On the data source page, select **Data** > **Paste Data as Connection** or **Paste Data as Data Source**.

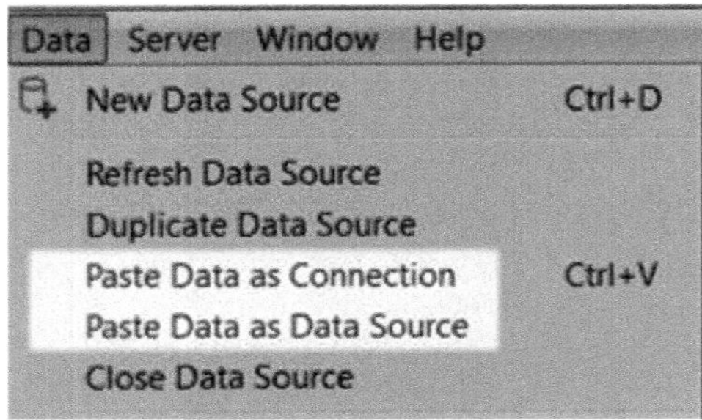

2. On the sheet, select **Data** > **Paste** to paste the data as a data source.

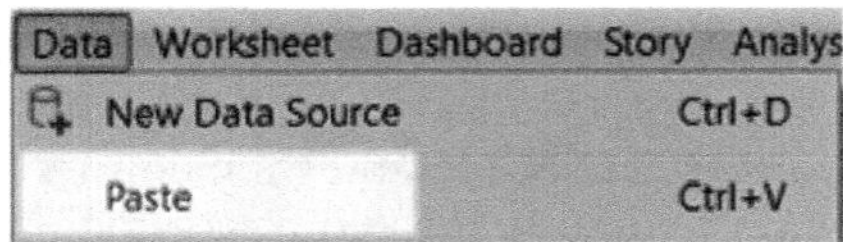

3. Select **File** > **Save** to save the data source.

When you save the workbook, the data source either becomes a part of the existing data source or is added to your repository, depending on which of the methods you choose. If you paste the data as a data source, the data source is saved with the workbook when you save the workbook as a packaged workbook (.twbx).

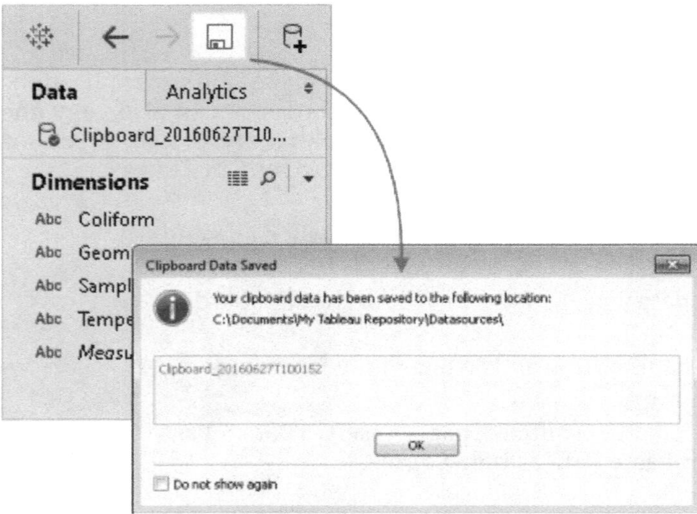

Connect to a Custom SQL Query

For most databases, you can connect to a specific query rather than the entire data set. Because databases have slightly different SQL syntax from each other, the custom SQL you use to connect to one database might be different from the custom SQL you might use to connect to another. However, using custom SQL can be useful when you know exactly the information you need and understand how to write SQL queries.

Though there are several common reasons why you might use custom SQL, you can use custom SQL to union your data across tables, recast fields to perform cross-database joins, restructure or reduce the size of your data for analysis, etc.

For Excel and text file data sources, this option is available only in workbooks that were created before Tableau Desktop 8.2 or when using Tableau Desktop on Windows with the legacy connection. To connect to Excel or text files using the legacy connection, connect to the file, and in the Open dialog box, click the **Open** drop-down menu, and then select **Open with Legacy Connection**.

Connect to a custom SQL query

1. After connecting to your data, double-click the **New Custom SQL** option on the Data Source page.

2. Type or paste the query into the text box. The query must be a single SELECT* statement.

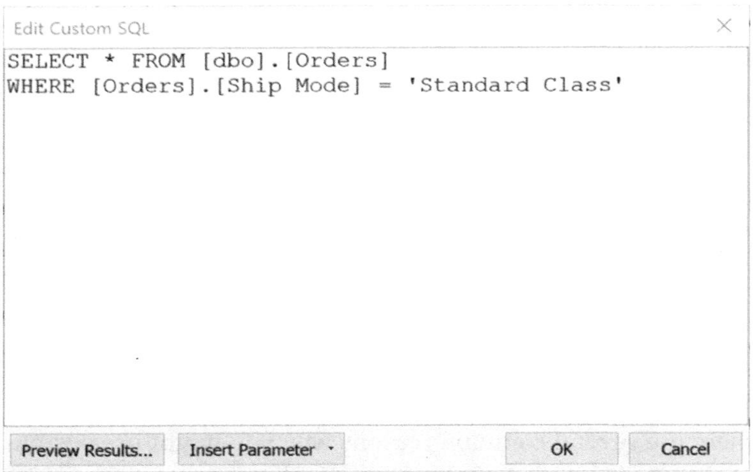

3. When finished, click **OK**.

When you click OK, the query runs and the custom SQL query table appears in the logical layer of the canvas. Only relevant fields from the custom SQL query display in the data grid on the Data Source page.

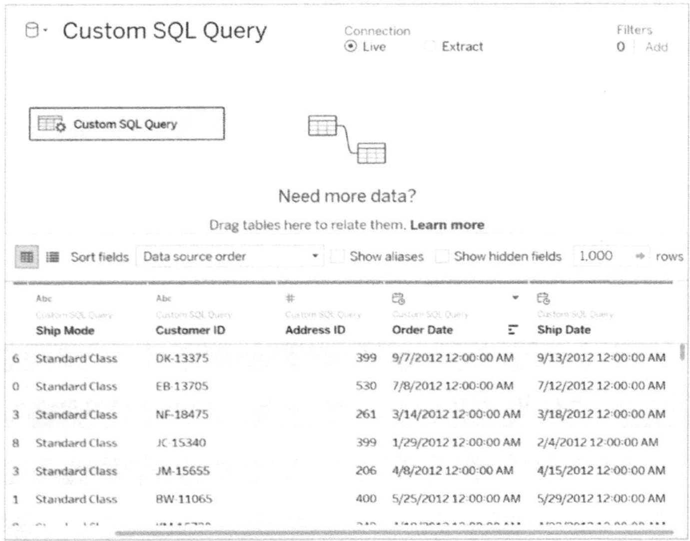

Edit a custom SQL query

To edit a custom SQL query

1. On the data source page, in the canvas, double-click the custom SQL query in the logical layer.

2. Hover over the custom SQL table in the physical layer until the arrow displays.

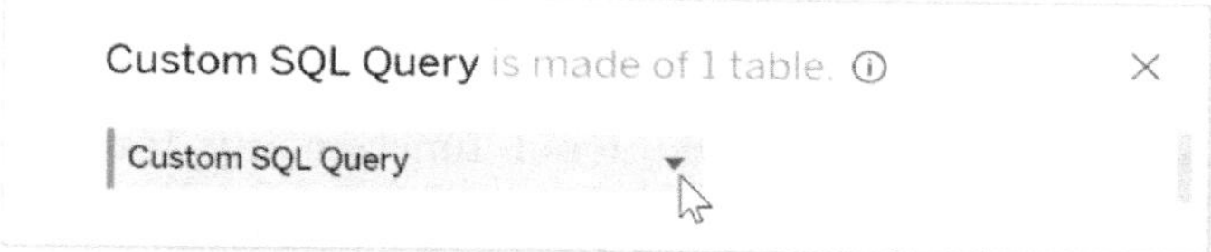

3. Click the arrow and then select **Edit Custom SQL Query**.

4. In the dialog box, edit the custom SQL query.

To change a custom SQL query name

When you drag a custom SQL query to the logical layer of the canvas, Tableau gives it a default name: Custom SQL Query, Custom SQL Query1, and so on. You can change the default name to something more meaningful.

1. On the data source page, in the logical layer of the canvas, select the drop-down arrow in the custom SQL query table and select **Rename**.

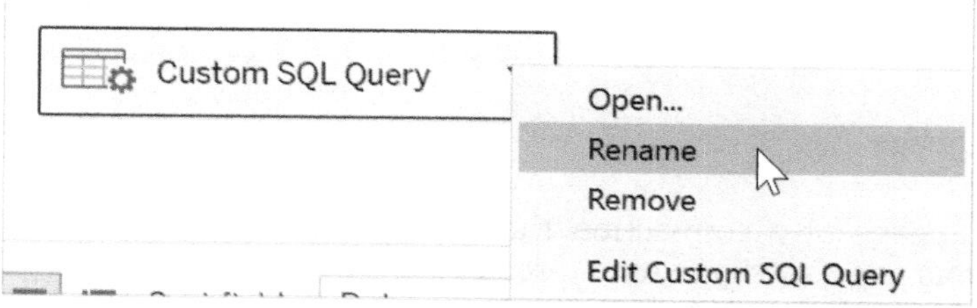

2. Enter the name you want to use for your custom SQL query.

Tableau Catalogue support for custom SQL

Supported queries

Catalogue currently supports custom SQL queries that meet the ANSI SQL-2003 standard, with three known exceptions:

- Time zone expressions
- Multiset expressions
- Tableau parameters

Supported features and functions

Catalogue supports the following additional functionality for data sources, workbooks and flows with connections that use the Microsoft SQL Server, MySQL or PostgreSQL drivers, for example, Amazon Aurora for MySQL, Amazon RedShift, Pivotal Greenplum Database, MemSQL, Denodo and others.

- SQL Server temp tables
- SQL Server table variables
- MySQL GROUP_CONCAT function
- PostgreSQL arrays
- PostgreSQL EXTRACT() function

Other custom SQL scenarios and functionality might work, but Tableau doesn't specifically test for or support them.

Supported lineage

To see the lineage of a connection that uses custom SQL, from the External Assets page, navigate to and select a table from the list. A page opens and shows information about the table, including name, type and description.

To the right of the table information is the Lineage pane, which shows the table's relationship to upstream and downstream assets. Note that

Catalogue doesn't support showing column information in the lineage for table metadata gathered using custom SQL.

In the following screenshot, the factAccountOpportunityByQuarter table was indexed because it's used by a data source. However, because it's referenced by a custom SQL query, the column information isn't available.

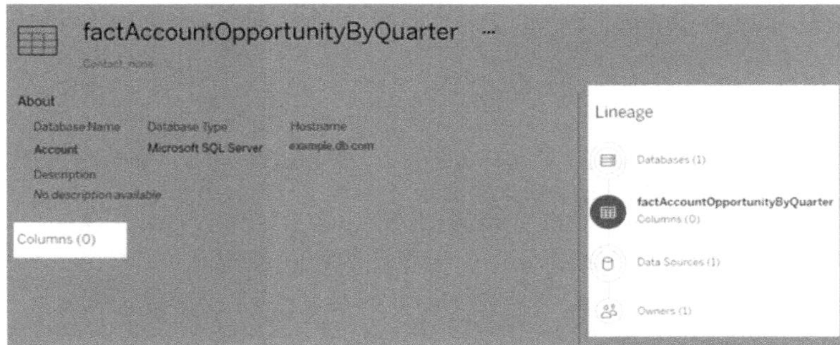

In a case where more than one data source, workbook or flow uses a table, any of the assets downstream from that table that use a custom SQL query are excluded when column-level filters are applied. As a result, fewer downstream assets show in the lineage than are actually used.

Dimensions and Measures - (Blue and Green)

We touched briefly on dimensions and measures when looking at the categorization of fields earlier in the book. Now, we will look at these concepts in greater details.

When you connect to a new data source, Tableau assigns each field in the data source as dimension or measure in the **Data** pane, depending on the type of data the field contains. You use these fields to build views of your data.

About data field roles and types

Data fields are made from the columns in your data source. Each field is automatically assigned a data type (such as integer, string, date), and a role: Discrete Dimension or Continuous Measure (more common), or Continuous Dimension or Discrete Measure (less common).

- As previously stated, d*imensions* contain qualitative values (such as names, dates or geographical data). You can use dimensions to categorize, segment, and reveal the details in your data. Dimensions affect the level of detail in the view.

- *Measures* contain numeric, quantitative values that you can measure. Measures can be aggregated. When you drag a measure into the view, Tableau applies an aggregation to that measure (by default).

Blue versus Green fields

Tableau represents data differently in the view depending on whether the field is discrete (*blue*), or continuous (*green*). *Continuous* and *discrete* are mathematical terms. Continuous means "forming an unbroken whole, without interruption"; discrete means "individually separate and distinct".

A visual cue that helps you know when a field is a measure is that the field is aggregated with a function, which is indicated with an abbreviation for the aggregation in the field name, such as: SUM(Profit).

Examples of continuous and discrete fields used in a view

In the example on the left (below), because the **Quantity** field is set to **Continuous**, it creates a horizontal axis along the bottom of the view. The green background and the axis help you to see that it's a continuous field.

In the example on the right, the **Quantity** field has been set to **Discrete**. It creates horizontal headers instead of an axis. The blue background and the horizontal headers help you to see that it's discrete.

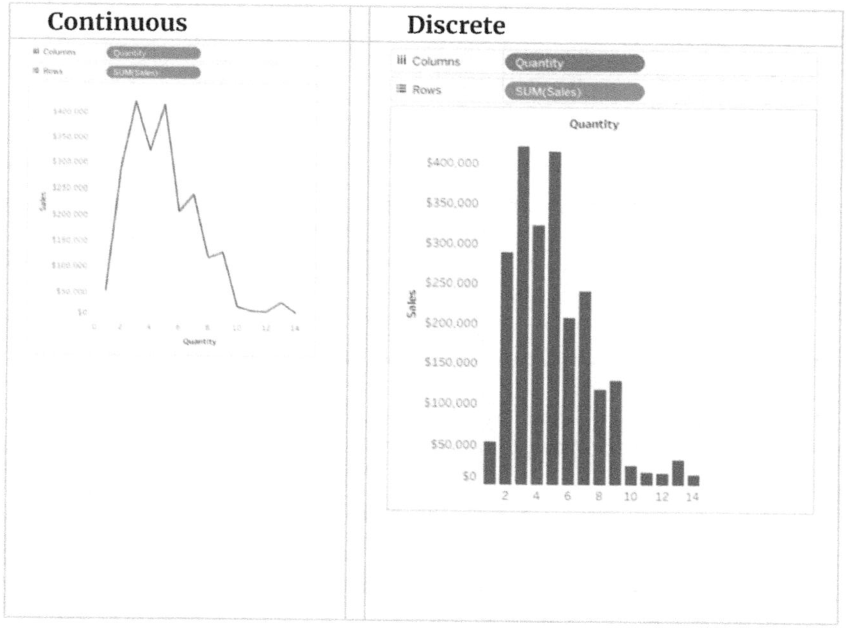

In both examples, the **Sales** field is set to **Continuous**. It creates a vertical axis because it continuous and it's been added to the Rows shelf. If it was on the Columns shelf, it would create a horizontal axis. The green background and aggregation function (in this case, SUM) help to indicate that it's a measure.

The absence of an aggregation function in the **Quantity** field name help to indicate that it's a dimension.

Dimension fields in the view

When you drag a discrete dimension field to **Rows** or **Columns**, Tableau creates column or row headers.

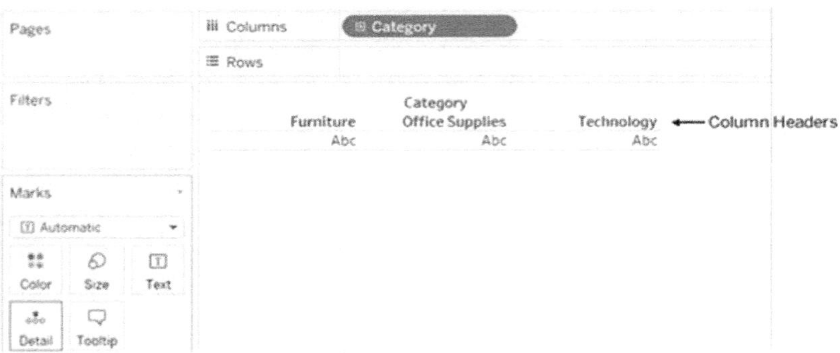

In many cases, fields from the **Dimension** area will initially be discrete when you add them to a view, with a blue background. Date dimensions and numeric dimensions can be discrete or continuous, and all measures can be discrete or continuous.

After you drag a dimension to **Rows** or **Columns**, you can change the field to a measure just by clicking the field and choosing **Measure**. Now the view will contain a continuous axis instead of column or row headers, and the field's background will become green:

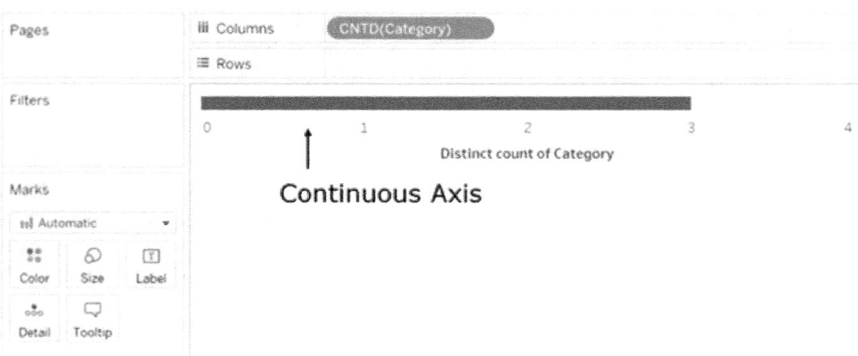

Date dimensions can be discrete or continuous. Dimensions containing strings or Boolean values cannot be continuous.

Chapter 5
Chart Types

Choose the Right Chart Type for Your Data

What chart or graph works best for your data? The visualization (or viz) you create depends on:

- The questions you are trying to ask
- The properties of your data
- How you want to present and communicate your insights to others

For example, showing the growth in sales each year requires a different visualization than showing the connection between discounted items and their profitability. Knowing what you need to show will help determine how you want to show it.

We will look at nine different types of information that you can display with a visualization. This isn't a comprehensive list, and there are bound to be exceptions to these categories. With experience you will be able to more quickly assess what chart type you want to create.

Change over time

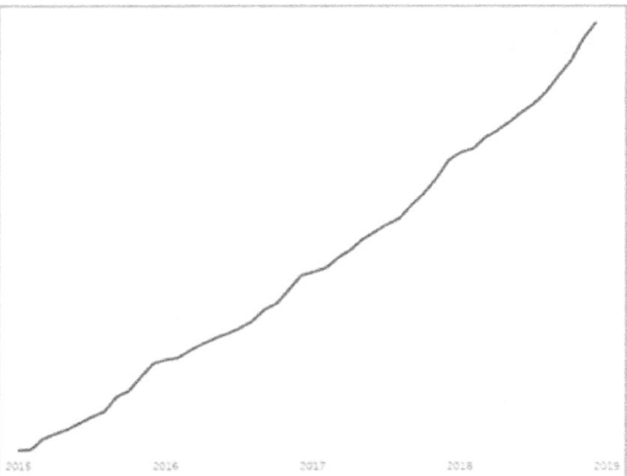

Showing a change over time for a measure is one of the fundamental categories of visualizations. There are many options for exploring change over time, including line charts, slope charts and highlight tables.

To show change over time, you need to know the value you expect to change, and how to work with Date fields in Tableau.

What kind of question does this chart answer?

- How has this measure changed in the past year?
- When did this measure change?
- How quickly has this measure changed?

Correlation

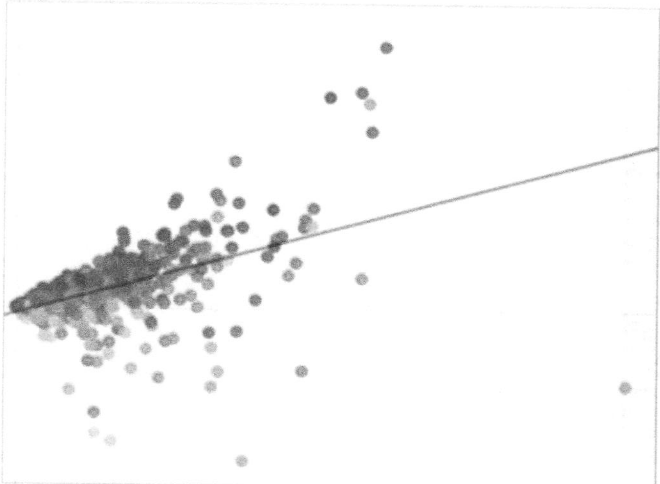

Sometimes you have two variables and are looking for the relationship between them. For example, you may be looking for the relationship between classroom size and school graduation rate, or how much lung capacity relates to endurance. (But remember, correlation does not always equal causation.)

Correlation can be shown with scatter plots or highlight tables, and you can use Tableau's analytics objects to show the strength of the correlation.

What types of question can this chart answer?

- Are these two measures related? How strongly?
- Are some measures more related than others?
- How strongly related are these measures?

Magnitude

Magnitude shows the relative size or value of two or more discrete items. If you are comparing sales for different regions, you are looking at magnitude.

Magnitude charts include bar charts, packed bubble charts, and line charts.

What types of question can this chart answer?

- Which of these dimension members has the highest measure?
- Are there any exceptional dimensions?
- How large of a gap is there between the lowest and highest measure between these dimensions?

Deviation

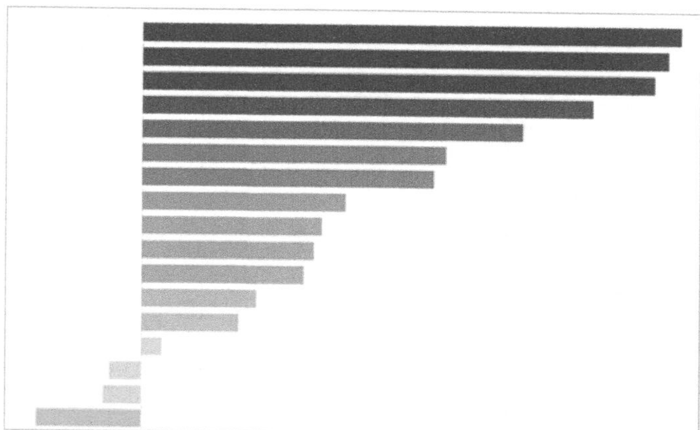

Deviation charts show how far a value varies from some baseline, such as the average or median. If you wanted to know which items had unusually high or low profit margins, you would use a deviation chart.

You can use bullet charts, bar charts, and combination charts to show deviation. You can also find the statistical significance of the deviation using a Z-score.

What types of question can this chart answer?

- How far from the norm does this measure stray?
- How important are the deviations in this measure?
- Is there a pattern to the deviations?

Distribution

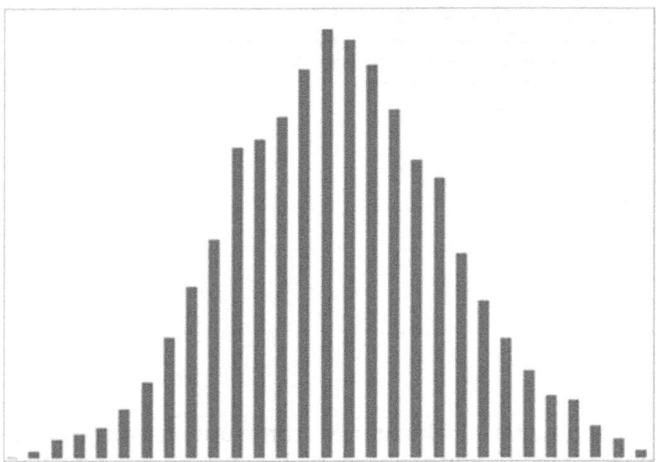

When you are trying to find the frequency of events within a population, you are looking at the distribution. If you are showing the number of respondents to a survey by age, or the frequency of incoming calls by day, a distribution chart might be the best choice.

Distribution charts include histograms, population pyramids, Pareto charts and box plots.

What types of question can this chart answer?

- Are events clustered around a certain probability?
- Which population group buys the most items?
- When are the busiest times in our work day?

Ranking

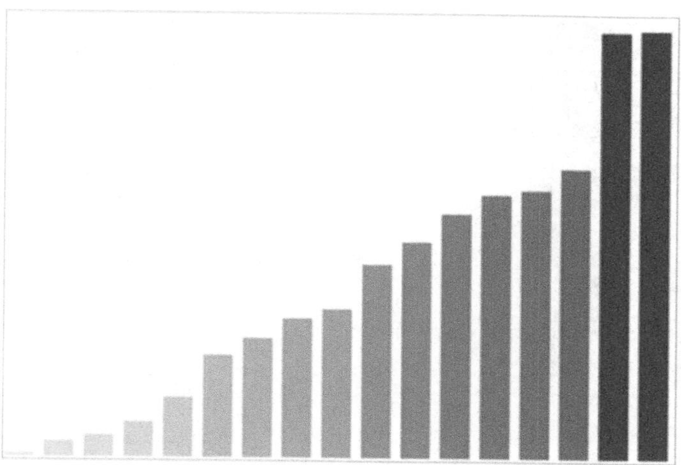

Sometimes you not only want to depict the magnitude of some value, but also the relative ranking of all the members of your dimension. Showing the top ten sales people or demonstrating the under-performing states use a ranking chart.

Ranking charts are usually bar charts that integrate rank calculations, top n sets, or key progress indicators.

What types of question can this chart answer?

- How many people are under-performing in the company?
- How much revenue is generated by our top ten customers?
- What is the value of our ten lowest revenue properties?

Part-to-Whole

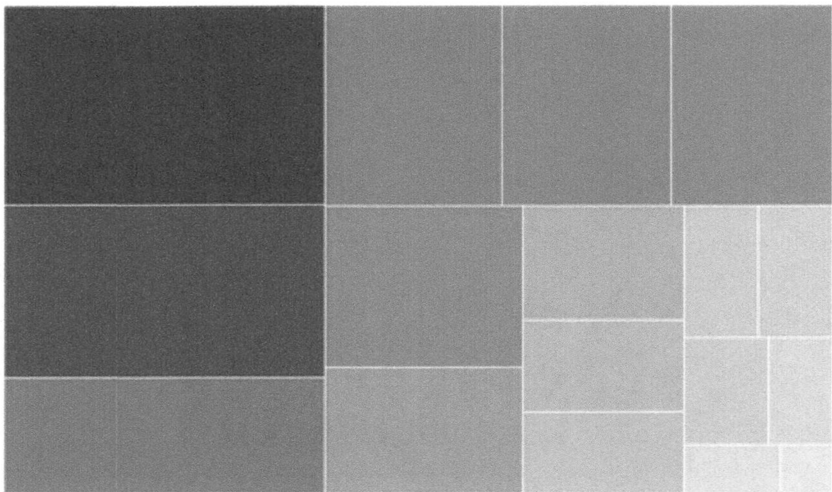

Part-to-Whole charts show how much of a whole an individual part takes up. For example, if you are showing how much each region contributes to overall sales, or how expensive each different shipping mode is for an individual product, you would use a part to whole chart.

Part-to-Whole charts can be pie charts, area charts, stacked bar charts, or treemaps.

What types of question can this chart answer?

- How much does this value contribute to the total?
- How does the distribution of costs change each year?
- Do different items contribute different amounts to sales by region?

Spatial

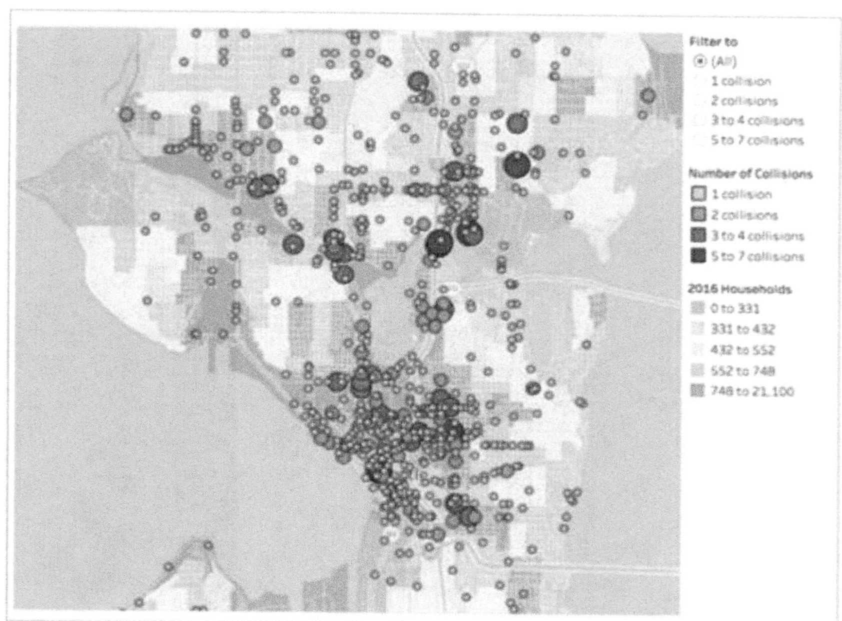

Spatial charts can precise locations and geographical patterns in your data. Showing the airport terminals with the most foot traffic or a map of all sales across the country are examples of spatial maps.

Spatial maps include filled maps, point distribution maps, symbol maps, and density maps.

What types of question can this chart answer?

- Which city has the highest sales?
- How far from distribution centers are our customers?
- How many people arrive at which gate?

Flow

Flow charts can be maps that convey movement over time, such as Sankey diagrams. Flow maps include path over time and path between origin and destination charts.

What types of question can this chart answer?

- What is the longest shipping route?
- How long are people lingering around gates?
- What are the bottlenecks to traffic in the city?

Build Common Chart Types in Data Views

Over the following pages, we will go through a series of detailed exercises that guide you through the steps involved in building some common chart types in data views. All exercises use the **Sample - Superstore** data source, which is included with Tableau Desktop.

Create an Area Chart

An area chart is a line chart where the area between the line and the axis are shaded with a color. These charts are typically used to represent accumulated totals over time and are the conventional way to display stacked lines. Follow the steps below to create an area chart.

The basic building blocks for an area chart are as follows:

Mark type:	Area
Columns shelf:	Dimension
Rows shelf:	Measure
Color:	Dimension

To create an area chart, follow the steps below:

1. Open Tableau Desktop and connect to the **Sample - Superstore** data source.

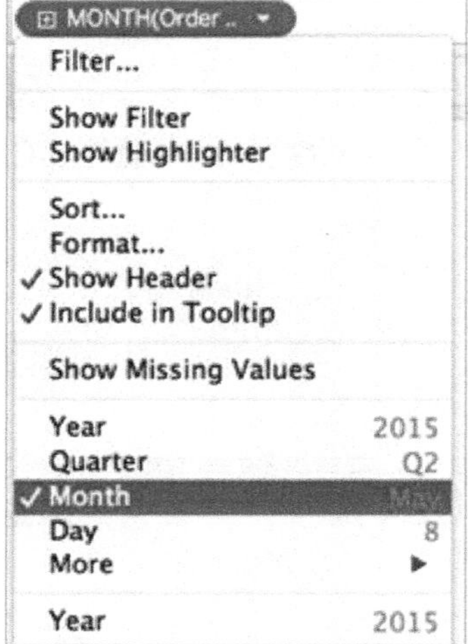

2. Navigate to a new worksheet.

3. From the **Data** pane, drag **Order Date** to the **Columns** shelf.

4. On the Columns shelf, right-click **YEAR(Order Date)** and select **Month**.

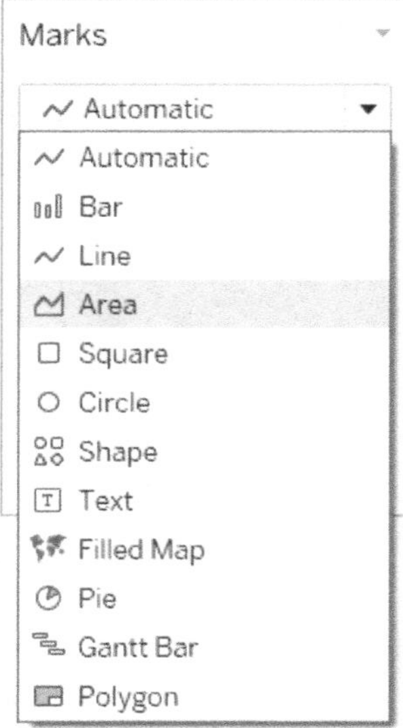

5. From the **Data** pane, drag **Quantity** to the **Rows** shelf.

6. From the **Data** pane, drag **Ship Mode** to **Color** on the Marks card.

7. On the Marks card, click the Mark Type drop-down and select **Area**.

The visualization updates to the following:

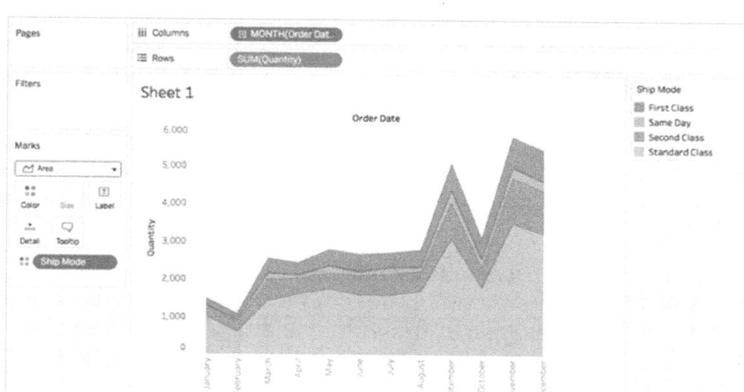

You can add formatting to an area chart. For example, you can edit the color legend and turn on mark labels and borders.

You can also use highlight actions with area charts. For example, selecting a color in the legend or turning on the highlighter will highlight the entire area instead of just the line.

Build a Bar Chart

Use bar charts to compare data across categories. You create a bar chart by placing a dimension on the **Rows** shelf and a measure on the **Columns** shelf, or vice versa.

A bar chart uses the **Bar** mark type.

Adding totals to the tops of bars in a chart is sometimes as simple as clicking the **Show Mark Labels** icon in the toolbar. But when the bars are broken down by color or size, each individual segment would labelled, rather than the total for the bar. With a few steps, you can add a total label at the top of every bar even when the bars are subdivided, as in the view you just created. In the following procedure you will technically be adding a reference line. But by configuring that "line" in a certain way, you end up with the labels you want.

1. From the **Analytics** pane, drag a **Reference Line** into the view and drop it on **Cell**.

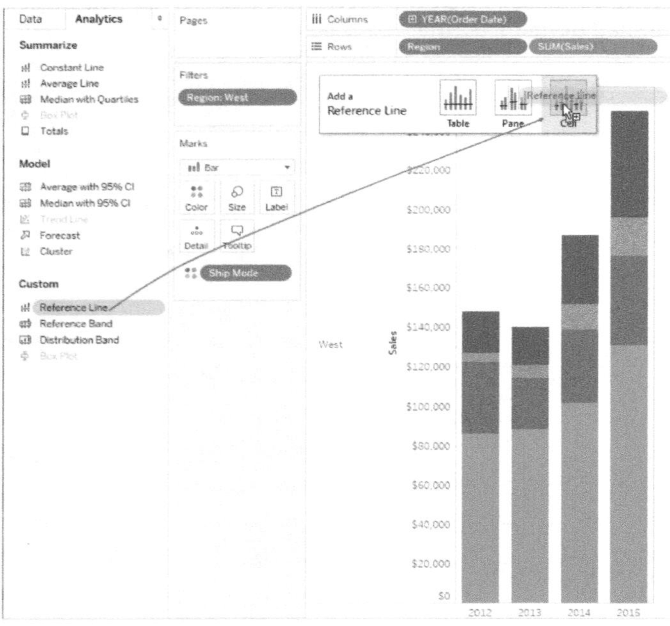

2. In the Edit Line, Band, or Box dialog box, set the aggregation for **SUM(Sales)** to **Sum**, set **Label** to **Value**, and set **Line** under Formatting to **None**:

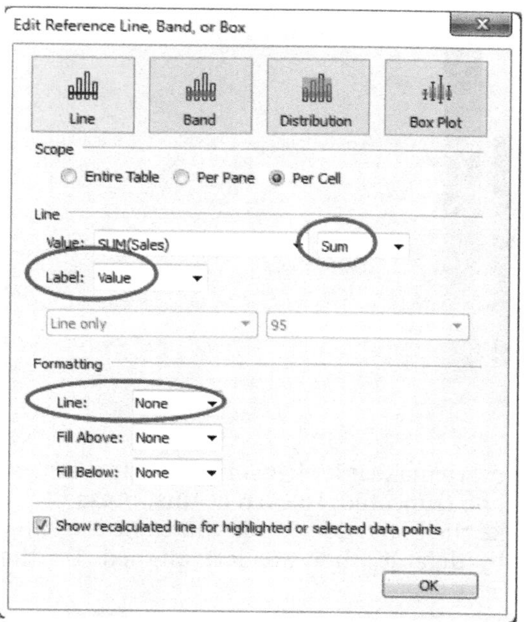

Then click **OK** to close the Edit Reference Line, Band, or Box dialog box.

Your view now has currency totals at the top of each bar:

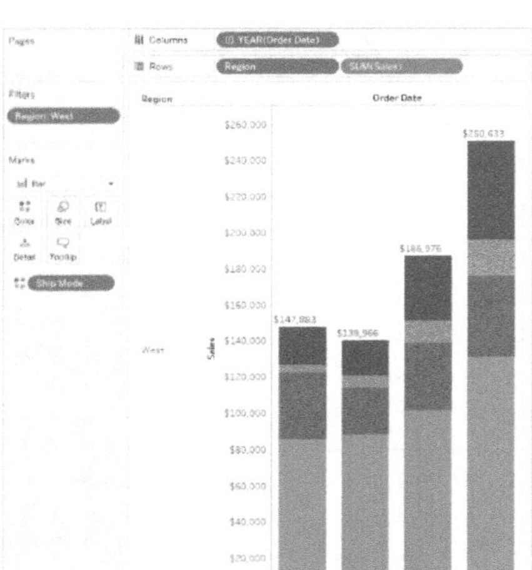

You may need to adjust the view to make it look just right. If the bars are too narrow, the numbers will be truncated; to correct this, press Ctrl + Right on the keyboard to make the bars wider. Or if you want to center the totals over the bars – by default, they are left-aligned. Do the following:

3. Right-click any of the totals on the bar chart and select **Format**.
4. In the Format window, in the **Reference Line Label** area, open the **Alignment** control and select the Center option for Horizontal alignment:

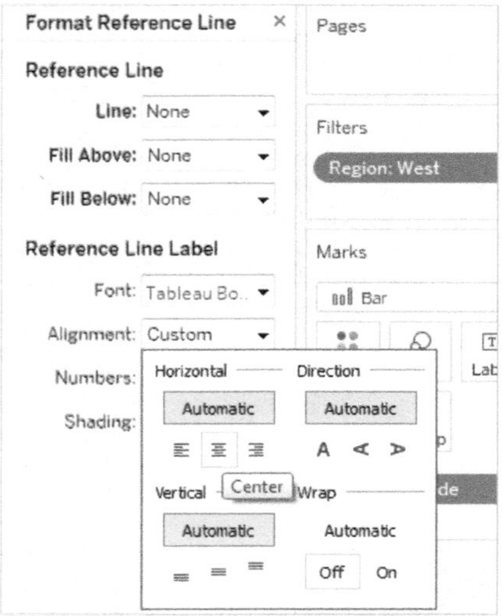

Build a Bullet Graph

A bullet graph is a variation of a bar graph developed to replace dashboard gauges and meters. A bullet graph is useful for comparing the performance of a primary measure to one or more other measures. Below is a single bullet graph showing how actual sales compared to estimated sales.

Follow the steps below to learn how to create a bullet graph.

1. Open Tableau Desktop and connect to the **World Indicators** data source.

2. Navigate to a new worksheet.

3. Hold down Shift on your keyboard and then, on the **Data** pane, under **Development**, select **Tourism Inbound** and **Tourism Outbound**.

4. In the upper-right corner of the application, click **Show Me**.

5. In Show Me, select the **Bullet Graph** image.

6. Click **Show Me** again to close it.

7. From the **Data** pane, drag **Region** to the **Rows** shelf.

The graph updates to look like the following:

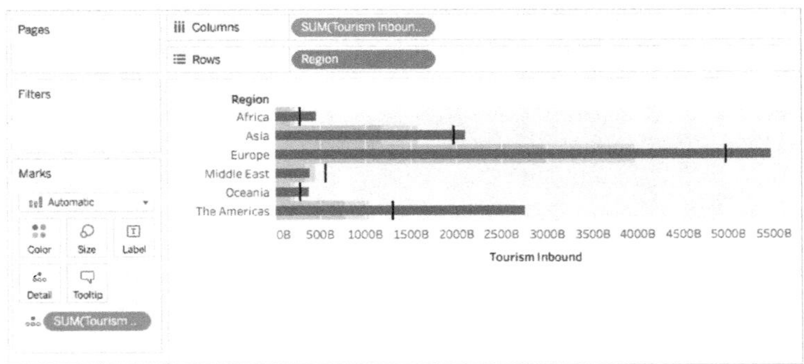

Swap reference line fields

Sometimes you might want to swap the reference lines fields. For example, the actual sales is shown as a reference distribution instead of a bar.

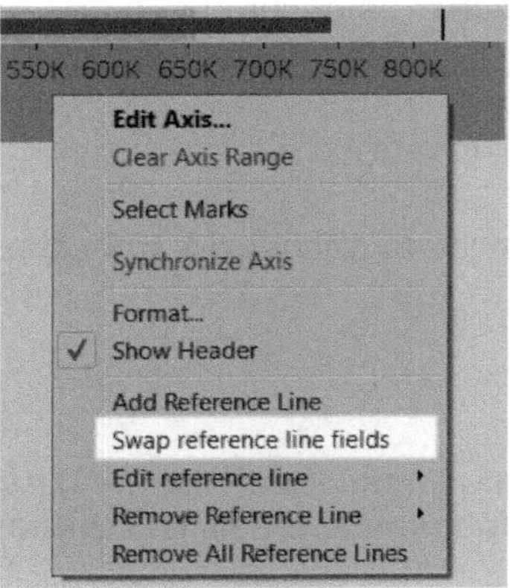

To swap the two measures, right-click (control-click on the Mac) the axis and select **Swap Reference Line Fields.**

Edit the distribution

Right-click (control-click on the Mac) the axis in the view and select **Edit Reference Line**, and then select one of the reference lines to modify.

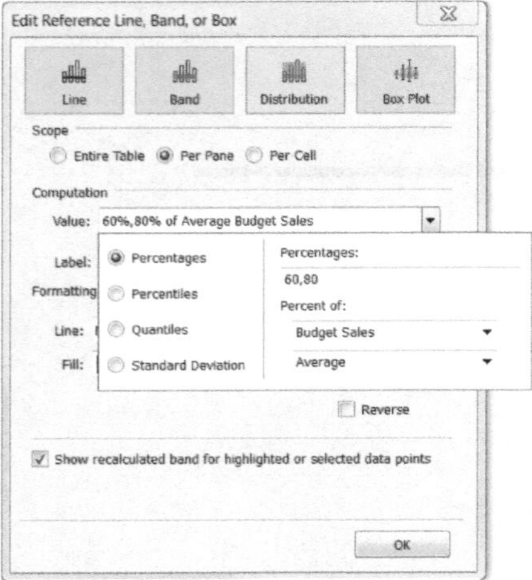

Build with Density Marks (Heatmap)

Use density chart to visualize patterns or trends in dense data with many overlapping marks. Tableau does this by grouping overlaying marks, and color-coding them based on the number of marks in the group.

Density maps help you identify locations with greater or fewer numbers of data points.

In Tableau, you can create a chart using the density mark by placing at least one continuous measure on the Columns shelf, and at least one dimension or measure on the Rows shelf (or vice versa), and then adding a field to the Marks card.

Note: Density charts work best when used with data sources containing many data points.

The basic building blocks for a density chart are as follows:

Mark type:	Density
Rows and Columns:	At least one continuous measure, and at least one measure or dimension
Marks card:	At least one continuous measure

Density charts use the **Density** mark type. By default, Tableau will use the automatic mark type.

To show how density charts can help make sense of overlapping marks in Tableau, we‘re going to start with a scatter plot with a large number of marks and re-create it as a density chart.

To use a density chart to see orders by date, follow these steps:

1. Open the **World Indicators** data source from the **Saved Data Sources** section of the Start screen.

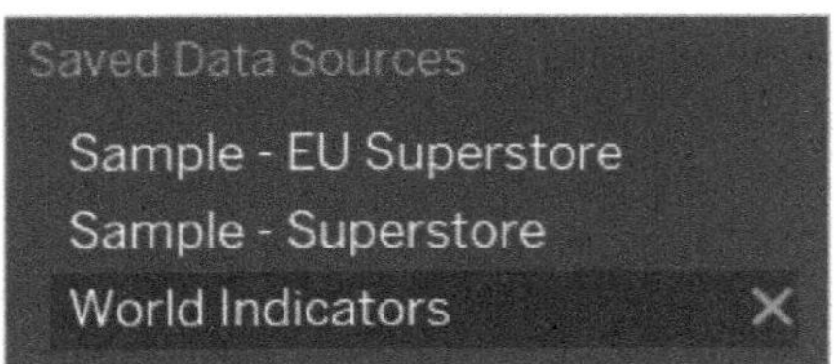

2. From the Health folder, drag **Infant Mortality** to the Columns shelf. Tableau aggregates the measure as a sum and creates a horizontal axis.

3. Drag the **Life Expectancy Female** to the **Rows** shelf.

Now you have a one-mark scatter plot.

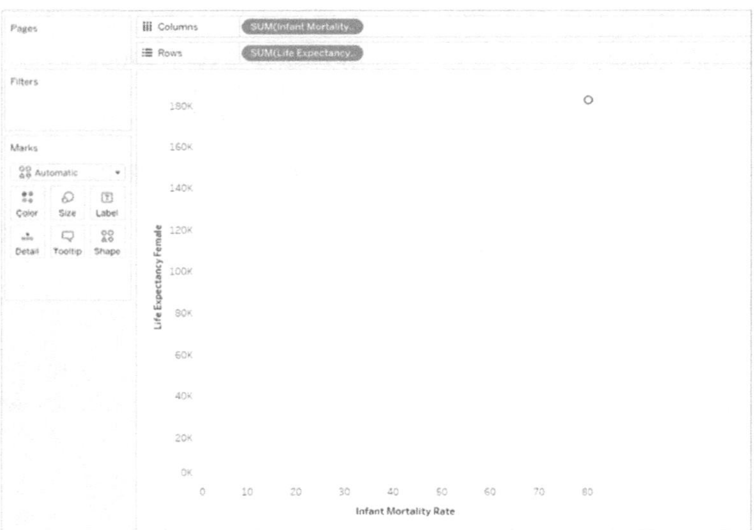

4. Both Infant Mortality and Life Expectancy are listed as a **Sum**, rather than average. Right click on both of these measures and to change Measure(Sum) to **Average**.

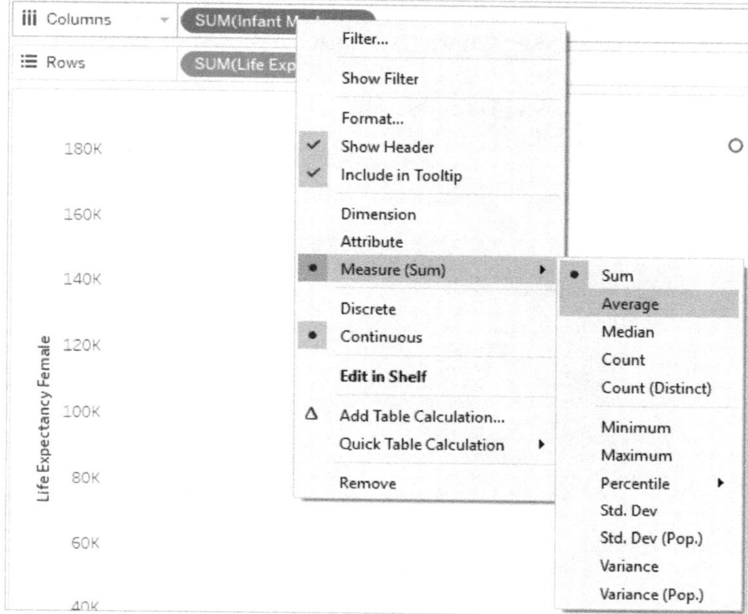

5. Drag the **Country** dimension to **Details** on the Marks card.

Now there are many more marks in your view. The number of marks in your view is now equal to the number of distinct countries in this data set. If you hover over a mark, you can see the country name, female life expectancy and infant mortality rate.

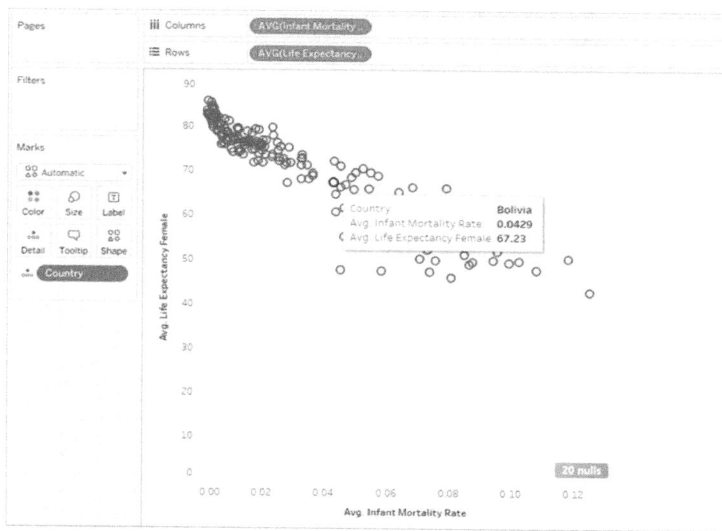

We've created a basic scatter plot, but there are lots of overlapping marks in the view and it's hard to see where the marks are most dense.

6. On the **Marks** card, select **Density** from the menu to change this scatter plot into a density chart.

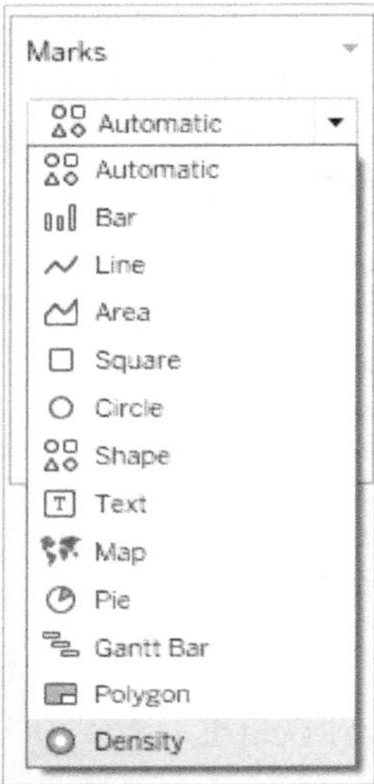

Tableau created a density chart by overlaying marks, called kernels, and color-coding where those kernels overlap. The more overlapping data points, the more intense the color is.

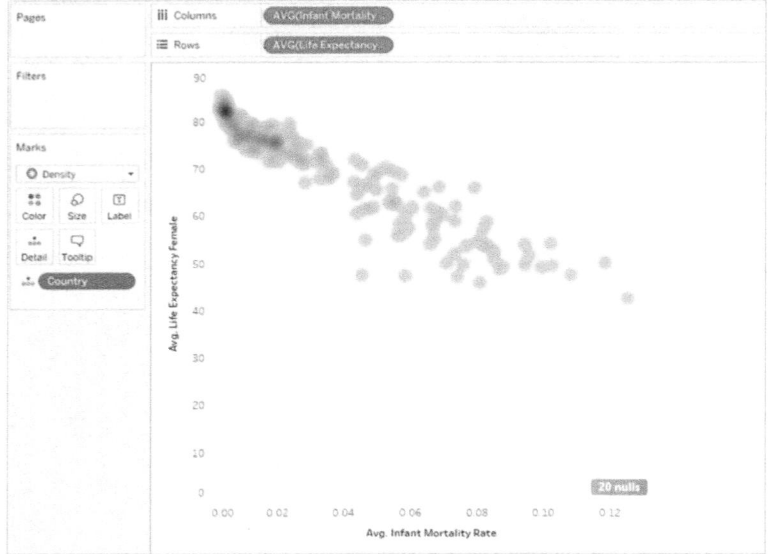

Tableau selected a blue color palette by default, but you can choose from ten density color palettes or any of the existing color palettes.

7. Select **Color** from the **Marks** card and select **Density Multi-color Light** from the menu.

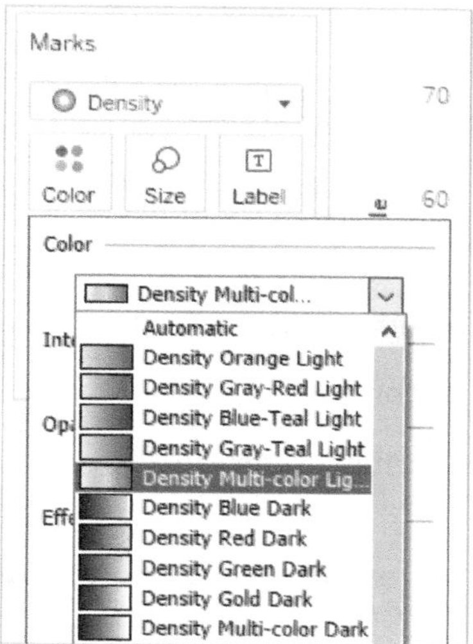

The names of the color palettes indicate whether they're designed for use on charts with dark or light backgrounds. Since our chart has a light background, we picked a "Light" palette.

This changes the color palette on your chart. More concentrated areas will appear red, while areas without overlapping marks will appear green.

Note: Color legends are not available for density marks.

8. In the Color menu, use the Intensity slider to increase or decrease the vividness of the density marks. For example, increasing intensity, or vividness, lowers the "max heat" spots in your data, so that more appear.

9. Select **Size** from the Marks card to adjust the size of the density's kernel.

10.

Build a Gantt Chart

Use Gantt charts to show the duration of events or activities.

In a Gantt chart, each separate mark (usually a bar) shows a duration. For example, you might use a Gantt chart to display average delivery time for a range of products.

The basic building blocks for a gantt chart are as follows:

Mark type:	Automatic or Gantt Bar
Columns shelf:	Date or Time field (continuous measure)
Rows shelf:	Dimension(s)
Size:	Continuous measure

To create a Gantt chart that shows how many days elapse on average between order date and ship date, follow these steps:

1. Connect to the **Sample - Superstore** data source.

2. Drag the **Order Date** dimension to **Columns**.

Tableau aggregates the dates by year and creates column headers with labels for the years.

3. On the **Columns** shelf, click the **Year (Order Date)** drop-down arrow, and then select **Week Number**.

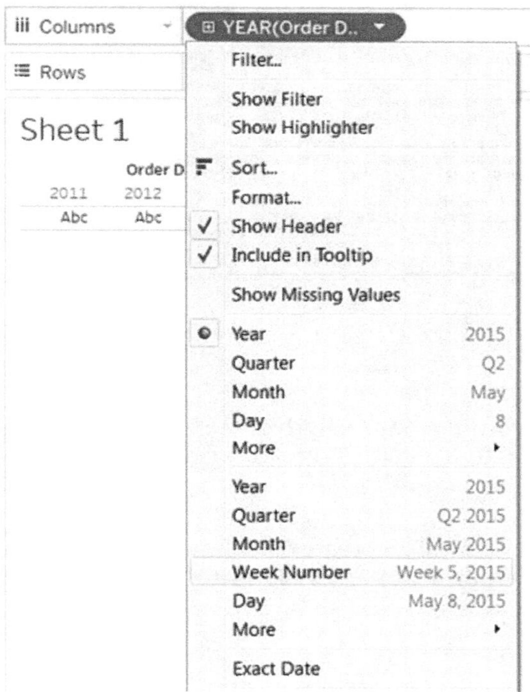

The column headers change. Individual weeks are indicated by tick marks because there are 208 weeks in a four-year span – too many to show as labels in the view.

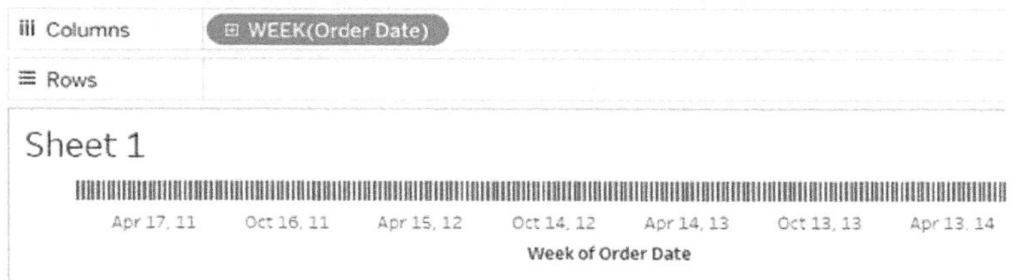

4. Drag the **Sub-Category** and **Ship Mode** dimensions to the **Rows** shelf. Drop **Ship Mode** to the right of **Sub-Category**.

This builds a two-level nested hierarchy of dimensions along the left axis.

Next, we'll size the marks according to the length of the interval between the order date and the ship date. To do this, create a calculated field to capture that interval.

5. In the toolbar menu, click **Analysis > Create Calculated Field**. You can also right-click (Control-click on Mac) any field in the **Data** pane and select **Create** > **Calculated Field**.

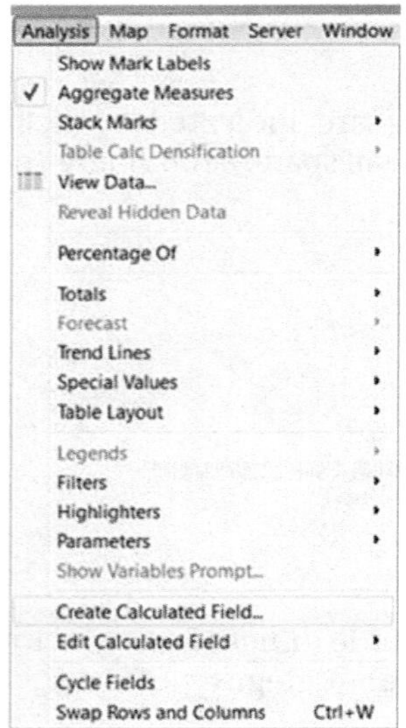

6. In the calculation dialog box, name your calculated field **OrderUntilShip**.

7. Clear any content that's in the **Formula** box by default.

8. In the **Formula** box, enter the following formula and then click **OK**:

DATEDIFF('day',[Order Date],[Ship Date])

The formula creates a custom measure that captures the difference between the **Order Date** and **Ship Date** values, in days.

9. Drag the **OrderUntilShip** measure to **Size** on the **Marks** card.

The default aggregation for **OrderUntilShip** is **Sum**, but in this case it makes more sense to average the values.

10. Right-click (Control-click on Mac) the **SUM(OrderUntilShip)** field on the **Marks** card, and then select **Measure (Sum)** > **Average**.

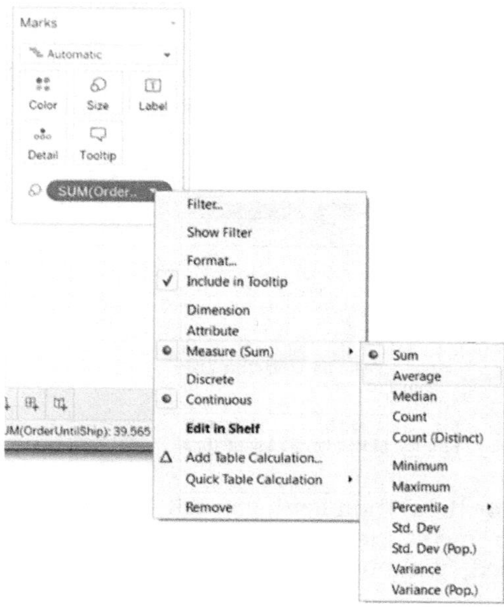

The view is coming along. But there are too many marks squeezed into the view.

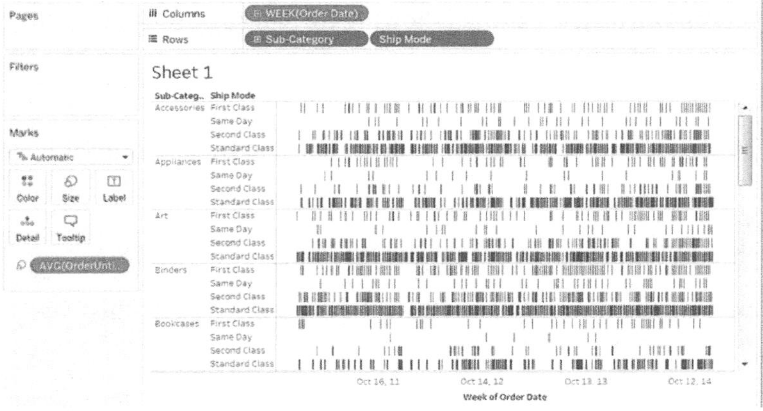

We can make our data more readable by filtering down to a smaller time window.

11. Hold down the Ctrl key (Option key on the Mac) and drag the **Week(Order Date)** field from the **Columns** shelf to the **Filter** shelf.

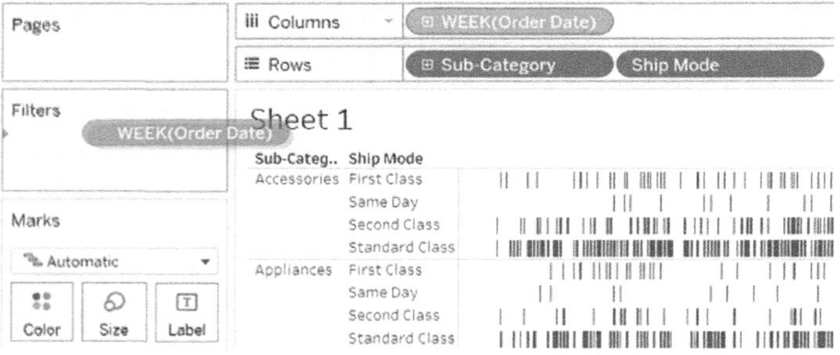

By holding down the Ctrl key (or the Option key), you tell Tableau that you want to copy the field to the new location, with whatever customizations you have added, without removing it from the old location.

12. In the Filter Field dialog box, select **Range of Dates** and then click **Next**.

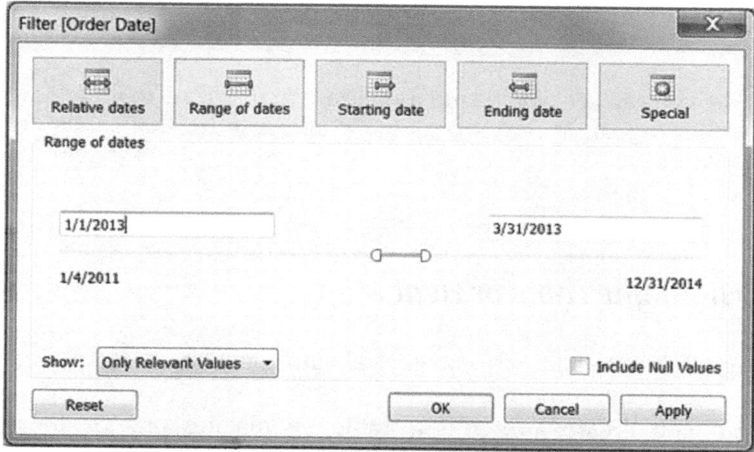

13. Set the range to a three-month time interval, such as 1/1/2013 to 3/31/2013, and then click **OK**.

It can be difficult to get the exact date using the sliders – it's easier just to enter the numbers you want directly into the date boxes or use the calendar to select the dates.

14. Drag the **Ship Mode** dimension to **Color** on the **Marks** card.

Now your view shows you all sorts of information about the lag between order times and ship times.

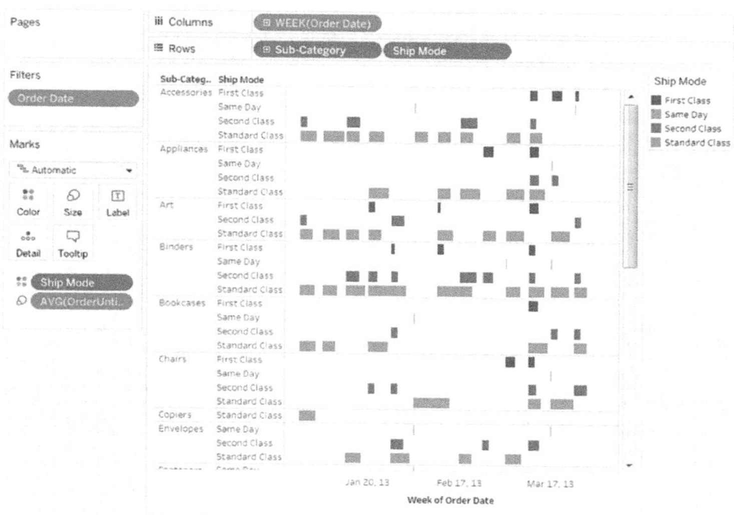

For example, you can see which ship modes are more prone to longer lag times, whether lag times vary by category and whether lag times are consistent over time.

Build a Highlight Table or Heat Map

Use highlight tables to compare categorical data using color.

In Tableau, you create a highlight table by placing one or more dimensions on the **Columns** shelf and one or more dimensions on the **Rows** shelf. You then select **Square** as the mark type and place a measure of interest on the **Color** shelf.

You can enhance this basic highlight table by setting the size and shape of the table cells to create a heat map.

To create a highlight table to explore how profit varies across regions, product sub-categories, and customer segments, follow these steps:

1. Connect to the **Sample - Superstore** data source.

2. Drag the **Segment** dimension to **Columns**.

Tableau creates headers with labels derived from the dimension member names.

3. Drag the **Region** and **Sub-Category** dimensions to **Rows**, dropping **Sub-Category** to the right of **Region**.

Now you have a nested table of categorical data (that is, the **Sub-Category** dimension is nested within the **Region** dimension).

4. Drag the **Profit** measure to **Color** on the **Marks** card.

Tableau aggregates the measure as a sum. The color legend reflects the continuous data range.

In this view, you can see data for only the Central region. Scroll down to see data for other regions.

In the Central region, copiers are shown to be the most profitable sub-category, and binders and appliances the least profitable.

5. Click **Color** on the **Marks** card to display configuration options. In the **Border** drop-down list, select a medium grey color for cell borders, as in the following image:

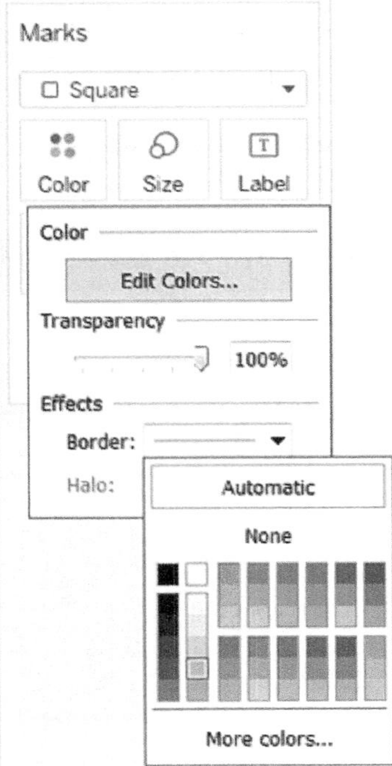

Now it's easier to see the individual cells in the view:

6. The default color palette is Orange-Blue Diverging. A Red-Green Diverging palette might be more appropriate for profit. To change the color palette and to make the colors more distinct, do the following:

o Hover over the **SUM(Profit)** color legend, then click the drop-down arrow that appears and select **Edit Colors**.

o In the **Edit Colors** dialog box, in the **Palette** field, select **Red-Green Diverging** from the drop-down list.

o Select the **Use Full Color Range** tick box and click **Apply** and then click **OK**.

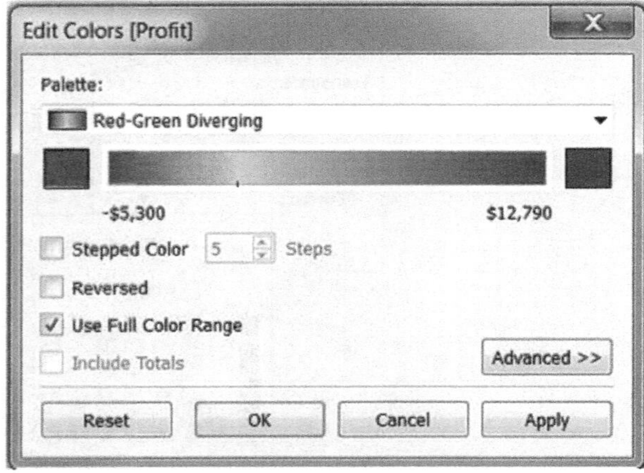

When you select this option, Tableau assigns the starting number a full intensity and the ending number a full intensity. If the range is from -10 to 100, the color representing negative numbers changes in shade much more quickly than the color representing positive numbers.

When you do not select **Use Full Color Range**, Tableau assigns the color intensity as if the range was from -100 to 100, so that the change in shade is the same on both sides of zero. The effect is to make the color contrasts in your view much more distinct.

Modify the size to create a heat map

7. Drag the **Sales** measure to **Size** on the **Marks** card to control the size of the boxes by the Sales measure. You can compare absolute sales numbers (by size of the boxes) and profit (by color).

Initially, the marks look like this:

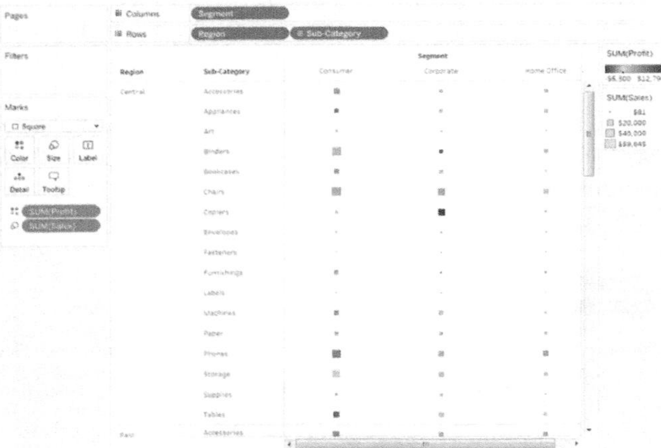

8. To enlarge the marks, click **Size** on the **Marks** card to display a size slider:

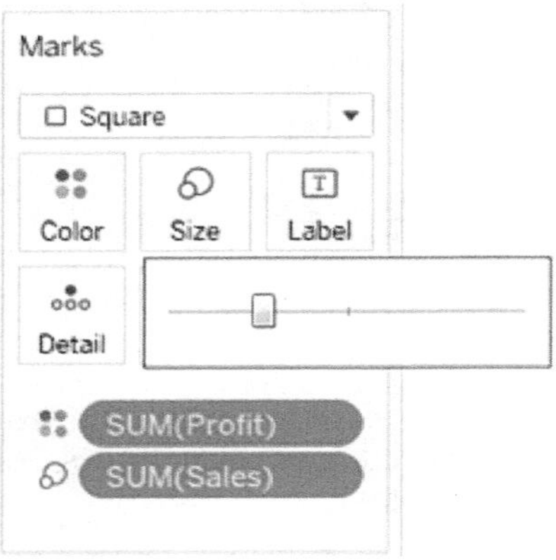

9. Drag the slider to the right until the boxes in the view are the optimal size. Now your view is complete:

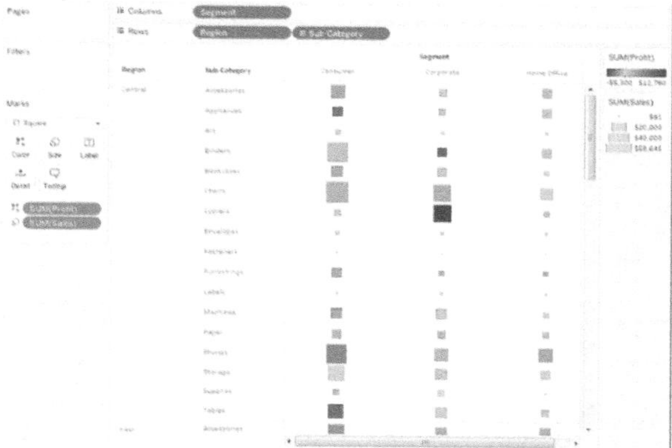

Build a Histogram

A histogram is a chart that displays the shape of a distribution. A histogram looks like a bar chart but groups values for a continuous measure into ranges, or bins.

The basic building blocks for a histogram are as follows:

Mark type:	Automatic
Rows shelf:	Continuous measure (aggregated by Count or Count Distinct)
Columns shelf:	Bin (continuous or discrete).

In Tableau you can create a histogram using **Show Me**.

1. Connect to the **Sample - Superstore** data source.
2. Drag **Quantity** to **Columns**.
3. Click **Show Me** on the toolbar, then select the histogram chart type.

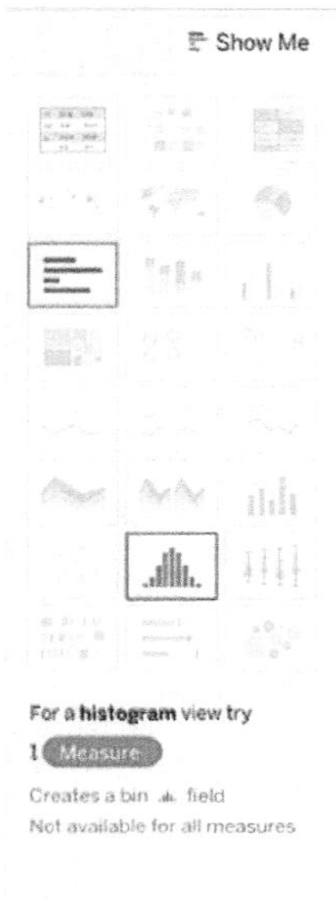

The histogram chart type is available in **Show Me** when the view contains a single measure and no dimensions.

Three things happen after you click the histogram icon in **Show Me**:

- The view changes to show vertical bars, with a continuous x-axis (1 - 14) and a continuous y-axis (0 - 5,000).

- The **Quantity** measure you placed on the **Columns** shelf, which had been aggregated as SUM, is replaced by a continuous **Quantity (bin)** dimension. (The green color of the field on the **Columns** shelf indicates that the field is continuous.)

To edit this bin: In the Data pane, right-click the bin and select **Edit**.

- The **Quantity** measure moves to the **Rows** shelf and the aggregation changes from SUM to CNT (Count).

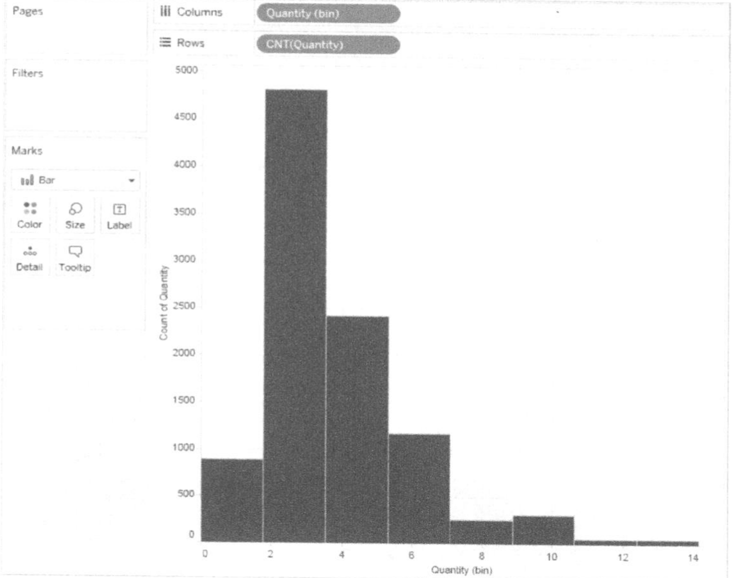

The **Quantity** measure captures the number of items in a particular order. The histogram shows that about 4,800 orders contained two items (the second bar), about 2,400 orders contained 4 items (the third bar), and so on.

Let's take this view one step further and add **Segment** to **Color** to see if we can detect a relationship between the customer segment (consumer, corporate or home office) and the quantity of items per order.

4. Drag **Segment** to **Color**.

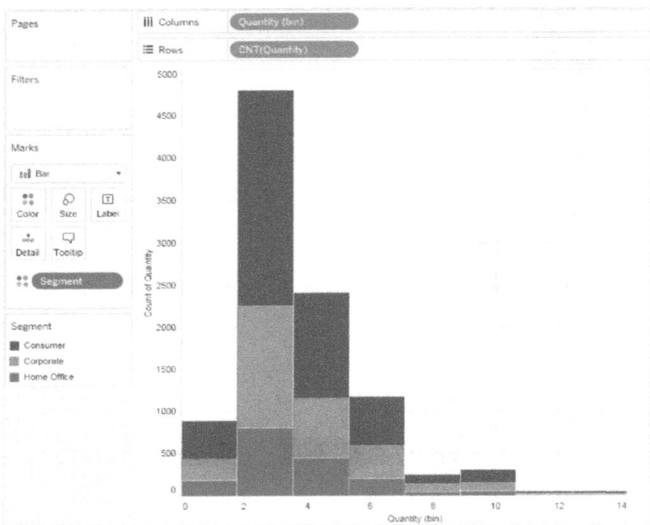

The colors don't show a clear trend. Let's show the percentage of each bar that belongs to each segment.

5. Hold down the Ctrl key and drag the **CNT(Quantity)** field from the **Rows** shelf to **Label**.

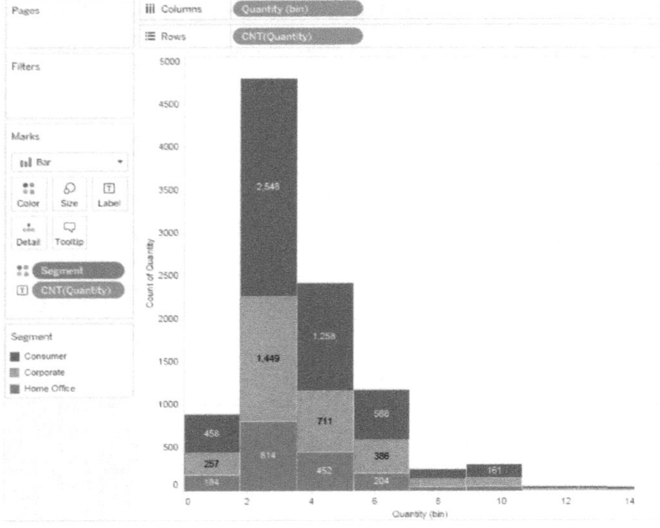

Holding down the Ctrl key copies the field to the new location without removing it from the original location.

6. Right-click (Control-click on a Mac) the **CNT(Quantity)** field on the **Marks** card and select **Quick Table Calculation** > **Percent of Total.**

Now each colored section of each bar shows its respective percentage of the total quantity:

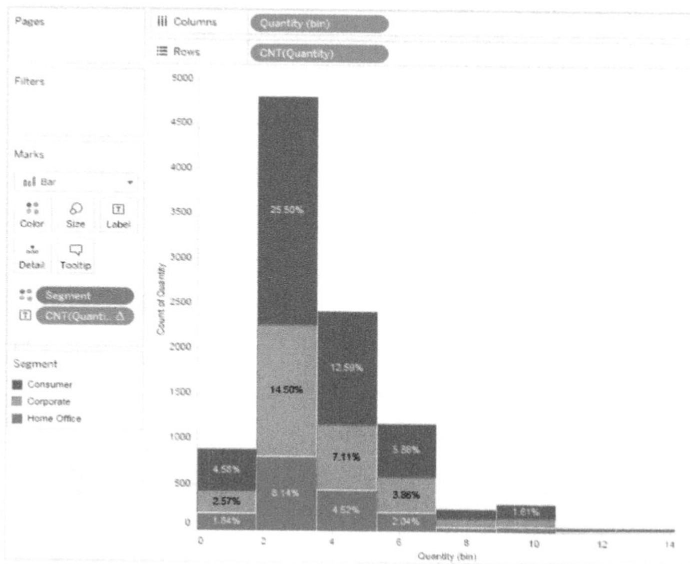

But we want the percentages to be on a per-bar basis.

7. Right-click the **CNT(Quantity)** field on the **Marks** card again and select **Edit Table Calculation.**

8. In the Table Calculation dialog box, change the value of the **Compute Using** field to **Cell**.

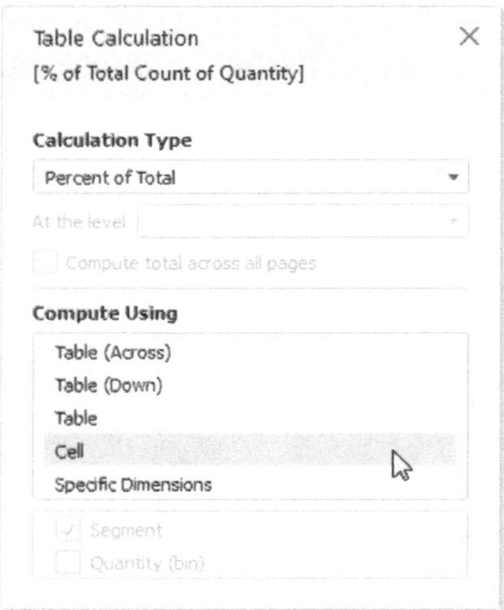

Now we have the view that we want:

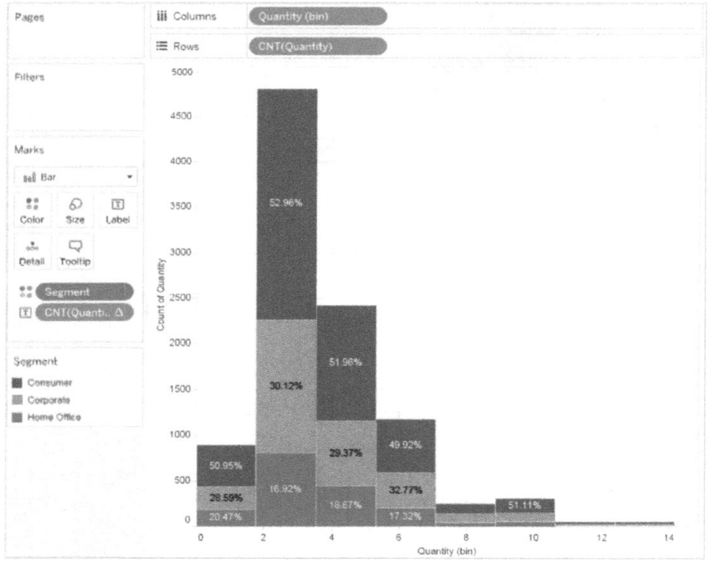

There is still no evidence that the percentages by customer segment show any trend as the number of items in an order increases.

Building Line Charts

Line charts connect individual data points in a view. They provide a simple way to visualize a sequence of values and are useful when you want to see trends over time, or to forecast future values.

To create a view that displays the sum of sales and the sum of profit for all years, and then uses forecasting to determine a trend, follow these steps:

1. Connect to the **Sample - Superstore** data source.

2. Drag the **Order Date** dimension to **Columns.**

Tableau aggregates the date by year, and creates column headers.

3. Drag the **Sales** measure to **Rows.**

Tableau aggregates **Sales** as SUM and displays a simple line chart.

4. Drag the **Profit** measure to **Rows** and drop it to the right of the **Sales** measure.

Tableau creates separate axes along the left margin for **Sales** and **Profit.**

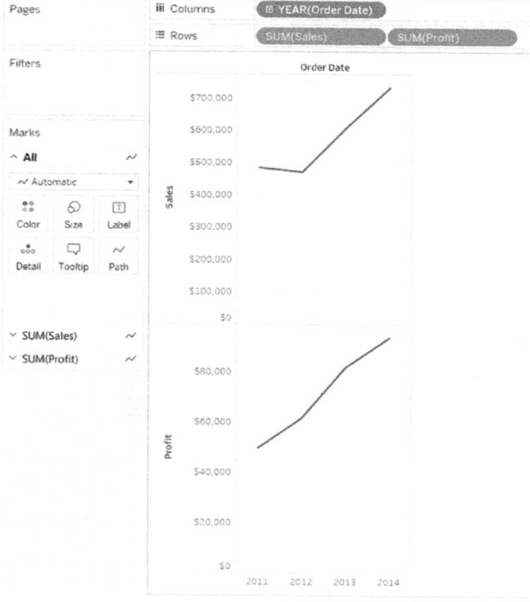

Notice that the scale of the two axes is different – the **Sales** axis scales from $0 to $700,000, whereas the **Profit** axis scales from $0 to $100,000. This can make it hard to see that sales values are much greater than profit values.

When you are displaying multiple measures in a line chart, you can align or merge axes to make it easier for users to compare values.

5. Drag the **SUM(Profit)** field from **Rows** to the **Sales** axis to create a blended axis. The two pale green parallel bars indicate that **Profit** and **Sales** will use a blended axis when you release the mouse button.

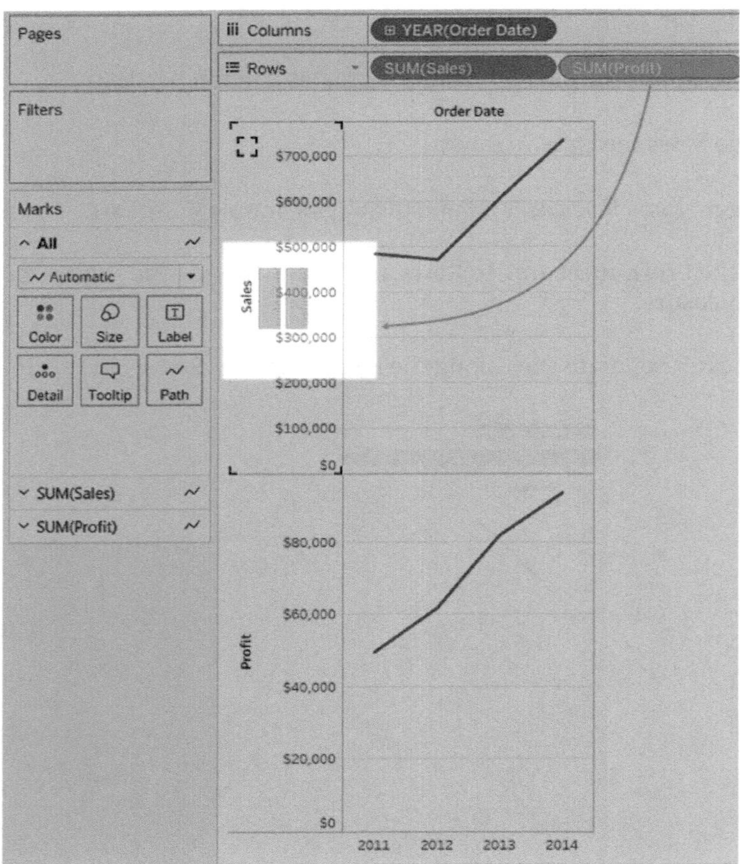

The view updates to look like this:

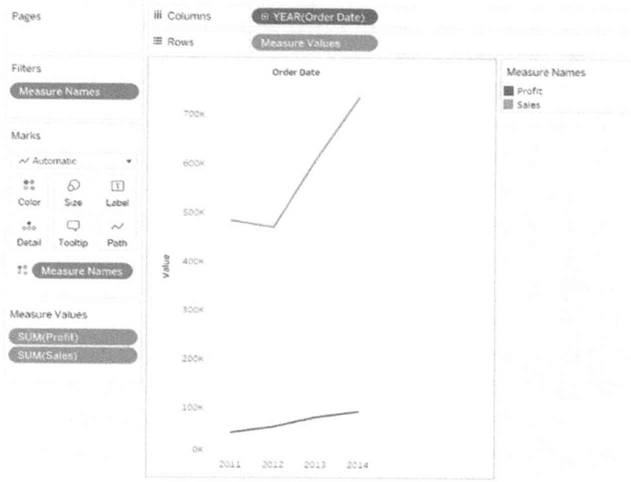

The view is rather sparse because we are looking at a summation of values on a per-year basis.

6. Click the drop-down arrow in the **Year (Order Date)** field on the **Columns** shelf and select **Month** in the lower part of the context menu to see a continuous range of values over the four-year period.

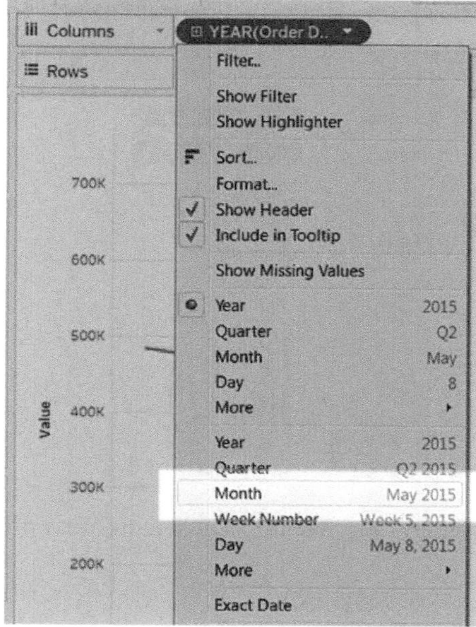

The resulting view is a lot more detailed than the original view:

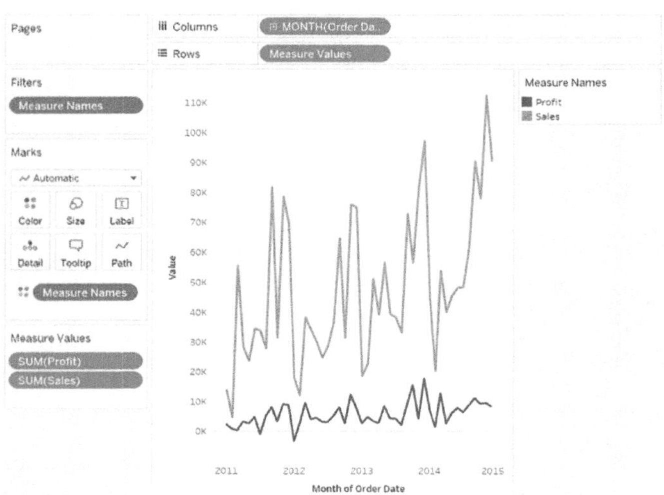

Notice that the values seem to go much higher just before the end of each year. A pattern like that is known as *seasonality*. If we turn on the forecasting feature in the view, we can see whether we should expect that the apparent seasonal trend will continue in the future.

7. To add a forecast, in the **Analytics** pane, drag the **Forecast** model to the view, and then drop it on **Forecast**.

We then see that, according to Tableau forecasting, the seasonal trend does continue into the future:

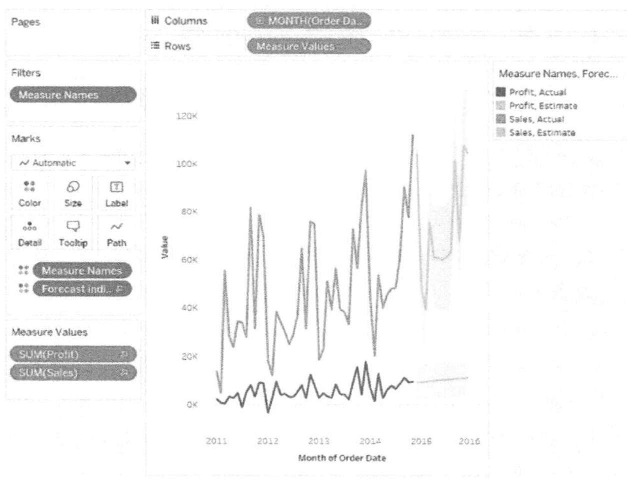

Build a Packed Bubble Chart

Use packed bubble charts to display data in a cluster of circles. Dimensions define the individual bubbles, and measures define the size and color of the individual circles.

The basic building blocks for a packed bubble chart are as follows:

Mark type:	Circle
Detail:	Dimension
Size:	Measure
Color:	Dimension or Measure
Label (optional):	Dimension or Measure

To create a basic packed bubble chart that shows sales and profit information for different product categories, follow these steps:

1. Connect to the **Sample - Superstore** data source.

2. Drag the **Category** dimension to **Columns**.

A horizontal axis displays product categories.

3. Drag the **Sales** measure to **Rows**.

The measure is aggregated as a sum and a vertical axis appears.

Tableau displays a bar chart – the default chart type when there is a dimension on the **Columns** shelf and a measure on the **Rows** shelf.

4. Click **Show Me** on the toolbar, then select the packed bubbles chart type.

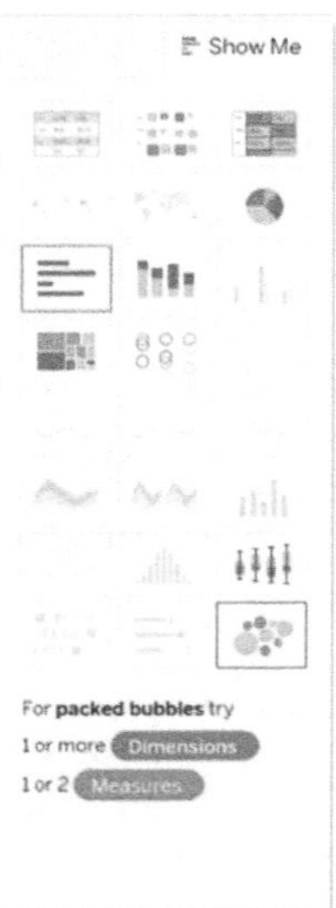

Tableau displays the following packed bubble chart:

5. Drag **Region** to **Detail** on the **Marks** card to include more bubbles in the view.

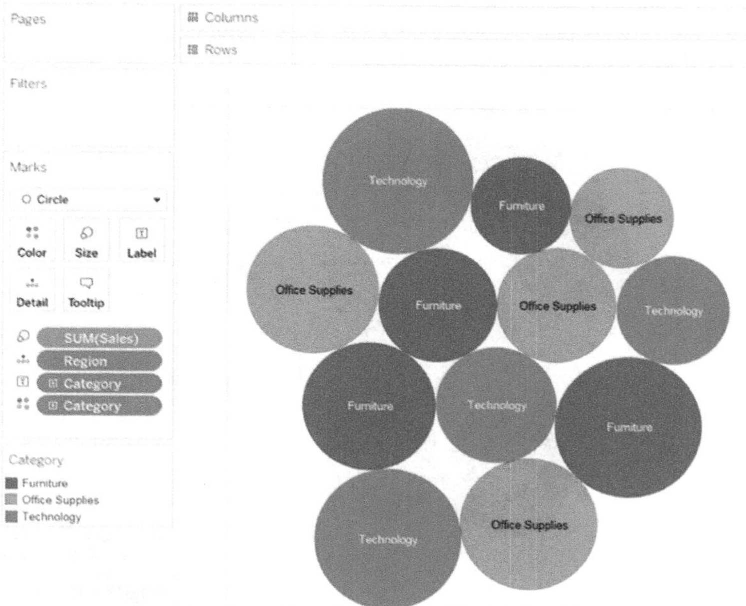

Next we'll add another layer of information to the view.

6. Drag **Profit** to **Color** on the **Marks** card:

7. Drag **Region** to **Label** on the **Marks** card to clarify what each bubble represents.

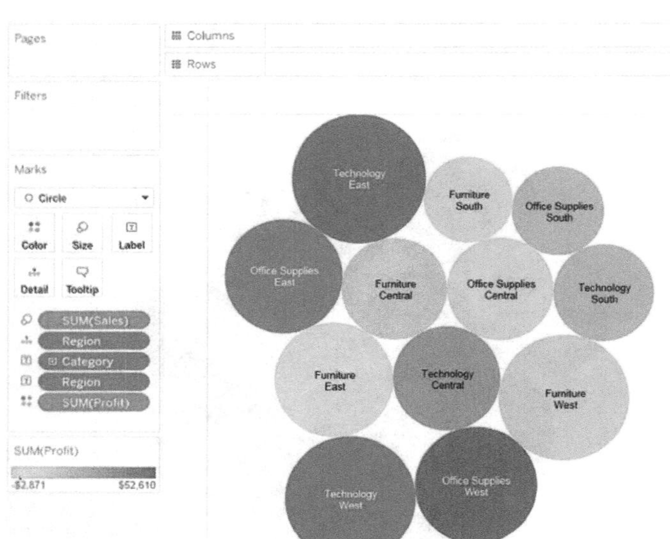

The size of the bubbles shows the sales for different combinations of region and category. The color of the bubbles shows the profit (the darker the green, the greater the profit).

To further develop this view, you might edit the colors for **Profit** to show negative profit in a different color, or create a calculated field to shows profit divided by sales (that is, profit margin) and then drop that on **Color** instead of absolute profit.

Build a Pie Chart

Use pie charts to show proportions of a whole.

The basic building blocks for a pie chart are as follows:

Mark type:	Pie
Color:	Dimension
Angle:	Measure

To create a pie chart view that shows how different product categories contribute to total sales, follow the steps below:

Step 1:

Connect to the **Sample - Superstore** data source.

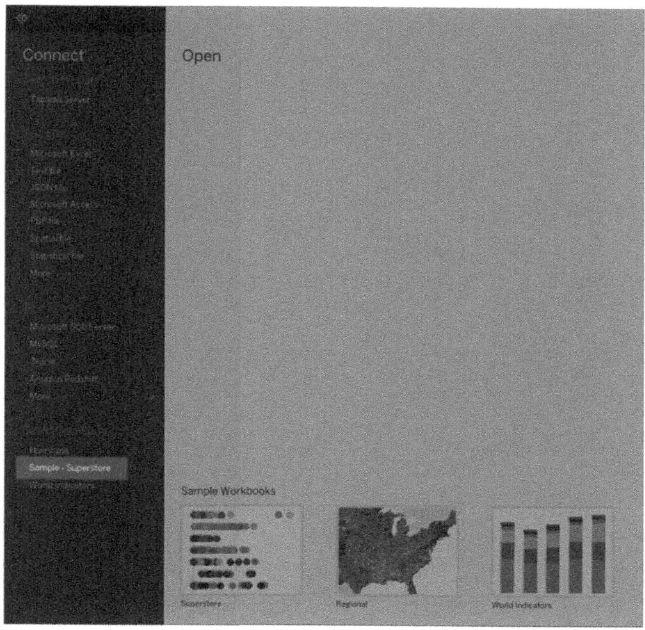

Step 2:

Drag the **Sales** measure to **Columns** and drag the **Sub-Category** dimension to **Rows**.

Tableau aggregates the **Sales** measure as a sum.

Also note that the default chart type is a bar chart.

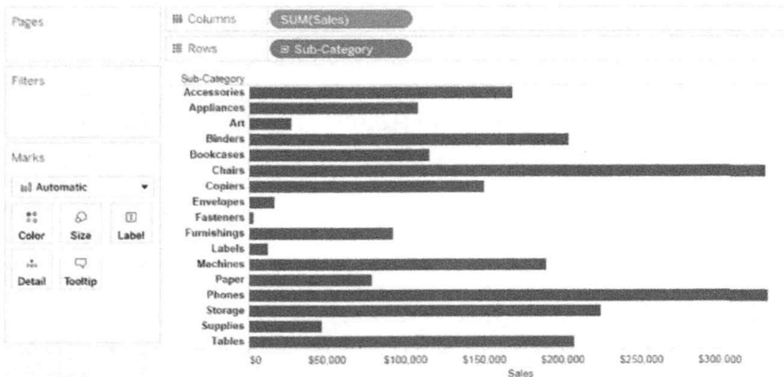

Step 3:

Click **Show Me** on the toolbar, then select the pie chart type.

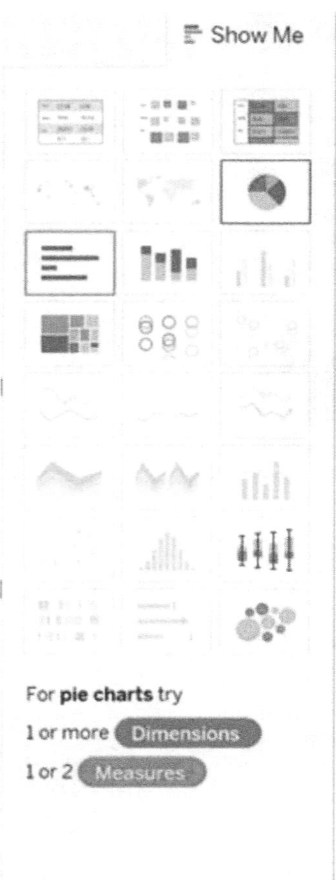

Step 4.

The result is a rather small pie. To make the chart bigger, hold down Ctrl + Shift (hold down ñ + z on a Mac) and press B several times.

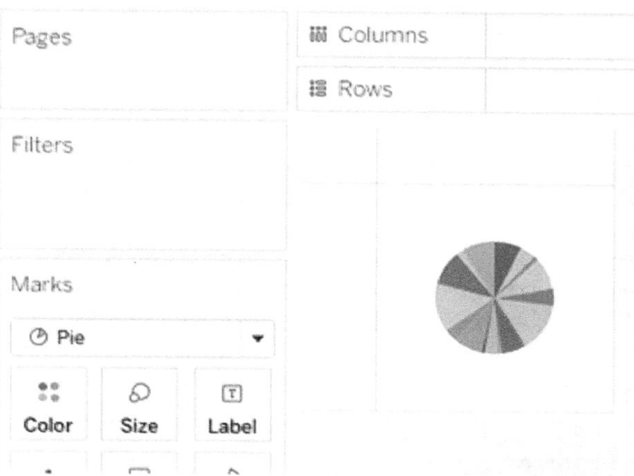

Step 5:

To add labels, drag the **Sub-Category** dimension from the **Data** pane to **Label** on the **Marks** card.

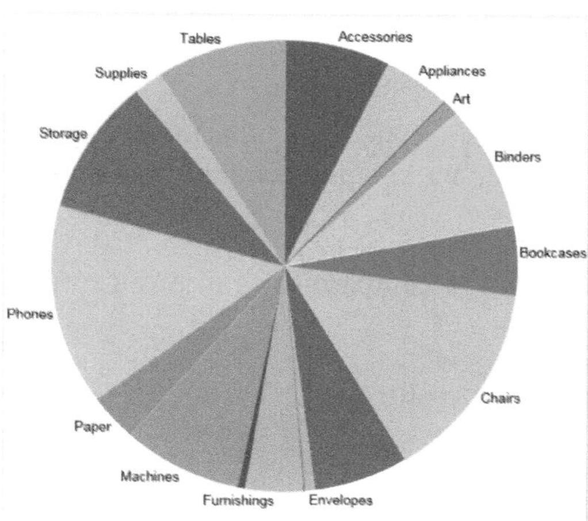

Step 6:

If you don't see labels, press Ctrl + Shift + B (press ñ + z + B on a Mac) to make sure most of the individual labels are visible.

Build a Scatter Plot

Use scatter plots to visualize relationships between numerical variables.

In Tableau, you create a scatter plot by placing at least one measure on the **Columns** shelf and at least one measure on the **Rows** shelf. If these shelves contain both dimensions and measures, Tableau places the measures as the innermost fields, which means that measures are always to the right of any dimensions that you have also placed on these shelves. The word "innermost" in this case refers to the table structure.

Creates Simple Scatter Plot

Creates Matrix of Scatter Plots

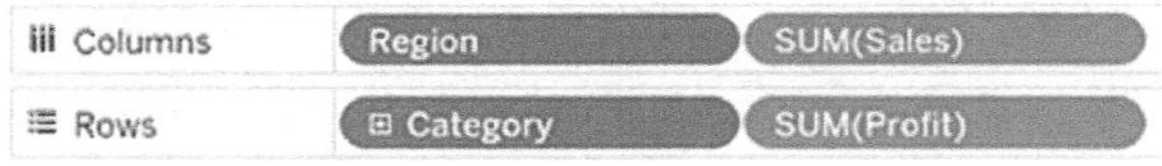

A scatter plot can use several mark types. By default, Tableau uses the shape mark type. Depending on your data, you might want to use another mark type, such as a circle or a square.

To use scatter plots and trend lines to compare sales to profit, follow these steps:

1. Open the **Sample - Superstore** data source.

2. Drag the **Profit** measure to **Columns**.

Tableau aggregates the measure as a sum and creates a horizontal axis.

3. Drag the **Sales** measure to **Rows**.

Tableau aggregates the measure as a sum and creates a vertical axis.

Measures can consist of continuous numerical data. When you plot one number against another, you are comparing two numbers; the resulting chart is analogous to a Cartesian chart, with x and y coordinates.

Now you have a one-mark scatter plot:

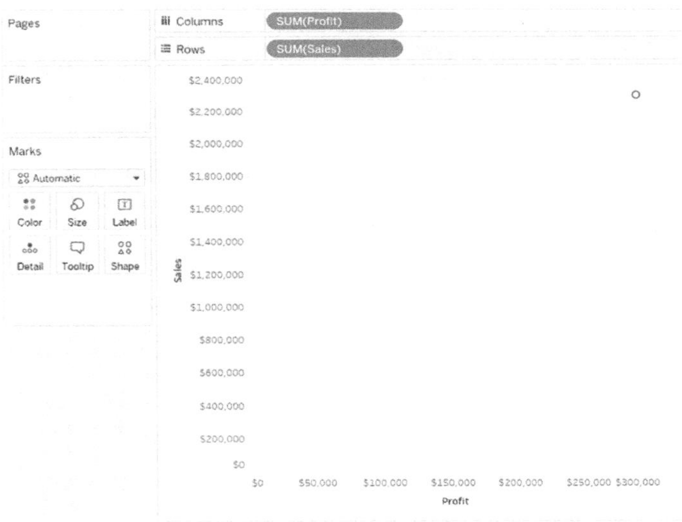

4. Drag the **Category** dimension to **Color** on the Marks card.

This separates the data into three marks – one for each dimension member – and encodes the marks using color.

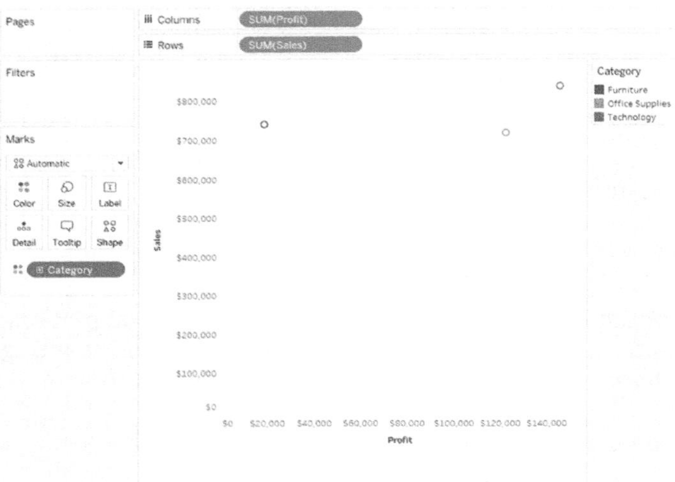

5. Drag the **Region** dimension to **Detail** on the **Marks** card.

Now there are many more marks in the view. The number of marks is equal to the number of distinct regions in the data source multiplied by the number of departments. (If you're curious, use the **Undo** button on the toolbar to see what would have happened if you'd dropped the **Region** dimension on **Shape** instead of **Detail**.)

6. To add trend lines, from the **Analytics** pane, drag the **Trend Line** model to the view, and then drop it on the model type.

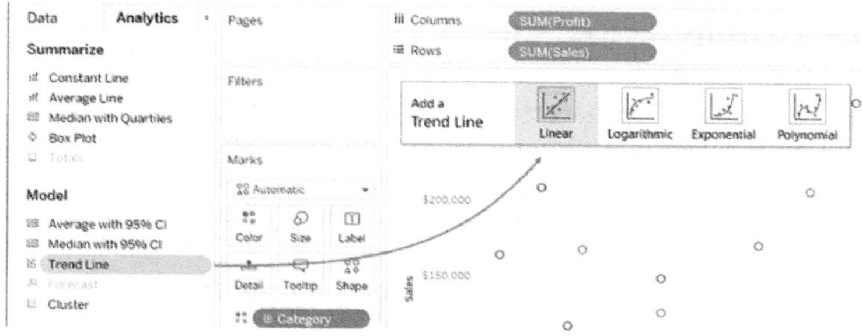

A trend line can provide a statistical definition of the relationship between two numerical values. To add trend lines to a view, both axes must contain a field that can be interpreted as a number – by definition, that is always the case with a scatter plot.

Tableau adds three linear trend lines – one for each color that you are using to distinguish the three categories.

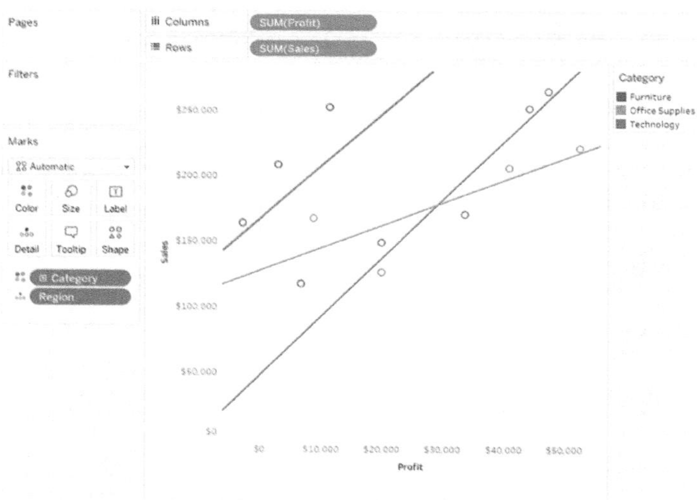

7. Hover the cursor over the trend lines to see statistical information about the model that was used to create the line:

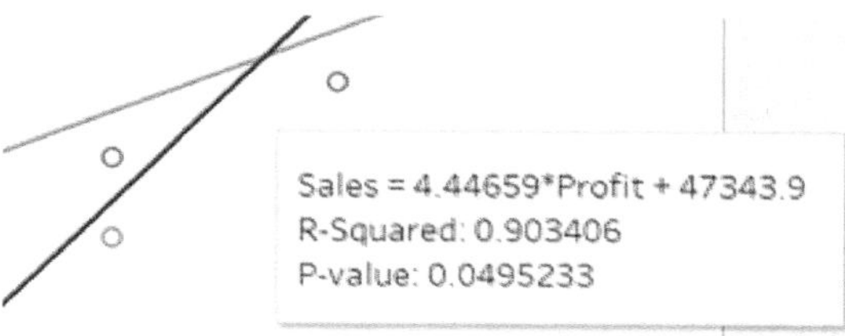

Build a Text Table

In Tableau, you typically create text tables (also called cross-tabs or pivot tables) by placing one dimension on the **Rows** shelf and another dimension on the **Columns** shelf. You then complete the view by dragging one or more measures to **Text** on the **Marks** card.

A text table uses the text mark type. Tableau uses this mark type automatically if the view is constructed using only dimensions (assuming the mark type is set to **Automatic**).

To create a text table that shows sales totals by year and category, follow these steps:

1. Connect to the **Sample - Superstore** data source.

2. Drag the **Order Date** dimension to **Columns**.

Tableau aggregates the date by year and creates column headers.

3. Drag the **Sub-Category** dimension to **Rows**.

Tableau creates row headers. Columns with headers plus rows with headers means that a valid table structure now exists.

Now you can add a measure to the view to see actual data.

4. Drag the **Sales** measure to **Text** on the **Marks** card.

Tableau aggregates the measure as a sum.

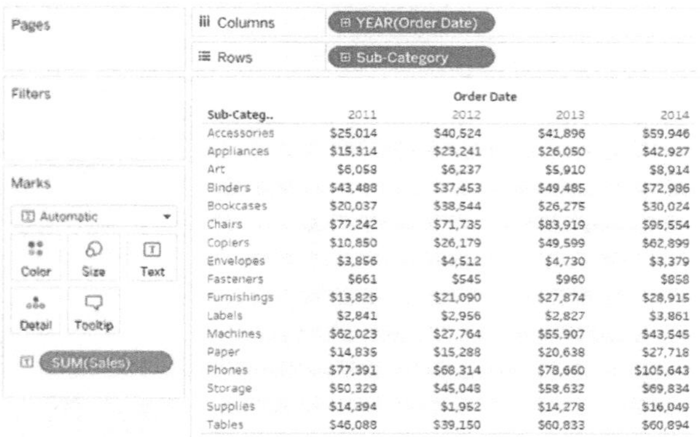

	Order Date			
Sub-Categ..	2011	2012	2013	2014
Accessories	$25,014	$40,524	$41,896	$59,946
Appliances	$15,314	$23,241	$26,050	$42,927
Art	$6,058	$6,237	$5,910	$8,914
Binders	$43,488	$37,453	$49,485	$72,986
Bookcases	$20,037	$38,544	$26,275	$30,024
Chairs	$77,242	$71,735	$83,919	$95,554
Copiers	$10,850	$26,179	$49,599	$62,899
Envelopes	$3,856	$4,512	$4,730	$3,379
Fasteners	$661	$545	$960	$858
Furnishings	$13,826	$21,090	$27,874	$28,915
Labels	$2,841	$2,956	$2,827	$3,861
Machines	$62,023	$27,764	$55,907	$43,545
Paper	$14,835	$15,288	$20,638	$27,718
Phones	$77,391	$68,314	$78,660	$105,643
Storage	$50,329	$45,048	$58,632	$69,834
Supplies	$14,394	$1,952	$14,278	$16,049
Tables	$46,088	$39,150	$60,833	$60,894

Tableau uses text as the mark type. Each cell in the table displays the sum of sales for a particular year and sub-category.

We can see that the chairs and phones sub-categories had the highest sales in every year.

5. Drag the **Region** dimension to **Rows** and drop it to the left of **Sub-Category**. A small triangle will appear to indicate that the new field will be inserted to the left of the existing field.

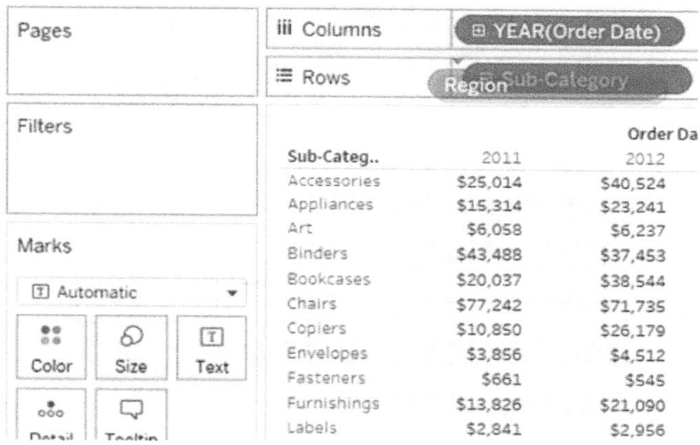

Sub-Categ..	2011	2012
Accessories	$25,014	$40,524
Appliances	$15,314	$23,241
Art	$6,058	$6,237
Binders	$43,488	$37,453
Bookcases	$20,037	$38,544
Chairs	$77,242	$71,735
Copiers	$10,850	$26,179
Envelopes	$3,856	$4,512
Fasteners	$661	$545
Furnishings	$13,826	$21,090
Labels	$2,841	$2,956

The view now breaks down sales by region, in addition to year and sub-category.

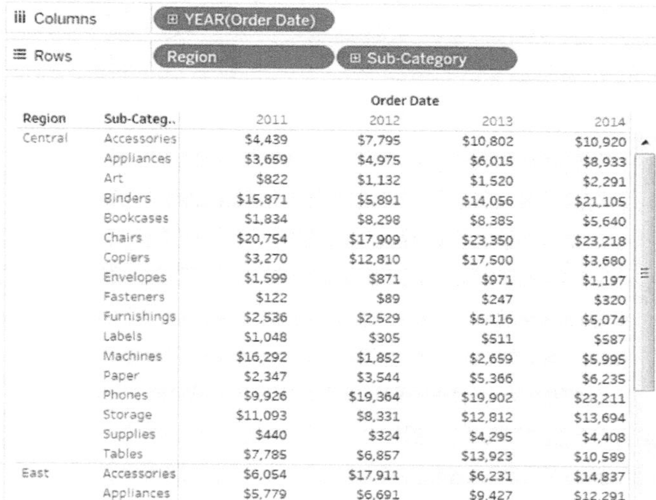

Region	Sub-Categ..	2011	2012	2013	2014
Central	Accessories	$4,439	$7,795	$10,802	$10,920
	Appliances	$3,659	$4,975	$6,015	$8,933
	Art	$822	$1,132	$1,520	$2,291
	Binders	$15,871	$5,891	$14,056	$21,105
	Bookcases	$1,834	$8,298	$8,385	$5,640
	Chairs	$20,754	$17,909	$23,350	$23,218
	Copiers	$3,270	$12,810	$17,500	$3,680
	Envelopes	$1,599	$871	$971	$1,197
	Fasteners	$122	$89	$247	$320
	Furnishings	$2,536	$2,529	$5,116	$5,074
	Labels	$1,048	$305	$511	$587
	Machines	$16,292	$1,852	$2,659	$5,995
	Paper	$2,347	$3,544	$5,366	$6,235
	Phones	$9,926	$19,364	$19,902	$23,211
	Storage	$11,093	$8,331	$12,812	$13,694
	Supplies	$440	$324	$4,295	$4,408
	Tables	$7,785	$6,857	$13,923	$10,589
East	Accessories	$6,054	$17,911	$6,231	$14,837
	Appliances	$5,779	$6,691	$9,427	$12,291

Regions are listed alphabetically. You can drag **Region** to the right of **Sub-Category** to organize the view first by sub-category, and then by region.

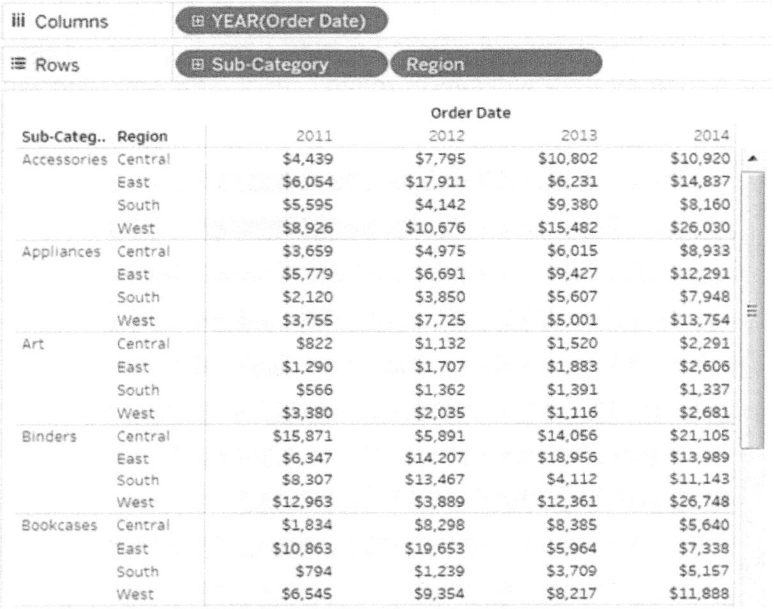

Columns: YEAR(Order Date)

Rows: Sub-Category, Region

Sub-Categ..	Region	Order Date 2011	2012	2013	2014
Accessories	Central	$4,439	$7,795	$10,802	$10,920
	East	$6,054	$17,911	$6,231	$14,837
	South	$5,595	$4,142	$9,380	$8,160
	West	$8,926	$10,676	$15,482	$26,030
Appliances	Central	$3,659	$4,975	$6,015	$8,933
	East	$5,779	$6,691	$9,427	$12,291
	South	$2,120	$3,850	$5,607	$7,948
	West	$3,755	$7,725	$5,001	$13,754
Art	Central	$822	$1,132	$1,520	$2,291
	East	$1,290	$1,707	$1,883	$2,606
	South	$566	$1,362	$1,391	$1,337
	West	$3,380	$2,035	$1,116	$2,681
Binders	Central	$15,871	$5,891	$14,056	$21,105
	East	$6,347	$14,207	$18,956	$13,989
	South	$8,307	$13,467	$4,112	$11,143
	West	$12,963	$3,889	$12,361	$26,748
Bookcases	Central	$1,834	$8,298	$8,385	$5,640
	East	$10,863	$19,653	$5,964	$7,338
	South	$794	$1,239	$3,709	$5,157
	West	$6,545	$9,354	$8,217	$11,888

You can use a table calculation to show percentages of the total instead of raw dollar values. First, you must determine how to frame the calculation.

In this case, there are three dimensions in the view: **Order Date**, **Sub-Category**, and **Region**.

You could show percentages of total for a single dimension, but that can be unwieldy. For example, if you show percentages just by region, the percentages would be calculated across the two remaining dimensions: **Sub-Category** (there are 17 sub-categories) and **Year(Order Date)** (there are 4 years). So you would be dividing the total 17 x 4 = 68 ways. That would make for some tiny percentages.

Instead, show percentages using two dimensions: **Year(Order Date)** and **Region**. Then the percentages are calculated on the remaining dimension, **Sub-Category**, that is, you calculate percent of total within each highlighted area shown below.

Columns: YEAR(Order Date)
Rows: Region, Sub-Category

Region	Sub-Categ..	2011	2012	2013	2014
Central	Accessories	$4,439	$7,795	$10,802	$10,920
	Appliances	$3,659	$4,975	$6,015	$8,933
	Art	$822	$1,132	$1,520	$2,291
	Binders	$15,871	$5,891	$14,056	$21,105
	Bookcases	$1,834	$8,298	$8,385	$5,640
	Chairs	$20,754	$17,909	$23,350	$23,218
	Copiers	$3,270	$12,810	$17,500	$3,680
	Envelopes	$1,599	$871	$971	$1,197
	Fasteners	$122	$89	$247	$320
	Furnishings	$2,536	$2,529	$5,116	$5,074
	Labels	$1,048	$305	$511	$587
	Machines	$16,292	$1,852	$2,659	$5,995
	Paper	$2,347	$3,544	$5,366	$6,235
	Phones	$9,926	$19,364	$19,902	$23,211
	Storage	$11,093	$8,331	$12,812	$13,694
	Supplies	$440	$324	$4,295	$4,408
	Tables	$7,785	$6,857	$13,923	$10,589
East	Accessories	$6,054	$17,911	$6,231	$14,837
	Appliances	$5,779	$6,691	$9,427	$12,291

The dimensions that you use to frame your calculation are called the *addressing fields*, and the fields in which you run your calculation are the *partition fields*.

6. To create a table calculation to show percentages, right-click (control-click on Mac) the **SUM(Sales)** field on the **Marks** card, and then select **Add Table Calculation**.

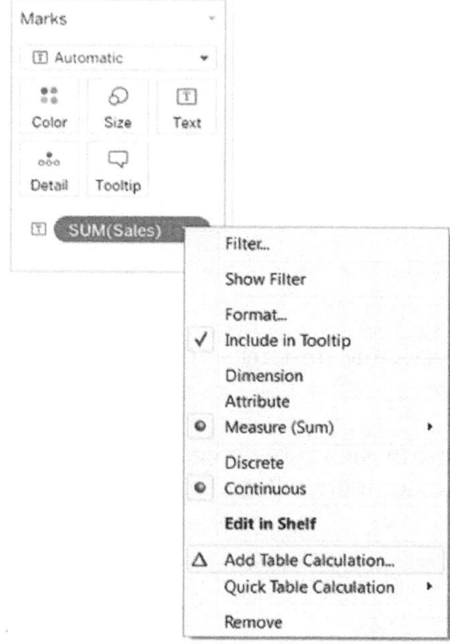

7. In the Table Calculation dialog box, set **Calculation Type** to **Percent of Total**.

The options in the dialog box change depending on the type of calculation you choose.

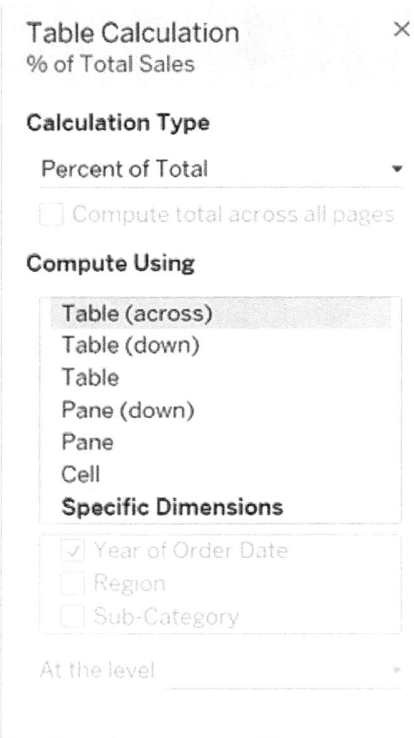

8. For the Calculation definition, select **Pane (Down)**, and then close the Table Calculation dialog box.

Now we see percentages calculated within each sub-category, duplicated for each year within each region. The numbers within each highlighted area add up to 100%.

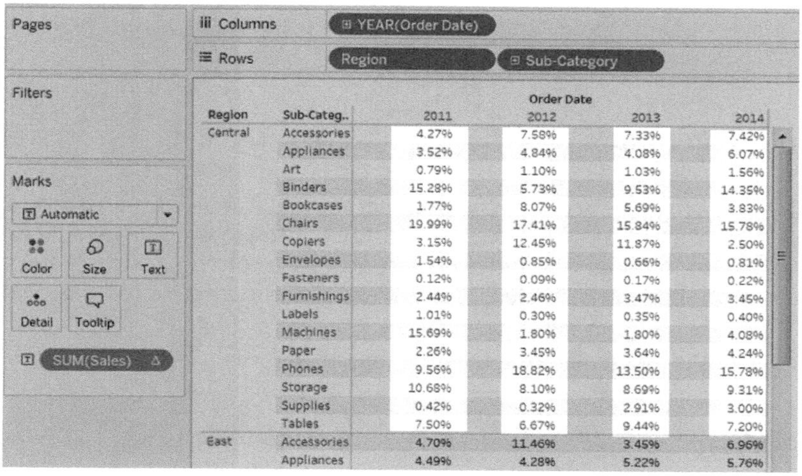

Pages

Columns: YEAR(Order Date)

Rows: Region | Sub-Category

Filters

Marks: Automatic — Color, Size, Text, Detail, Tooltip — SUM(Sales) Δ

Region	Sub-Categ..	Order Date 2011	2012	2013	2014
Central	Accessories	4.27%	7.58%	7.33%	7.42%
	Appliances	3.52%	4.84%	4.08%	6.07%
	Art	0.79%	1.10%	1.03%	1.56%
	Binders	15.28%	5.73%	9.53%	14.35%
	Bookcases	1.77%	8.07%	5.69%	3.83%
	Chairs	19.99%	17.41%	15.84%	15.78%
	Copiers	3.15%	12.45%	11.87%	2.50%
	Envelopes	1.54%	0.85%	0.66%	0.81%
	Fasteners	0.12%	0.09%	0.17%	0.22%
	Furnishings	2.44%	2.46%	3.47%	3.45%
	Labels	1.01%	0.30%	0.35%	0.40%
	Machines	15.69%	1.80%	1.80%	4.08%
	Paper	2.26%	3.45%	3.64%	4.24%
	Phones	9.56%	18.82%	13.50%	15.78%
	Storage	10.68%	8.10%	8.69%	9.31%
	Supplies	0.42%	0.32%	2.91%	3.00%
	Tables	7.50%	6.67%	9.44%	7.20%
East	Accessories	4.70%	11.46%	3.45%	6.96%
	Appliances	4.49%	4.28%	5.22%	5.76%

Pane (Down) is the appropriate choice because it specifies that the calculation should be performed from top to bottom within each pane of the table. The table has two vertical dimensions, so **Table (Down)** would have calculated the percent of total from top to bottom for the entire table, ignoring the **Region** dimension.

The pane is always the finest level of detail for the relevant direction (across or down). If you had three dimensions on the vertical axis, you might have had to use field names to define the calculation, because only the dimension furthest to the left on the **Rows** shelf (defined as Table) and the dimension furthest to the right (defined as Pane) could be captured with the structural options.

Build a Treemap

Use treemaps to display data in nested rectangles. You use dimensions to define the structure of the treemap, and measures to define the size or color of the individual rectangles. Treemaps are a relatively simple data visualization that can provide insight in a visually attractive format.

The basic building blocks for a treemap are as follows:

Mark type:	Automatic or Square
Color:	Dimension or Measure
Size	Measure
Label or **Detail**:	Dimension(s)

To create a treemap that shows aggregated sales totals across a range of product categories, follow the steps below.

1. Connect to the **Sample - Superstore** data source.

2. Drag the **Sub-Category** dimension to **Columns**.

A horizontal axis appears, which shows product categories.

3. Drag the **Sales** measure to **Rows**.

Tableau aggregates the measure as a sum and creates a vertical axis.

Tableau displays a bar chart – the default chart type when there is a dimension on the **Columns** shelf and a measure on the **Rows** shelf.

4. Click **Show Me** on the toolbar, then select the treemap chart type.

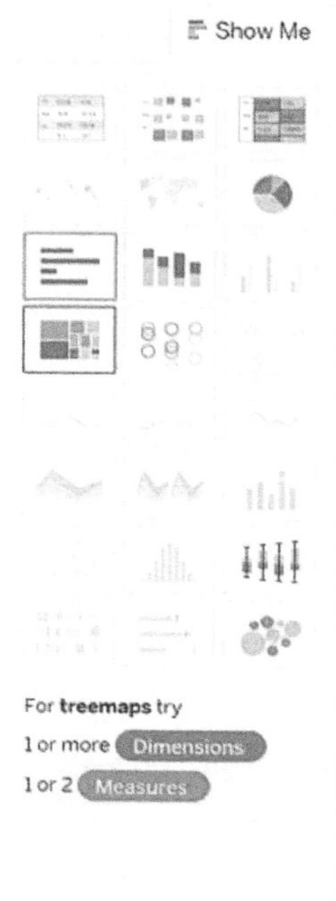

Tableau displays the following treemap:

In this treemap, both the size of the rectangles and their color are determined by the value of **Sales** – the greater the sum of sales for each category, the darker and larger its box.

5. Drag the **Ship Mode** dimension to **Color** on the **Marks** card. In the resulting view, **Ship Mode** determines the color of the rectangles – and sorts them into four separate areas accordingly. **Sales** determines the size of the rectangles:

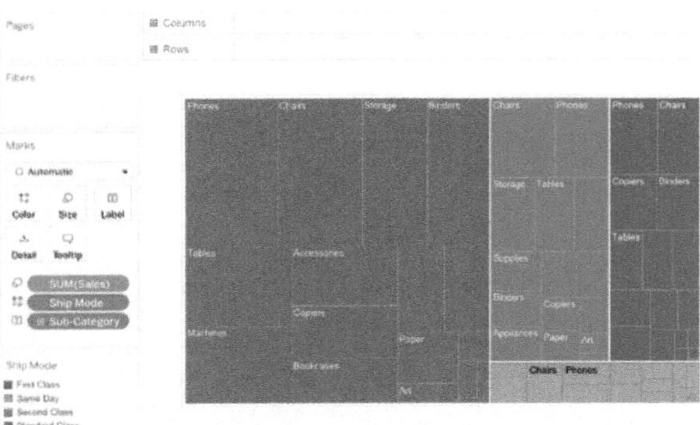

6. Try another option to modify the treemap: click the **Undo** button to remove **Ship Mode** from view.

7. Drag the **Profit** measure to **Color** on the **Marks** card. Now **Profit** determines the color of the rectangles, and **Sales** determines their size:

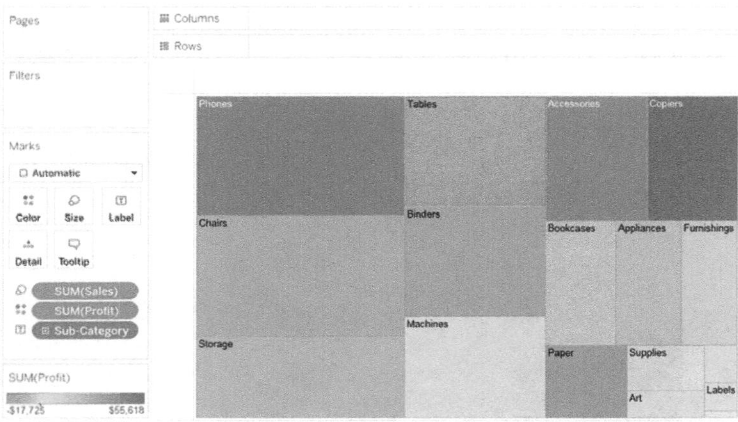

With treemaps, **Size** and **Color** are the crucial elements. You can place measures on **Size** and **Color**, but placing a measure anywhere else has no effect. Treemaps can accommodate any number of dimensions, including one or even two on **Color**. But beyond that, adding dimensions only breaks the map into an ever greater number of smaller rectangles.

Build a Combination Chart

Combination charts are views that use multiple mark types in the same visualization. For example, you may show sum of profit as bars with a line across the bars showing sum of sales. You can also use combination charts to show multiple levels of detail in the same view. For example, you can have a line chart with individual lines showing average sales over time for each customer segment, then you can have another line that shows the combined average across all customer segments.

To create a combination chart, follow the steps below:

1. Open Tableau Desktop and connect to the **Sample - Superstore** data source.

2. Navigate to a new worksheet.

3. From the **Data** pane, drag **Order Date** to the **Columns** shelf.

4. On the Columns shelf, right-click **YEAR(Order Date)** and select **Month**.

5. From the **Data** pane, drag **Sales** to the **Rows** shelf.

6. From the **Data** pane, drag **Profit** to the **Rows** shelf and place it to the right of SUM(Sales).

7. On the Rows shelf, right-click **SUM(Profit)** and select **Dual-Axis**.

The view updates. Measure Names is added to Color on the Marks card to differentiate the lines.

Note: Some marks can be hidden behind others. To move the marks forward or backward, right-click one of the axes in the visualization and select Move Marks to Back or Move Marks to Front.

8. On the SUM(Profit) Marks card, click the Mark Type drop-down and select **Bar**.

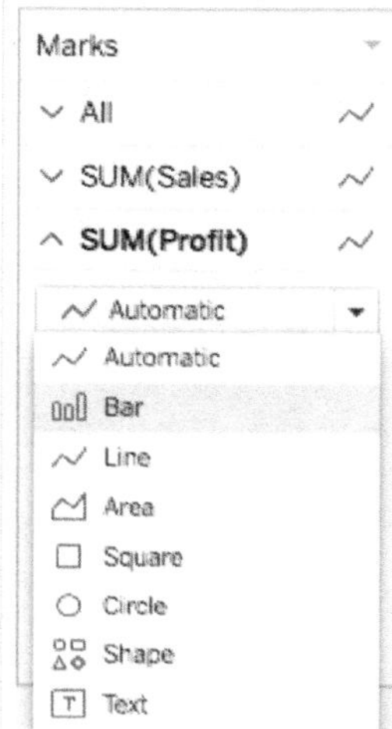

9. In the visualization, right-click the **Profit** axis and select **Synchronise Axis**.

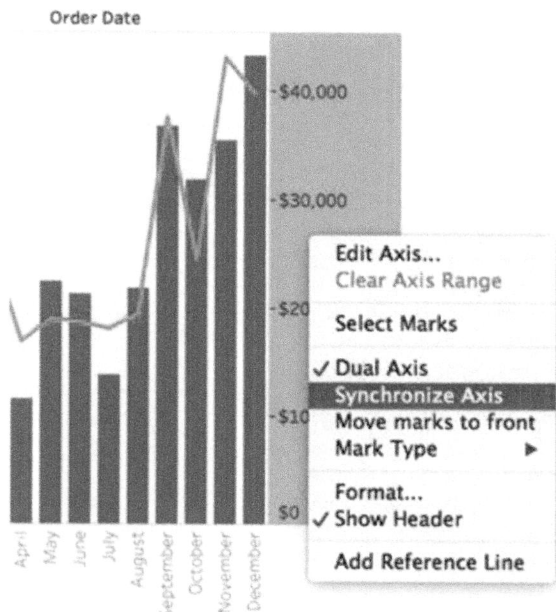

The view updates to look like this:

Chapter 6
Extracting Your Data

Extract Your Data

Extracts are saved subsets of data that you can use to improve performance or to take advantage of Tableau functionality not available or supported in your original data. When you create an extract of your data, you can reduce the total amount of data by using filters and configuring other limits. After you create an extract, you can refresh it with data from the original data. When refreshing the data, you have the option to either do a full refresh, which replaces all of the contents in the extract, or you can do an incremental refresh, which only adds rows that are new since the previous refresh.

Extracts are advantageous for several reasons:

Supports large data sets: You can create extracts that contain billions of rows of data.

Help improve performance: When you interact with views that use extract data sources, you generally experience better performance than when interacting with views based on connections to the original data.

Support additional functionality: Extracts allow you to take advantage of Tableau functionality that's not available or supported by the original data, such as the ability to compute Count Distinct.

Provide offline access to your data: If you are using Tableau Desktop, extracts allow you to save and work with the data locally when the original data is not available. For example, when you are travelling.

Create an extract

Though there are several options in your Tableau workflow for creating an extract, the primary method is described below.

After you connect to your data and set up the data source on the Data Source page, in the upper-right corner, select **Extract**, and then click the **Edit** link to open the Extract Data dialog box.

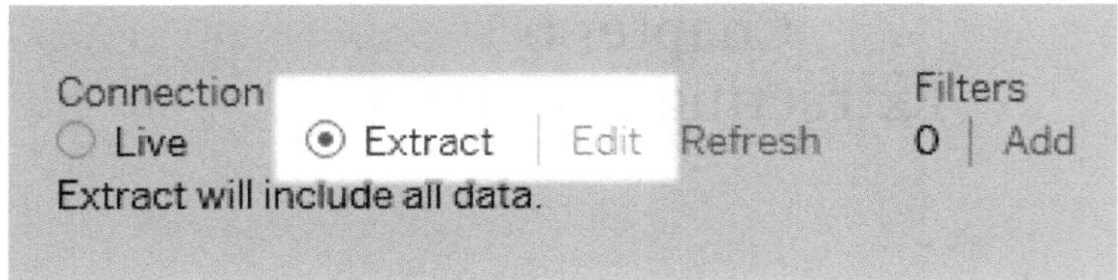

General tips for working with extracts

Save your workbook to preserve the connection to the extract

After you create an extract, the workbook begins to use the extract version of your data. However, the connection to the extract version of your data is not preserved until you **save** the workbook. This means if you close the workbook without saving the workbook first, the workbook will connect to the original data source the next time you open it.

Toggle between sampled data and entire extract

When you're working with a large extract, you might want to create an extract with a sample of the data so you can set up the view while avoiding long queries every time you place a field on a shelf on the sheet tab. You can then toggle between using the extract (with sample data) and using the entire data source by selecting a data source on the **Data** menu and then selecting **Use Extract**.

Don't connect directly to the extract

Because extracts are saved to your file system, it is possible to connect directly to them with a new Tableau Desktop instance. This is not recommended for a few reasons:

The table names will be different. Tables stored in your extract use special naming to guarantee name uniqueness, and it may not be human-readable.

You cannot refresh the extract. When connecting directly to an extract, Tableau treats that file as the true source, as opposed to a clone of underlying data. So, it's not possible to relate it back to your source data.

The data model and relationships will be lost. The data model and relationships between the tables is stored in the .tds file and not in the .hyper file, so this information is lost when connecting directly to the .hyper file. Additionally, if you extract using logical tables storage, you will not see any references to the original underlying physical tables.

Remove the extract from the workbook

You can remove an extract at anytime by selecting the extract data source on the **Data** menu and then selecting **Extract** > **Remove**. When you remove an extract, you can choose to **Remove the extract from the workbook only** or **Remove and delete the extract file**. The latter option will delete the extract from your hard drive.

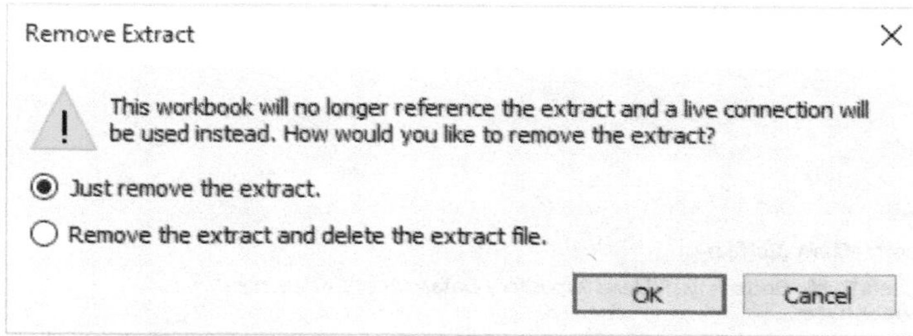

See extract history

You can see when the extract was last updated and other details by selecting a data source on the **Data** menu and then selecting **Extract** > **History**.

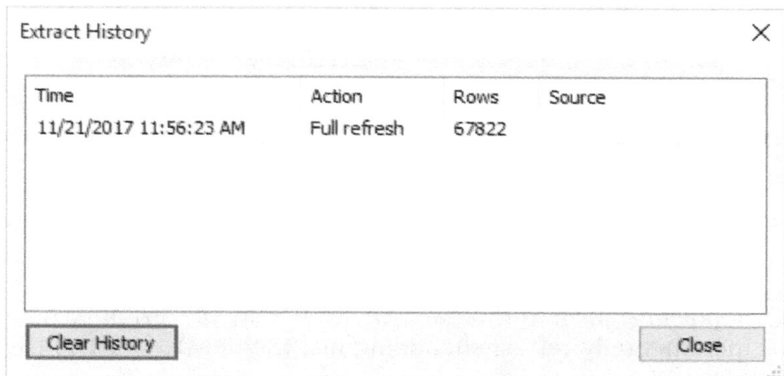

If you open a workbook that is saved with an extract and Tableau cannot locate the extract, select one of the following options in the Extract Not Found dialog box when prompted:

Locate the extract: Select this option if the extract exists but not in the location where Tableau originally saved it. Click **OK** to open an Open File dialog box where you can specify the new location for the extract file.

Remove the extract: Select this option if you have no further need for the extract. This is equivalent to closing the data source. All open worksheets that reference the data source are deleted.

Deactivate the extract: Use the original data source from which the extract was created, instead of the extract.

Regenerate the extract: Recreates the extract. All filters and other customizations you specified when you originally created the extract are automatically applied.

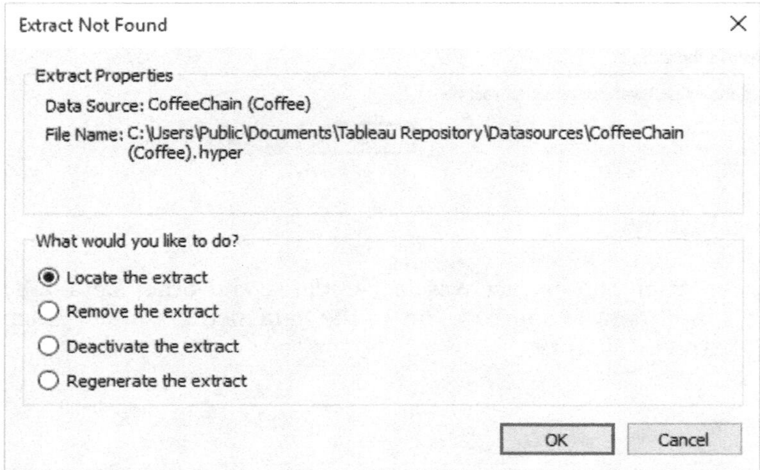

Refresh Extracts

When the original data changes, you can refresh the extract using Desktop by selecting a data source on the **Data** menu and then selecting **Extract** > **Refresh**. Extracts can be configured to be fully refreshed, replacing all of the data with what's in the original data source, or incrementally refreshed, adding just the new rows since the previous refresh.

Before you refresh extracts

If you want to refresh an extract, make note of the file format of the extract before you perform an extract refresh. If you perform a refresh on an .tde extract using version 2021.3, the extract is upgraded to .hyper extract automatically. While there are many benefits of upgrading to a

.hyper extract, you will be unable to open the extract with previous versions of Tableau Desktop.

Configure a full extract refresh

By default, extracts are configured to fully refresh. This means that every time you refresh the extract, all of the rows are replaced with the data in the original data source. While this kind of refresh ensures that you have an exact copy of what is in the original data, depending on the size of the extract, a full refresh can sometimes take a long time and be expensive on the database. If an extract is not configured for an incremental refresh, selecting to refresh the extract will perform a full refresh of the extract.

Publish to Tableau Server

If you plan to publish the extract as a data source to Tableau Server, you can specify a schedule for the extract refresh during publishing.

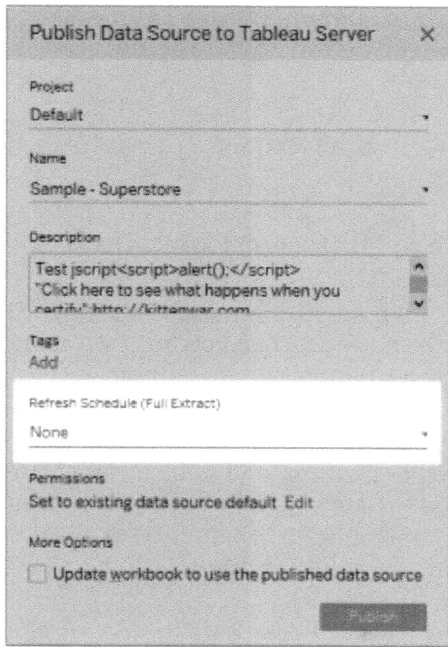

Similarly, if you are publishing the extract in a workbook to Tableau Server, you can also specify a schedule for the extract refresh during publishing.

Publish to Tableau Online

If you plan to publish the extract as a data source to Tableau Online, your options for refreshing your data depend on the characteristics of your data sources.

Configure an incremental extract refresh

Most data sources support an incremental refresh. Rather than refreshing the entire extract, you can configure a refresh to add only the rows that are new since the previous time you extracted the data. For example, you may have a data source that is updated daily with new sales transactions. Rather than rebuild the entire extract each day, you can just add the new transactions that occurred that day. Then once a week you might want to do a full refresh just to be sure you have the most up to date data.

Note: If the data structure of the source data changes (for example, a new column is added), you will need to do a full extract refresh before you can start doing incremental refreshes again.

You can follow the steps below to set up an extract to be refreshed incrementally.

Select a data source on the **Data** menu and then select **Extract Data**.

In the Extract Data dialog box, select **All rows** as the number of Rows to extract. Incremental refresh can only be defined when you are extracting all rows in the database. You cannot increment a sample extract.

Select **Incremental refresh** and then specify a column in the database that will be used to identify new rows. For example, if you select a Date field, refreshing will add all rows whose date is after that last time you refreshed. Alternatively, you can use an ID column that increases as rows are added to the database.

Note: A Full Refresh replaces all of the rows with the data in the original data source every time you refresh the extract. A Full Refresh can take longer and be expensive on the database.

When finished, click **Extract**.

The steps above can be used to define a new extract or edit an existing extract for an incremental refresh. If you are editing an existing extract, the last refresh is shown so you can be sure you are updating the extract with the correct data.

See extract history

You can see a history of when the extract was refreshed by selecting a data source on the **Data** menu and then select **Extract** > **History**.

The Extract History dialog box shows the date and time for each refresh, whether it was full or incremental, and the number of rows that were added. If the refresh was from a file, it also shows the source file name.

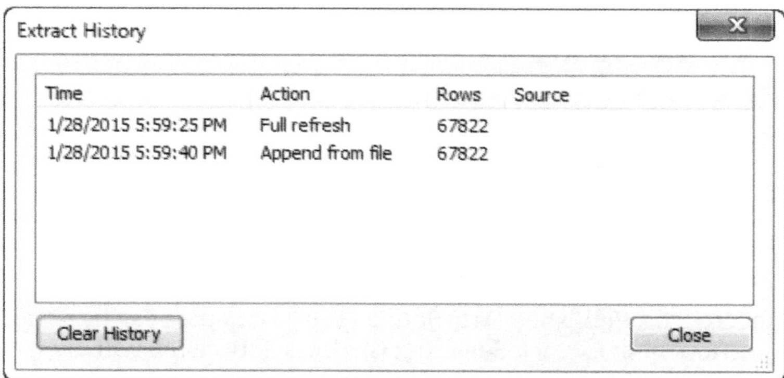

Refresh Data Sources

If you are connected to a data source that has been modified, you can immediately update Tableau Desktop with the changes by selecting a data source on the **Data** menu and then selecting **Refresh**.

Not every connection will behave in the same way. There are three primary connection types: Live Connection, Extract and Published Data Source. The type of connection is displayed by the icon next to your data source in the Data Pane.

Live Connection

A live connection sends queries to the database and updates the view depending on the results. However, the specific fields queried are defined when the connection is initially created. Refreshing the data source will update any new or changed fields.

Extract

Refreshing an extract will query the data source the extract was created from and rebuild the extract. This process might take some time, depending upon the size of the extract.

Published Data Source

When connected to a Published Data Source, the data source can be either a live connection or an extract. Selecting the **Data Source** tab will display whether the Published Data Source is a live connection or an extract. If the data source is an Extract, all refreshes of the extract are managed by Tableau Server and can only be refreshed by the server.

Changes to underlying data

If a field that is used in a Tableau worksheet is removed from the underlying data of the data source and then the data source is refreshed, a warning message displays indicating that the field will be removed from the view and the worksheet will not display correctly because of the missing field.

If the underlying data changes – for example, if new fields or rows are added, data values or field names are changed, or data is deleted, Tableau will reflect those changes the next time you connect to the data source. However, because Tableau Desktop queries the data and does not import the data, you can immediately update Tableau to reflect the data modifications without disconnecting, provided the changes have been saved in the underlying data first.

Replace Data Sources

There are times when you may want to update a workbook or sheet to use a different data source. Rather than rebuild your workbook using a new data source, you can replace the data source.

Replacing a data source does not merge or edit the data sources. Rather, replacing a data source simply redirects fields used in the worksheet to map to corresponding fields in the new data source. Any fields that the user creates in the *original* data source (for example, calculated fields, groups, sets, etc.), that are included in the view are successfully copied over to the new data source. Fields that are not included in the view that don't exist in the *new* data source are not automatically copied and will need to be manually copied and pasted to the *new* data source before replacing the old one. Folder structures will also not be copied over.

The two data sources do not have to be identical, however, any differences between the data sources will affect the sheets in the workbook and the fields in the view. More specifically, any fields, groups, sets and calculated fields that do not exist in the new data source (or have a different name) are removed from the Data pane.

Open a workbook that connects to the *original* data source.

Select **Data** > **New Data Source** and then connect to the *new* data source.

On the Data Source page, drag a table to the canvas to set up the data source (if this is not automatically done for you).

Go to the sheet tab and select **Data** > **Replace Data Source**.

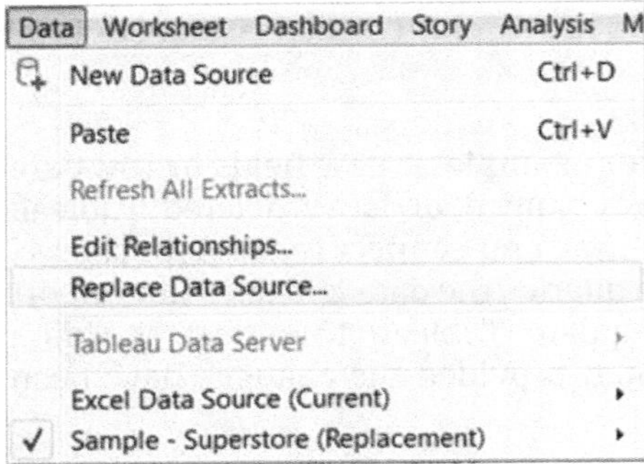

In the Replace Data Source dialog box, select the **Current** data source and the **Replacement** data source.

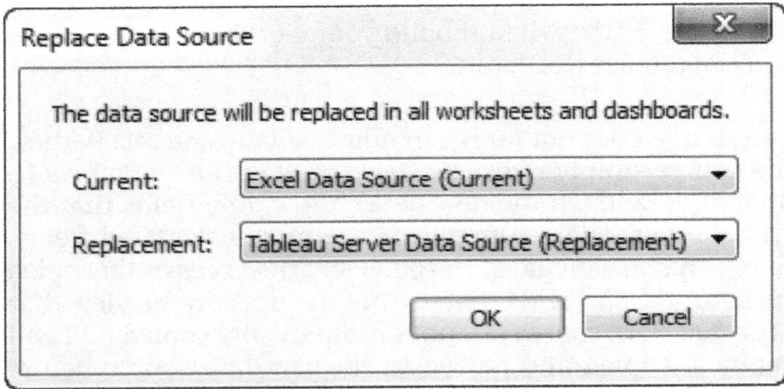

When finished, click **OK**.

All worksheets, dashboards, and stories that used the *original* data source are updated to use the *new* data source. You can click **Undo** on the toolbar to revert the change and return to the original data source.

You can only replace one data source with another data source when both data sources are relational data sources, or when both data sources are cube (multidimensional) data sources. In Tableau, cube data sources are supported for Windows only.

Published data sources

When you publish a data source from a workbook, the current workbook in Tableau Desktop will automatically connect to the published data source, and automatically close the local data source. So it is not necessary to replace the data source when you publish a data source.

In addition, replacing a data source is not currently available for web authoring in Tableau Online or Tableau Server.

Save Data Sources

If you've created a data connection that you might want to use with other workbooks or share with colleagues, you can export (save) the data source to a file. You might want to do this also if you've added joined tables, default properties or custom fields – such as groups, sets, calculated fields and binned fields – to the Data pane.

Options for saving a local data source

You can save a data source to either of the following formats:

Data Source (.tds) – contains only the information you need to connect to the data source, including the following:

Data source type

Connection information specified on the data source page; for example, database server address, port, location of local files, tables

Groups, sets, calculated fields, bins

Default field properties; for example, number formats, aggregation and sort order

Use this format if everyone who will use the data source has access to the underlying file or database defined in the connection information. For example, the underlying data is a CSV file on your computer, and you are the only person who will use it; or the data is hosted on a cloud platform, and your colleagues all have the same access you do.

Packaged Data Source (.tdsx) – contains all information in the data source (.tds) file, as well as a copy of any local file-based data or extracts.

A packaged data source is a single zipped file. Use this format if you want to share your data source with people who do not have access to the underlying data that is defined in the connection information.

Save a data source

In Tableau Desktop, open the workbook that has the connection to the data you want to save as a file.

At the top of the **Data** pane, right-click (Control-click on Mac) the name of the data source, and then select **Add to Saved Data Sources**.

Enter a file name, select the file type (.tds or .tdsx) and then click **Save**.

Connect to your data source

By default, Tableau saves .tds and .tdsx files to the **Datasources** folder under your Tableau repository. When you use the default location, you can connect to the data source on the **Connect** pane.

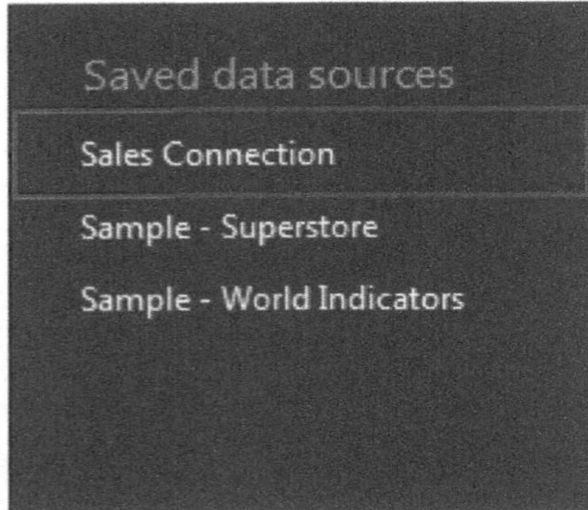

If you specified a different location, you can connect to the data source by selecting **File** > **Open** and navigating to it.

Updating a data source after the underlying data location changes

If you move a local data file that a .tds file contains a reference to, when you try to open the data source in Tableau, you will be prompted to locate or replace the original data source. If you replace the original data source, the replacement data must be of the same type (for example, Excel or MySQL). To avoid saving a specific file path, save the data source as a .tdsx file.

Close Data Sources

You can close a data source at any time. Doing so does not modify the data source. Instead, it disconnects Tableau from the data so that you can no longer query it. Additionally, the data source is cleared from the Data pane and all open worksheets associated with the data source are cleared. If you accidentally close a data source, use the Undo button to reopen it. Close a data source by doing one of the following:

Right-click (control-click on a Mac) the data source at the top of the Data pane and select **Close**.

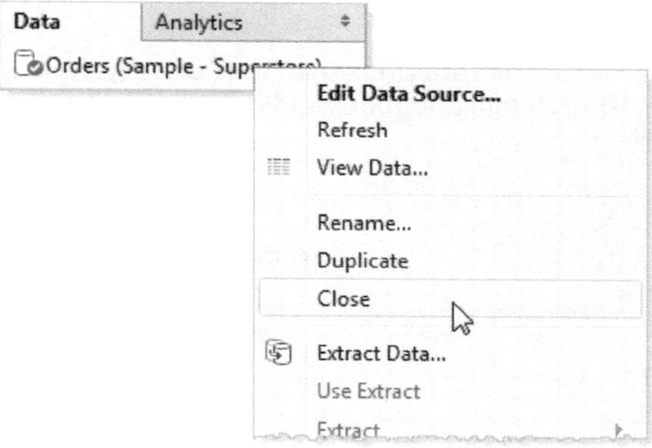

Select a data source on the **Data** menu and then select **Close**.

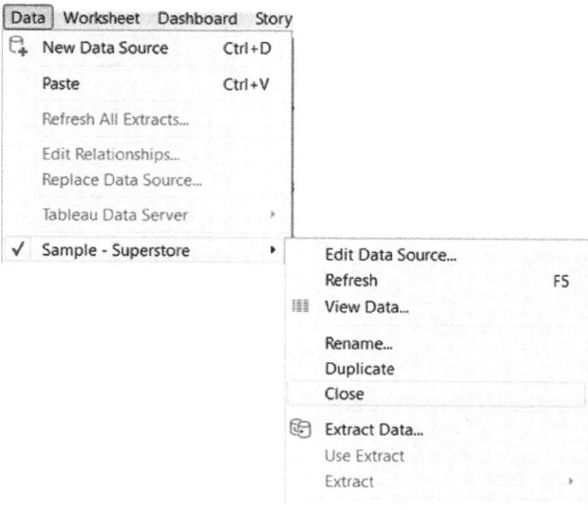

Chapter 7
Tableau Manipulations

Organize and Customize Fields in the Data Pane

The Data pane has many features and functions to help you organize and customize your data fields, find fields, and hide fields.

Organize the Data Pane

You can reorganize the items in the Data pane from its default layout using folders or through sorting.

Group fields in folders

To make data sources with many fields easier to work with, you can organize the Data pane items into folders. Items like fields, parameters, and sets can be grouped into folders.

Click the **Group by Folder** option in the Data pane menu, or in a field's context menu.

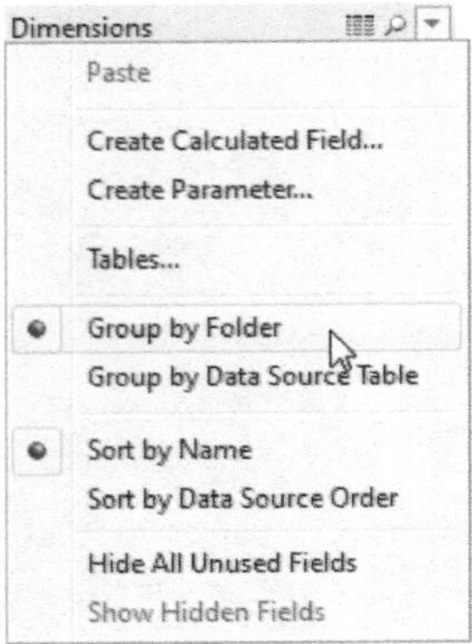

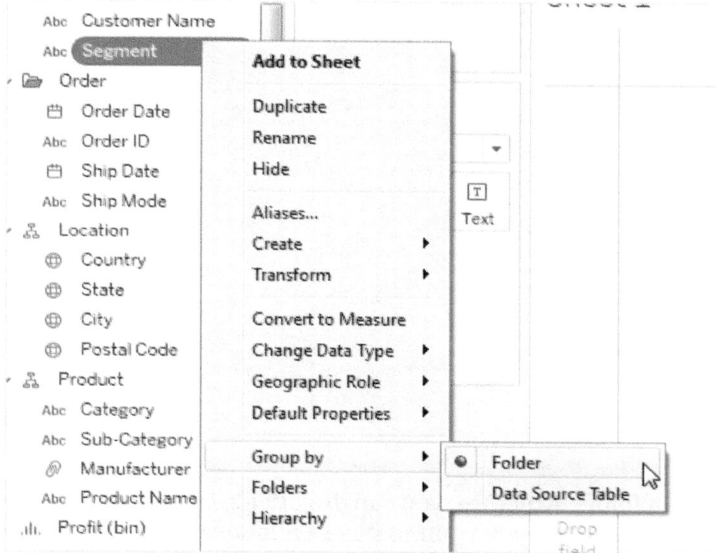

Notes on grouping options

- When you connect to a single table in your data source, grouping by folder is enabled by default.

- When you connect to a data source with multiple tables, grouping by table is enabled.

- When the **Group by Data Source Table** option is selected, the dimensions and measures are grouped according to the database table they belong to. This is especially useful when you have several joined tables.

- "Group by" options are only available for relational data sources – not for multidimensional (cube) data sources.

Group fields into folders

1. In the Data pane, select the fields you want to group together or right-click (control-click on Mac) an empty area in the Data pane.

2. Click **Folders** > **Create Folder**.

3. When prompted, name the new folder.

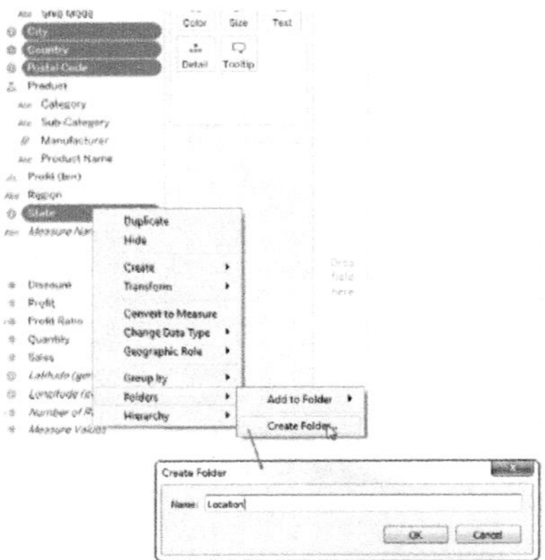

After you create a folder structure, you can drag fields from one folder to another or duplicate a field you want to have available in more than one folder.

Add a field to a folder

- Drag a field on top of the folder name to add the field to the folder. If the folder is expanded, you can drag the field into the general area of the folder.

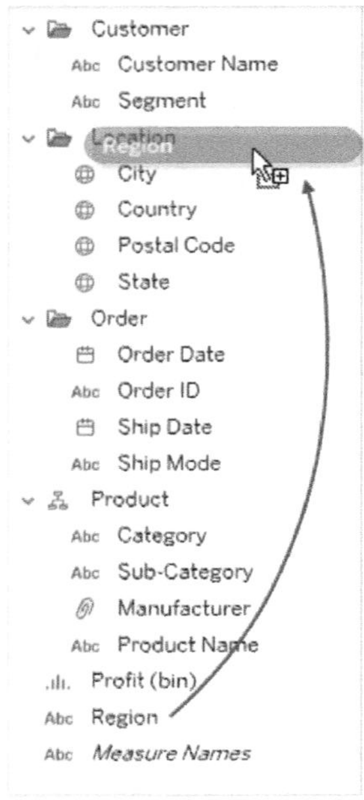

Sort fields in the Data pane

When organizing the Data pane with or without folders, you can have Tableau sort the items. These **Sort by** options are also located in the Data pane menu.

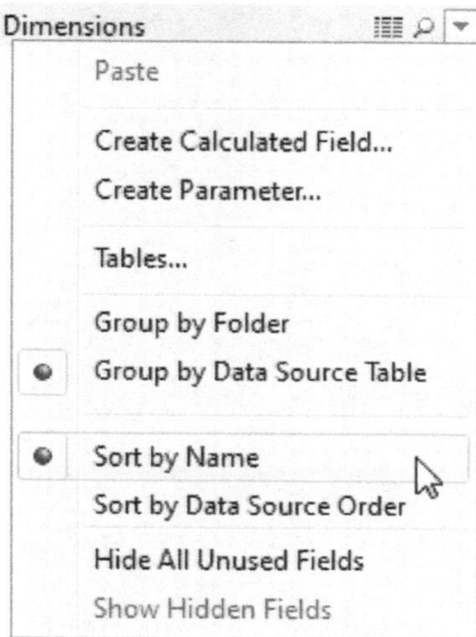

Sort options are only available for relational data sources, not for multidimensional (cube) data sources. You can sort by one of the following options:

- **Sort by Name** – lists the dimensions and measures in alphabetical order according to their field aliases.

- **Sort by Data Source Order** – lists the dimensions and measures in the order they are listed in the underlying data source.

Find fields

You can search for fields, folders and hierarchies in the Data pane. When there are many fields in your data source it can be difficult to find a specific one like "Date" or "Customer" or "Profit," or to find all fields that end in "xyz." To find an item, do the following:

Click the **Find Field** icon at the top of the Data pane (**Ctrl + F** in Windows, **Command-F** on a Mac) and enter the name of the item you want to search for. You can also enter a string of characters, to search for all item names that contain that string.

As you type in the search box, search filters the contents of the Data pane to show all fields, folders or hierarchies that contain the typed string.

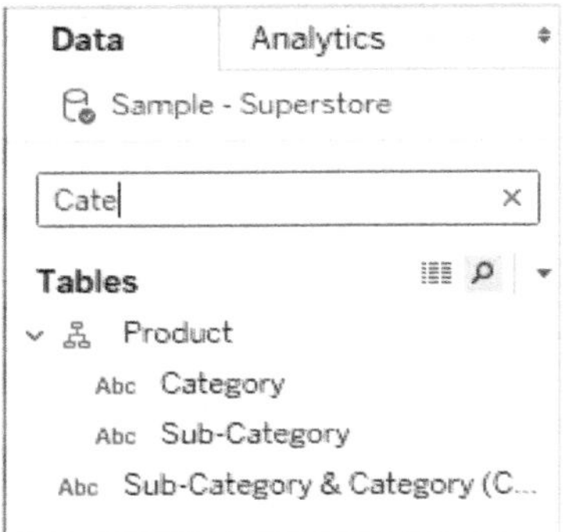

Search remains open until you click the **Find Field** icon or press **Ctrl + F** again.

Rename Fields

You can rename fields in the Data pane. For example, you could rename a field named **Customer Segment** in the data source to be **Business Segment** in Tableau. You can also rename user-created fields. Renaming a field does not change the name of the field in the underlying data source, rather it is given a special name that appears only in Tableau workbooks. The changed field name is saved with the workbook as well as when you export the data source. You can rename any type of field: dimensions, measures, sets, or parameters.

Revert to the Default Field Name

If the field you renamed was from the original data source you can click the field name in the Data pane and hold the mouse button down until the field name is shown in the box. At the right of the edit field is a small circular arrow that you can click to restore the original data source field name.

To revert the names of multiple fields that were in the original data source, select them all, right-click, and then choose **Reset Names**.

Combine Fields

Combine fields to create a cross product of members from different dimensions. You can combine dimensions if you want to encode a data view using multiple dimensions.

To combine the fields, select multiple dimensions in the Data pane and then right-click (control-click on a Mac) the fields and select **Create** > **Combined Field**.

Note: For cube (multidimensional) data sources, you must select levels from different hierarchies. In Tableau, cube data sources are supported only in Windows.

For example, the selections shown below will produce a new field that consists of the Category and Sub-Category dimensions.

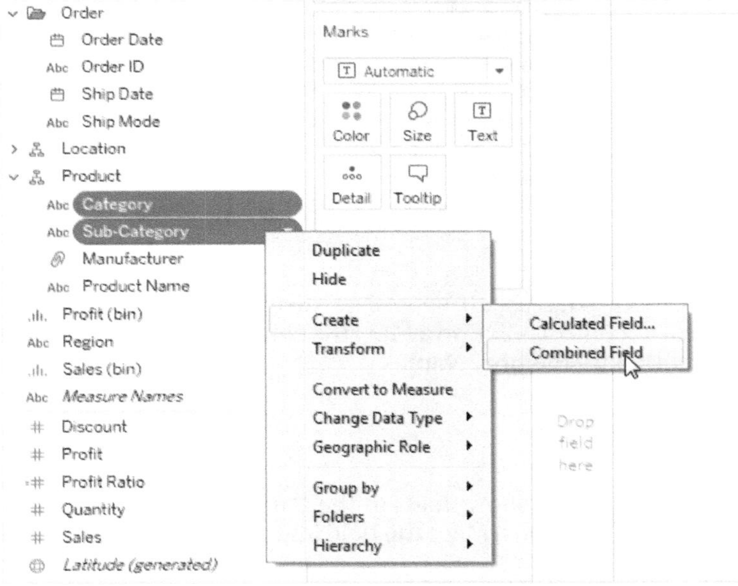

The two dimensions are combined into a new dimension. The name of the field is automatically created from the names of the original fields. Right-click (control-click on a Mac) the new field and select **Rename** to change the name.

When you use the new field in a view, a header is created for each combination of the two original dimensions. For example, the view below shows the members of the combined Category and Sub-Category fields.

	Region		
Sub-Category & Category ..	Central	East	South
Accessories, Technology	$33,956	$45,033	$27,277
Appliances, Office Supplies	$23,582	$34,188	$19,525
Art, Office Supplies	$5,765	$7,486	$4,656
Binders, Office Supplies	$56,923	$53,498	$37,030
Bookcases, Furniture	$24,157	$43,819	$10,899
Chairs, Furniture	$85,231	$96,261	$45,176
Copiers, Technology	$37,260	$53,219	$9,300
Envelopes, Office Supplies	$4,637	$4,376	$3,346
Fasteners, Office Supplies	$778	$820	$503
Furnishings, Furniture	$15,254	$29,071	$17,307
Labels, Office Supplies	$2,451	$2,603	$2,353

Note: For cube data sources, to choose to display the fully qualified name, right-click (control-click on a Mac) the combined field in the Data pane and select **Qualify Member Names**.

Hide or Unhide Fields

You can selectively hide or show fields in the Data pane. To hide a field, right-click (control-click on a Mac) the field and select **Hide**.

When you want to change your fields from hidden to visible, select **Show Hidden Fields** on the Data pane menu.

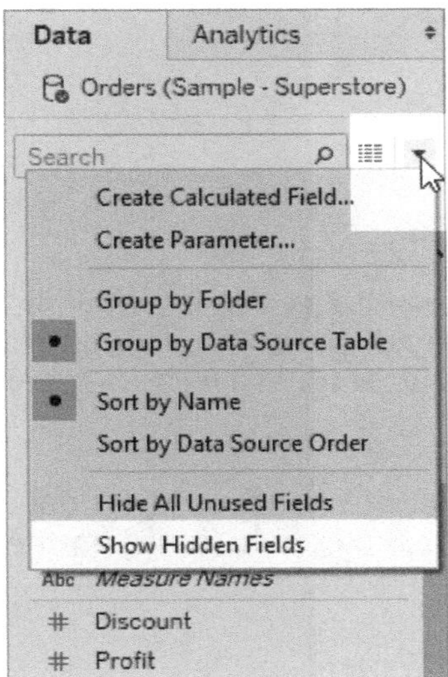

The hidden fields are then shown in grey in the Data pane. You can then select one or more hidden fields, right-click (control-click on a Mac) and select **Unhide**.

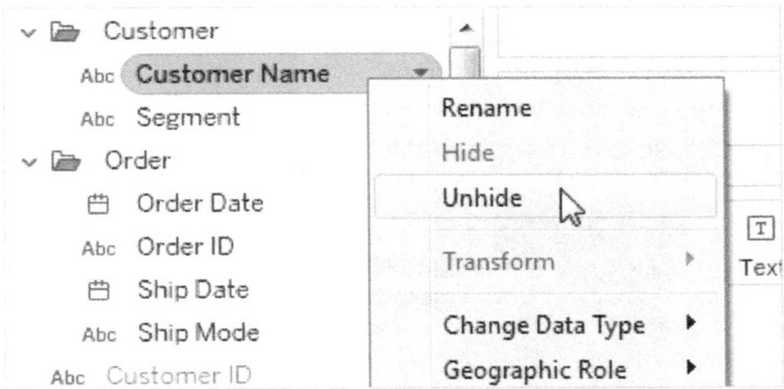

Select **Hide All Unused Fields** on the Data pane menu to quickly hide all of the fields that are not being used in the workbook.

Note: Hiding fields can be a good way to decrease the size of a data extract file because hidden fields are automatically excluded from the extract.

Add Calculated Fields to the Data Pane

You can create calculated fields that appear in the Data pane. These new computed fields can be used like any other field. Select **Create Calculated**

Field on the Data pane menu. Alternatively, select **Analysis** > **Create Calculated Field**.

Edit Default Settings for Fields

When you drag fields to shelves, the data is represented as marks in the view. The fields and their marks are initially displayed based on their default settings. You can control these default settings by clicking the drop-down arrow on a field.

The **Default Properties** menu includes default settings for aggregation, comments, number formatting, color, shape, and totals (based on the type of field).

Set the default aggregation for a measure

You can specify a default aggregation for any measure. The default aggregation will be used automatically when the measure is first totalled in the view.

1. Right-click (control-click on a Mac) any measure in the Data pane and select **Default Properties** > **Aggregation**.

2. In the Aggregation list, select an aggregation.

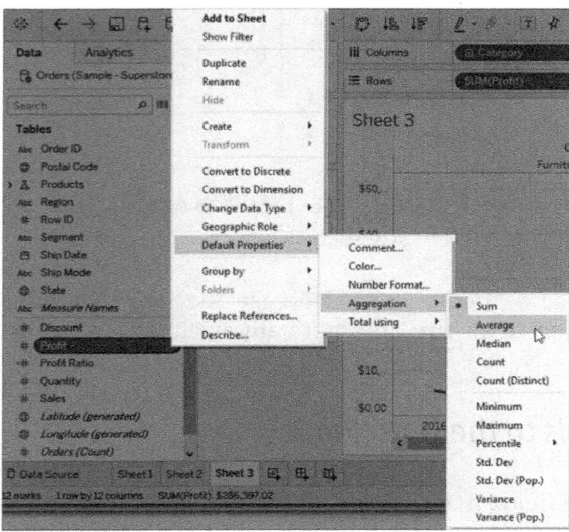

Whether you are specifying the aggregation for a field on a shelf or the default aggregation in the Data pane, you can select from several aggregations.

Add default comments for specific fields

Fields can have comments that describe them. The comments display in a tooltip in the Data pane and in the Calculated fields dialog box. Field comments are a good way to give more context to the data in your data source. Comments are especially useful when you are building a workbook for others to use.

To add a default comment for a field

1. Right-click (control-click on a Mac) a field in the Data pane and select **Default Properties** > **Comment**.

2. Write a comment in the subsequent dialog box. Comments support rich text formatting that will be represented in the tooltip.

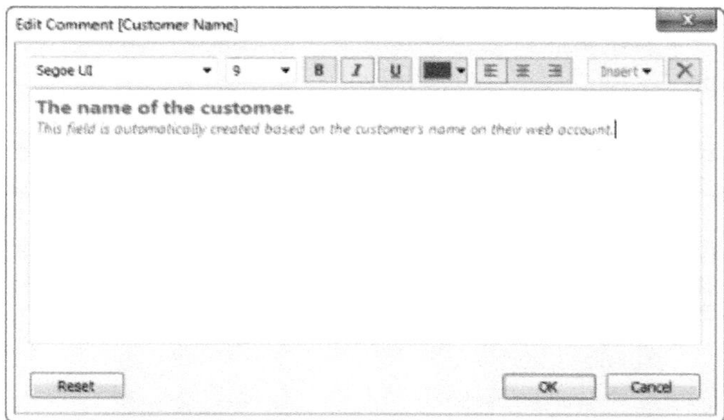

3. When finished, click **OK**.

Now when you hover the cursor over the field in the Data pane, you will see the comment.

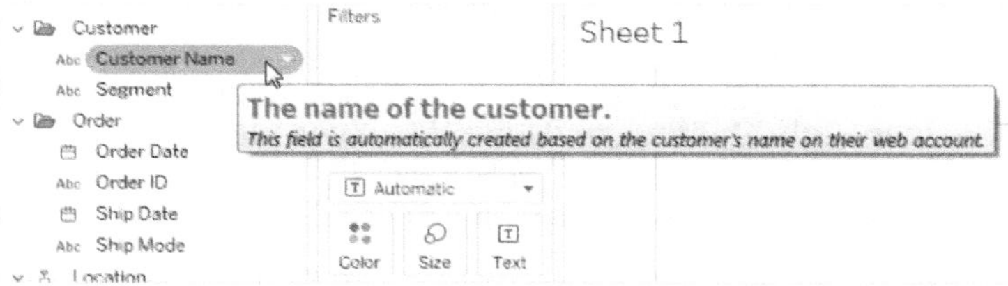

Set the default number format

You can set the default number format for date and number fields. For example, you may want to always show the Sales values as currency using the U.S. dollar sign and two decimal places. Or you may want to always show Discount as a percentage.

To set the default formats, right-click (control-click on Mac) a date or number field and select either **Date Format** or **Number Format** on the Default Properties menu. A dialog box will open, where you can specify a default format.

Set the default color

When you use a dimension to color encode the view, default colors are assigned to the field's values. Color encodings are shared across multiple worksheets that use the same data source to help you create consistent displays of your data. For example, if you define the Western region to be green, it will automatically be green in all other views in the workbook. To set the default color encodings for a field, right-click (control-click on Mac) the field in the Data pane and select **Default Properties** > **Color**.

Set the default shape

When you use a dimension to shape encode the view, default shapes are assigned to the field's values. Shape encodings are shared across multiple worksheets that use the same data source to help you create consistent displays of your data. For example, if you define that Furniture products are represented with a square mark, it will automatically be changed to a square mark in all other views in the workbook.

To set the default shape encodings for a field, right-click (control-click on Mac) the field in the Data pane and select **Default Properties** > **Shape**.

Set the default sort order for the values within a categorical field

You can set a default sort order for the values within a categorical field so that every time you use the field in the view, the values will be sorted correctly. For example, let's say you have an Order Priority field that contains the values High, Medium, and Low. When you place these in the view, by default they will be listed as High, Low, Medium because they are shown in alphabetical order. You can set a default sort so that these values are always listed correctly.

To set the default sort order, right-click (control-click on a Mac) a dimension and select **Default Properties** > **Sort**. Then use the sort dialog box to specify a sort order.

Note: The default sort order also controls how the field values are listed in a filter in the view.

Create Aliases to Rename Members in the View

You can create aliases (alternate names) for members in a dimension so that their labels appear differently in the view.

Aliases can be created for the members of discrete dimensions only. They cannot be created for continuous dimensions, dates, or measures.

Create an alias

1. In the Data pane, right-click a dimension and select **Aliases**.

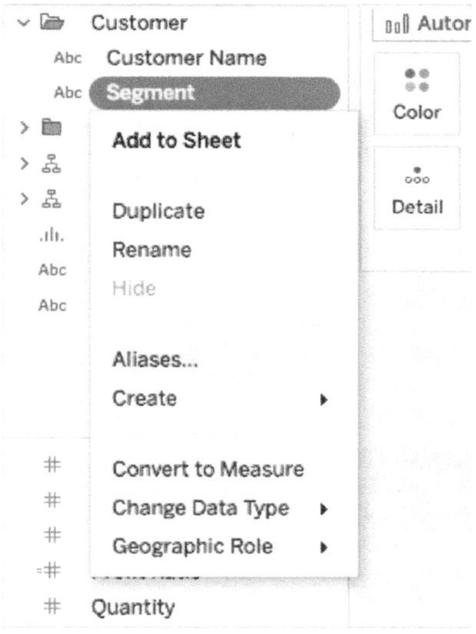

Tip: If **Aliases** does not appear in the dialog, verify that you are not connected to a published data source and the field you are trying to alias is a discrete dimension.

2. In the Edit Aliases dialog box, under **Value (Alias)**, select a member and enter a new name.

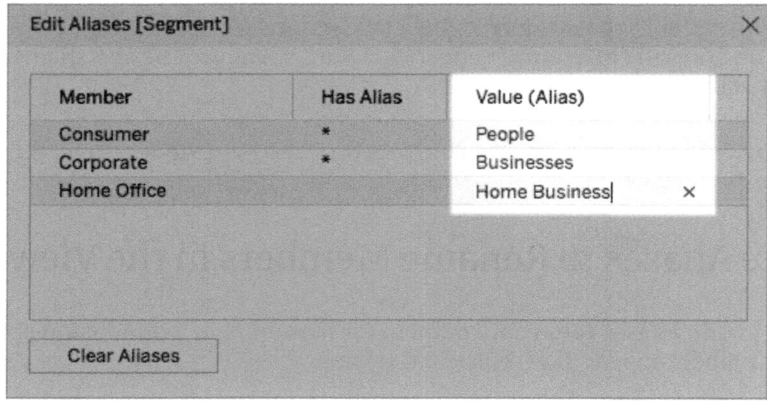

Tip: To reset the member names back to their original names, click **Clear Aliases**.

3. To save your changes:

- In Tableau Desktop, click **OK**.

- On Tableau Server or Tableau Online, click the **X** icon in the top-right corner of the dialog box.

When you add the field to the view, the alias names appear as labels in the view. For example,

When the Alias option is not available

Measures can't be re-aliased

Tableau does not permit re-aliasing measures as this would involve modifying data values themselves. If you have a field in your data that contains values such as *0* and *1* but actually encodes information such as *no* and *yes*, Tableau will interpret this as a continuous measure. You can convert it to a discrete dimension and then re-alias the values.

Published data sources

Alternatively, the Alias option may be missing for a discrete dimension because you are connected to a published data source. When using a published data source, you cannot create or edit aliases. You can only change aliases on fields that you create in your workbook. If you didn't publish the data source, you can duplicate the field (right click > **Duplicate**) and edit aliases for the duplicate field without restriction.

Convert Fields between Discrete and Continuous

You can convert measures from discrete to continuous or from continuous to discrete. And you can convert date dimensions and other numeric dimensions to be either discrete or continuous.

Convert measures

You can convert measures from discrete to continuous or from continuous to discrete. Click the field and choose **Discrete** or **Continuous**. The field is green when it is continuous, and blue when it is discrete.

For measures in the **Data** pane, right-click the field and choose **Convert to Discrete** or **Convert to Continuous**. The color of the field changes accordingly.

Convert date fields

You can convert Date fields between discrete and continuous. Discrete dates act as labels and continuous dates will have an axis similar to a measure.

Click any Date field in the view and choose one of the options on the context menu to change it from discrete to continuous or from continuous to discrete.

To convert a Date field in the **Data** pane (and thus to determine the default result when you drag it into a view), right-click the field and choose **Convert to Discrete** or **Convert to Continuous**.

Create Hierarchies

When you connect to a data source, Tableau automatically separates date fields into hierarchies so you can easily break down the viz. You can also create your own custom hierarchies. For example, if you have a set of fields named Region, State, and County, you can create a hierarchy from these fields so that you can quickly drill down between levels in the viz.

To create a hierarchy:

1. In the **Data** pane, drag a field and drop it directly on top of another field.

Note: When you want to create a hierarchy from a field inside a folder, right-click (control-click on a Mac) the field and then select **Create Hierarchy**.

2. When prompted, enter a name for the hierarchy and click **OK**.

3. Drag additional fields into the hierarchy as needed. You can also re-order fields in the hierarchy by dragging them to a new position.

Drill up or down in a hierarchy

When you add a field from a hierarchy to the visualization, you can quickly drill up or down in the hierarchy to add or subtract more levels of detail.

To drill up or down in a hierarchy in Tableau Desktop or in web authoring:

- In the visualization, click the + or - icon on the hierarchy field.

When you are editing or viewing the visualization on the web, you have the option of clicking the + or - icon next to a field label.

Remove a hierarchy

To remove a hierarchy:

- In the **Data** pane, right-click (control-click on a Mac) the hierarchy and select **Remove Hierarchy**.

The fields in the hierarchy are removed from the hierarchy and the hierarchy disappears from the Data pane.

Group Your Data

You can create a group to combine related members in a field. For example, if you are working with a view that shows average test scores by major, you might want to group certain majors together to create major categories. English and History might be combined into a group called Liberal Arts Majors, while Biology and Physics might be grouped as Science Majors.

Groups are useful for both correcting data errors (e.g. combining CA, Calif., and California into one data point) as well as answering "what if" type questions (e.g. "What if we combined the East and West regions?).

Create a group

There are multiple ways to create a group. You can create a group from a field in the **Data** pane, or by selecting data in the view and then clicking the group icon.

Create a group by selecting data in the view

1. In the view, select one or more data points and then, on the tooltip that appears, click the group icon .

Note: You can also select the group icon on the toolbar at the top of the workspace.

If there are multiple levels of detail in the view, you must select a level to group the members. You can select to group all dimensions, or just one.

Create a group from a field in the Data pane

1. In the **Data** pane, right-click a field and select **Create** > **Group**.

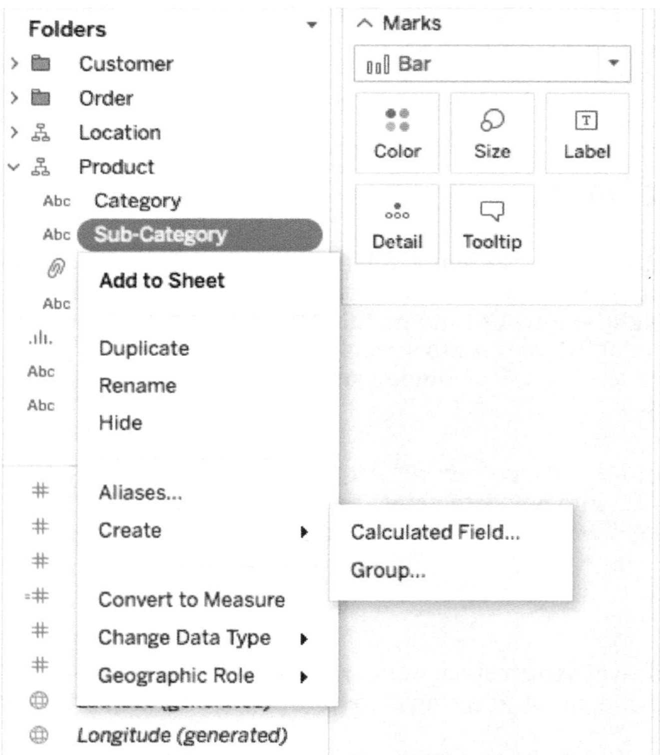

2. In the Create Group dialog box, select several members that you want to group, and then click **Group**.

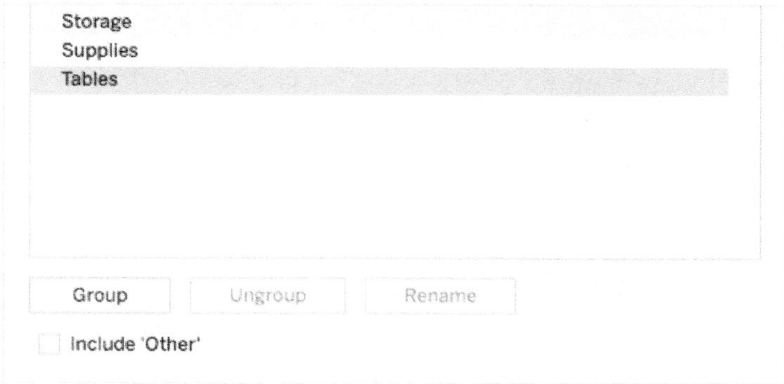

The selected members are combined into a single group. A default name is created using the combined member names.

To rename the group, select it in the list and click **Rename**.

Tip: You can search for members using the **Find** option near the bottom-right of the dialog box. (Tableau Desktop only)

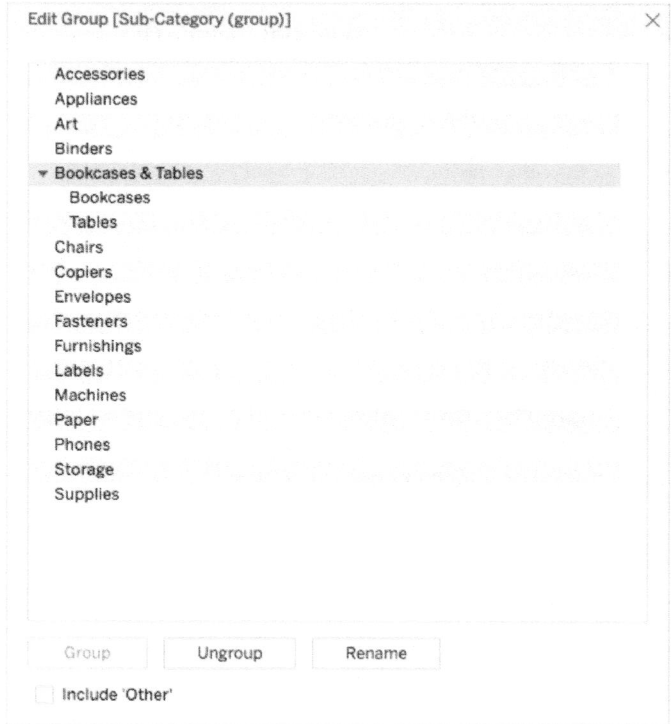

Include an Other Group

When you create groups in Tableau, you have the option to group all remaining, or non-grouped members in an Other group.

The Include Other option is useful for highlighting certain groups or comparing specific groups against everything else. For example, if have a view that shows sales versus profit product category, you might want to highlight the high and low performing categories in the view, and group all the other categories into an "Other" group.

Includes Other

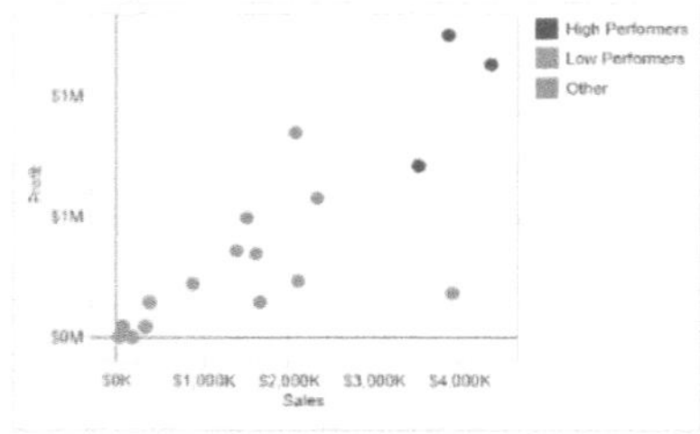

Does not include Other

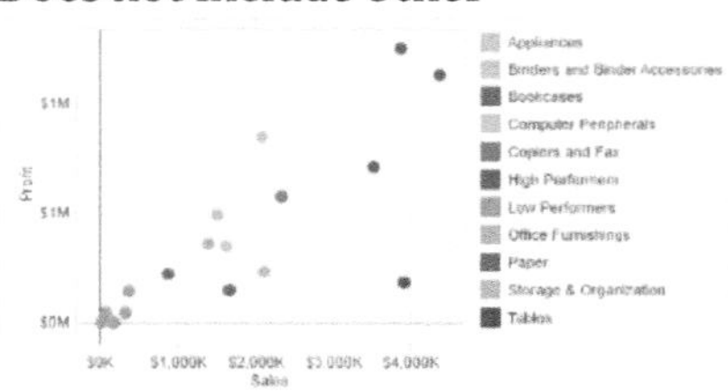

To include an Other group:

1. In the **Data** pane, right-click the group field and select **Edit Group**.
2. In the Edit Group dialog box, select **Include 'Other'**.

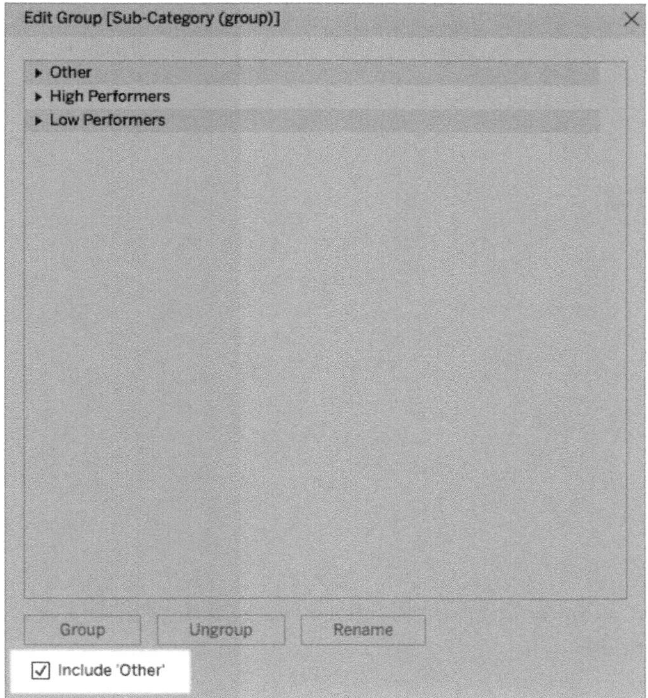

Edit a Group

After you have created a grouped field, you can add and remove members from the groups, create new groups, change the default group names and change the name of the grouped field. You can make some changes directly in the view, and others through the Edit Group dialog box.

To add members to an existing group:

- In the **Data** pane, right-click the group field, and then click **Edit Group**.

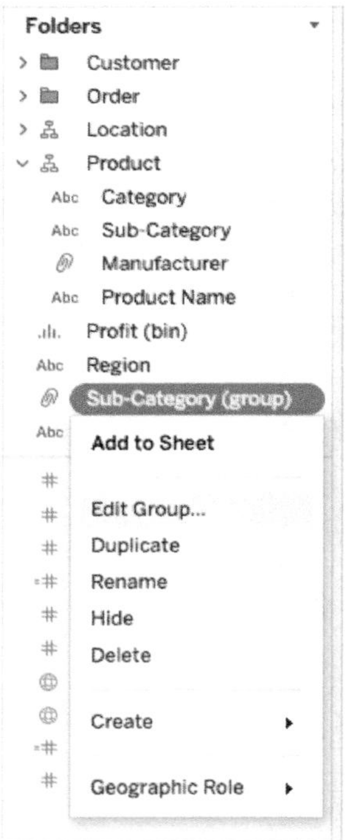

- In the Edit Group dialog box, select one or more members and drag them into the group you want.

- Click **OK**.

To remove members from an existing group:

- In the **Data** pane, right-click the group field, and then click **Edit Group**.

- In the Edit Group dialog box, select one or more members, and then click **Ungroup**.

The members are removed from the current group. If you have an Other group, the members are added to it.

- Click **OK**.

To create a new group in a group field:

- In the **Data** pane, right-click the group field, and then click **Edit Group**.

- In the Edit Group dialog box, select one or more members, and then click **Group**.

- Click **OK**.

Note: To rename a group, select the group in the Edit Group dialog box, and then click **Rename**.

Create Sets

You can use sets to compare and ask questions about a subset of data. Sets are custom fields that define a subset of data based on some conditions.

You can make sets more dynamic and interactive by using them in Set Actions. Set actions let your audience interact directly with a viz or dashboard to control aspects of their analysis. When someone selects marks in the view, set actions can change the values in a set.

In addition to a Set Action, you can also allow users to change the membership of a set by using a filter-like interface known as a Set Control, which makes it easy for you to designate inputs into calculations that drive interactive analysis.

Create a dynamic set

There are two types of sets: dynamic sets and fixed sets. The members of a dynamic set change when the underlying data changes. Dynamic sets can only be based on a single dimension.

To create a dynamic set:

In the Data pane, right-click a dimension and select **Create** > **Set**.

In the Create Set dialog box, configure your set. You can configure your set using the following tabs:

General: Use the General tab to select one or more values that will be considered when computing the set.

You can alternatively select the **Use all** option to always consider all members even when new members are added or removed.

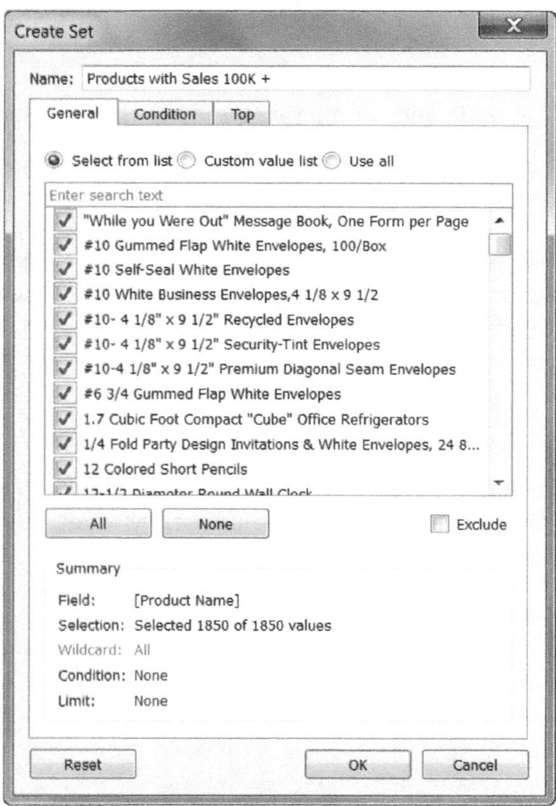

Condition: Use the Condition tab to define rules that determine which members to include in the set.

For example, you might specify a condition that is based on total sales that only includes products with sales over £100,000.

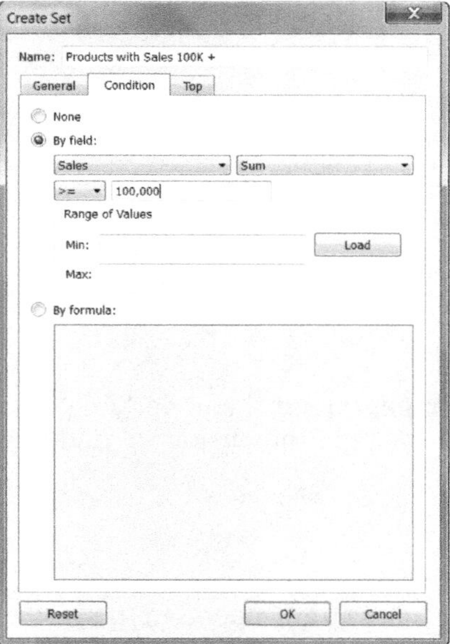

Top: Use the Top tab to define limits on what members to include in the set.

For example, you might specify a limit that is based on total sales that only includes the top 5 products based on their sales.

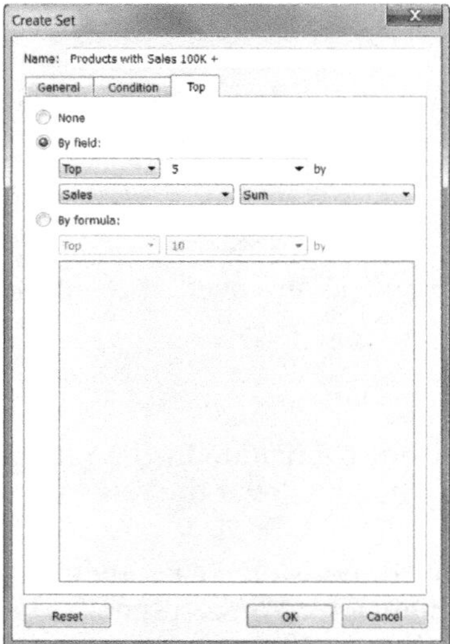

When finished, click **OK**.

The new set is added to the bottom of the Data pane, under the Sets section. A set icon indicates the field is a set.

Sets

State - High Sales & Profit

Top Customers by Profit

Create a fixed set

The members of a fixed set do not change, even if the underlying data changes. A fixed set can be based on a single dimension or multiple dimensions.

To create a fixed set:

In the visualization, select one or more marks (or headers) in the view.

Right-click the mark(s) and select **Create Set**.

In the Create Set dialog box, type a name for the set.

Optionally complete any of the following:

By default, the set includes the members listed in the dialog box. You can select the option to **Exclude** these members instead. When you exclude, the set will include all of the members you didn't select.

Remove any dimensions that you don't want to be considered by clicking the red 'x' icon that appears when you hover over a column heading 

.

Remove any specific rows that you don't want to include in the set by clicking the red 'x' icon that appears when you hover over the row ✕.

If the marks you selected represent multiple dimensions, each member of the set will be a combination of those dimensions. You can specify the character that separates the dimension values. To do so, for **Separate members by**, enter a character of your choice.

Select **Add to Filters shelf** to automatically move the set to the Filters shelf once it is created.

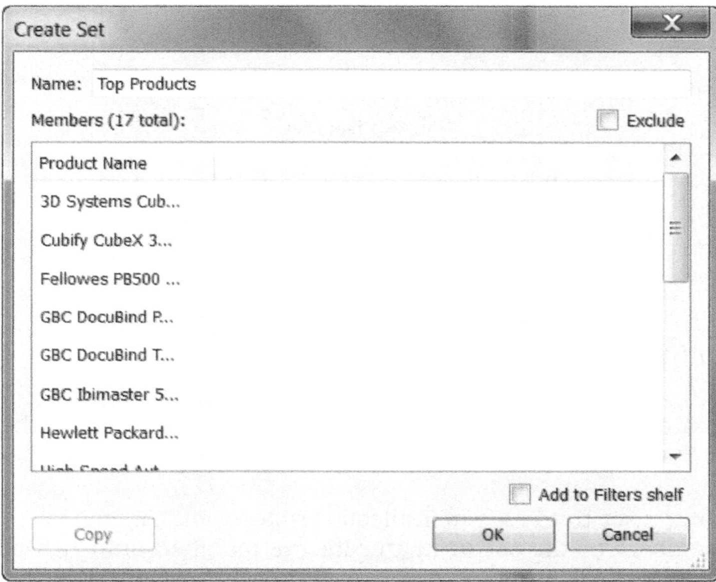

When finished, click **OK**.

The new set is added to the bottom of the Data pane, under the Sets section. A set icon indicates the field is a set.

Sets

State - High Sales & Profit

Top Customers by Profit

Add or remove data points from sets

If you created a set using specific data points, you can add more data to or subtract data from the set.

To add or remove data points from a set:

In the visualization, select the data points you want to add or remove.

In the tooltip that appears, click the Sets drop-down menu icon, and then select **Add to [set name]** or **Remove from [set name]** to add or remove data from a particular set.

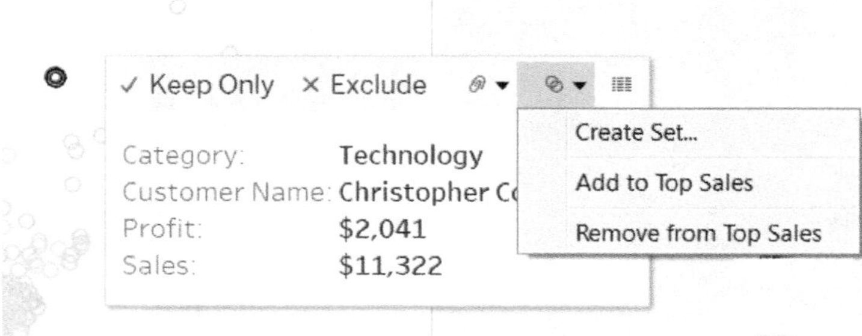

Use sets in the visualization

After you create a set, it displays at the bottom of the Data pane in the Sets section. You can drag it into the viz like any other field.

When you drag a set to the viz in Tableau Desktop, you can choose to show the members of the set or aggregate the members into In/Out categories.

In Tableau Server or Tableau Online you can only aggregate the members of the set into In/Out categories.

Show In/Out members in a set

In most cases, when you drag a set to the viz, Tableau displays the set using the In/Out mode. This mode separates the set into two categories:

In - The members in the set.

Out - The members that aren't part of the set.

For example, in a set defined for the top 25 customers, the top customers would be part of the In category and all other customers would be part of the Out category.

Using the In/Out mode makes it easy to compare the members in the set to everything else.

To show In/Out members in the visualization:

In Tableau Desktop, right-click the set in the visualization workspace and select **Show In/Out of Set**.

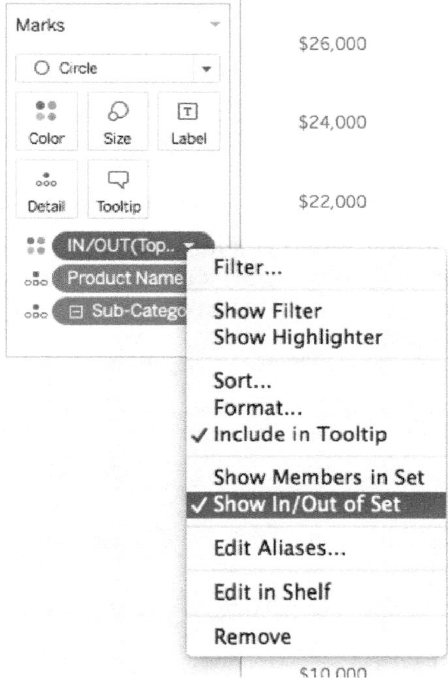

When a set is in In/Out mode, the field on the shelf is prefaced by the text, "IN/OUT", followed by the set name.

Show members in a set

As an alternative to showing the set using In/Out mode, you can list the members in the set. Showing the members in the set automatically adds a filter to the view that includes only the members of the set.

To switch a set to list the individual members:

In the visualization workspace, right-click the set and select **Show Members in Set**.

Note: To display the fully qualified member names for cubes, right-click the set in the Data pane and select **Qualify Member Names**.

Let users change set values

Add a set action

You can use set actions to give your audience more control over their analysis of your visualization.

Set actions take an existing set and update the values contained in that set based on a user's action in the viz. As the author, you can use a set or sets that you have already created to define the scope of the set action.

Show a set control in the view

To give your audience the ability to quickly modify members of a set, you can also display a Set Control. A set control is a worksheet card that is very similar to a parameter control or filter card. You can add set controls to worksheets and dashboards and they are included when you publish to Tableau Server or Tableau Online, or save to the web on Tableau Public.

To display the set control, right-click (Control-click) the set in the Data pane and select **Show Set**.

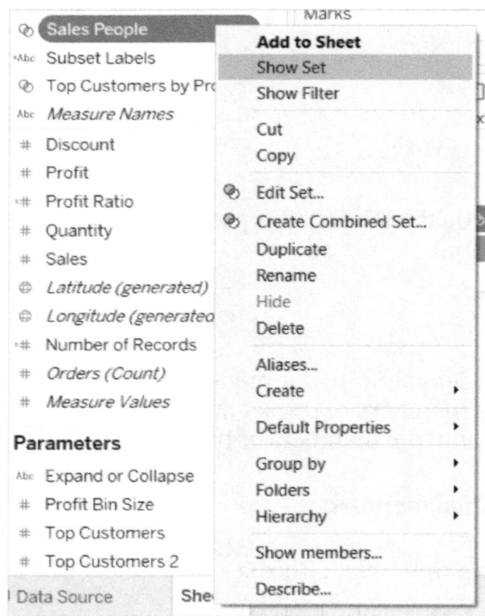

Like other cards, set controls have a menu that you can open using the drop-down arrow in the upper right corner of the card. Use this menu to customize the display of the control, which supports both single-value and multiple-value selection modes. For example, you can show radio buttons for individual selection, or a drop-down list that supports multiple selections.

Note: You can only display a set control for dynamic sets – not fixed sets. This is by design, as fixed sets aren't meant to change in membership. In addition, if the dynamic set is not in play in the view (that is, if it's not referenced in a calculation or instantiated on the sheet), the context menu item will be disabled, reminding you to add the set to the view.

Combine sets

You can combine two sets to compare the members. When you combine sets you create a new set containing either the combination of all members, just the members that exist in both, or members that exist in one set but not the other.

Combining sets allows you to answer complex questions and compare cohorts of your data. For example, to determine the percentage of customers who purchased both last year and this year, you can combine two sets containing the customers from each year and return only the customers that exist in both sets.

To combine two sets, they must be based on the same dimensions. That is, you can combine a set containing the top customers with another set containing the customers that purchased last year. However, you cannot combine the top customers set with a top products set.

To combine sets:

In the Data pane, under Sets, select the two sets you want to combine.

Right-click the sets and select **Create Combined Set**.

In the Create Set dialog box, do the following

Type a name for the new combined set.

Verify that the two sets you want to combine are selected in the two drop-down menus.

Select one of the following options for how to combine the sets:

All Members in Both Sets - the combined set will contain all of the members from both sets.

Shared Members in Both Sets - the combined set will only contain members that exist in both sets.

Except Shared Members - the combined set will contain all members from the specified set that don't exist in the second set. These options are equivalent to subtracting one set from another. For example, if the first set contains Apples, Oranges and Pears and the second set contains Pears and Nuts; combining the first set except the shared members would contain just Apples and Oranges. Pears is removed because it exists in the second set.

Optionally specify a character that will separate the members if the sets represent multiple dimensions.

When finished, click **OK**.

Note: This functionality is not available in workbooks created before version 8.2 that use Microsoft Excel or text file data sources, workbooks that use the legacy connection or workbooks that use Microsoft Access data sources.

Examples of sets

There are many ways you can use sets to answer complex questions and compare cohorts of data. Below are some examples of ways you can use sets to define and compare subsets of data.

How do members of a set contribute to the total?

You may have all kinds of questions surrounding how the members in a set contribute to the overall total. For example, what percent of total sales come from repeat customers? You can answer these types of questions using the IN/OUT mode for a set.

The example below uses sales data to create a set for customers who have purchased 5,000 USD or more in products.

Create the set

Right-click (control-click on Mac) the **Customer Name** dimension in the Data pane and select **Create** > **Set**.

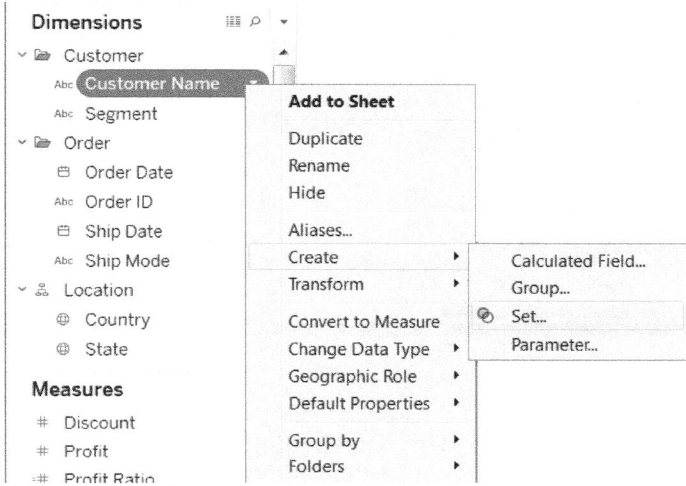

In the Create Set dialog box, type a name for the set. In this example, we'll call the set, 'Customers'

Select the **Use all** option so the condition always applies to all values even when new customers are added.

On the Condition tab, click **By field**, and then define a condition that only includes customers when **Sum** of **Sales** is greater than or equal to **5,000**.

Click **OK**.

Create the visualization

Drag the new set from the **Sets** area at the bottom of the **Data** pane to the **Rows** shelf.

Drag **Sales** to the **Columns** shelf. The view now shows the total sales for customers who have purchased more than 5,000 USD of product and the total sales for all other customers.

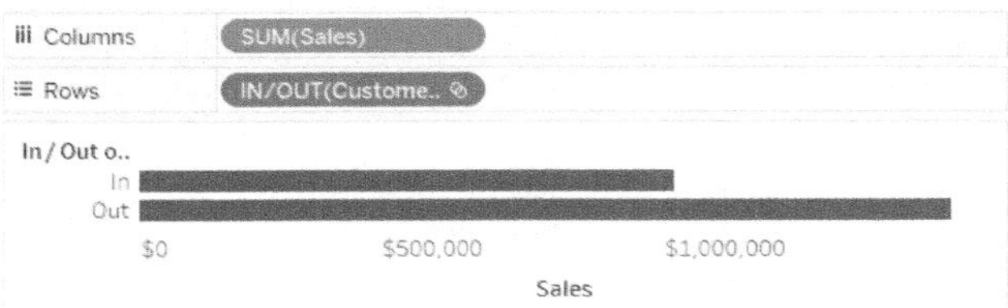

Finally, click on the drop-down arrow on the **Sum (Sales)** field on the Column shelf and select **Quick Table Calculation** > **Percent of Total** on the context menu.

The view now shows that customers with sales greater than or equal to 5,000 make up about 39% of the overall sales.

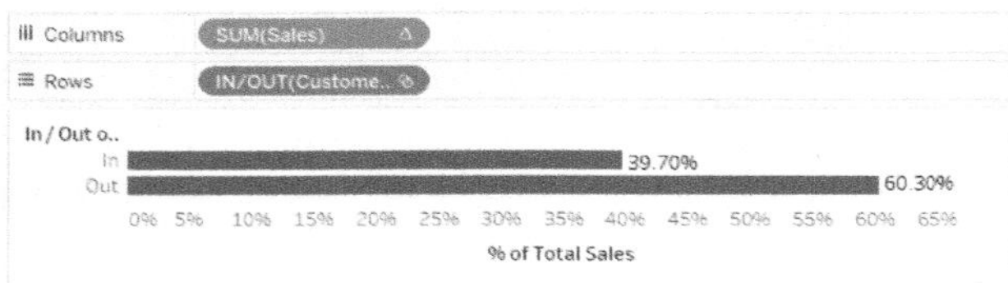

How many members of a set exist in another set?

Another common use of sets is to compare subsets of data or cohorts. For example, you may wonder how many customers that purchased last year also purchased this year. Or if a customer purchased a specific product, what other products did they buy? You can answer these types of questions by creating multiple sets and combining them. The example below uses sales data to determine how many customers who purchased in 2012 also purchased in 2013.

Create a combined set

Drag the **Customer Name** field to the Rows shelf.

Drag the **Order Date** field to the Filters shelf.

In the Filter Field dialog box, select **Years** and click **Next**.

In the Filter dialog box, select **2012** and click **OK**.

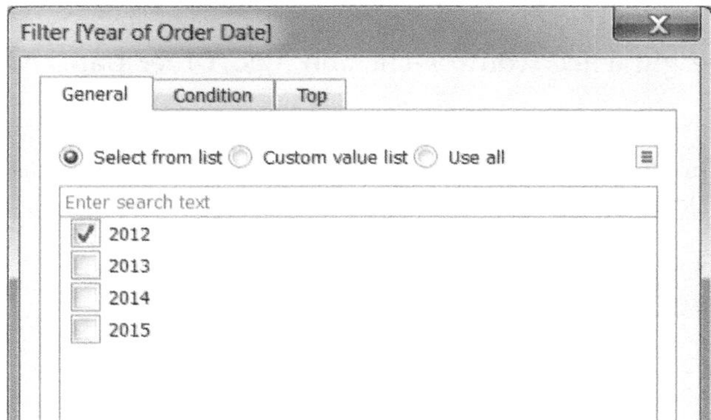

Back in the view, press CTRL + A (Command-A on a Mac) on your keyboard to select all of the customers.

Right-click (control-click on Mac) the selection and select **Create Set**.

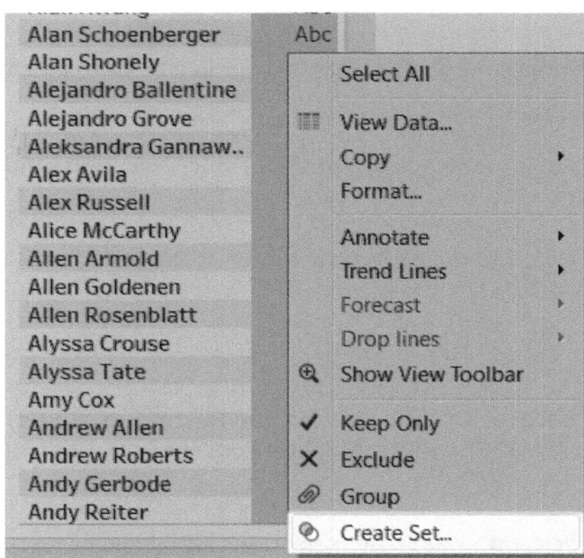

In the Create Set dialog box that opens, type a name for the set. In this example, we'll call the set 'Customers (2012)'.

Click **OK**.

On the **Filters** shelf, right-click (control-click on Mac) **Order Date** and select **Edit Filter**.

In the Filter dialog box, change the filter to only include **2013** instead of **2012**, and then click **OK**.

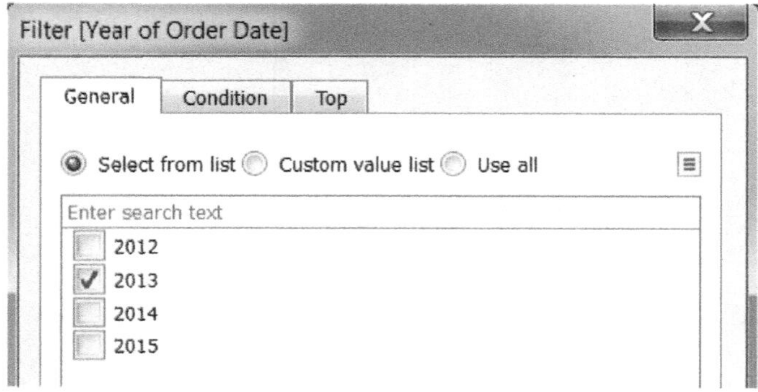

Again, press CTRL + A (Command-A on a Mac) on your keyboard to select all of the customers.

In the view, right-click (control-click on Mac) the selection and select **Create Set**.

In the Create set dialog box that opens, type a name for the set. This set will be called 'Customers (2013)'.

Click **OK**.

In the **Data** pane, select both the **Customers 2012** and **Customers 2013** by holding the Ctrl key (Command key on a Mac) on your keyboard as you select.

Right-click (control-click on Mac) the selection and select **Create Combined Set**.

In the Create Set dialog box, type a name for the new set. In this example, we'll call the set 'Customers (2012 & 2013)'.

Make sure the correct two sets are selected in the drop-down menus.

Select the option to include **Shared Members in Both Sets**.

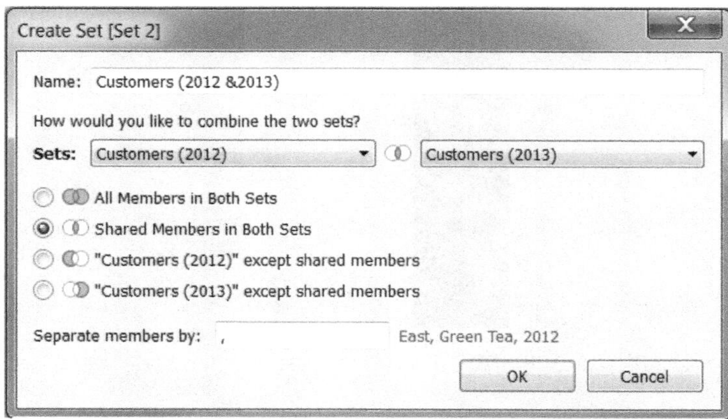

Click **OK**.
Create the visualization

At the bottom of the workbook, click the New Worksheet icon.

In the new worksheet, drag the **Customer Name** dimension to the **Rows** shelf.

Click the drop-down arrow on the Customer Name field on the Rows shelf and select **Measure** > **Count (Distinct)** from the context menu.

Finally, from the **Sets** area of the **Data** pane, drag the **Customers (2012 & 2013)** field to the **Filters** shelf. You can see that 437 customers purchased products in both 2012 and 2013.

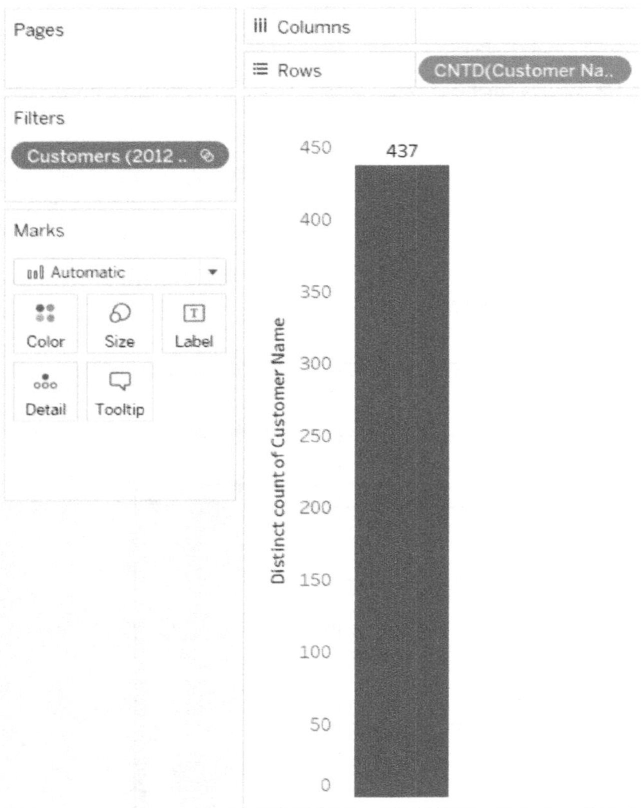

Hierarchical sets and descendants

A hierarchical set filters data to the selected members and all of their descendants. They are unique to multidimensional (cube) data sources and are defined within the data source prior to connecting to Tableau Desktop.

When you create sets in Tableau from a cube data source, descendants and any hierarchical structures are automatically included with the selected members.

For example, a set named **Dairy** is created from the **Product** hierarchy. As shown below, it includes only the Dairy product department.

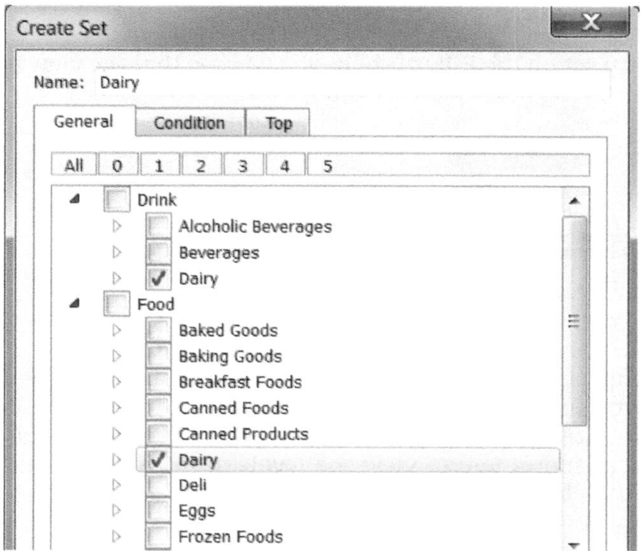

Consider the following view. The **Product Department** dimension is placed on the **Rows** shelf and the **Store Sales** measure is placed on the **Columns** shelf.

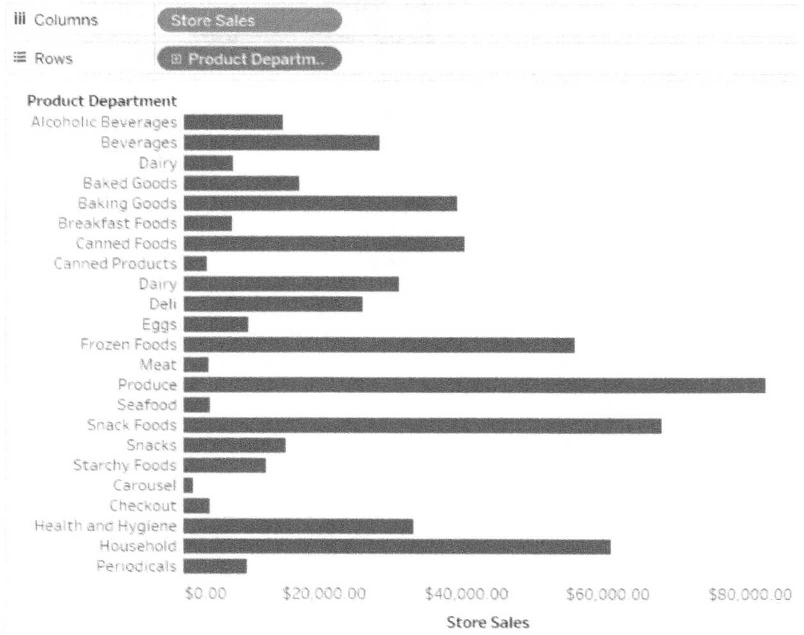

If you place the **Dairy** set on the **Filters** shelf, you can see that the view is filtered to include only the Dairy product categories.

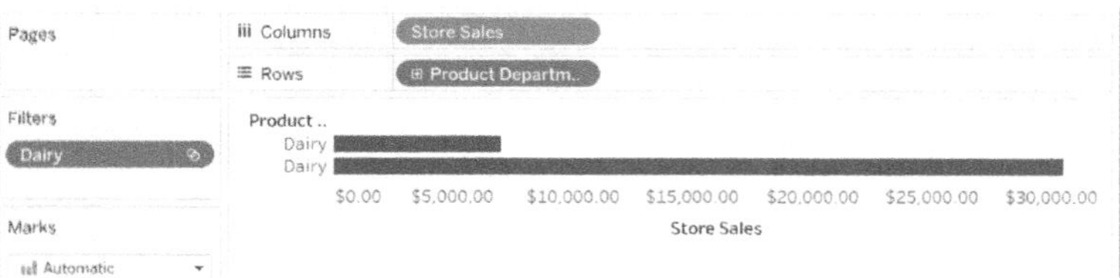

As shown below, you can drill down into **Product Department** to reveal the **Product Category**, **Product Subcategory**, and **Brand Name** levels. As these descendants are revealed, row headers are added to the view. This is because a set filter allows you to view the levels of detail contained within the filtered members.

Create Parameters

A parameter is a workbook variable such as a number, date or string that can replace a constant value in a calculation, filter or reference line.

For example, you may create a calculated field that returns True if Sales is greater than $500,000 and otherwise returns False. You can replace the constant value of "500000" in the formula with a parameter. Then, using the parameter control, you can dynamically change the threshold in your calculation.

You can even create a *dynamic* parameter that's set to automatically refresh its current value (to the result of a single-value, view-independent calculation), list of values (based on a data source column) or range of values. This will happen each time the workbook is opened and Tableau connects to the data source referenced by the parameter, or whenever you select **Refresh** from the data source's context menu.

You can make your parameters more dynamic and interactive by using them in Parameter Actions. Parameter actions let your audience change a parameter value through direct interaction with a viz, such as clicking or selecting a mark.

Create a parameter

Follow the instructions below to create a new parameter from the Data pane.

In the Data pane, click the drop-down arrow in the upper right corner and select **Create Parameter**.

In the Create Parameter dialog box, give the field a **Name**.

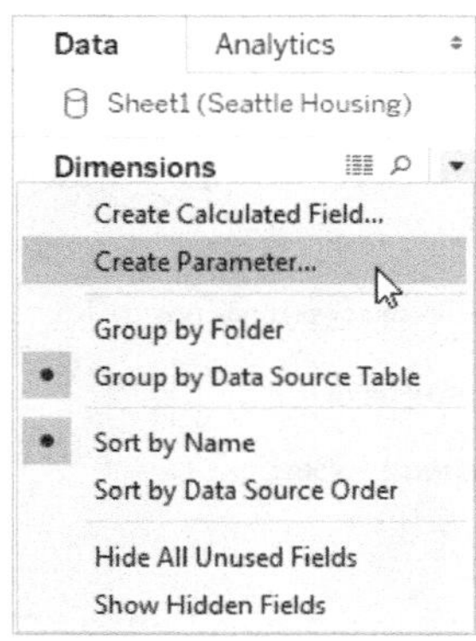

Specify the data type for the values it will accept:

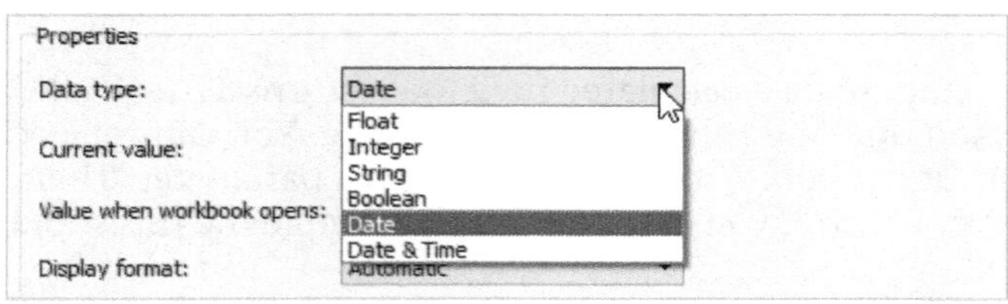

Specify a current value. This is the default value for the parameter. In this case, let's leave the field as is because we'll be using the latest data, which we'll configure in the next step.

Specify a value when the workbook opens. In this case, let's create a dynamic parameter by setting the parameter's default value to the result of a single-value, view-independent calculation.

Note: If there is more than one value, the workbook would not be able to choose a default value. The calculation must also be view-independent so that the value won't change as the viz changes. To do this, you can use a FIXED level of detail (LOD) expression that is not dependent on the structure of the viz. All parts of the calculation must be inside the FIXED LOD expression. If you use a FIXED LOD expression as the default value and are using context filters, the dynamic parameter will not reflect any context filters.

For this dynamic parameter, let's use **Latest Month**. This means that if the connected data source is updated and the workbook is opened, the parameter will automatically update when the workbook is opened.

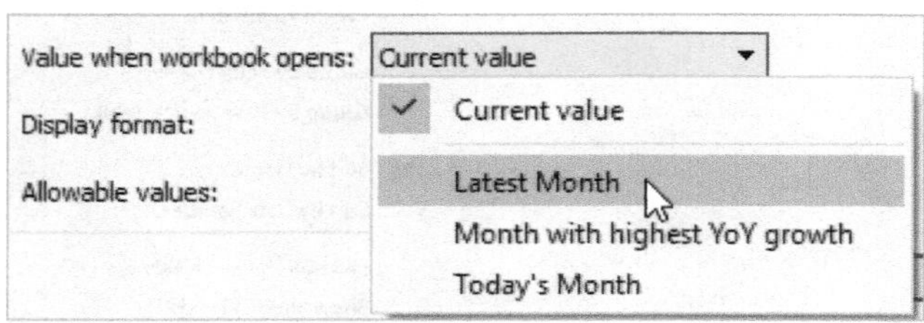

Specify the display format to use in the parameter control (Tableau Desktop only).

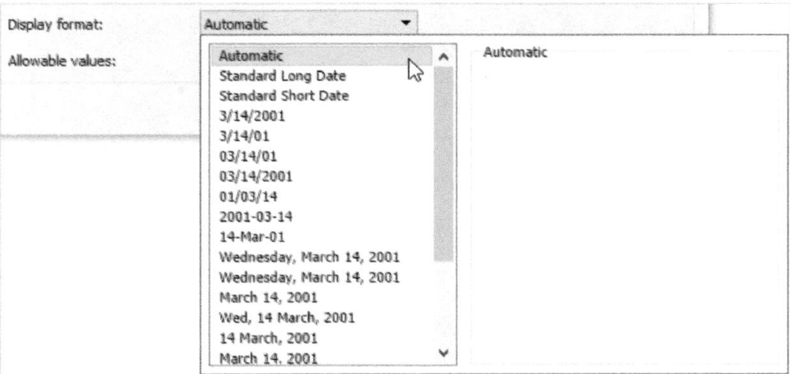

Specify how the parameter will accept values. You can select from the following options:

All - The parameter control is a simple text field.

List - The parameter control provides a list of possible values for you to select from.

Range - The parameter control lets you select values within a specified range.

The availability of these options is determined by the data type. For example, a string parameter can only accept all values or a list. It does not support a range.

If you select List, you must specify the list of values. Click in the left column to type your list of values, or you can add members of a field by selecting **Add values from**.

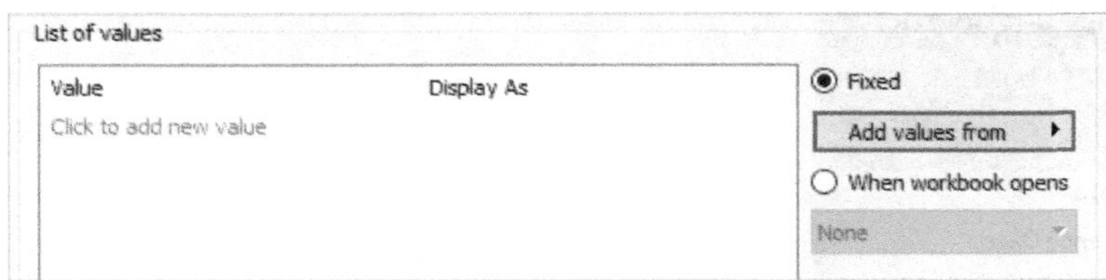

If you select Range, you must specify a minimum, maximum and step size. For example, you can define a date range between 1 January 2019

and 31 December 2019, with the step size set to 1 month to create a parameter control that lets you select each month in 2019.

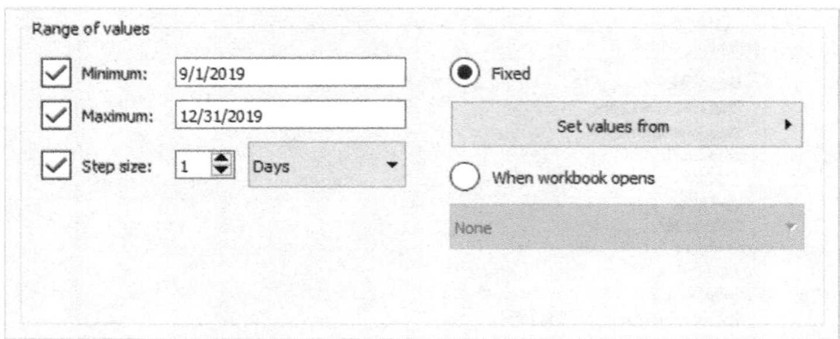

In this case, to refresh the parameter's list of values (or domain) whenever the workbook opens, select **List**, and then select **When workbook opens**. Notice that the list of values on the left is greyed out because the workbook is dynamically pulling values from the data source.

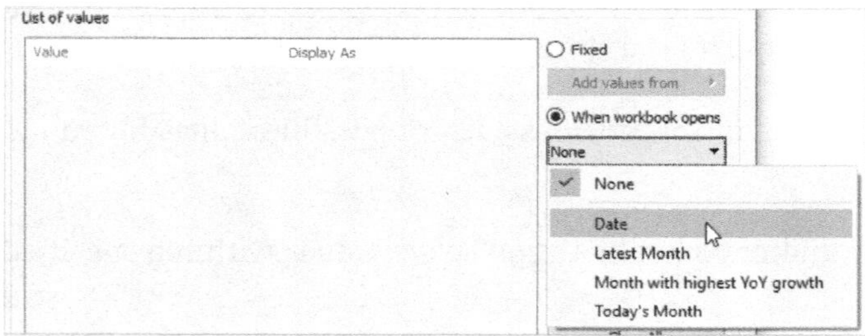

When finished, click **OK**.

The parameter is now listed in the Parameters section at the bottom of the **Data** pane.

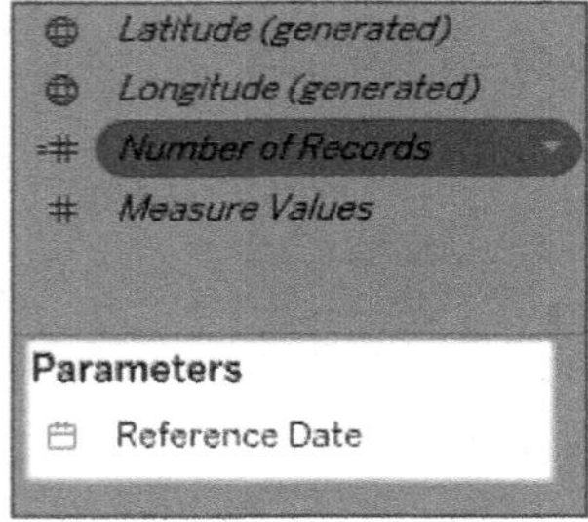

The parameter is also available everywhere else you can use a parameter – for example, on the Top tab in the Filter dialog box, or in the Reference

Line dialog box. Parameters are global across the workbook and can be used in any worksheet.

When the parameter value or list of values can't refresh

Below are a few scenarios in which a default parameter value or a refreshable list of parameter values (domain) will not update as expected:

The default field returns a value whose data is incompatible with the parameter's data type.

The default field doesn't return a single value (for the parameter's current value).

The default field returns null.

The default field is in a data source that's not yet connected.

The default field is no longer found in the workbook's namespace (i.e. it's been deleted).

The user cancels the query to the data source while Tableau is attempting to connect.

Edit a parameter

You can edit parameters from the Data pane or the parameter control. Follow the instructions below to edit a parameter:

Do one of the following:

Right-click (Control-click on a Mac) the parameter in the **Data** pane and select **Edit**.

Select **Edit Parameter** on the parameter control card menu.

In the Edit Parameter dialog box, make the modifications as necessary.

When finished, click **OK**. The parameter is updated along with any calculations that use it.

To delete a parameter, right-click it in the Data pane and select **Delete**. Any calculated fields that use the deleted parameter will become invalid.

Use a parameter in a calculation

Parameters give you a way to dynamically modify values in a calculation. Rather than manually editing the calculation (and all dependent calculations), you can use a parameter. Then when you want to change the value, you open the parameter control, change the value, and all of the calculations that use that parameter are updated.

To use a parameter in a calculation, drag the parameter from the Data pane and drop it in the calculation editor, either at a new location in the formula or to replace a part of the current formula:

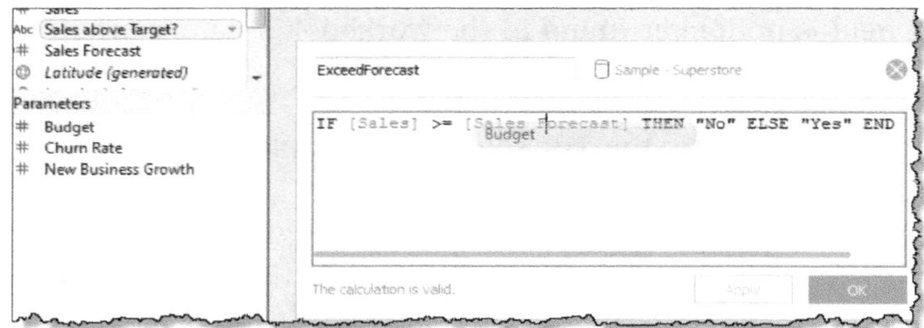

Use a parameter in a filter

Parameters give you a way to dynamically modify values in a Top N filter. Rather than manually setting the number of values you want to show in the filter, you can use a parameter. Then when you want to change the value, you open the parameter control and the filter updates. For example, when creating a filter to show the Top 10 products based on total profit, you may want to use a parameter instead of the fixed "10" value. That way, you can quickly update the filter to show the top 10, 20, or 30 products.

A list of parameters is available in the drop-down lists on the **Top** tab of the Filter dialog box. Select the parameter you want to use in the filter.

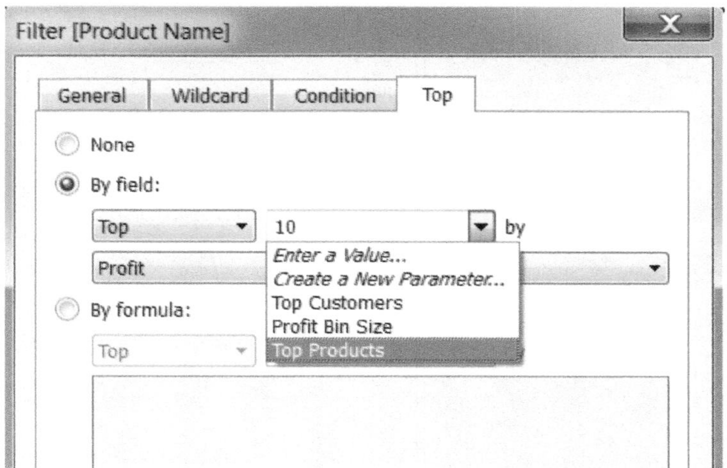

To show the parameter control, right-click the parameter in the **Data** pane and select **Show Parameter**. Use the parameter control to modify the filter to show the top 10 products, 15 products, 20 products, and so on.

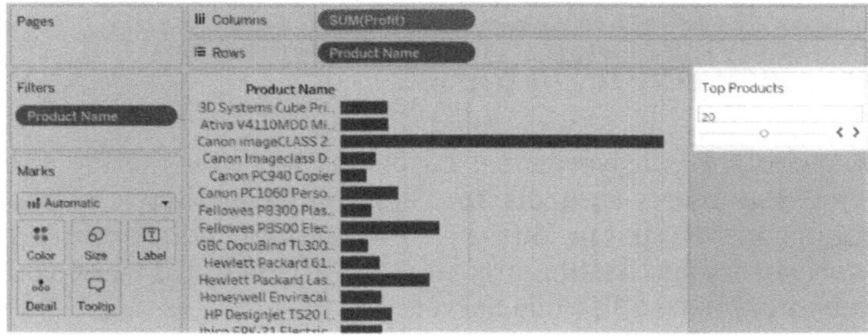

Use a parameter in a reference line

Parameters give you a way to dynamically modify a reference line, band, or box. For example, instead of showing a reference line at a fixed location on the axis, you can reference a parameter. Then you can use the parameter control to move the reference line.

A list of parameters is available in the Value drop-down list in the Add Reference Line, Band, or Box dialog box. Select the parameter you want to use.

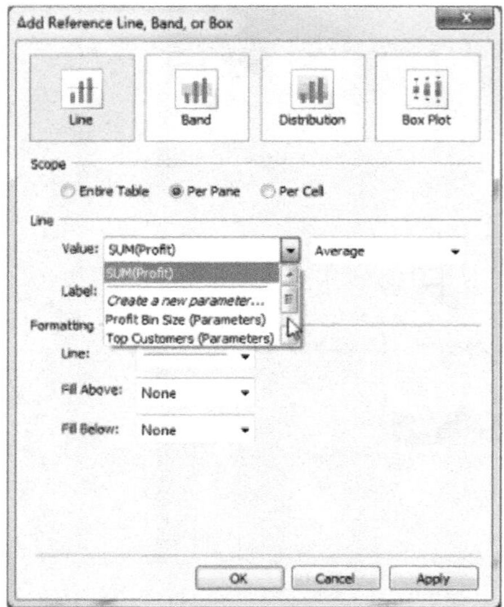

The reference line is drawn at the Current Value specified by the parameter. To open the parameter control, right-click (Control-click on a Mac) the parameter in the **Data** pane and then select **Show Parameter**. Use the parameter control to change where the reference line is drawn.

Show a parameter control in the viz

The parameter control is a worksheet card that lets you modify the parameter value. Parameter controls are very similar to filter cards in that they contain controls that modify the view. You can open parameter controls on worksheets and dashboards and they are included when you save to the web or publish to Tableau Server.

To open the parameter control, right-click (Control-click) the parameter in the **Data** pane and select **Show Parameter**.

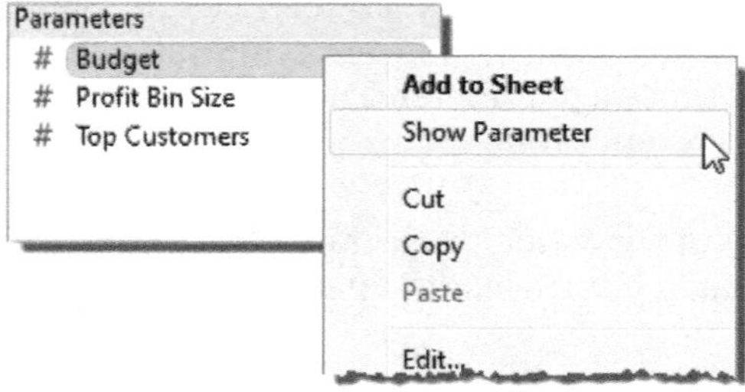

Like other cards, parameter controls have a menu that you can open using the drop-down arrow in the upper right corner of the card. Use this menu to customize the display of the control. For example, you can show a list of values as radio buttons, a compact list, a slider, or a type in field. The options available on this menu depend on the data type of the parameter as well as whether it accepts all, a list, or a range of values.

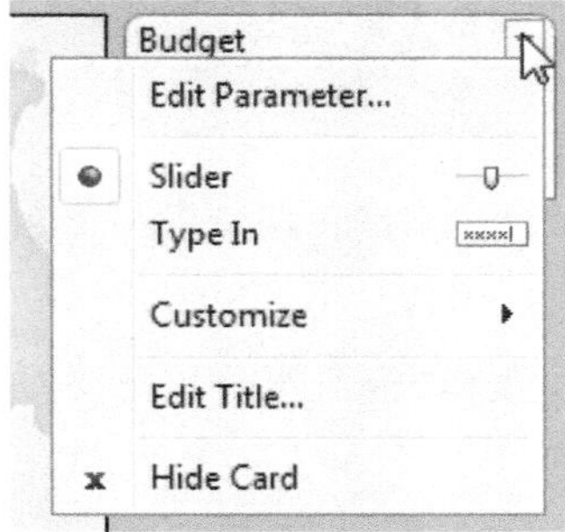

Sort Data in a Visualization

There are many ways to sort data in Tableau. When viewing a visualization, data can be sorted using single click options from an axis, header or field label. In the authoring environment, additional sorting options include sorting manually in headers and legends, using the toolbar sort icons or sorting from the sort menu.

Quickly sort from an axis, header or field label

There are multiple ways to sort a visualization with single click sort buttons.

In all cases, **one** click sorts ascending, **two** clicks sorts descending and **three** clicks clear the sort.

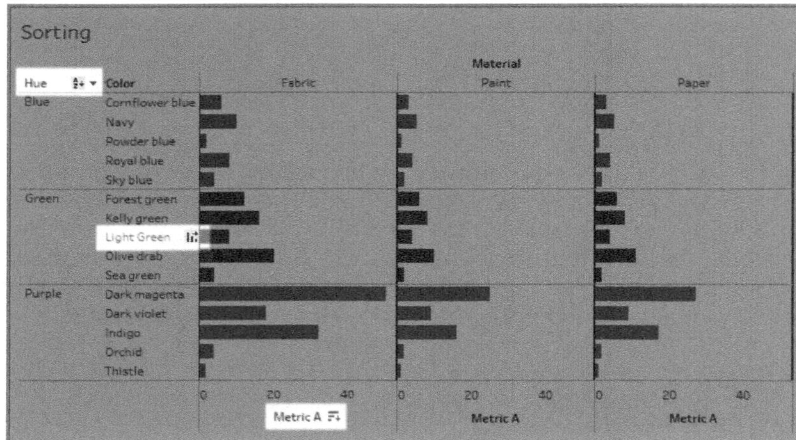

Sort icons may appear on an axis (Metric A), header (Light Green) or field label (Hue)

The sort will update correctly if the underlying data changes.

Sort from an axis

1. Hover over a numerical axis to bring up the sort icon.
2. Click the icon to sort.

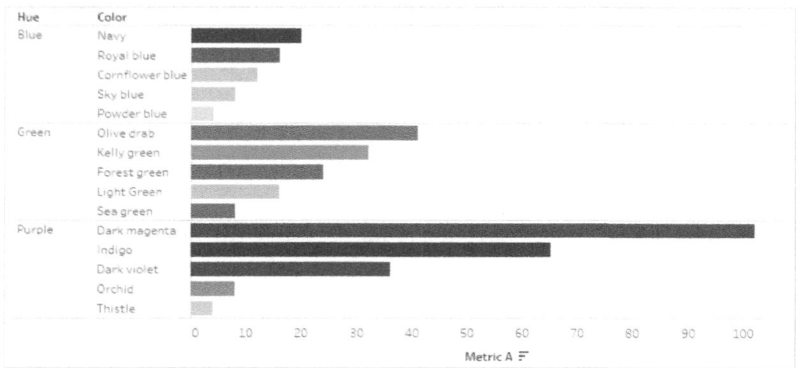

Sort: Color is sorted within each Hue in decreasing order of Metric A

In this example, the sort is applied to **Color** (sorting the rows) based on the values for **Metric A**. If there are hierarchical dimensions like above, the sort is applied to the innermost dimension. Here, that means that **Color** will sort inside **Hue**. Dark magenta cannot sort to the top of the viz because it must stay inside the pane for the Purple hue.

Sort from a header

1. Hover over a header to bring up the sort icon.

2. Click the icon to sort.

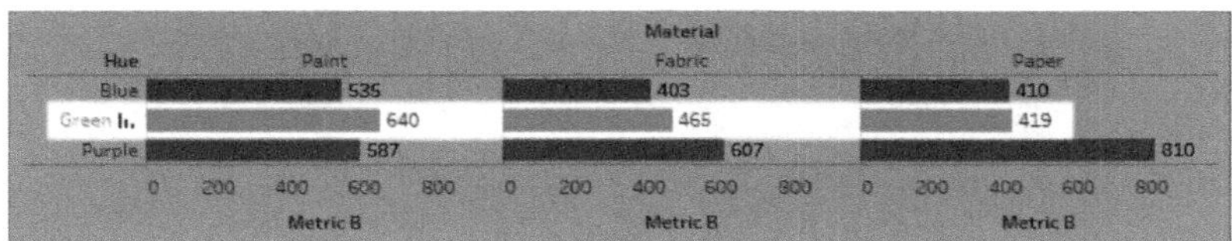

Sort: Materials are arranged in decreasing order of Metric B for Green.

In this example, the sort is applied to **Material** (sorting the order of the columns – Paint, Fabric and Paper) based on the values for Green, since that header was used for the sort.

Sort from a field label

1. Hover over a field label to bring up the sort icon.

The sort icon for a field label is slightly different from a header or axis. The default option is alphabetical sorting, but there is also a menu where you can choose to sort by a field in the view.

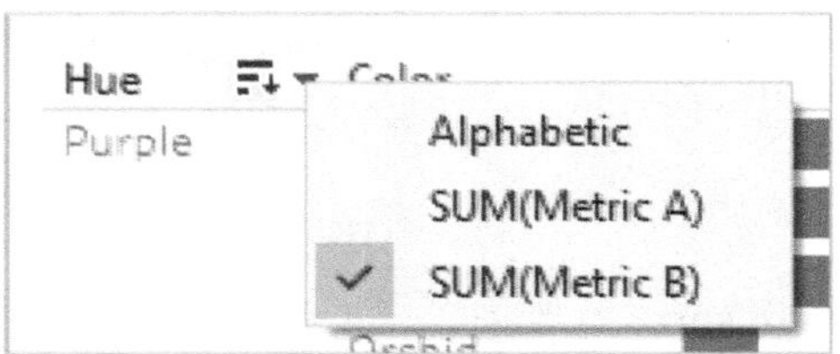

2. Click the A-Z icon to sort alphabetically, or open the menu to see a list of fields it is possible to sort by then chose a field. The icon switches to the bar icon and you can click to sort.

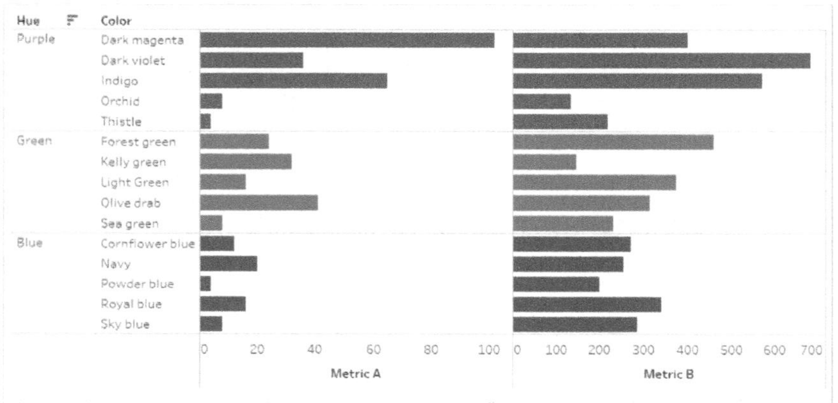

Sort: Hues are arranged in descending order by Metric B.

In this example, the sort is applied to the outermost dimension (Hue) based on total Metric B. (Metric B is aggregated for all the colors within each hue and Hue is sorted. Therefore, Purple is first, then Green, then Blue.)

Missing sort icons

If the sort icons do not appear, this functionality may have been turned off or it might not be possible to sort the view. For example, scatterplots cannot be sorted from a numerical axis because the position of the marks are fully determined by the data. No sort icon will appear on the axes in scatterplots.

Sort options while authoring

In an authoring environment, there are additional sorting options to those available on published content.

Sort from the toolbar

1. Select the dimension you wish to sort.

If you do not select a field before sorting, the default behavior is to sort the deepest dimension.

2. Choose the appropriate sort button (ascending or descending) in the toolbar.

Sort by drag and drop

To manually sort, select a header in a viz or on a legend and drag it to the correct location – a heavy black line indicates where it will go.

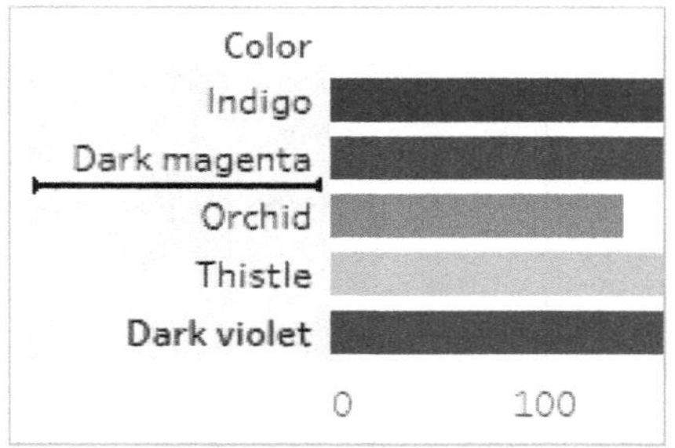

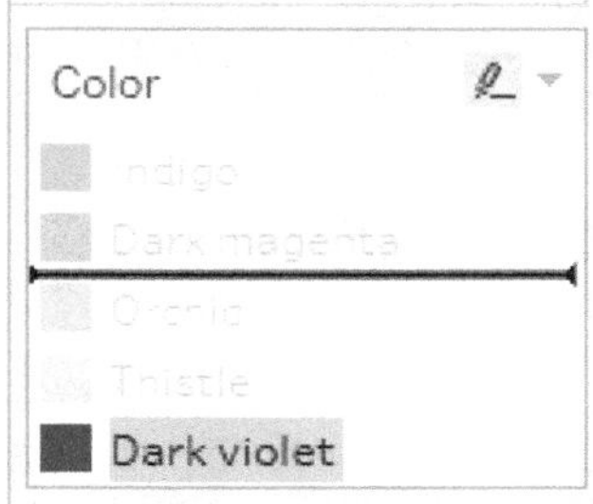

Note: Sorting on a legend also changes the order of the marks, not simply how the legend is displayed. Whatever is bottommost in the legend becomes the bottommost mark in the viz. This can either mean closest to the axis or header, or actually underneath in the case of scatterplots and other viz types that may have overlapping marks.

Sort specific fields in the viz

Customize sorting by using the Sort menu for specific fields. (The Sort menu is not available for continuous measures.)

1. Right-click (Windows) or control-click (Mac) the field you want to sort, and select **Sort**.

2. Select a **Sort By** option, and configure its behavior:

○ **Data Source Order** sorts based on how the data is sorted in the data source. Generally for relational data sources, this tends to be natural sort order. Natural sort order is an alphabetic sort where multi-digit numbers are treated as a single character. For example, natural sorting puts 2 before 19 because 2 is less than 19, whereas alphabetic sorting puts 19 before 2 because 1 is less than 2.

If you are using a cube, data source order is the defined hierarchical order of the members within a dimension.

- **Alphabetic** sorts the data alphabetically. This sort is case sensitive, sorts [A-Z] before [a-z], and treats digits individually (that is, 19 comes before 2).

To create a non-case sensitive sort, create a calculated field using the UPPER() or LOWER() functions to remove variation in capitalisation.

- **Field** lets you select the field whose value will be used to determine the sort order. The field does not need to be used in the visualization. You can also select an aggregation for the sorting field. The aggregation options available depend on the field type.

- **Manual** lets you select a value and move it to the desired position, either by dragging it in the list or using the arrows to the right.

- **Nested** lets you select the field whose value will be used to determine the sort order. The field does not need to be used in the visualization. You can also select an aggregation for the sorting field. The aggregation options available depend on the field type.

Actions

One of the best ways to add interaction to a dashboard is through using dashboard actions. This allows the user to really engage with the data in front of them. The dashboard actions invite the user to play with the dashboard.
There are six different types of actions that we can apply to our sheets within our dashboard.

1. Filter actions
2. Highlight actions
3. URL actions
4. Go to action
5. Set actions
6. Parameter actions

For example, in a dashboard showing home sales by neighborhood, you could use actions to display relevant information for a selected neighborhood. Selecting a neighborhood in one view can trigger an action that highlights the related houses in a map view, filters a list of the houses sold, then opens an external web page showing census data for the neighborhood.

Here's how you use the different types of actions:

- **Filter**. Use the data from one view to filter data in another to help guide analysis.

- **Highlight**. Call attention to marks of interest by coloring specific marks and dimming all others.

- **Go to URL**. Create hyperlinks to external resources, such as a web page, file or another Tableau worksheet.

- **Go to Sheet**. Simplify navigation to other worksheets, dashboards or stories.

- **Change Parameter**. Let users change parameter values by directly interacting with marks on a viz.

- **Change Set Values**. Let users change the values in a set by directly interacting with marks on a viz.

Filter actions send information between worksheets. Typically, a filter action sends information from a selected mark to another sheet showing related information. Behind the scenes, filter actions send data values from the relevant source fields as filters to the target sheet.

For example, in a view showing the sales price of houses, when you select a particular house, a filter action can show all comparable houses in a different view. The source fields for the filter might contain sales price and square footage.

Create or edit a filter action

1. Do either of the following:

   - On a worksheet, select **Worksheet** > **Actions**.

   - On a dashboard, select **Dashboard** > **Actions**.

From the drop-down menu of a dashboard sheet, you can also select **Use as Filter**. In the Actions dialog box, "generated" appears in the default names of actions created this way.

2. In the Actions dialog box, click **Add Action**, and then select **Filter**. Or select an existing action, and choose **Edit**.

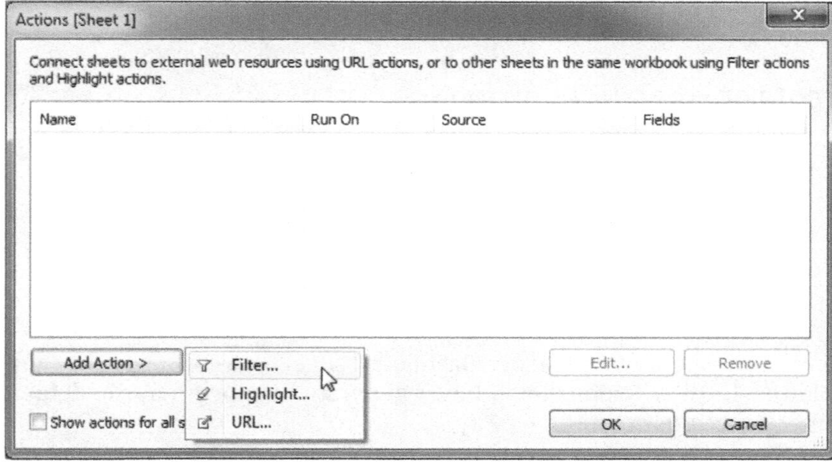

3. Specify a name for the action.

4. Select a source sheet or data source. If you select a data source or dashboard, you can select related sheets you want to launch the action from.

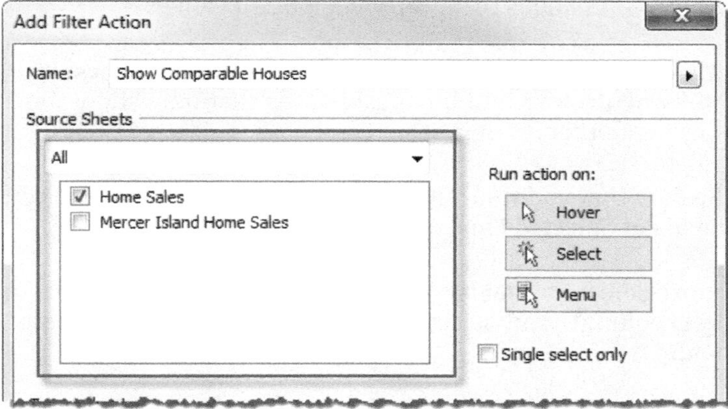

5. Specify how the action runs:

○ **Hover** - Runs when you mouse over marks in the view.

○ **Select** - Runs when you click marks in the view. If you want to avoid running the action when multiple marks are selected, also select **Single-select only**.

○ **Menu** - Runs when you right-click (Windows) or Control-click (macOS) a mark in the view, and then click an option in the tooltip menu.

6. Select a target sheet. When you select a dashboard, you can select one or more sheets within it.

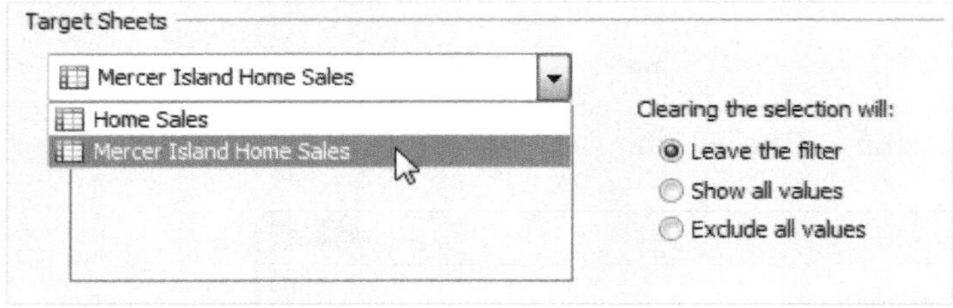

7. Specify what happens when the selection is cleared in the view:

○ **Leave the filter** – Continues to show filtered results on the target sheets. (In web-authoring mode, this is labelled **Keep filtered values.**)

○ **Show all values** – Changes the filter to include all values.

○ **Exclude all values** – Changes the filter to exclude all values. This option is useful when you're building dashboards that only show some sheets if a value in another sheet is selected.

8. Specify the data that you want to show on the target sheets. You can filter on **All Fields** or **Selected Fields.**

9. If you chose **Selected Fields**, click on a drop-down menu in the **Source Field** column, and select a field. Then select a target data source and field.

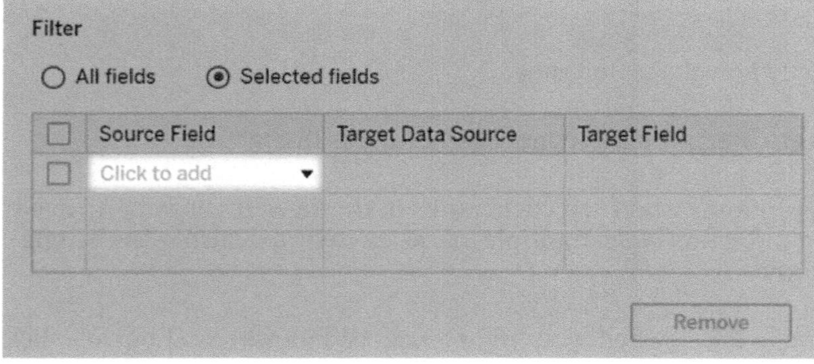

Understanding available target fields

In the Add Filter dialog box, the fields available in the Target Field drop-down list are limited to the data type of the Source Field. For example, if you select a text field for the source, only text fields are available as targets.

If you are connected to a relational data source, you can add sheet links across data sources even if the field names don't match. For example, if one data source has a Latitude field while another has a Lat field, you can associate the fields using the drop down lists in the Add Filter dialog box. When using a multidimensional data source, the destination sheet must use the same data source as the source sheet, and the source and target field names must match. (In Tableau, multidimensional data sources are supported only in Windows.)

Highlight actions allow you to call attention to marks of interest by coloring specific marks and dimming all others. You can highlight marks in the view using a variety of tools. For example, you can manually select the marks you want to highlight, use the legend to select related marks, use the highlighter to search for marks in context or create an advanced highlight action.

Create Advanced Highlight Actions

You can define more advanced highlight actions using the Actions dialog box. There you can specify source and target sheets and the fields you want to use for highlighting. Follow the steps below to create a highlight action.

1. On a worksheet select **Worksheet >Actions**. From a dashboard, select **Dashboard >Actions**.

2. In the Actions dialog box click the **Add Action** button and then select **Highlight**.

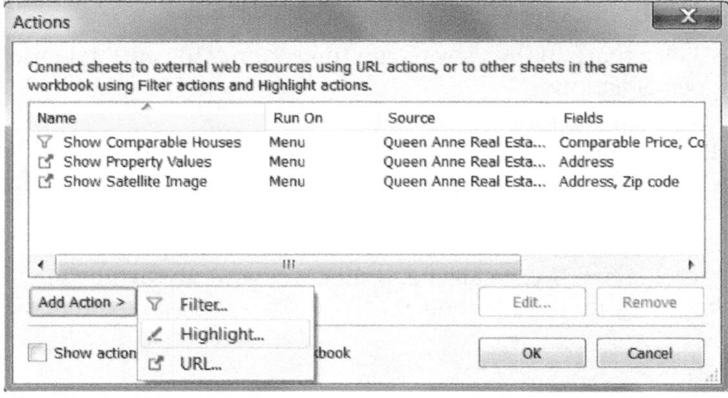

3. Name the action to identify it in the Actions dialog box. Try to make the name descriptive, such as, *Highlight Products Shipped by Delivery Truck*. You can select variables from a drop-down list and use them in the name. Then they are filled in based on the values of the selected field.

4. Use the drop-down list to select the source sheet or data source. If you select a data source or a dashboard sheet, you can further select individual sheets within them.

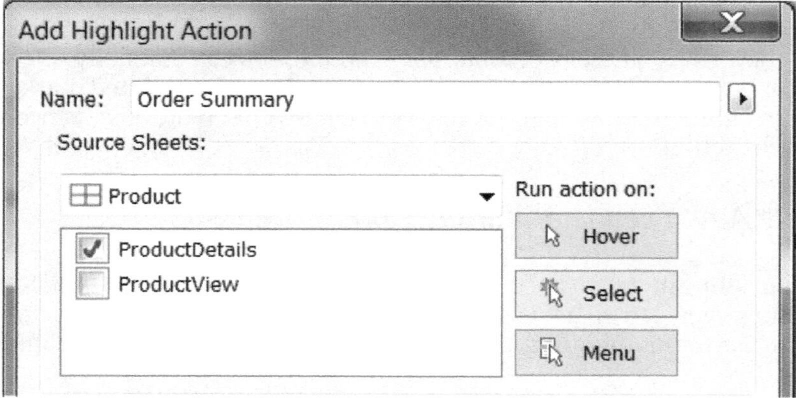

5. Select how you want to trigger the action. You can select from the following options:

- **Hover** - Rest the pointer over a mark in the view to run the action. This option works well for highlight and filter actions within a dashboard.

- **Select** – Click a mark in the view to run the action. This option works well for all types of actions.

- **Menu** - Right-click (control-click on Mac) a selected mark in the view and then select an option on the context menu. This option works well for filter and URL actions.

6. Select a target sheet. If you select a dashboard, you can further select individual sheets within the dashboard.

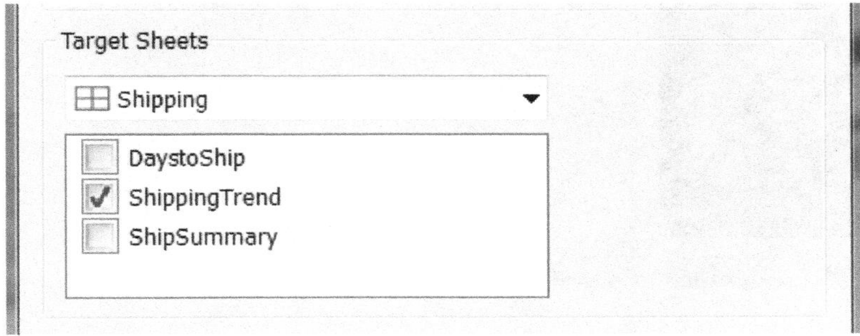

7. Select the fields you want to use for highlighting. Select from the following options:

○ **All Fields** - Marks in the target sheet are highlighted when they match the marks selected in the source sheet. All fields are considered when determining a match.

○ **Dates and Times** - Marks in the target sheet are highlighted when their date and time match those of the marks selected in the source sheet. The source and target worksheets can only have one date field each, however the date fields can have different names.

○ **Selected Fields** - Marks in the target sheet are highlighted based on select fields. For example, highlighting using the Ship Mode field will result in an action that highlights all marks in the target sheet that have the same ship mode as the selected mark in the source sheet.

8. When finished, click **OK** twice to close the dialog boxes and return to the view.

A URL action is a hyperlink that points to a web page, file, or other web-based resource outside of Tableau. You can use URL actions to create an email or link to additional information about your data. To customize links based on your data, you can automatically enter field values as parameters in URLs.

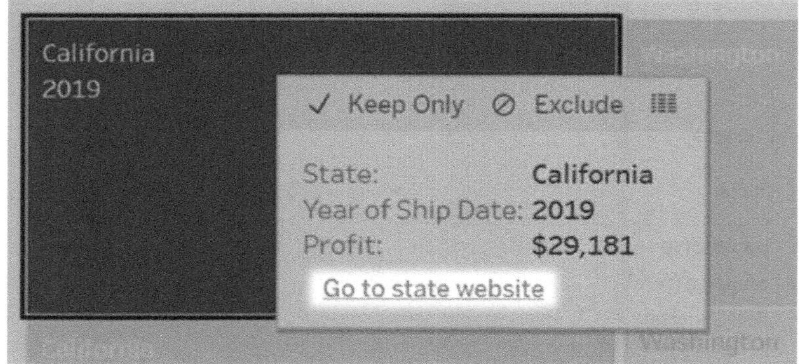

A URL action run from a tooltip menu. The link reflects the action name, not the target URL.

Open a web page with a URL action

1. On a worksheet, select **Worksheet** > **Actions**. From a dashboard, select **Dashboard** > **Actions**.

2. In the Actions dialog box, click **Add Action** and then select **Go to URL**.

3. In the next dialog box, enter a name for the action. To enter field variables in the name, click the **Insert** menu to the right of the **Name** box.

Note: Give the action a descriptive name, because in tooltip menus the link reflects that name, not the URL. For example, when linking to more product details, a good name could be "Show More Details".

4. Use the drop-down list to select a source sheet or data source. If you select a data source or dashboard you can select individual sheets within it.

5. Select how users will run the action.

6. For URL Target, specify where the link will open:

○ **New Tab if No Web Page Object Exists** – Ensures that the URL opens in a browser on sheets that lack web page objects. This is a good choice when Source Sheets is set to All or a data source.

○ **New Browser Tab** – Opens in the default browser.

○ **Web Page Object** – (Available only for dashboards with Web Page objects) Opens in the web page object you select.

7. Enter a URL with one of the following prefixes:

○ http, https, ftp, mailto, news, gopher, tsc, tsl, sms, tel, file

○ Tableau Desktop also supports local paths like C:\Example folder\example.txt

To enter field and filter values as parameters in the URL, click the **Insert** menu to the right of the URL. Be aware that any referenced fields must be present in the view, not just a related data source.

Note: On a dashboard, you can specify an ftp address only if the dashboard doesn't contain a web object. If a web object exists, the ftp address won't load.

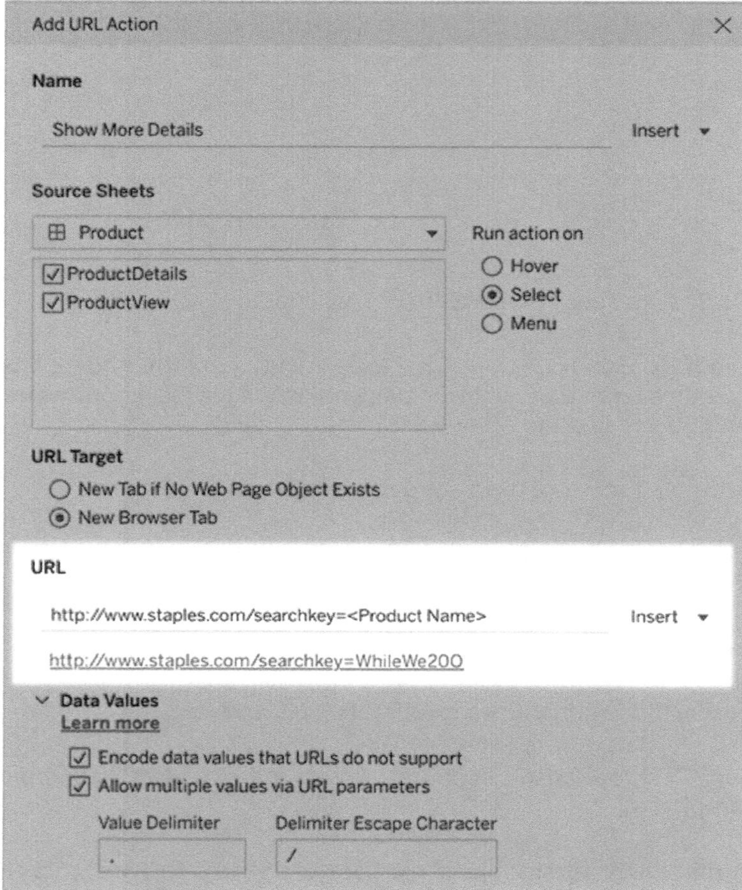

Below the URL you enter is a hyperlinked example you can click for testing.

8. (Optional) In the Data Values section, select any of the following options:

○ **Encode Data Values that URLs Do Not Support** – Select this option if your data contains values with characters that browsers don't allow in URLs. For example, if one of your data values contains an ampersand, such as "Sales & Finance", the ampersand must be translated into characters that your browser understands.

○ **Allow Multiple Values via URL Parameters** – Select this option if you are linking to a web page that can receive lists of values via parameters in the URL. For example, say you select several products in a view and you want to see each product's details hosted on a webpage. If the server can load multiple product details based on a list of identifiers (product ID or product name), you could use multi-select to send the list of identifiers as parameters.

When you allow multiple values, you must also define the delimiter escape character, which is the character that separates each item in the list (for example, a comma). You must also define the Delimiter Escape, which is used if the delimiter character is used in a data value.

Create an email with a URL action

1. On a worksheet, select **Worksheet** > **Actions**. From a dashboard, select **Dashboard** > **Actions**.

2. In the Actions dialog box, click **Add Action**, and select **Go to URL**.

3. In the Source Sheets drop-down list, select the sheet that contains the field with the email addresses you want to send to.

4. In the URL box, do the following:

- Type **mailto:**, and click the **Insert** menu at right to select the data field that contains email addresses.

- Type **?subject=**, and enter text for the Subject line.

- Type **&body=**, and click the **Insert** menu at right to select the fields of information that you want to include in the body of the email.

In the example below, the "Email" field contains the email addresses, the subject is "City Information", and the body text of the email consists of the city and state data that is associated with the email address.

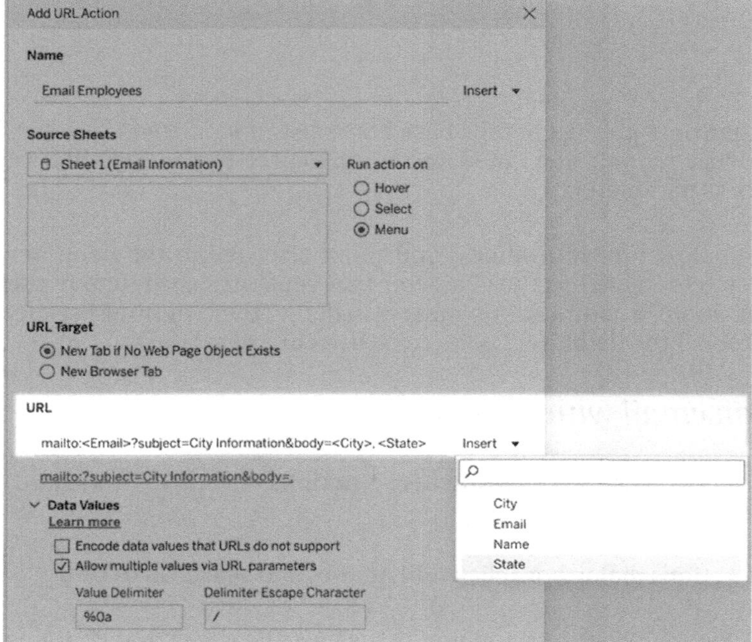

:

5. (Optional) Display data from your workbook in the body of your email as a vertical list instead of the default horizontal list. For example, suppose you have a horizontal list of cities, such as Chicago, Paris, Barcelona, which you would rather display vertically, like this:

Chicago
Paris
Barcelona

To make the list vertical, in the Data Values section, do the following:

- Deselect **Encode Data Values that URLs Do Not Support**
- Select **Allow Multiple Values via URL Parameters**.
- Type **%0a** in the **Value Delimiter** text box to add line breaks between each item in the list. (These are the URL-encoded characters for a line break.)

Using field and filter values in URLs

When users trigger URL actions from selected marks, Tableau can send field, filter and parameter values as variables in the URL. For example, if a URL action links to a mapping website, you could insert the address field to automatically open the currently selected address on the website.

1. In the Edit URL Action dialog box, begin typing the URL for the link.

2. Place the cursor where you want to insert a field, parameter or filter value.

3. Click the **Insert** menu to the right of the text box and select the field, parameter, or filter you want to insert. The variable appears within angle brackets. You can continue adding as many variables as you need.

Note: Any referenced fields must be present in the view, not just a related data source. Otherwise, the link won't display in the viz, even if it functions when you click Test Link.

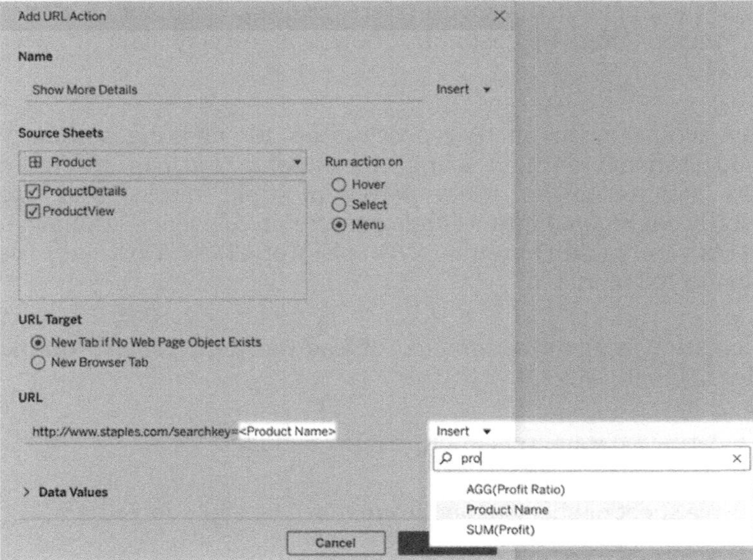

Including aggregated fields

The list of available fields includes only non-aggregated fields. To use aggregated field values as link parameters, first create a related calculated field, and add that field to the view. (If you don't need the calculated field in the visualization, drag it to Detail on the Marks card.)

Inserting parameter values

When inserting parameter values, URL actions send the Display As value by default. To instead send the actual value, add the characters ~na after the parameter name.

For example, say you have a parameter that includes IP addresses, with Actual Value strings such as 10.1.1.195 and Display As strings with more friendly values such as Computer A (10.1.1.195). To send the actual value, you'd revise the parameter in the URL to look like this: http://<IPAddress~na>/page.htm.

Parameter Actions

One way to utilize parameter actions is what we call dynamic highlighting. Now this is going to use a parameter action.

Use parameter actions to let your audience change a parameter value through direct interaction with a viz, such as clicking or selecting a mark. You can use parameter actions with reference lines, calculations, filters and SQL queries, and to customize how you display data in your visualizations.

Parameter actions open up new possibilities for creating summary values and statistics without using calculations. You can configure parameter actions to let users select multiple marks that are automatically aggregated into a single parameter value. For example, a parameter action could show the AVG(Sales) or COUNTD(Orders) for currently selected marks.

You can create parameter actions in Tableau Desktop, Tableau Online and Tableau Server.

When you define a parameter action, it must include:

- the source sheet or sheets it applies to.
- the user behavior that runs the action (hover, select or menu).
- the target parameter, the source field and the respective aggregation (if applicable).

The parameter referenced in the action must also be referenced in some part of the visualization. You can do this in different ways, such as referencing the parameter in a calculated field or reference line that is used in the viz. You can also build a view that uses a source field that is referred to in the parameter action.

General steps for creating parameter actions

1. Create one or more parameters..

2. **Optional**: Depending on the behavior you want to make available to users for their analysis, you might want to create a calculated field that uses the parameter.

3. Build a visualization that will make use of parameter actions.

For example, if you created a calculated field that uses the parameter, build the view using that calculated field. Or, drag a field that you plan to tie to the parameter into the view.

4. Create a parameter action that uses a parameter. You can create multiple parameter actions for different purposes. The parameter action must refer to the sheet name of the visualization, the parameter name and the source field that the parameter will be associated with.

5. Test the parameter action and adjust its settings or other related elements in your visualization as needed to get the behavior you want your audience to experience.

Create a parameter action

1. In a worksheet, select **Worksheet >Actions**. In a dashboard, select **Dashboard >Actions**.

2. In the Actions dialog box, click **Add Action** and then select **Change Parameter**.

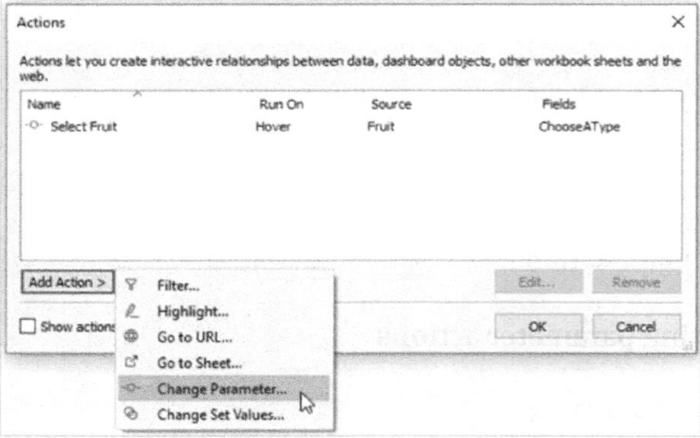

3. In the **Actions** dialog box, specify a meaningful name for the action.

4. Select a source sheet or data source. The current sheet is selected by default. If you select a data source or dashboard you can select individual sheets within it.

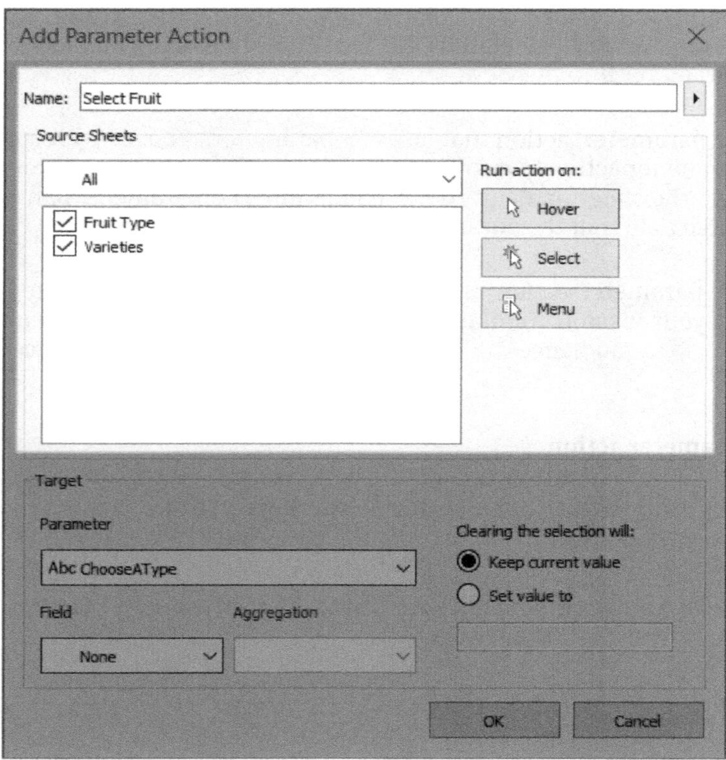

5. Select how users will run the action.

○ **Hover** - Runs when a user hovers the mouse cursor over a mark in the view. Also exposes an option for the action in the mark's tooltip.

○ **Select** - Runs when a user clicks a mark or selects multiple marks in the view.

○ **Menu** - Runs when a user right-clicks (macOS: control-clicks) a selected mark in the view, then selects an option on the context menu. Also exposes an option for the action in the mark's tooltip.

6. Under **Target**, specify the target parameter and a source field. All parameters in the workbook are available in the **Parameter** list.

To let your users select multiple marks that get aggregated into a single parameter value, select an aggregation type.

Note: If you want your users to be able to select multiple marks, you will need to select an aggregation. If **Aggregation** is set to **None**, and multiple marks that contain different values for the source field are selected, the parameter action will not run.

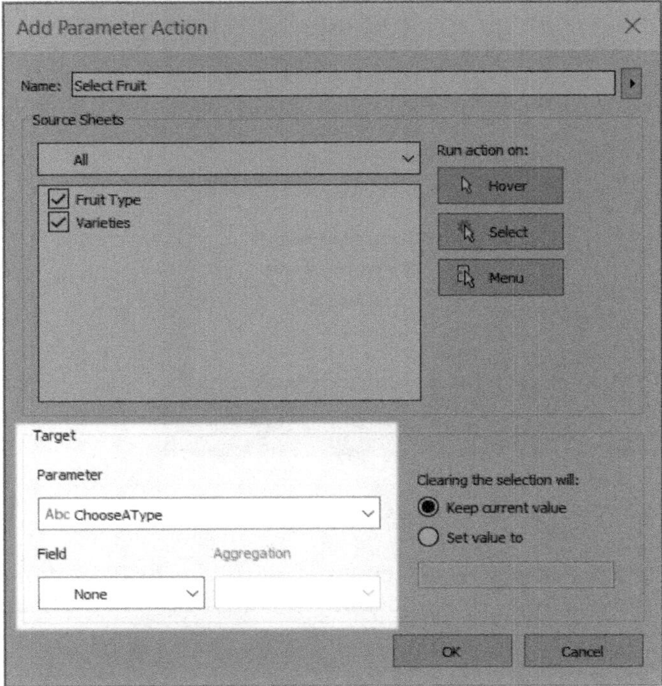

The aggregation that you choose for the parameter action can be different than the aggregation used for that field in the view. For example, you could create a view that uses SUM(Sales), but set the Sales source field referenced in the parameter action to use Average for the aggregation. Note that if you then change the aggregation of the Sales field in the view to AVG(Sales), you will need to update the parameter action to reference the Sales field again.

7. Specify what will happen when the selection is cleared.

- **Keep current value** - Current parameter value will remain in the view.

- **Set value to** - Parameter value will revert to the indicated value.

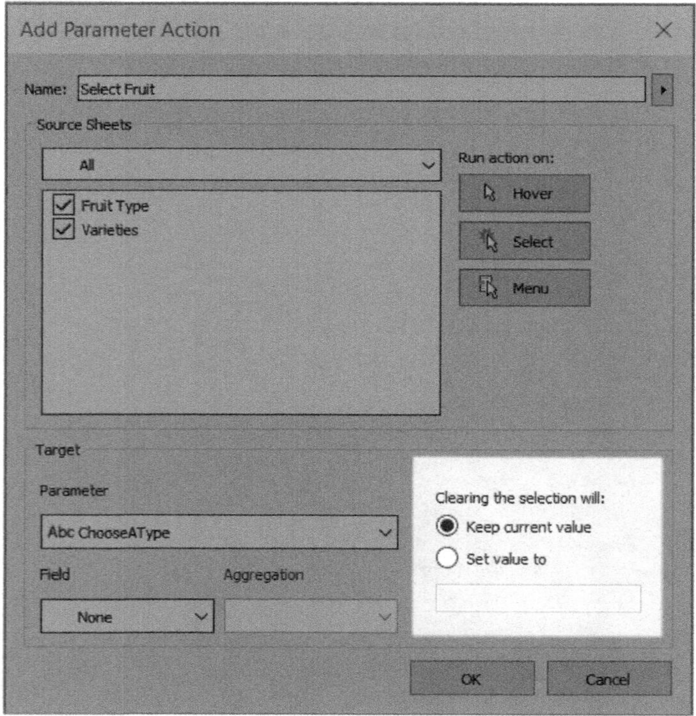

8. Click **OK** to save your changes and return to the view.

9. Test the parameter action by interacting with the visualization. Tweak some of the settings for the action to adjust the behavior as needed.

Set Actions

Use set actions to let your audience interact directly with a viz or dashboard to control aspects of their analysis. When someone selects marks in the view, set actions can change the values in a set.

Set actions take an existing set and update the values contained in that set based on user actions in a viz. You can define the set action to include:

- the source sheet or sheets it applies to.
- the user behavior that runs the action (hover, select or menu).
- the target set (the data source and set to be used).
- what happens when the selection is cleared.

To change or affect a visualization, the set referenced in the action must be used somehow in the visualization. You can do this in different ways, such as using the set in a calculated field that you then use to build the viz, or by placing the set in the view or on a Marks card property.

You can create set actions in Tableau Desktop, Tableau Online and Tableau Server.

General steps for set actions

1. Create one or more sets. The sets you create will be associated with the data source that is currently selected.

2. Create a set action that uses one of the sets you created. You can create multiple set actions for different purposes.

3. Depending on the behavior you want to make available to users for their analysis, you might want to create a calculated field that uses the set.

4. Build a visualization that uses a set referenced by a set action. For example, if you create a calculated field that uses the set, build the view using that calculated field. Or, drag the set to Color in the Marks card.

5. Test the set action and adjust its settings as needed to get the behavior you want your audience to experience.

Create a set action

1. In a worksheet, select **Worksheet >Actions**. In a dashboard, select **Dashboard >Actions**.

2. In the Actions dialog box, click **Add Action** and then select **Change Set Values**.

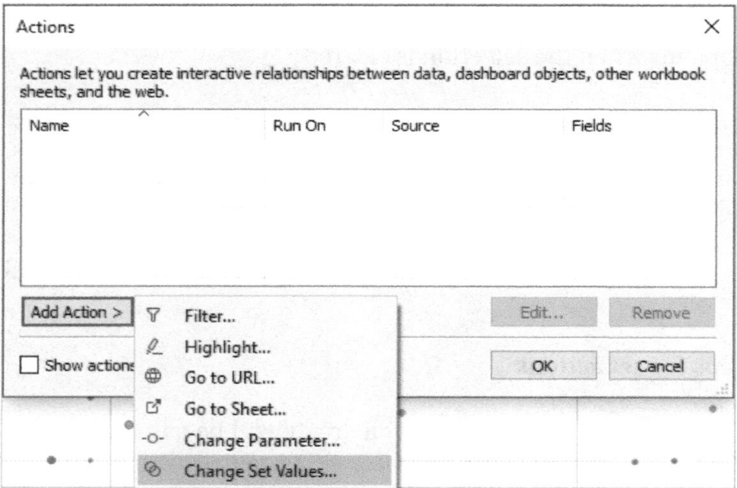

3. In the **Add/Edit Set Action** dialog box, specify a meaningful name for the action.

4. Select a source sheet or data source. The current sheet is selected by default. If you select a data source or dashboard you can select individual sheets within it.

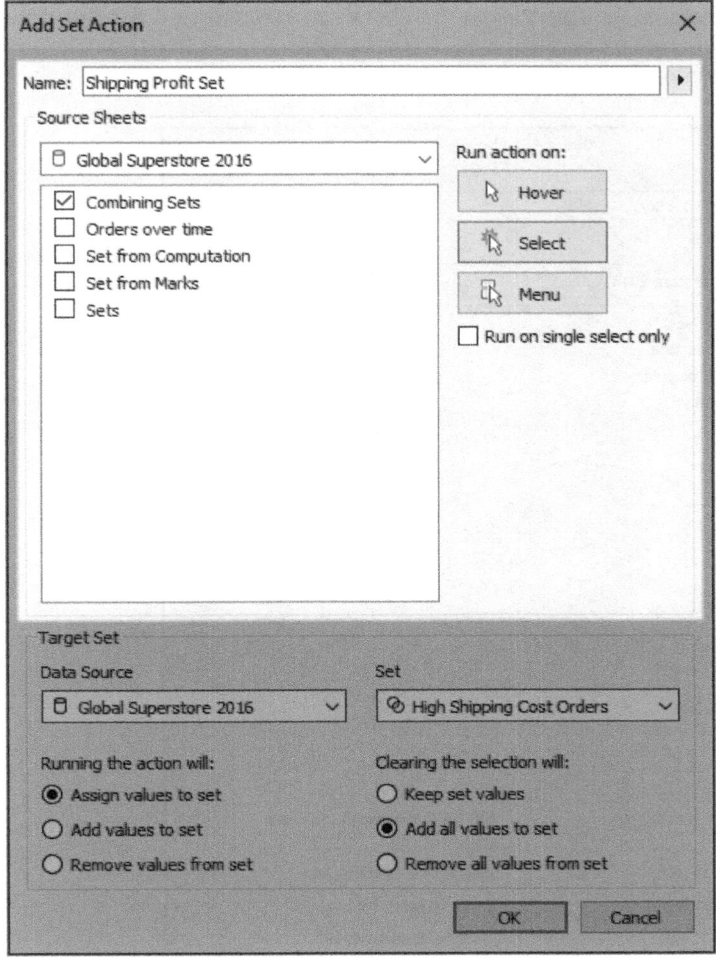

5. Select how users will run the action.

○ **Hover** - Runs when a user hovers the mouse cursor over a mark in the view.

○ **Select** - Runs when a user clicks a mark in the view. This option works well for set actions.

○ **Menu** - Runs when a user right-clicks (control-clicks on Mac) a selected mark in the view, then selects an option on the context menu.

6. Specify the target set. First, select the data source, and then select the set.

The sets available in the Target Set lists are determined by the data source that you select and the sets that you have created in the workbook that are associated with that data source.

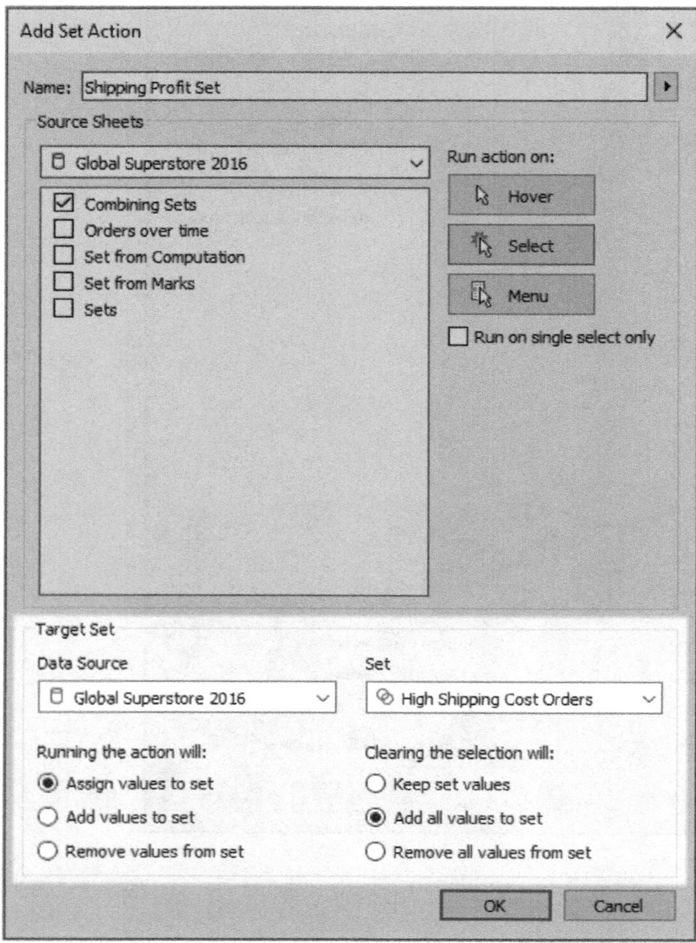

In this example, the target set is using *Global Superstore 2016* as the data source and *High Delivery Cost Orders* as the set.

7. Specify what happens when the action is run in the view:

- **Assign values to set** – Replaces all values in the set with the values selected.

- **Add values to set** – Adds individually selected values to the set.

- **Remove values from set** – Removes individually selected values from the set.

Note: Selecting **Add values to set** or **Remove values from set** via the Set Action dialog modifies the values selected in the General tab of the set's definition – just like **Assign values to set** does. This differs from the **Add to** and **Remove from** functionality available only in authoring mode via the set's context menu in the tooltip. The latter unions or removes values to and from the set after the condition specified has been applied.

8. Specify what happens when the selection is cleared in the view:

- **Keep set values** - Current values in the set remain in the set.
- **Add all values to set** - Adds all possible values to the set.
- **Remove all values from set** - Removes previously selected values from the set.

9. Click **OK** to save your changes and return to the view.

10. Test the set action by interacting with the visualization. Tweak some of the settings for the action to adjust the selection behavior as needed.

Running Actions

Depending on how the action is created, you can run an action using one of the following three methods:

- **Hover** - Rest the pointer over a mark in the view to run the action. This option works well for highlight and filter actions within a dashboard.
- **Select** - Click on a mark in the view to run the action. This option works well for all types of actions.
- **Menu** - On Tableau Desktop, right-click (control-click on Mac) a selected mark in the view and then select an option on the context menu. On Tableau Server or Online, left-click (click on Mac) a selected mark in the view to see the context menu. This option works well for filter and URL actions.

Actions and Dashboards

Actions often have unique behavior when the source or destination is a dashboard. Because a dashboard can contain multiple views, a single filter or highlight action can have broad impact. Dashboards can also contain web page objects, which you can target with interactive URL actions.

Use a single view to filter other views in a dashboard

Imagine you have a dashboard that contains three views about profitability: a map, a bar chart, and a table of customer names. You can use a filter action to make one of the views in your dashboard, such as the map, the controlling view for the filter action. When your users select a region in the map, the data in the other views is filtered so that it relates to just that region.

1. On the dashboard, select the view you want to use as a filter.

2. In the shortcut menu of the view, choose **Use as Filter**. You can perform the same action by clicking the Use as Filter icon .

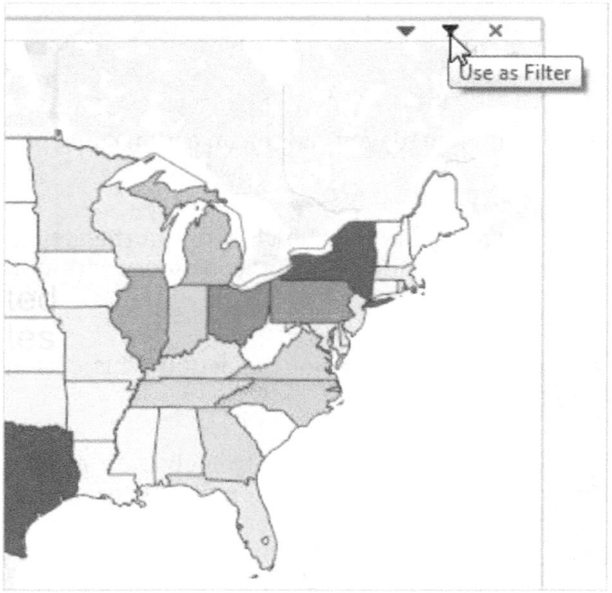

You can also use filter actions to filter the data on a dashboard when the data comes from multiple data sources.

Use multiple views to filter other views in a dashboard

Just as you can use a single view to filter other views in a dashboard, you can also use multiple views as a filter. The trick is to not only use these views as filters, but to also disable their ability to be filtered themselves.

1. Create or open a dashboard that has at least three views.

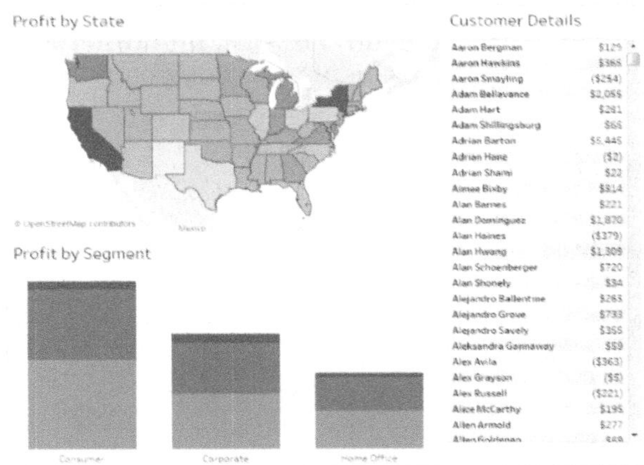

2. Select the first view that you want to use as a filter (such as a map), and from its shortcut menu, select **Use as Filter**.

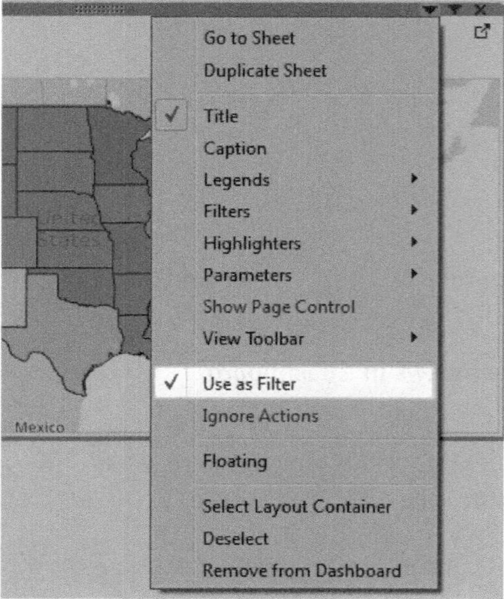

3. Open the same view's shortcut menu again and select **Ignore Actions**. This ensures that other filter actions, including the one you'll create next, will not affect this view.

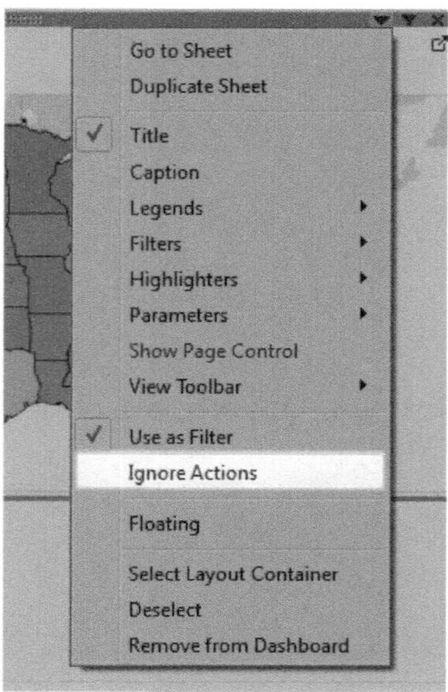

4. Repeat the steps 2 and 3 for any other views you want to use as a filter.

Now, selecting marks in these controlling views filters data in one or more detail views – all without affecting any other controlling views.

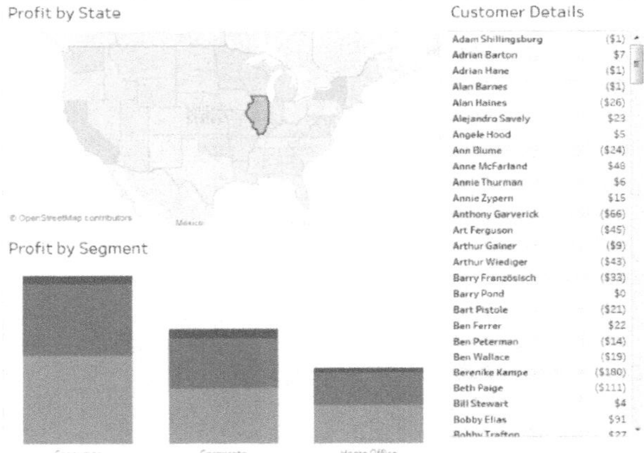

Navigate from one view to another view, dashboard or story

Use the Go to Sheet action to let users quickly navigate to a related visualization – a dashboard, sheet, or story – when they click on a mark or a tooltip menu item in the original view.

1. From your dashboard, select **Dashboard** > **Actions**.

2. In the Actions dialog box, click **Add Action** and then select **Go to Sheet**.

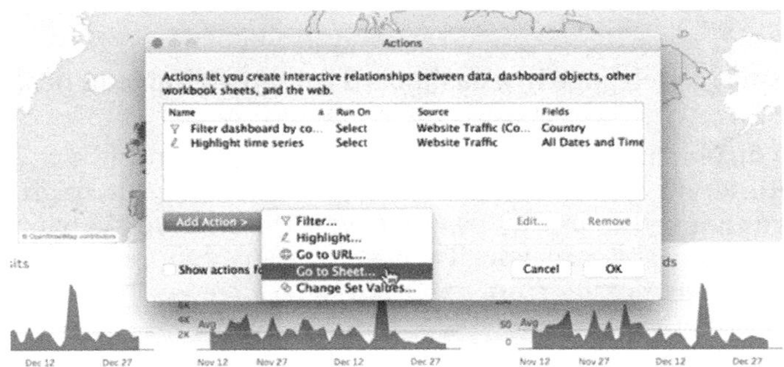

3. Specify a name for the action. (If you choose to run the action using a tooltip menu, the name you specify here is what the tooltip displays.)

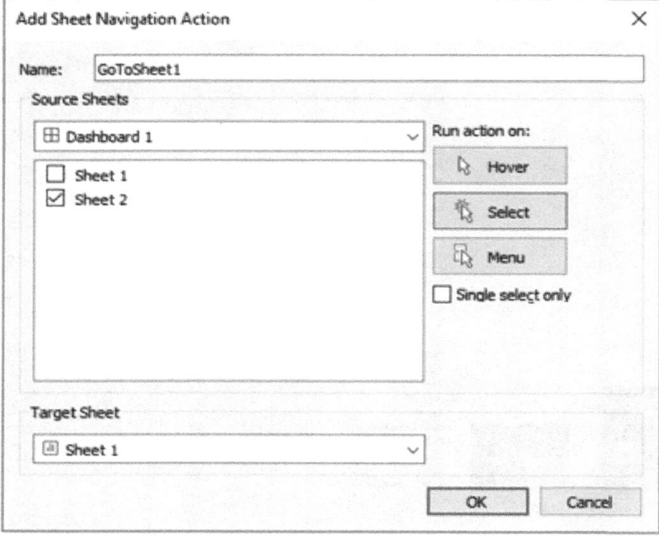

4. Select a source sheet that will initiate the action.

5. Specify how people viewing your dashboard will run the action. **Select** or **Menu** are the best choices for a navigation action.

If you choose **Select**, consider selecting **Single-select only** so users won't navigate away from the view when multiple marks are selected.

6. For the target sheet, select the navigation destination that appears when users click marks or tooltip menu items in the source sheet. Then click **OK**.

Interactively display a web page in a dashboard (Create in Tableau Desktop)

To interactively display information from the web inside a dashboard, you can use a URL action with a web page object. For example, you might have a dashboard that shows profits by country. In addition to showing the profit data in your dashboard, you also want to display supplemental information about the countries from a web site.

1. Drag a **Web Page** object onto your dashboard, and enter a URL.

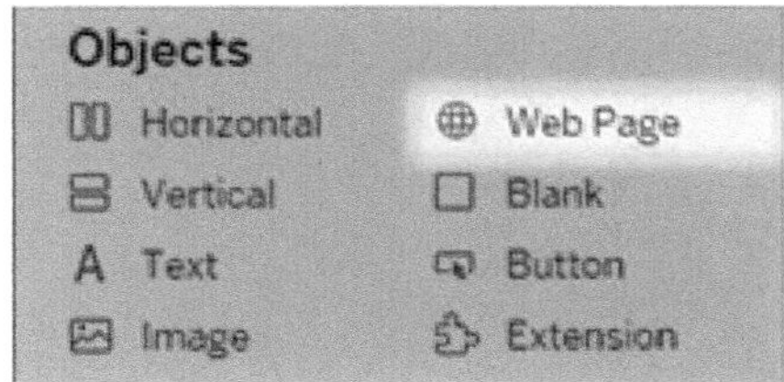

2. From your dashboard, select **Dashboard** > **Actions**.

3. In the Actions dialog box, click **Add Action** and then select **Go to URL**.

4. Specify a name for the link. If you choose to run the action using a menu, such as a menu option on a tooltip, the name you specify here is what's displayed.

5. Under Source Sheets, select the view or data source that will initiate the action. For example, if you want the action to be initiated when a user clicks a link on a map's tooltip, select the map view.

6. Specify whether people viewing your dashboard will run the action on hover, select, or menu.

7. Enter the URL, starting with the http:// or https:// prefix, such as http://www.example.com.

You can use field values as parameters in your URL. For example, if Country is a field used by a view in your dashboard, you can use <Country> as a parameter in your URL.

8. For URL Target, select **Web Page Object**, and select the object you created in step 1.

When you launch the action, a web page automatically loads within the dashboard rather than opening a separate browser window.

Using Field and Filter Values in Action Names

In addition to using field, parameter, and filter values in URLs, you can use this information as variables in the action names. The name of the action displays on the context menu when an action is launched using the menu. Using field and filter variables in the name is useful in making the action specific to the selected mark. In a view showing real estate information, you could name a URL action that points at satellite images from an online mapping service, "Show satellite image of <Address>". When you right-click (control-click on Mac) a specific mark, the <Address> tag is replaced with the location value associated with that mark.

1. In the Add Action dialog box, begin typing the name for the action.

2. Place the cursor where you want to insert the field or filter value.

3. Click the arrow to the right of the text box and select the field or filter you want to add as a variable. The field or filter name is added between angle brackets.

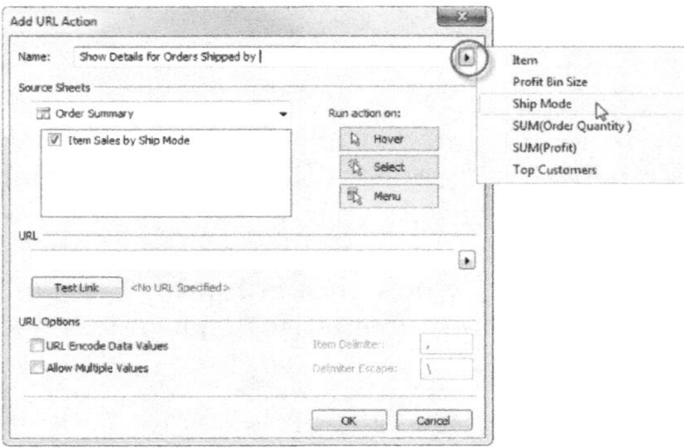

Here's a finished example for an action run from a tooltip menu:

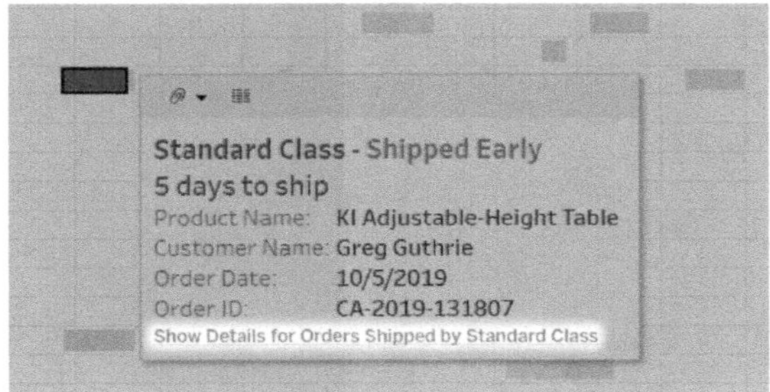

Maps and Geographic Data Analysis in Tableau

This example walks you through some of the most common tasks you might perform when creating maps in Tableau.

You'll learn how to connect to and join geographic data; format that data in Tableau; create location hierarchies; build and present a basic map view; and apply key mapping features along the way.

If you're new to building maps in Tableau, this a great place to start.

Step 1: Connect to your geographic data

Geographic data comes in many shapes and formats. When you open Tableau Desktop, the start page shows you the connectors available in the left **Connect** pane. These are how you will connect to your data.

You can work with geographic data by connecting to spatial files, or you can connect to location data stored in spreadsheets, text files or on a server.

Spatial files, such as a shapefile or geoJSON file, contain actual geometries (points, lines or polygons), whereas text files or spreadsheets contain point locations in latitude and longitude coordinates, or named locations that, when brought into Tableau, connect to the Tableau geocoding (stored geometries that your data references).

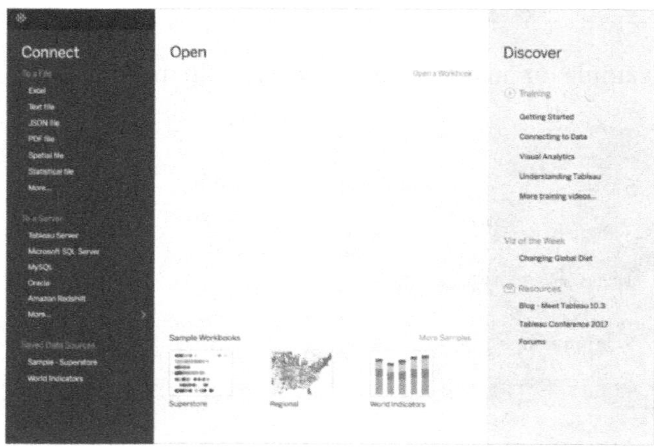

For this example, you are going to connect to an Excel file that comes with Tableau Desktop. It contains location names that Tableau can geocode. When you build a map view, the location names reference the geometries stored in the Tableau Map Service based on the geographic role you assign to the field. You'll learn more about geographic roles later in this example.

1. Open Tableau Desktop.

2. In the Connect pane, click **Excel**.

3. Navigate to **Documents** > **My Tableau Repository** > **Data Sources**, and then open the **Sample - Superstore.xls** file.

Once you connect to the data source, your screen will look like this:

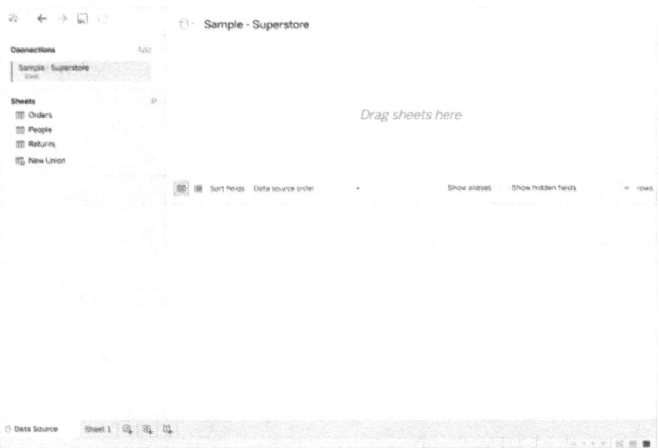

This is called the Data Source page, and it is where you can prepare your location data for use in Tableau.

Some of the tasks you can perform on the Data Source page include the following, but you don't have to do all these things to create a map view:

- Adding additional connections and joining your data
- Adding multiple sheets to your data source
- Assigning or changing geographic roles to your fields
- Changing the data type of your columns (from numbers to strings, for example)
- Renaming columns
- Splitting columns, such as splitting a full address into multiple columns for street, city, state and postcode

Step 2: Join your data

Your data is often held in multiple data sources or sheets. As long as those data sources or sheets have a column in common, you can join them in Tableau. Joining is a method for combining the related data on those common fields. The result of combining data using a join is a virtual table that is typically extended horizontally by adding columns of data.

Joining is often necessary with geographic data, particularly spatial data. For example, you can join a KML file that contains custom geographies for school districts in Oregon, U.S. with an Excel spreadsheet that contains demographic information about those school districts.

For this example, you will join two sheets in the Sample-Superstore data source.

1. On the left side of the Data Source page, under Sheets, double-click **Orders**.

2. Under Sheets, double-click **People**.

Tableau creates an inner-join between the two spreadsheets, using the Region column from both spreadsheets as the joining field. Now there is a sales person assigned to every location in your data source, as well as to regions.

To edit this join, click the join icon (the two circles). You can edit the join in the Join dialog box that opens.

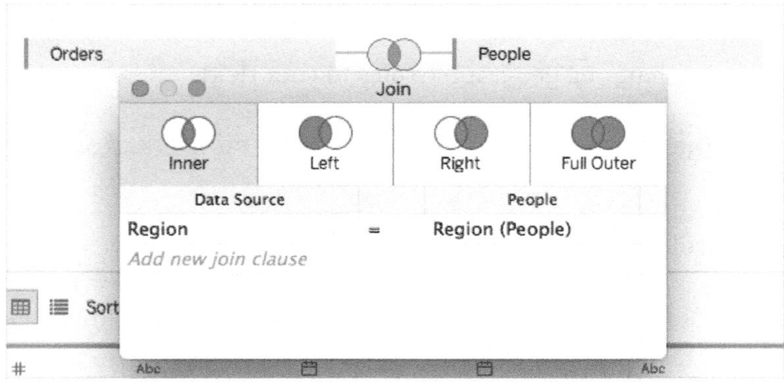

Step 3: Format your geographic data in Tableau

After you set up your data source, you might need to prepare your geographic data for use in Tableau. Not all of these procedures will always be necessary to create a map view, but it's important information to know when it comes to preparing geographic data for use in Tableau.

Depending on the type of map you want to create, you must assign certain data types, data roles and geographic roles to your fields (or columns).

For example, in most cases, your latitude and longitude fields should have a *data type* of **number (decimal)**, a *data role* of **measure**, and be assigned the **Latitude** and **Longitude***geographic roles*. All other geographic fields should have a *data type* of **string**, a *data role* of **dimension** and be assigned the appropriate geographic roles.

Note: If you are connecting to a spatial file, a Geometry field is created. It should have a data role of measure.

This step demonstrates how to format your geographic data to meet this criteria.

Change the data type of a column

When you first connect to geographic data, Tableau assigns data types to all of your columns. These data types include Number (decimal), Number (whole), Date and Time, Date, String and Boolean. Sometimes Tableau does not get these data types right, and you must edit them. For example, Tableau might assign a Postcode column a data type of Number (whole). To create map views, your Postcode data must have a data type of String.

To change the data type of a column:

1. On the Data Source page, click the data type icon (the globe) for Postcode and select **String**.

Assign geographic roles to your geographic data

In Tableau, a *geographic role* associates each value in a field with a latitude and longitude value. When you assign the correct geographic role to a field, Tableau assigns latitude and longitude values to each location in that field by finding a match that is already built in to the installed geocoding database. This is how Tableau knows where to plot your locations on the map.

When you assign a geographic role to a field, such as State, Tableau creates a Latitude (generated) field and a Longitude (generated) field.

Geographic roles are sometimes automatically assigned to your data, such as in this example. You can tell a geographic role has been assigned to your data because the column includes a globe icon.

If a geographic role is not automatically assigned, you can manually assign one to your field. You don't need to do so for this example, but it's important to know how so you can do it for your own data.

To assign or edit a geographic role:

1. On the Data Source page, click the globe icon.

2. Select **Geographic Role**, and then select a role that best matches your data.

For example, in this case, the Country column does not have a geographic role assigned to it, so the Country/Region geographic role is assigned.

Change from dimensions to measures

When you connect to geographic data, Tableau also assigns data roles to all of your columns. A column can be a *dimension* or *measure*. In most cases, your latitude and longitude columns should be measures. For special cases, such as if you want to plot every location in your data source on a map without the ability to drill up or down a level of detail (such as from City to State), they can be dimensions.

The rest of your geographic data should be dimensions.

You don't need to change the data role of a column for this example, but it's important to know how so you can do it for your own data. Feel free to practise here. You can always undo any changes you make.

To change the data role of a column:

1. On the Data Source page, click **Sheet 1**.

Your workspace updates to look like this:

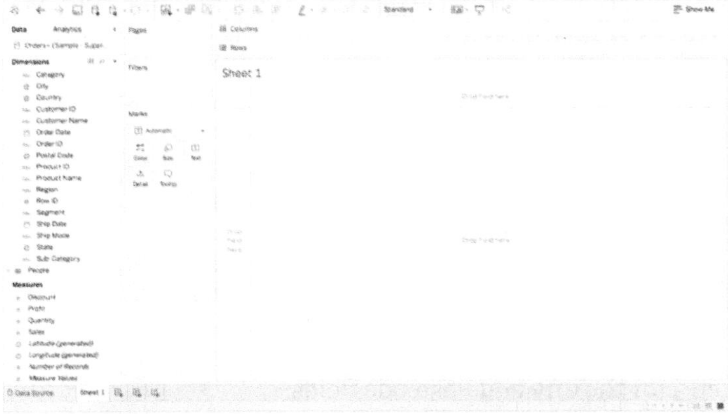

This is called a worksheet, and it is where you will build your map. On the left-side of the screen is the **Data** pane. All of the columns in your data source are listed as fields in this pane. For example, Country and State. These fields contain all the raw data in your columns. Note that Tableau has generated a Latitude and Longitude field (*Latitude (generated)* and *Longitude (generated)*). This is because you assigned geographic roles to your data.

The fields in the data pane are divided into measures and dimensions. The fields placed in the Dimensions section of the Data pane are often categorical data, such as Date and Customer ID, while the fields placed in the Measures section of the Data pane are often quantitative data, such as Sales and Quantity.

2. In the **Data** pane, under Dimensions, select a field, such as Row ID, and drag it down to the Measures section.

The field is added to the Measures section and changes from blue to green. You just converted a Dimension to a Measure. To convert a field from a measure to a dimension, drag the field from the Measures section up to the Dimensions section.

Step 4: Create a geographic hierarchy

Now that you are in the worksheet space, you can create geographic hierarchies. This is not required to create a map view, but creating a geographic hierarchy will allow you to quickly drill into the levels of geographic detail your data contains, in the order you specify.

To create a geographic hierarchy:

1. In the Data pane, right-click the geographic field, **Country**, and then select **Hierarchy** > **Create Hierarchy**.

2. In the Create Hierarchy dialog box that opens, give the hierarchy a name, such as Mapping Items, and then click **OK**.

At the bottom of the Dimensions section, the Mapping Items hierarchy is created with the Country field.

3. In the Data pane, drag the State field to the hierarchy and place it below the Country field.

4. Repeat step 3 for the City and Postcode fields.

When you are finished, your hierarchy should be in the following order:

- Country
- State
- City
- Postcode

Step 5: Build a basic map

Now that you have connected to and joined your data, formatted your data and built a geographic hierarchy, you are now ready to start building your map. You will start by building a basic map view.

1. In the Data pane, double-click **Country**.

The Country field is added to Detail on the Marks card, and Latitude (generated) and Longitude (generated) are added to the Columns and Rows shelves. A map view with one data point is created. Since a geographic role is assigned to Country, Tableau creates a map view. If you double-click any other field, such as a dimension or measure, Tableau adds that field to the Rows or Columns shelf, or the Marks card, depending on what you already have in the view. Geographic fields are always placed on Detail on the Marks card, however.

Since this data source only contains one country, (United Kingdom), that is the only data point shown. You will need to add more levels of detail to see additional data points. Since you created a geographic hierarchy, this is easy.

2. On the Marks card, click the + icon on the **Country** field.

The State field is added to Detail on the Marks card and the map updates to include a data point for every state in the data source.

If you did not create a hierarchy, the + icon on the Country field will not be available. In this case, to add State as another level of detail, manually drag **State** from the **Data** pane to **Detail** on the Marks card.

Congratulations! You now have a basic map view that you can customize and build upon in the next steps.

Step 6: Change from points to polygons

The default map type in Tableau is often a point map. When you have geographic roles assigned to your geographic data, however, it's easy to change those data points to polygons.

1. On the Marks card, click the Mark Type drop-down and select **Filled Map**.

The map updates to a polygon map.

Step 7: Add visual detail

You can add measures and dimensions to the Marks card to add visual detail to your view. In this example, you will add color and labels to the view.

Add color

- From Measures, drag **Sales** to **Color** on the Marks card.

Each state is colored by sum of sales. Since Sales is a measure, a qualitative color palette is used. If you place a dimension on color, then a categorical color palette is used.

Add labels

1. From Measures, drag **Sales** to **Label** on the Marks card.

Each state is labelled with sum of sales. The numbers need a little bit of formatting, however.

2. In the Data pane, right-click **Sales** and select **Default Properties** > **Number Format**.

3. In the Default Number Format dialog box that opens, select **Number (Custom)**, and then do the following:

- For **Decimal Places**, enter **0**.
- For **Units**, select **Thousands (K)**.
- Click **OK**.

The labels and the color legend update with the specified format.

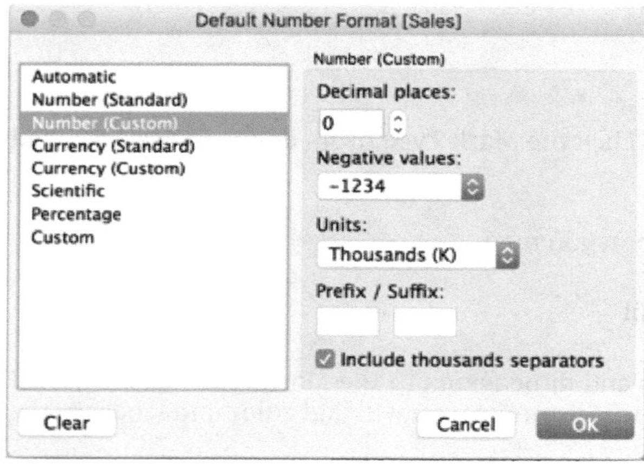

Step 8: Customize your background map

The background map is everything behind your marks (borders, oceans, location names, etc.) You can customize the style of this background map, as well as add map layers and data layers. In addition to customising the background maps, you can also connect to your own WMS server or Mapbox map.

To customize your background map:

1. Select **Map** > **Map Layers**.

The Map Layers pane appears on the left side of the workspace. This is where all background map customisation happens.

2. In the Map Layers pane, click the **Style** drop-down and select **Normal**.

The background map updates to look like this:

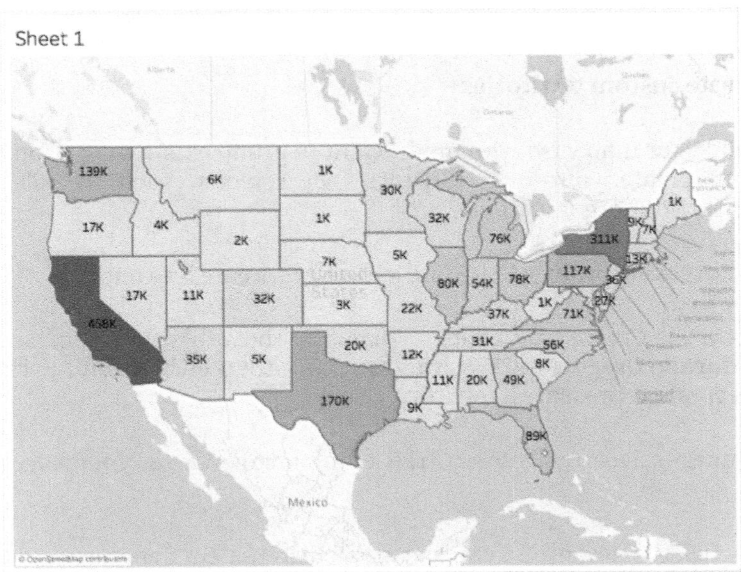

3. In the Map Layers pane, under Map Layers, select **Coastlines**, and then clear **Country/Region Borders**, **Country/Region Names**, **State/Province Borders**, and **State/Province Names**.

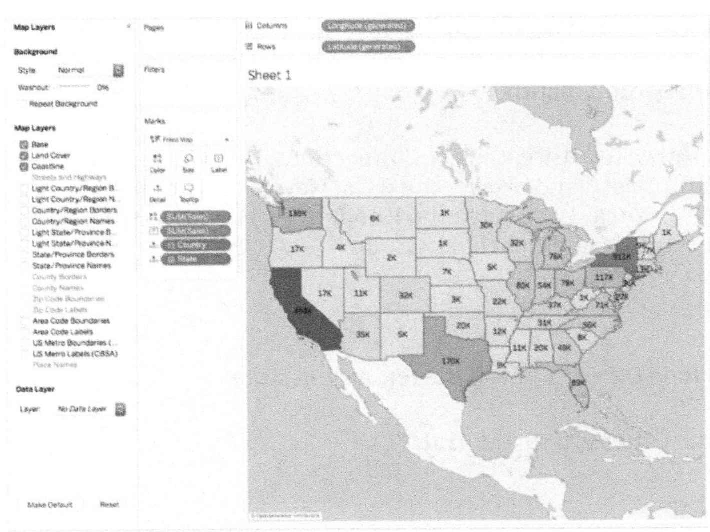

4. At the top of the Map Layers pane, click the **X** to return to the **Data** pane.

The background map is now simplified to draw attention to your data.

Step 9: Create custom territories

As you build your map view, you might want to group existing locations together to create your own territories or regions, such as sales territories for your organization.

1. In the Data pane, right-click **State** and select **Create** > **Group**.

2. In the Create Group dialog box that opens, select **California**, **Oregon** and **Washington** , and then click **Group**. Each group you create represents a territory.

Note: To multi-select, hold down Ctrl (Command on Mac) as your select states.

3. Right-click the new group you just created and select **Rename**.

4. Rename the group, **West Coast**.

5. For the next territory, select **Alabama**, **Florida**, **Georgia**, **Louisiana**, **Mississippi**, **South Carolina** and **Texas**, and then click **Group**.

6. Rename this group, **South**.

7. For the third territory, select **Connecticut**, **Delaware**, **District of Columbia**, **Main**, **Maryland**, **Massachusetts**, **New Hampshire**, **New Jersey**, **New York**, **Pennsylvania**, **Rhode Island**, **Vermont** and, finally, **West Virginia** and then click **Group**.

8. Rename this group, **East Coast**.

9. Select **Include Other** to group the remaining states.

10. Rename the **Other** group, **Central**.

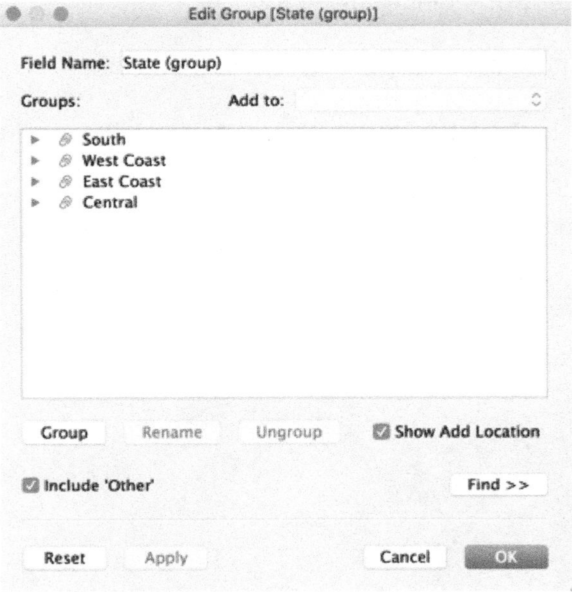

11. Click **OK**.

A State (group) field appears in the **Data** pane beneath your other mapping items.

12. From the Data pane, drag **State (group)** to **Color** on the Marks card.

The view updates to look like this:

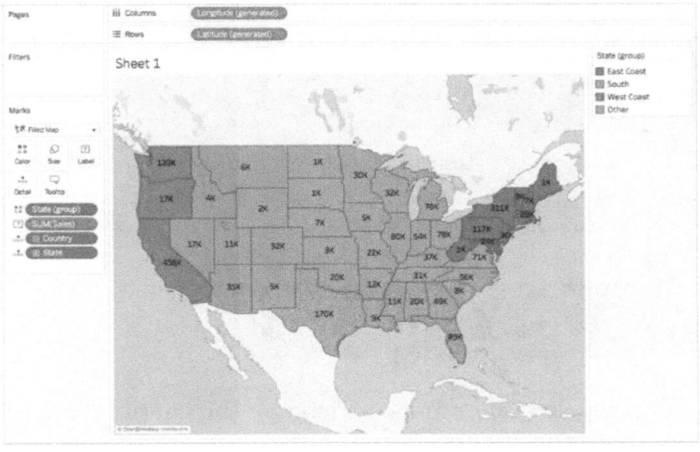

Notice that each group has a different color.

13. On the Marks card, click the **Color** icon and select **Edit Colors**.

14. In the Edit Colors dialog box that appears, select **Assign Palette**, and then click **OK**.

The marks update with new colors.

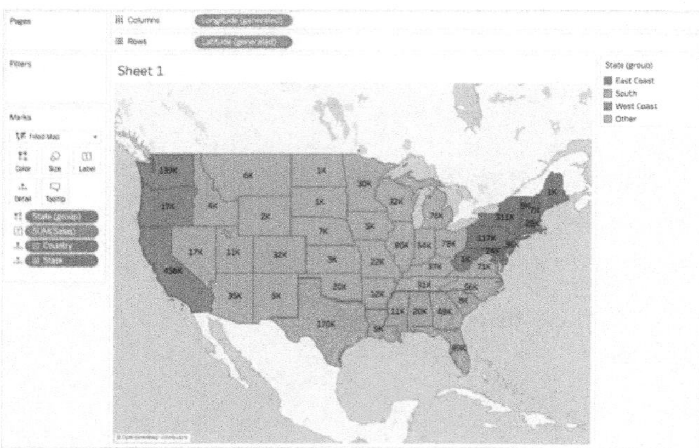

15. From Measures, drag **Sales** to **Tooltip** on the Marks card.

When you hover over a state, a tooltip appears with the sales for that state, among other information. You'll learn how to edit this tooltip later.

16. On the Marks card, click the minus (-) icon on the **Country** field to remove State from the level of detail.

If you did not create a hierarchy, you can drag **State** from the view to remove it. You can remove any field by dragging it from the view.

The states no longer appear on the map. Notice how the sum of sales has updated for the labels and in the tooltip? This is because custom territories aggregate at the level of the group, rather than separately for each location within the group. So the sum of sales your are seeing in the West Coast group, for example, are the total sales for California, Oregon and Washington combined.

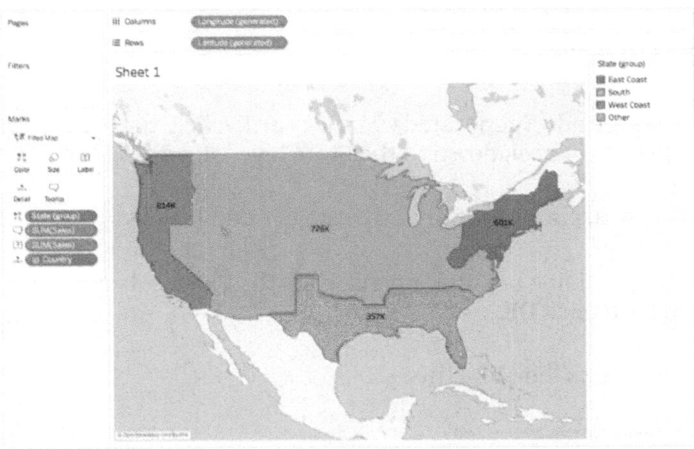

Step 10: Create a dual axis map

So far you have created two map views: one that shows the sales per state, and one that shows the sales per region. Could you layer these maps on top of one another? Yes! In Tableau, you can create a map with two layers of marks. This is called a dual axis map in Tableau, and is often used to layer points over polygons. In this example, you will layer two polygons maps.

To create a dual axis map:

1. From the Data pane, drag **Longitude (generated)** to the **Columns** shelf and place it to the right of the first Longitude field.

The view updates with two identical maps.

There are now three tabs on the Marks card: one for each map view, and one for both views (All). You can use these to control the visual detail of the map views. The top Longitude tab corresponds to the map on the left of the view, and the bottom Longitude tab corresponds to the map on the right of the view.

2. On the Marks card, select the top **Longitude (generated)** tab.

3. From Measures, drag **Sales** to **Color**on the top Longitude (generated) Marks card.

The map on the left updates.

4. On the top Longitude (generated) Marks card, click the + icon on the **Country** field to drill back down to the State level of detail.

5. On the Marks card, click **Color**, and then select **Edit Colors**.

6. In the Edit Colors dialog box that opens, click the Palette drop-down, select **Grey**, and then click **OK**.

At this point, your maps look like this:

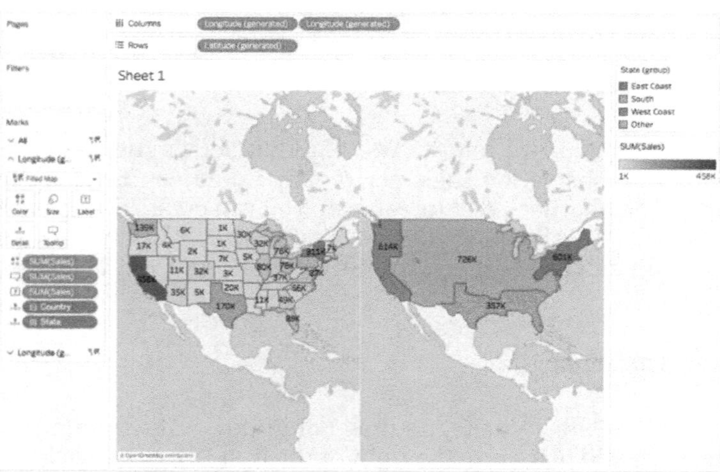

7. On the Columns shelf, right-click the **Longitude (generated)** field on the right and select **Dual Axis**.

8. On the Marks card, select the bottom **Longitude (generated)** tab.

9. On the bottom **Longitude (generated)** Marks card, drag both **SUM(Sales)** fields from the view to remove them.

The labels for each map no longer overlap.

10. On the bottom **Longitude (generated)** Marks card, click **Color**, and then, for **Opacity**, enter **50%**.

This is a crucial step if you want to be able to see the map on the bottom layer.

The map view updates to look like this:

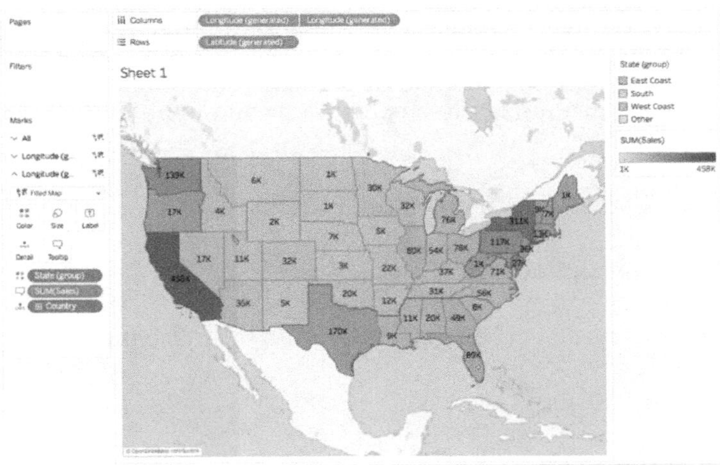

You can now see how each state performed within each group.

11. On the bottom **Longitude (generated)** Marks card, click **Tooltip**.

An Edit Tooltip dialog box opens.

12. Copy the following text and paste it into the Edit Tooltip dialog box, and then click **OK**:

Total <State (group)> region sales: **<SUM(Sales)>**

The tooltip looks similar to this:

Congrats! You've created a dual axis map! There's only one thing left to do.

Step 11: Customize how others can interact with your map

Now that you have created your map view, you can customize how people will interact with it. For example, you might now want anyone to be able to zoom in or out of your map, or pan. Or perhaps you want to display a map scale? You can customize these two options and more in the Map Options dialog box.

To customize how others can interact with your map:

1. Select **Map** > **Map Options**.

2. In the Map Options dialog box that appears, do the following:

- Select **Show Map Scale**.
- Clear **Show Map Search**.
- Clear **Show View Toolbar**.

A scale appears in the bottom-right corner of the map, and the map search icon and the toolbar in the top left corner of the map disappear. You can still pan and zoom using keyboard shortcuts.

And that's a wrap! Your map view is now ready to be presented or combined with another view in a dashboard.

Chapter 8
Drilldown On Dashboards

Drilldown on Dashboards

As we have previously seen, a dashboard is a collection of several views, letting you compare a variety of data simultaneously. If you have a set of views that you review every day, for example, you can create a dashboard that displays all the views at once, rather than navigate to separate worksheets.

Like worksheets, you access dashboards from tabs at the bottom of a workbook. Data in sheets and dashboards is connected; when you modify a sheet, any dashboards containing it change, and vice versa. Both sheets and dashboards update with the latest available data from the data source.

Elements of a Good Dashboard

Whatever dashboard you're going to build in Tableau, you have to consider four important questions.
The answers to these questions are going to impact the design choice, that goes into building that dashboard.

1. Who is your target audience for this dashboard? - Who is the dashboard for? Who is the intended audience for this dashboard?
2. Where is that audience member actually going to view your dashboard? Desktop or tablet? Understanding where impacts things like the dashboard size.
3. Why? Why are we building this dashboard in the first place? What is the purpose of that dashboard?
4. What question do you want to answer? - What do we want to exclude?

Creation of the Dashboard

After you've created one or more sheets, you can combine them in a dashboard, add interactivity and much more.

Create a dashboard, and add or replace sheets

You create a dashboard in much the same way you create a new worksheet.

1. At the bottom of the workbook, click the **New Dashboard** icon:

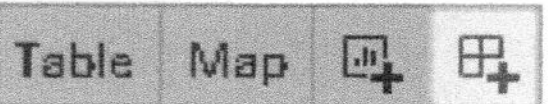

2. From the **Sheets** list at left, drag views to your dashboard at right.

3. To replace a sheet, select it in the dashboard at right. In the Sheets list at left, hover over the replacement sheet, and click the **Swap Sheets** button.

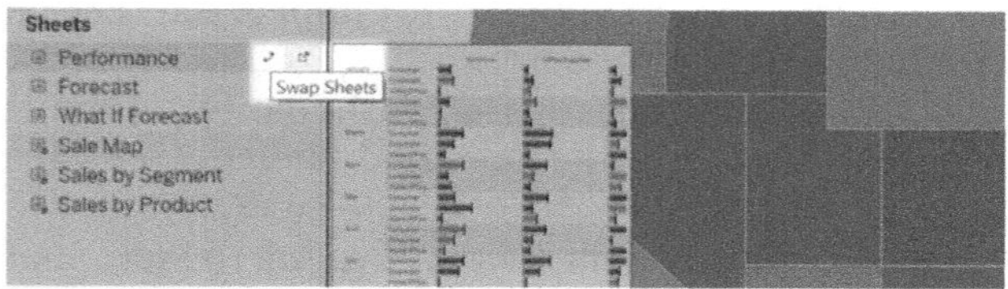

Note: When you replace a sheet, Tableau retains any padding, border or background color. However, you may need to adjust sheet size if content differs significantly. You may also need to delete dashboard items specific to the previous sheet, such as filters, which become blank.

Add interactivity

You can add interactivity to dashboards to enhance users' data insights. Try these techniques:

- In the upper corner of sheet, enable the **Use as Filter** option to use selected marks in the sheet as filters for other sheets in the dashboard.

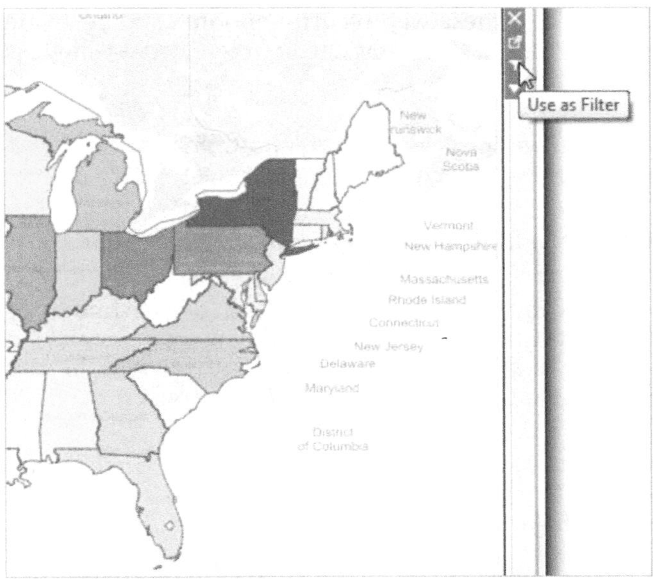

- When authoring in Tableau Desktop, add actions to use multiple sheets as filters, navigate from one sheet to another, display web pages and more.

Add dashboard objects and set their options

In addition to sheets, you can add dashboard objects that add visual appeal and interactivity. Here is some guidance about each type:

- **Horizontal** and **Vertical** objects provide **layout containers** that let you group related objects together and fine-tune how your dashboard resizes when users interact with them.

- **Text** objects can provide headers, explanations and other information.

- **Image** objects add to the visual flavor of a dashboard, and you can link them to specific target URLs. (While Web Page objects can also be used for images, they are better for complete web pages. The Image object provides image-specific fitting, linking and alt-text options.)

- **Web Page** objects display target pages in the context of your dashboard. Be sure to review **these web security options**, and be aware that some web pages don't allow themselves to be embedded – Google is one example.

Note: For security reasons, your Tableau administrator may prevent Web Page and Image objects from displaying target URLs.

- **Blank** objects help you adjust spacing between dashboard items.

- **Navigation** objects let your audience navigate from one dashboard to another, or to other sheets or stories. You can display text or an image to indicate the button's destination to your users, specify custom border and background colors and provide informational tooltips.

- **Download** objects let your audience quickly create a PDF file, PowerPoint slide or PNG image of an entire dashboard, or a crosstab of selected sheets. Formatting options are similar to Navigation objects.

Note: Crosstab download is possible only after publishing to Tableau Online or Tableau Server.

- **Extension** objects let you add unique features to dashboards or integrate them with applications outside Tableau.

- **Ask Data** objects let users enter conversational queries for specific data source fields, which authors optimize for specific audiences such as sales, marketing and support staff.

Add an object

From the **Objects** section at left, and drag an item to the dashboard on the right:

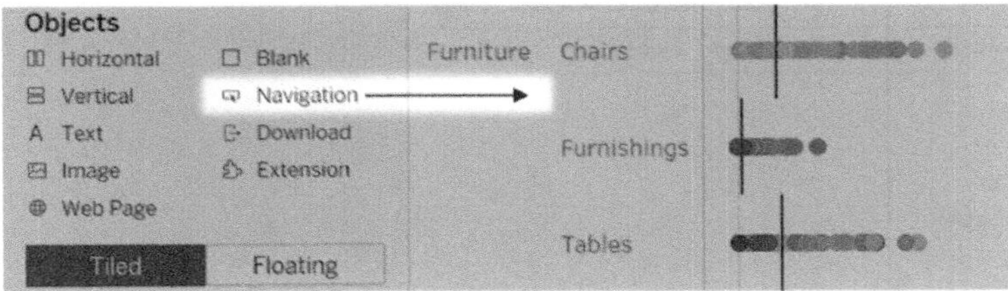

Set options for objects

Click the object to select it. Then click the arrow in the upper corner to open the shortcut menu. (The menu options vary depending on the object.)

Detailed options for Image objects

With the Image object, you can either insert image files into dashboards or link to images posted on the web. In either case, you can specify a URL the image opens when clicked, adding interactivity to your dashboard.

1. From the Objects section at left, drag an Image object to your dashboard at right. Or, on an existing Image object in a dashboard, click the pop-up menu in the upper corner, and choose **Edit Image**.

2. Click either **Insert Image File** to embed an image file into the workbook or **Link to Image** to link to a web-based image.

Consider linking to a web-based image when:

○ The image is very large and your dashboard audience will view it in a browser. (Unlike web-based images, inserted images must be downloaded every time a sheet opens, slowing performance.)

○ The image is an animated GIF file. (Inserted images don't support animated GIFs.)

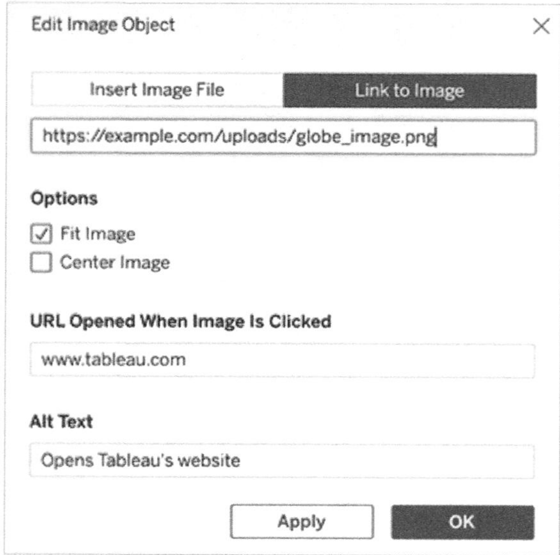

3. If you're inserting an image, click **Choose** to select the file. If you're linking to an image, enter its web URL.

4. Set remaining image fitting, URL linking and alt text options. (Alt text describes the image in screen-reading applications for improved accessibility.)

Detailed options for Navigation and Download objects

Navigation and Download objects have several unique options that help you visually indicate a navigation destination or file format.

A navigation button using text for the button style

1. In the upper corner of the object, click the object menu and choose **Edit Button**.

2. Do one of the following:

○ From the **Navigate to** menu, choose a sheet outside the current dashboard.

○ From the **Export to** menu, choose a file format.

3. Choose image or text for **Button Style**, specify the image or text you want to appear, and then set related formatting options.

4. For **Tooltip text**, add explanatory text that appears when viewers hover over the button. This text is optional and typically best used with image buttons. (For example, you might enter "Open Sales viz" to clarify the destination for a navigation button that appears as a miniature sales chart.)

Note: When viewing a published dashboard, simply clicking a button navigates or exports. When authoring a dashboard, however, you need to Alt-click (Windows) or Option-click (macOS).

Show and hide objects by clicking a button

Show/Hide buttons let dashboard viewers toggle the visibility of dashboard objects, revealing them only when necessary.

How hidden objects affect layouts

When a floating object is hidden, it simply reveals any objects beneath it. Show/Hide buttons can be particularly helpful when you want to temporarily hide a floating group of filters to reveal more of a visualization.

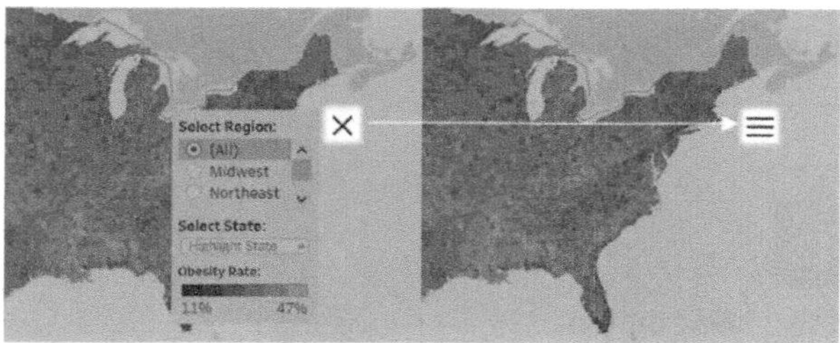

When a tiled object is hidden, the results depend on the object's level in the layout hierarchy.

- In most cases, you'll want to place objects you plan to hide in a Horizontal or Vertical layout container, because hidden objects will have their space filled in by other objects in the container.

- By contrast, in the Tiled layout container at the very top of the layout hierarchy, a hidden object leaves blank space behind.

Add and configure a Show/Hide button

1. Select a dashboard object.

2. From the pop-up menu in the upper corner of the object, select **Add Show/Hide Button**.

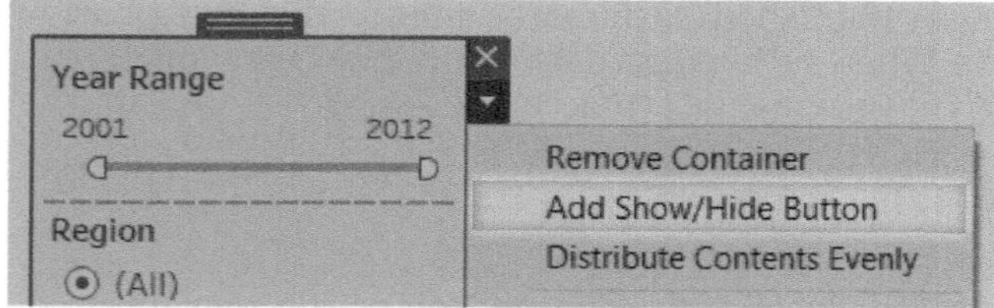

3. From the button menu, choose **Edit Button**.

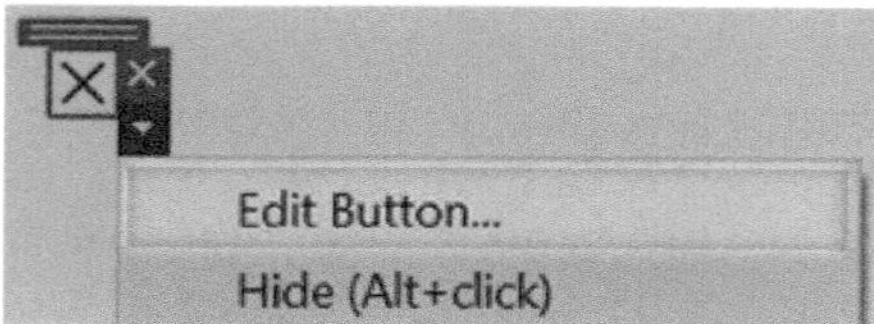

4. Set these options:

○ **Dashboard Item to Show/Hide** specifies the target object. (An object can be the target of only one Show/Hide button at a time. Choose **None** if you want to target the object with another Show/Hide button.)

○ **Button Style** specifies whether image or text displays for the button.

○ **Button Appearance** specifies how the button looks when the item is both shown and hidden. Click **Item Shown** and **Item Hidden** to choose different images or text for each state.

○ **Tooltip text** provides explanatory text that appears when viewers hover over the button. (For example, you might enter "Show or hide filters" for a container with filter menus.)

5. If necessary, drag the button to a different location or resize it to better fit your layout.

Note: When viewing a published dashboard, simply clicking a Show/Hide button toggles object visibility. When authoring a dashboard, however, you need to Alt-click (Windows) or Option-click (macOS).

Security for Web Page objects

If you include Web Page objects in your dashboard, you can optimize security by doing the following.

Use HTTPS protocol when possible

As a best practice, use HTTPS (https://) in your URLs. This ensures that the connection from your dashboard to the web page is encrypted. Also, if Tableau Server is running HTTPS and you use HTTP in the URL, your users' browsers won't be able to display the web page that the URL points to. If you don't specify a protocol, HTTP will be assumed.

Security options for Web Page objects (Tableau Desktop only)

Choose **Help** > **Settings and Performance** > **Set Dashboard Web View Security**, and set the options below. (In some organizations, these options are controlled across all machines by a Tableau administrator.)

Note: Any changes you make to these security options apply to both existing and newly created web page objects.

• **Enable JavaScript** Allows JavaScript support in the web view. Clearing this option may cause some web pages that require JavaScript to function improperly in the dashboard.

• **Enable Plug-ins** Enables any plug-ins the web page uses, such as an Adobe Flash or QuickTime player.

• **Block Pop-ups** When selected, blocks pop-ups.

• **Enable URL Hover Actions** Allows URL hover actions.

• **Enable Web Page Objects and Web Images** Allows the display of target URLs in Web Page and Image objects. If you deselect this option, Web Page objects and Image objects that link to the web remain in the dashboard but show no content.

Accelerators for Cloud-based Data

Accelerators are pre-built dashboards that help you get started quickly on your data analysis for uses across departments, industries and even cloud-based systems like Salesforce, ServiceNow ITSM, LinkedIn Sales Navigator, Marketo and Oracle Eloqua. You can use the Accelerator for inspiration and ideas, and even swap out sample data for your own.

Simply choose one of the beautiful, informative designs tailored to your industry or function in the Tableau Exchange. If you're a Creator in Tableau Online, you can also create a new workbook and choose an Accelerator when you create a new workbook.

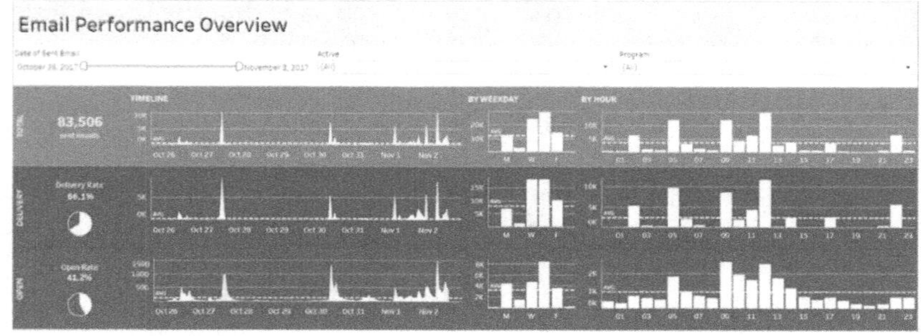

Use an Accelerator from Tableau Exchange

Download an Accelerator in Tableau Exchange that fits your industry, role or enterprise application. Accelerators download as packaged workbooks.

Double-click on the workbook to open it in Tableau Desktop.

To use the Accelerator in Tableau Online or Tableau Server:

1. Navigate to the Home or Explore pages, then click **New** > **Upload Workbook** to upload the packaged workbook to your Tableau site.

2. Specify a name and project for the workbook. Select **Upload** to publish the dashboard with sample data.

Get your data into the dashboards

Once you've opened the Accelerator in Tableau, you can edit the workbook and connect to the appropriate data source to view the Accelerator with your data.

1. Select the **Data Source** tab. In the dialog that appears, enter your application credentials to sign in. For example, for a Salesforce Accelerator, enter your Salesforce name and password. If you are using the Salesforce Accelerator, make sure your account has API access to your Salesforce instance.

2. Select the dashboard tab. While Tableau prepares an extract of your data, sample data appears so you can explore the layout. You might want to start with one or two weeks of data so that the extract can be created quickly.

3. If any worksheets appear blank, navigate to the worksheet. Replace reference fields by right-clicking on the fields with red exclamation marks as necessary.

Now you're ready to explore your data and gain insights at the speed of thought.

Use an Accelerator in Tableau Online

It's easy to use an Accelerator within Tableau Online for cloud-based data like Salesforce, ServiceNow ITSM, LinkedIn Sales Navigator, Marketo and Oracle Eloqua. When the process is complete, you can **edit the resulting workbook** just like any other, quickly customizing it for your needs.

1. If you're a Creator in Tableau Online, navigate to the Home or Explore page, then click the **New** button and select **Workbook**.

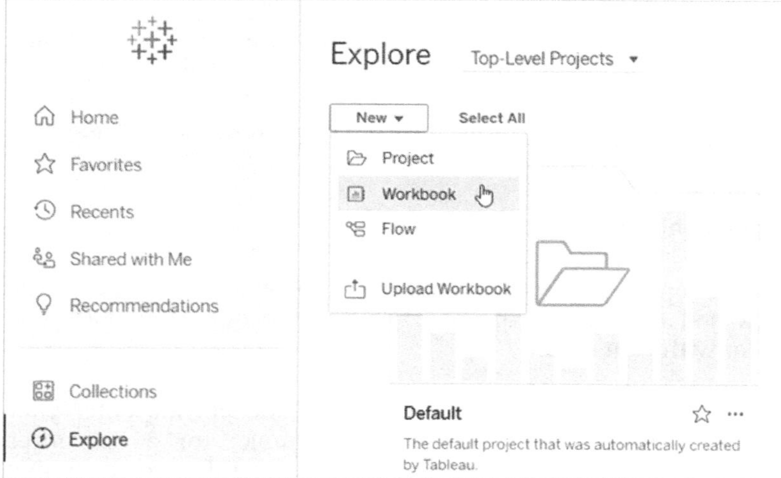

2. At the top of the Connect to Data window, click **Accelerator**.

3. From the list of pre-built designs, find an option that reflects the data source and business metrics you need, and click **Use Dashboard**.

4. To quickly see how a workbook looks with sample data, click **Continue without signing in**. Or click **Continue** to create a workbook with your data.

5. Specify a name and containing project for the workbook.

6. If you chose to create a workbook with your data, connect to your data source. While Tableau prepares an extract of your data, sample data appears so you can explore the layout.

That's it – you've created a rich, interactive dashboard in seconds!

Change permissions to share Accelerators with colleagues

To avoid exposure of confidential data, workbooks for Accelerators are visible only to authors and administrators by default. To share an Accelerator with your colleagues, follow these simple steps:

1. In Tableau Online, **navigate to the workbook** for the Accelerator.

2. Select the workbook, click **Actions**, and choose **Permissions**.

3. Give **View** permissions to any user or group you want to see the dashboard.

Replace sample data with your data

If you chose to quickly load sample data in a dashboard, you can replace it with your data at any time.

1. In Tableau Online, **navigate to the workbook** for the Accelerator.

2. On the **Data Sources** tab, select the data source. From the Actions menu, choose **Edit Connection**.

3. For authentication, select **Embedded credentials in the connection**, and either choose an existing user account or add a new one. Then click **Save**.

4. On the **Refresh Schedules** tab, select the schedule. From the Actions menu, choose **Run Now**.

Fix greyed-out views by replacing field names

If your organization has customized the data structure for a cloud-based system, you may need to match those changes in Accelerators after your data loads in them. For example, if your organization has renamed the Salesforce "Account" field to "Customer", you'll need to make a corresponding change in Accelerators to avoid greyed-out views like this:

Fortunately, the fix is pretty straightforward:

1. Above the dashboard, click **Edit**.

2. Navigate directly to the greyed-out sheet.

3. In the Data pane on the left, look for red exclamation points (!) next to field names, which indicate that your organization uses different names.

4. Right-click each of those fields, and choose **Replace References**. Then select the correct field name from the list.

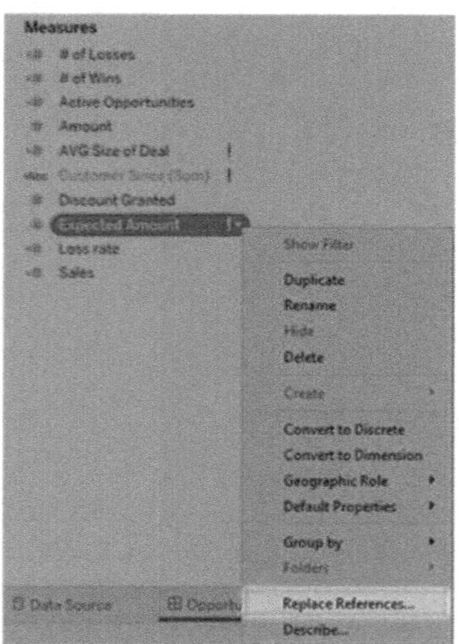

Fix empty dashboards by changing default date ranges

If a dashboard looks completely empty, the likely cause is a default date range that doesn't correspond to the dates in your source data.

1. **Download the workbook**, and open it in Tableau Desktop.

2. Click the **Data Source** tab.

3. In the upper-left corner, click the arrow next to the data source name, and choose **Edit Connection**. Then sign in.

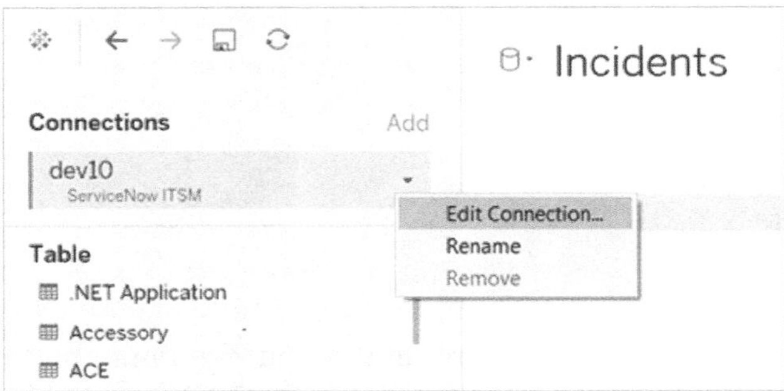

4. Specify a date range that reflects the dates in your data, and click **Connect**.

5. Choose **Server** > **Publish Data Source** to update extracts of the data on Tableau Online.

Size and Lay Out Your Dashboard

After you create a dashboard, you might need to resize and reorganize it to work better for your users.

Dashboard size options

Fixed size (default): The dashboard remains the same size, regardless of the size of the window used to display it. If the dashboard is larger than the window, it becomes scrollable. You can pick from a preset size, such as Desktop Browser (the default), Small Blog and iPad.

Fixed size dashboards let you specify the exact location and position of objects, which can be useful if there are floating objects. Select this setting if you know the precise size at which your dashboard will be displayed. Published dashboards that use a fixed size can load faster because they're more likely to use a cached version on the server. (Dashboards with variable sizes need to be freshly rendered for every browser request.).

Range: The dashboard scales between minimum and maximum sizes that you specify. If the window used to display the dashboard is smaller than the minimum size, scroll bars are displayed. If it's larger than the maximum size, white space is displayed.

Use this setting when you're designing for two different display sizes that need the same content and have similar shapes – such as small- and medium-sized browser windows. Range also works well for mobile dashboards with vertical layouts, where the width may change to account for different mobile device widths, but the height is fixed to allow for vertical scrolling.

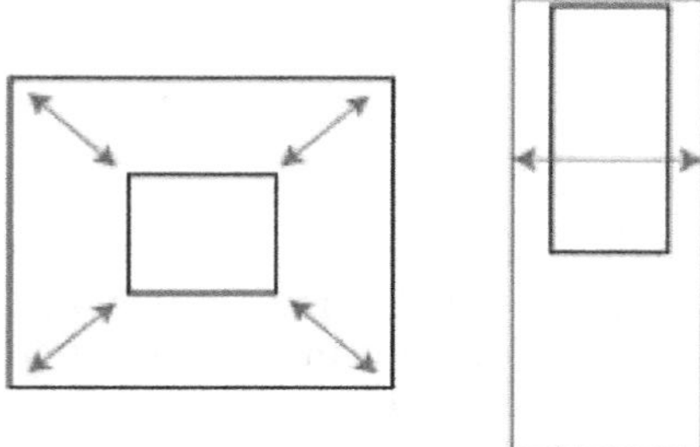

Automatic: The dashboard automatically resizes to fill the window used to display it.

Use this setting if you want Tableau to take care of any resizing. For best results, use a tiled dashboard layout.

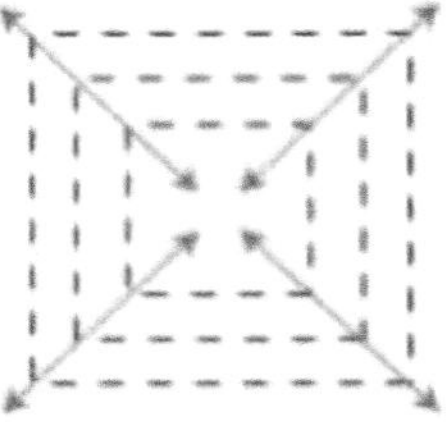

Set overall dashboard size

- Under **Size** on the Dashboard pane, select the dashboard's dimensions (such as **Desktop Browser**) or sizing behavior (for example, **Automatic**).

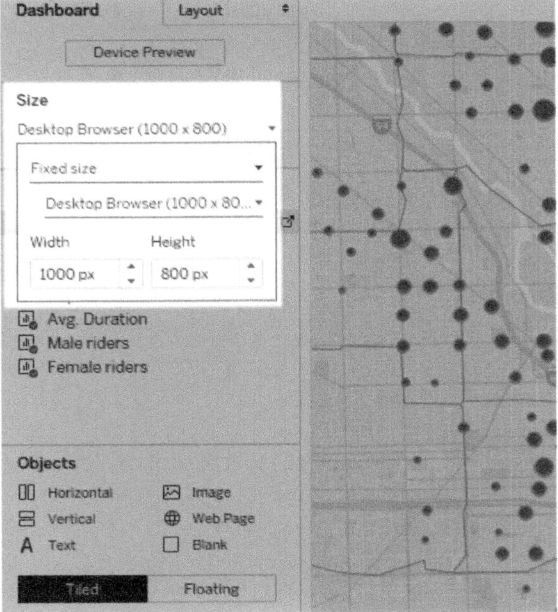

Group items using layout containers

Layout containers let you group related dashboard items together so you can quickly position them. As you change the size and placement of items inside a container, other container items automatically adjust.

Layout container types

A horizontal layout container resizes the width of the views and objects it contains; a vertical layout container adjusts height.

Horizontal layout container

The two views below are arranged in a horizontal layout container.

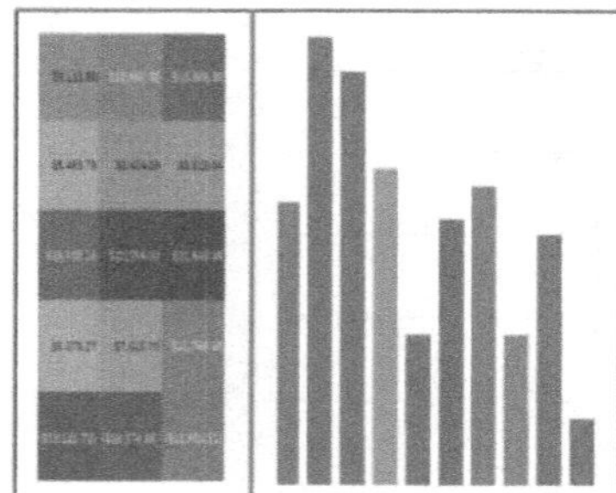

Vertical layout container

The three views below are stacked in a vertical layout container.

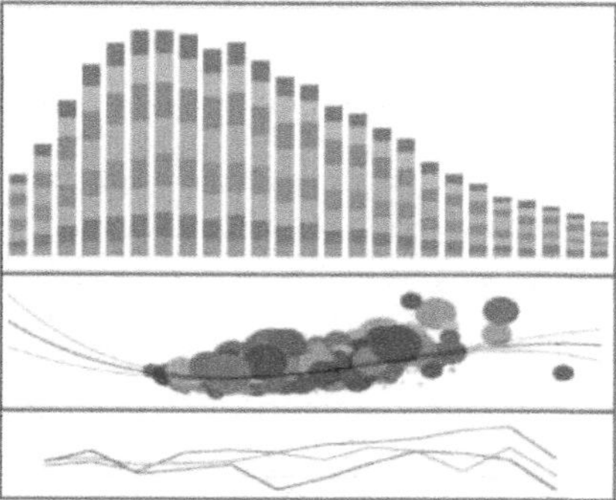

Add a layout container

1. Under **Objects** on the Dashboard pane, select **Horizontal** or **Vertical**.

2. Drag the container to the dashboard.

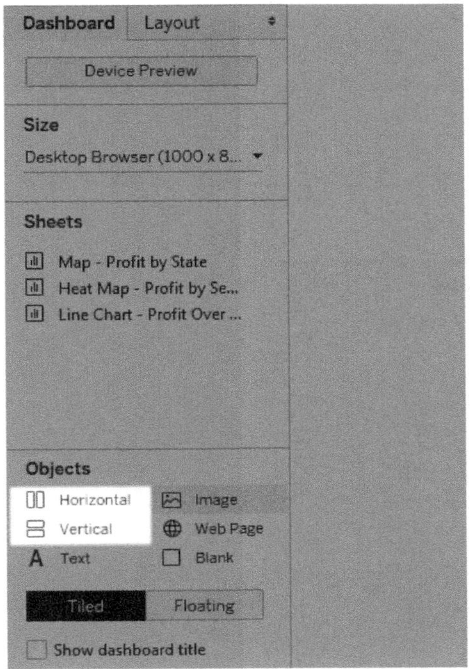

3. Add views and objects to the layout container.

Evenly distribute a layout container's items

1. Select the layout container. If you have trouble doing this, select an individual item within the container and choose **Select Container** from its shortcut menu.

2. With the layout container selected, choose **Distribute Evenly** from its shortcut menu:

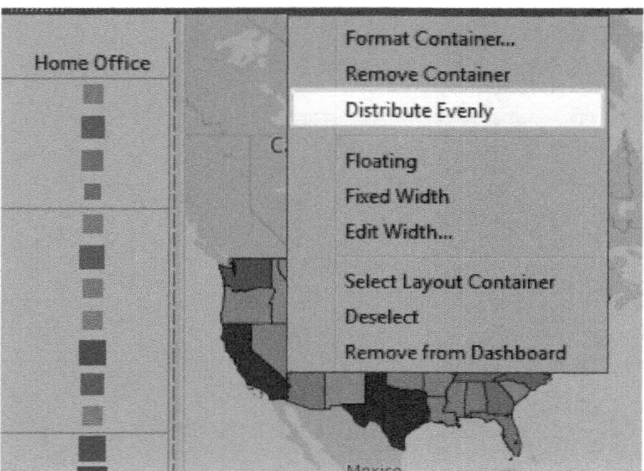

Items that are already within the layout container arrange themselves evenly; any items you add will do the same.

Automatically resize sheets in layout containers

If you add multiple sheets with related data to a layout container, whenever marks are selected in one sheet, you can automatically resize related sheets.

In this example, when a mark is selected in the map, the bar chart updates to display profit and sales for that mark; when no marks are selected in the map, it automatically expands to fill the layout container.

With mark selected

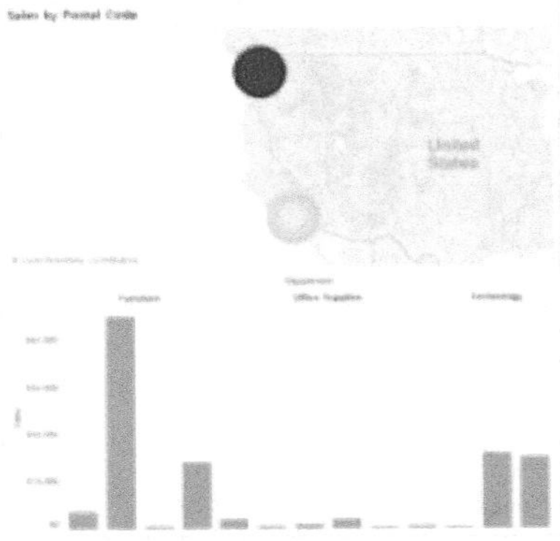

Without a selection

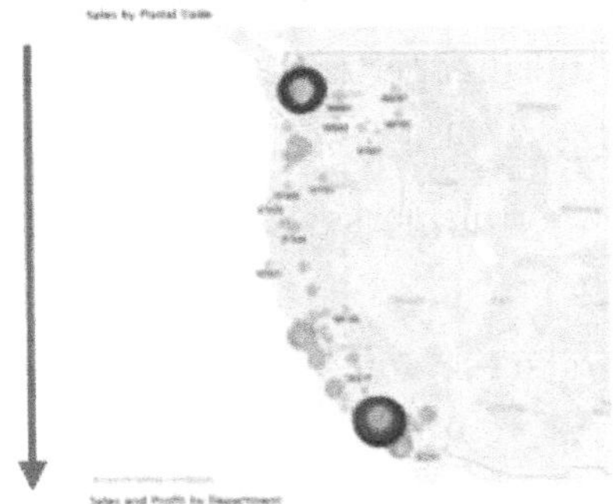

1. Add multiple sheets with related data to a layout container.

2. From the drop-down menu of the sheet you want to expand, choose **Use as Filter**.

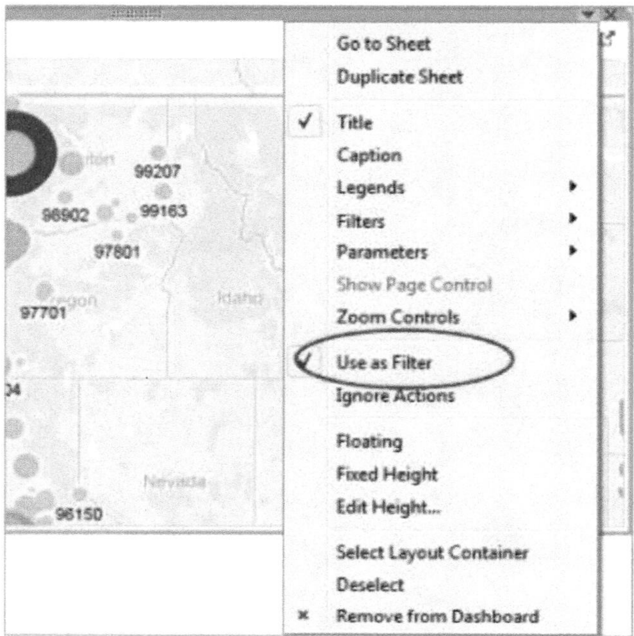

3. Choose **Dashboard** > **Actions**, and double-click the generated filter you just created.

4. In the **Target Sheets** section of the Edit Filter Action dialog box, select the other sheets in the layout container.

5. To control how target sheets resize when no marks are selected in the source sheet, select one of the following:

- **Show all values** returns target sheets to their original size, showing all data.

- **Exclude all values** collapses target sheets under their titles, hiding all data.

Remove a layout container to independently edit items it contains

1. Select the container either on the dashboard or in the **Item hierarchy** area of the Layout pane.

2. From the drop-down menu at the top of the container, select **Remove Container**.

Tile or float dashboard items

Tiled vs. floating layouts

Each object, layout container, and view that you place on a dashboard is either tiled (the default) or floating.

Tiled layout

Tiled items don't overlap; they become part of a single-layer grid that resizes based on the overall dashboard size.

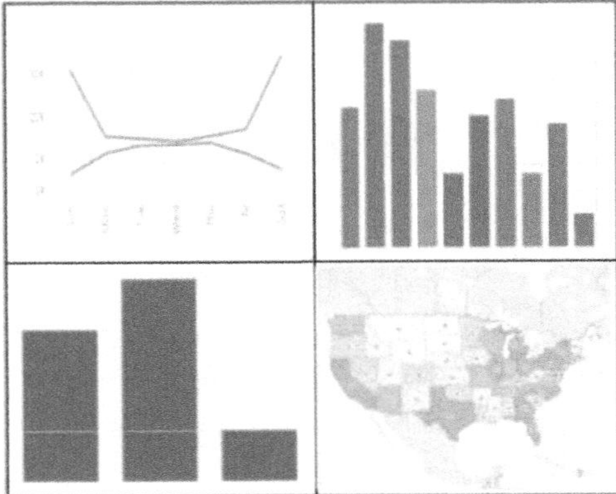

Floating layout

Floating items can be layered over other objects. In the example below, a map floats over tiled views.

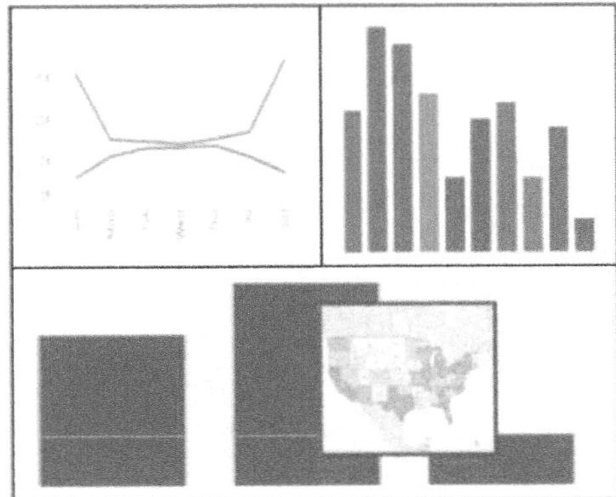

For best results, give floating objects and views a fixed size and position.

Float or tile a new item

1. Under **Objects** in the Dashboard pane, click the layout option you want to use: **Floating** or **Tiled**.

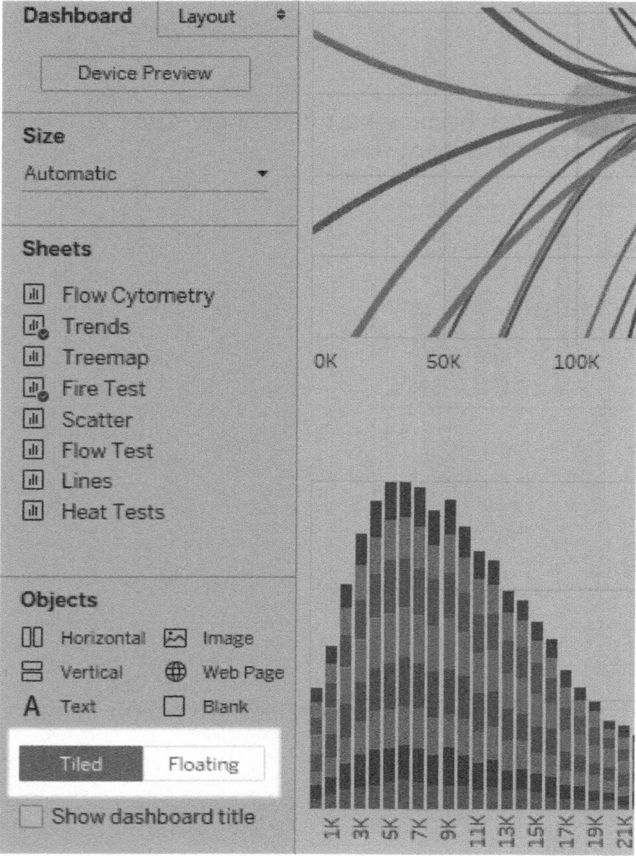

2. Drag the view or object onto the dashboard on the right.

Tip: You can also assign a floating layout to an item by holding down **Shift** on your keyboard as you drag it onto the dashboard.

Switch an existing item from tiled to floating

1. Select the item in the dashboard.

2. In the item's shortcut menu, select **Floating**:

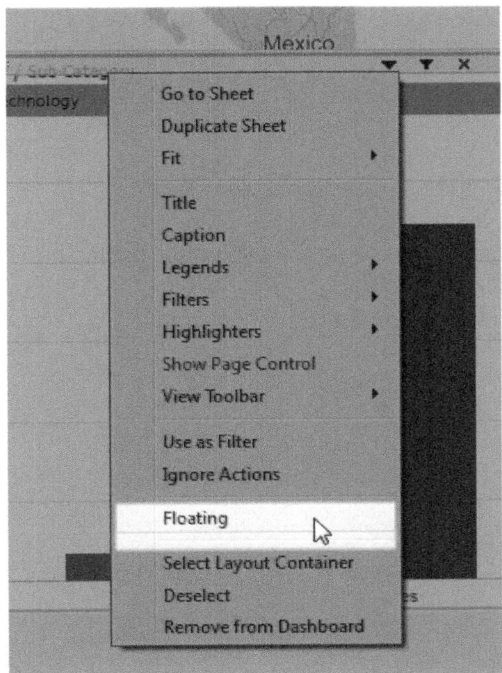

Add padding, borders and background colors around items

Padding lets you precisely space items on dashboard, while borders and background colors let you visually highlight them. Inner padding sets the spacing between item contents and the perimeter of the border and background color; outer padding provides additional spacing beyond the border and background color.

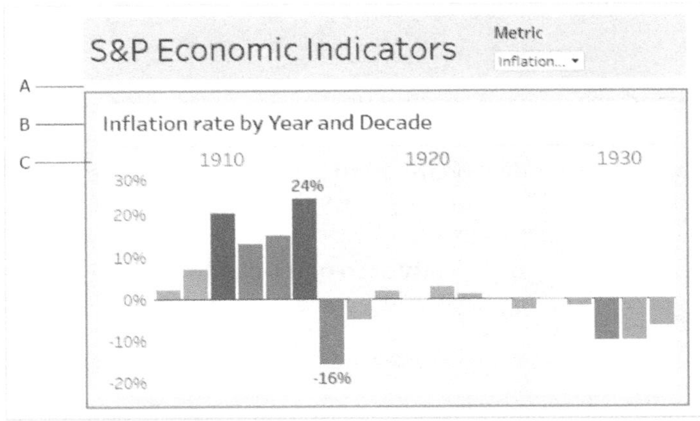

A. Outer padding B. Blue border C. Inner padding with light blue background

1. Select an individual item, or your entire dashboard.

2. On the **Layout** tab at left, specify border style and color, background color and opacity, or padding size in pixels.

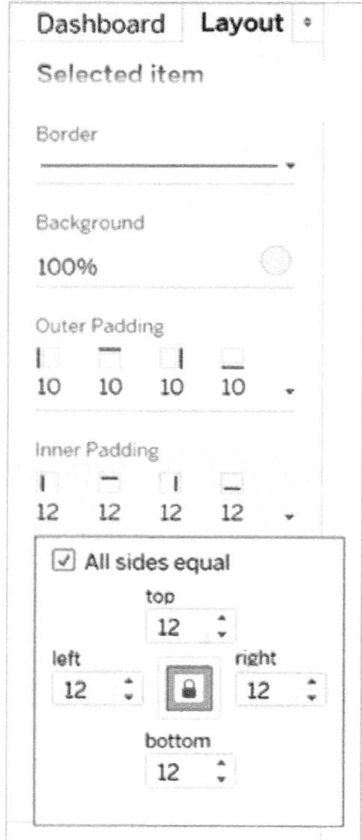

Here are some handy dashboard spacing tips:

- To precisely align one dashboard item with another, deselect **All sides equal**, and adjust padding for only one side.

- To create seamless designs, specify zero outer padding for adjoining items.

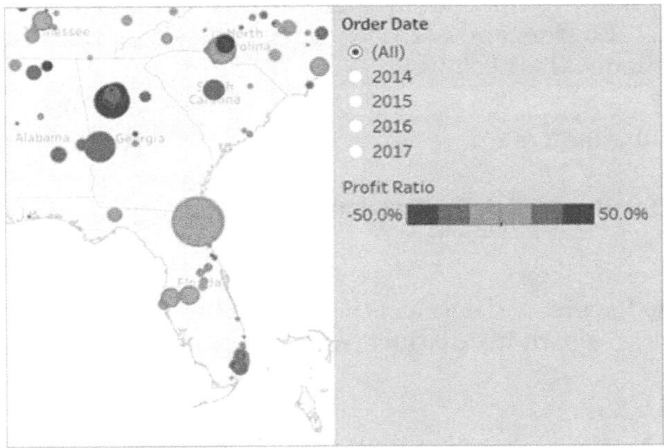

Visually integrate elements with transparency

Transparent elements create a seamless visual look for your dashboards, revealing underlying objects and images.

Make worksheet backgrounds transparent

1. In your dashboard, select the sheet.

2. Choose **Format** > **Shading**, click the **Worksheet** menu, and choose **None** for the background color.

If the sheet appears opaque, change the background color to None for the underlying dashboard, object or layout container. You can quickly adjust these items on the Layout tab for the dashboard.

3. To smoothly integrate the transparent sheet with other dashboard items, choose **Format** > **Borders** and **Format** > **Lines**, and either remove borders and lines or change their colors.

Additional steps for transparent maps

1. Choose **Format** > **Shading**, click the **Pane** menu, and choose **None** for the color.

2. Choose **Map** > **Map Layers**, and deselect the opaque **Base** layer. Then, to make transparent maps more distinct when zoomed out, select the **Coastline** layer.

Depending on the map style, you also may need to experiment with turning other layers on or off.

Make a sheet partially transparent

1. In the **Layout** pane for the dashboard, select the sheet.

2. Click the **Background** color, and set the color and opacity.

Float transparent legends, filters, highlighters and parameters

To visually connect filters, parameters and highlighters to related data, float these items, which are transparent by default. Text always remains fully opaque, maintaining legibility.

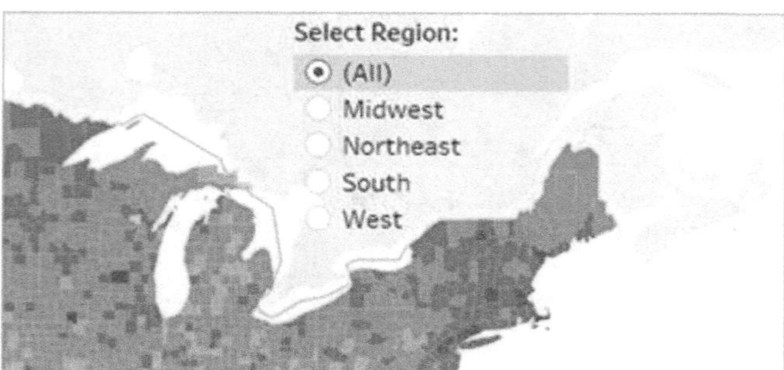

If a floating object continues to display a color, check these object- and worksheet-level settings:

- Select the object, and on the **Layout** tab, click the **Background** color, and choose **None**.

- Click the **Format** menu, and then choose **Legends**, **Filters**, **Highlighters**, or **Parameters**. Then, in the Format pane at left, choose **Shading** > **None**.

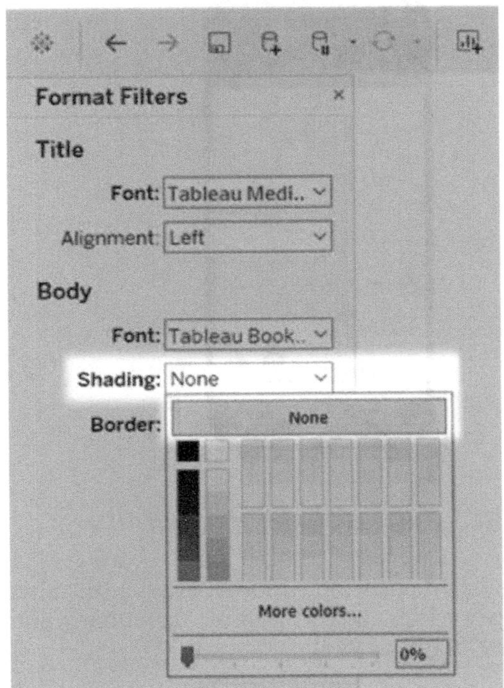

Create Dashboard Layouts for Different Device Types

Dashboards can include layouts for different types of devices that span a wide range of screen sizes. When you publish these layouts to Tableau Server or Tableau Online, people viewing your dashboard experience a design optimized for their phone, tablet or desktop. As the author, you only have to create a single dashboard and deliver a single URL.

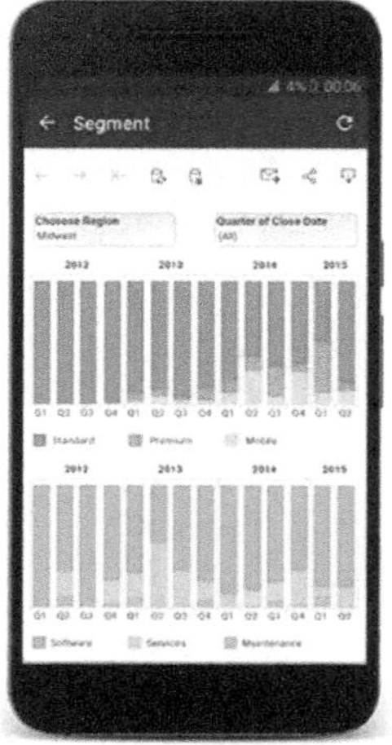

How the Default dashboard relates to device layouts

Device layouts appear on the Dashboard tab, under Default. Initially, each device layout contains every item in the Default dashboard and derives its size and layout from Default as well.

Think of the Default dashboard as the parent, and the device layouts (desktop, tablet, and phone) as its children. Any view, filter, action, legend or parameter that you want to add to a device layout must first exist in the Default dashboard.

Phone layouts and the Default dashboard

To save time with a unique Phone layout option that automatically reflects changes to the Default dashboard, either click the open lock icon, or choose **Auto-Generate Layout** from the pop-up menu.

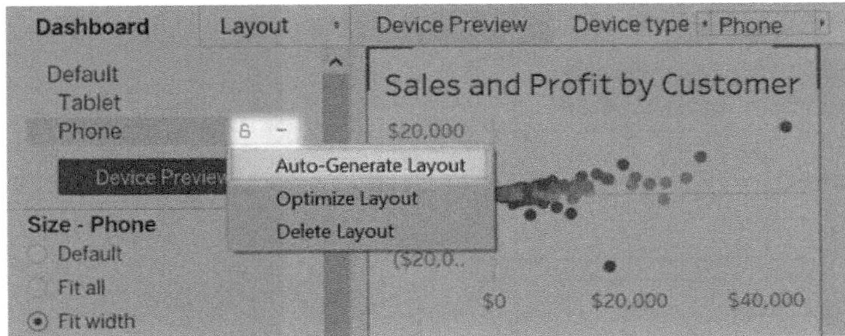

If you instead click the closed lock icon 🔒 or choose **Edit Layout** from the menu, the Phone layout becomes fully independent, so you'll need to manually add and arrange items to reflect changes to the Default dashboard.

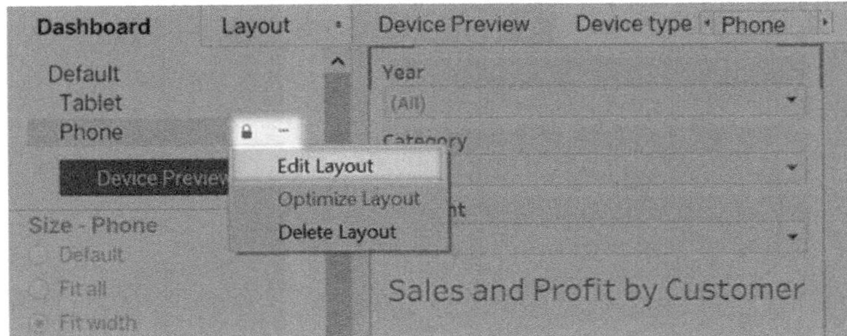

Desktop and Tablet layouts and the Default dashboard

Unlike Phone layouts, you need to manually add Desktop and Tablet layouts to a dashboard. Desktop and Tablet layouts are always fully independent from the Default dashboard, so each device layout can contain a unique arrangement of objects.

Automatically add phone layouts

Two options let you automatically add phone layouts:

- To create phone layouts whenever you open old dashboards that lack them, choose **Dashboard** > **Add Phone Layouts to Existing Dashboards**

- To create phone layouts whenever you create a new dashboard, choose **Dashboard** > **Add Phone Layouts to New Dashboards**. (This option is on by default.)

Preview and manually add device layouts

1. Open a dashboard.

2. On the **Dashboard** tab on the left, click **Device Preview**.

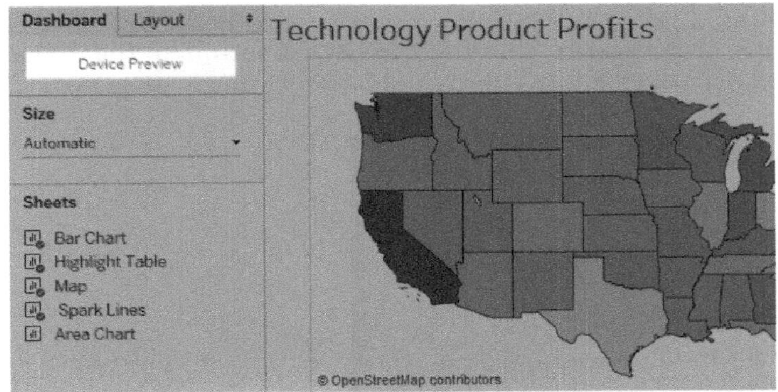

In device preview mode, these options appear above the dashboard:

3. Take a moment to click through the **Device types** and **Models** and explore the different screen sizes. Then set these options:

○ To see how the dashboard will look in landscape vs. portrait mode, click . Usually, landscape is optimal for tablets and portrait is best for phones.

○ Select **Tableau Mobile app** to see how the dashboard will look with the app instead of the browser. This option is available for iOS or Android devices and shrinks the dashboard slightly, leaving space for the app controls.

4. Choose a **Device type**, such as **Tablet**.

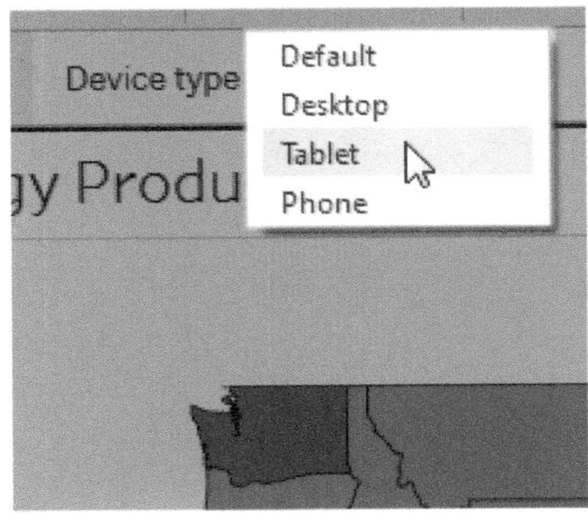

5. In the upper-right corner, click the **Add Layout** button for the device type you selected (for example, **Add Tablet Layout**).

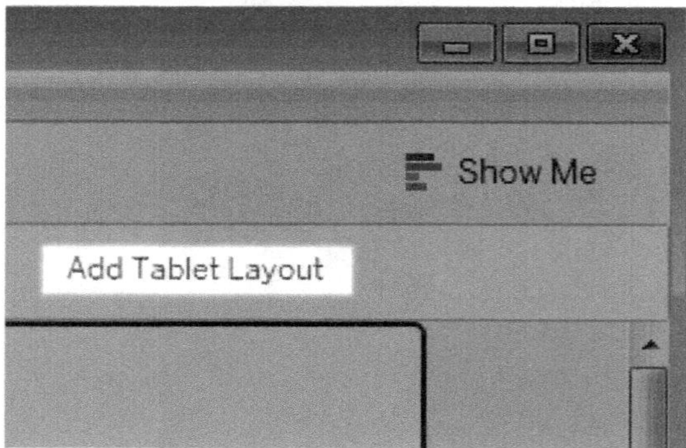

6. Add an additional layout by selecting a new **Device type** and clicking **Add Layout**.

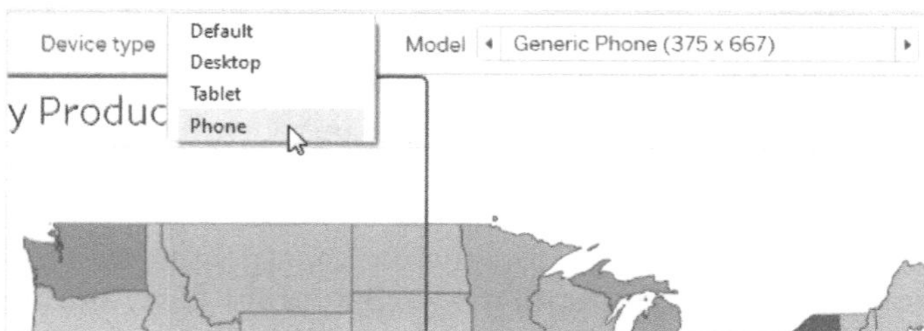

Creating a layout for each device type gives you the most control over your users' experience as they view your dashboard from different devices. After you publish a dashboard with all three layouts, users won't see the default dashboard layout; instead, they'll always see the appropriate device-specific layout.

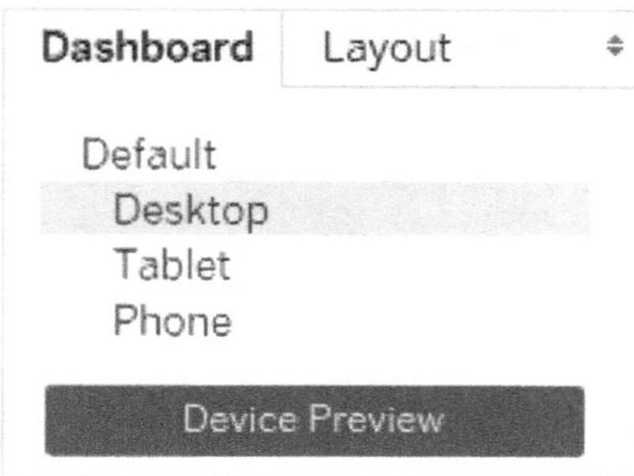

Note: If you make changes to a view, double-check related devices layouts to ensure that they look as you expect.

Customize a device layout

After you've added a device layout to your dashboard, you can start rearranging objects to create the look you want.

1. For Desktop and Tablet layouts, click **Custom**:

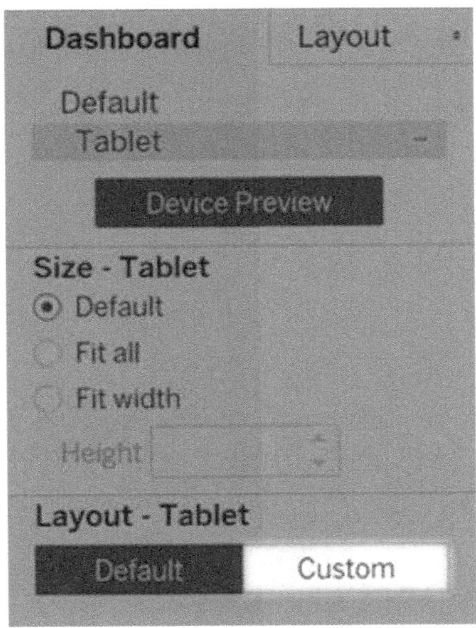

For Phone layouts, either click the lock icon 🔒, or choose **Edit Layout** from the pop-up menu:

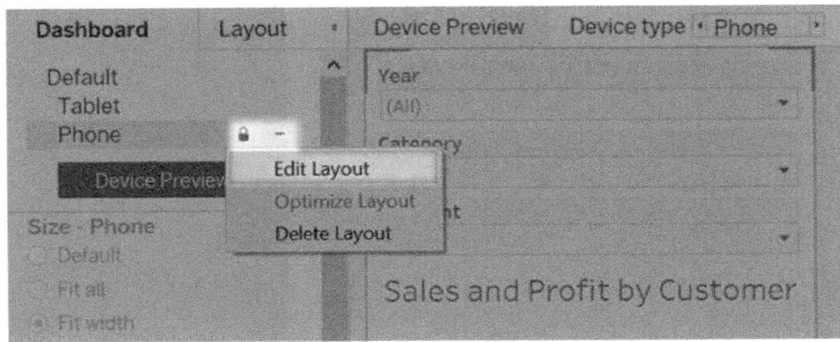

2. Anything you can add to your layout is listed on the left, under **Layout**. If an item has a blue check mark, it means that it's part of the device layout that you're currently working on.

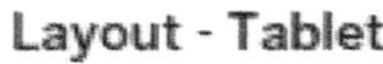

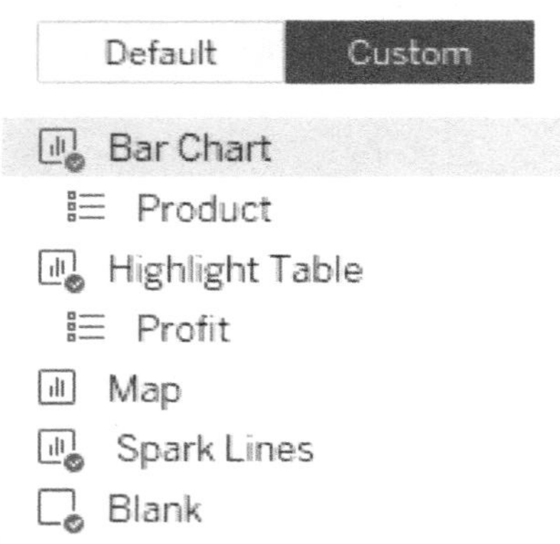

3. If you remove an item, it's only removed from the current device layout. It still exists on the default dashboard and can be added to the device layout again.

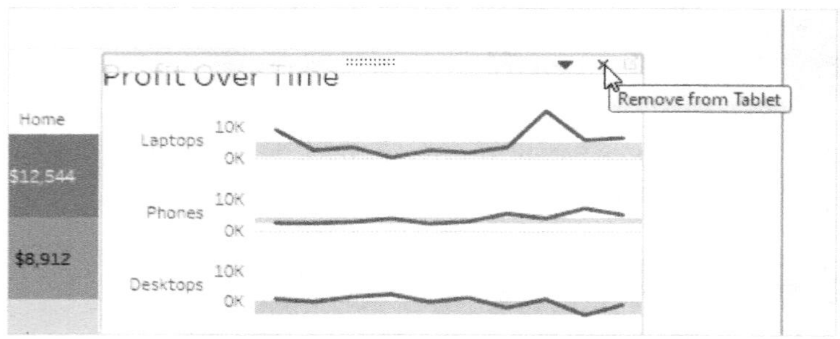

4. Click through the **Device model** options to see how the layout will appear on different models.

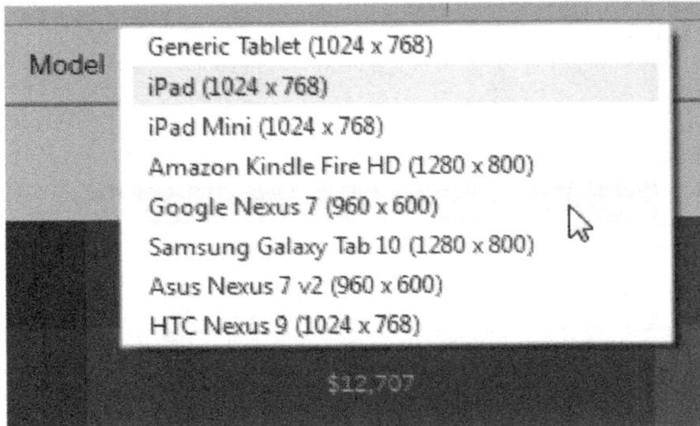

Ultimately, it's the size of the web browser that loads the dashboard that determines which layout appears on the device..

5. At left, explore the options under **Size**.

Default: The height and width of the device layout mimics whatever the default dashboard is using. For example, if you're creating a tablet layout and the default dashboard is set to a fixed size of Desktop Browser (1000 x 800), setting Size to Default for the tablet layout will make it use 1000 x 800 as well.

Fit all: All items are automatically resized to fit the device frame size. The device frame size is determined by the Device type, Model, and orientation (portrait or landscape) settings.

Fit width (recommended for phones): Items are automatically resized to fit the width of the device frame, but the height is fixed. This is a great option for phone layouts and vertical scrolling.

Optimize for phones

The small screens of mobile phones benefit from further optimisation. Try these techniques.

Optimize manual phone layouts

If you've chosen to edit a phone layout yourself, you can quickly optimize the placement of filters, remove white space and more. On the **Dashboard** tab, click the pop-up menu to the right of **Phone**, and select **Optimize Layout**.

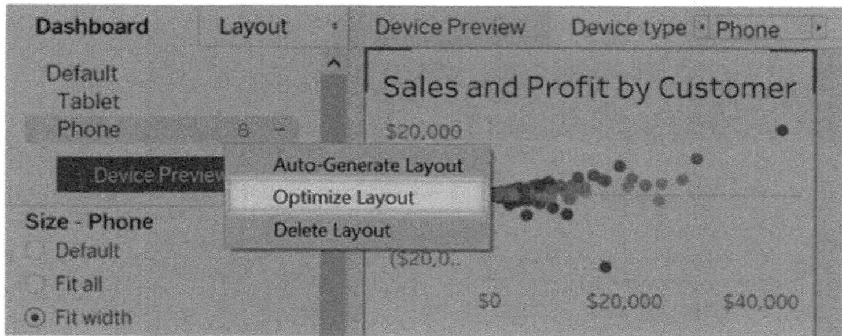

Be aware that this command only rearranges items currently in the phone layout. If you want to continuously update the phone layout to reflect all changes to the default dashboard, select **Auto-Generate Layout**.

Add links that trigger instant messages and phone calls

To let phone users quickly contact key people about dashboard content, add URL actions to objects that automatically trigger SMS messages and telephone calls. Use the link format sms:*phone-number* or tel:*phone-number*. Be sure to include country and area codes if necessary.

Create phone-specific versions of views

Create duplicates of certain views in the default dashboard – one optimized for desktop viewing and a second optimized for phones.

1. Go to the worksheet for a view, click its tab, and select **Duplicate Sheet**.

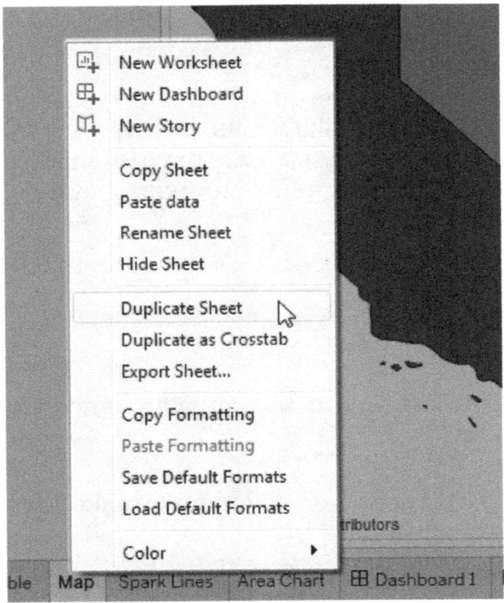

2. Customize the view for mobile viewing.

For maps for example, you may want to zoom in to a specific region by default, or you may want to disable panning, zooming, and other functionality.

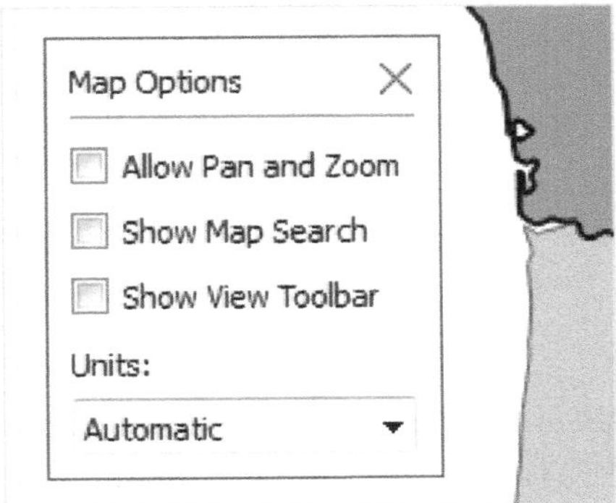

3. Now add the new view to the default dashboard so that it can be available to the device layouts you're creating.

Shorten titles

Short titles work best for mobile viewing. To edit a title, double-click it.

Optimize white space

White space is another visual element to consider. While screen real estate on a phone is scarce and you want to make the most of it, you may also want to provide additional safe places for your users to tap or initiate scrolling, so they don't select filters and other items unintentionally.

To add white space, use padding or Blank objects..

Publish the dashboard

1. Click **Server** > **Publish Workbook**. If you're not already signed in, you're prompted for your credentials.

2. In the Publish Workbook to Tableau Server dialog box, make sure the **Show sheets as tabs** check box is cleared.

When this check box is selected for device-specific dashboards, the tabs' sizing requirements interfere with the server's ability to correctly detect the size of the web browser and load the correct layout.

3. Click **Publish**.

Test the dashboard

After you publish the dashboard to Tableau Server or Tableau Online, test the dashboard by viewing it from different browser sizes.

1. Open the dashboard on Tableau Server or Tableau Online.

2. In the upper-right corner of the page, click **Share** and copy the contents of the **Link** text box.

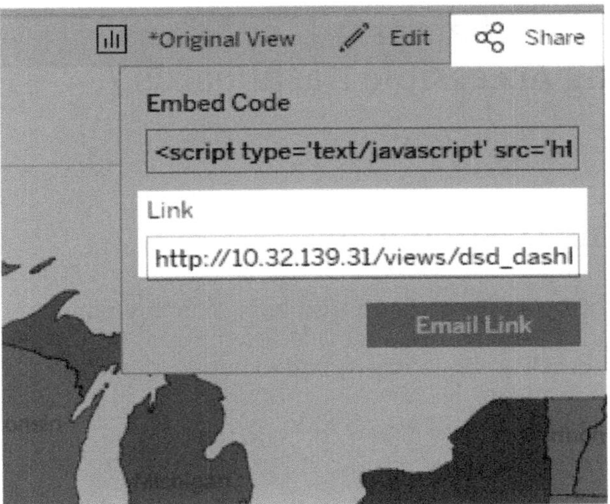

3. Paste the string into a web browser URL. The string should include the following: embed=y

4. With the embed code string as your browser URL, test the different layouts by changing the size of your web browser window and refreshing it.

Confirm which layout a device will display

The dashboard layout a device displays is based on the smallest dimension (height or width) of the iframe in which the Tableau view appears. Sometimes Desktop, Tablet or Phone layouts may appear on other types of devices. For example, a Tablet layout may appear on a desktop computer if the display or browser window is small.

If Tableau Online and Tableau Server users find a Phone or Tablet layout too limiting, they can click **See Desktop Layout** in the toolbar. This toggle button lets users switch back to the mobile device layout at any time.

Chapter 9
Building Accessible Dashboards

Build Accessible Dashboards

If you want to make your dashboards accessible to as many people as possible, or if you work in an environment that is subject to US Section 508 requirements, or other accessibility-related laws and regulations, you can use Tableau to create dashboards that conform to the Web Content Accessibility guidelines (WCAG 2.0 AA).

To make an accessible dashboard:

1. Create a dashboard in either Tableau Desktop or in web authoring on Tableau Server or Tableau Online

2. Publish and embed that dashboard into a web page that conforms to Web Content Accessibility guidelines (WCAG 2.0 AA)

This topic explains how screen readers help users to navigate dashboards, the order that screen readers read objects or views in a dashboard, what items in a dashboard are accessible and how to take an existing dashboard and make it more accessible for all users.

Dashboard keyboard navigation and focus order

Tableau contains keyboard shortcuts that helps users navigate using only a keyboard.

When creating a dashboard, note that screen readers read views or objects in a dashboard in the order in which they were added. For example, if your dashboard contains a text object containing information that helps explain the dashboard, add this object to your dashboard first.

You can also edit the dashboard hierarchy directly by editing the XML directly.

Create accessible dashboards

Many items and objects in the Tableau workspace support keyboard navigation and are compatible with assistive technologies like screen reading software. You can use the following items on a dashboard you want to be accessible:

- **Add dashboard objects and set their options**
  - Text objects
  - Web page objects
  - Button objects
  - Image objects
- Toolbar
- Dashboard titles
- Views, specifically:
  - Title
  - Workbook tabs
  - View Data window
  - Captions (when visible)
  - Categorical legends
  - Single and multi-value filters

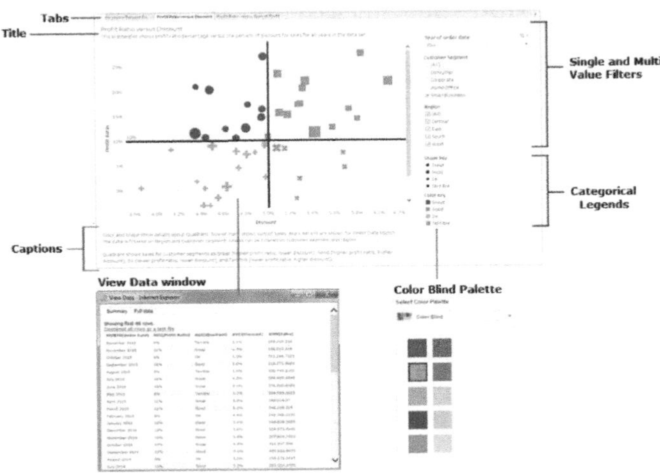

Note: Interactivity within a view (mark selection, tooltips, etc) is not accessible.

Walkthrough: make existing dashboards more accessible

Let’s start with a finished workbook and work backward to make it more accessible.

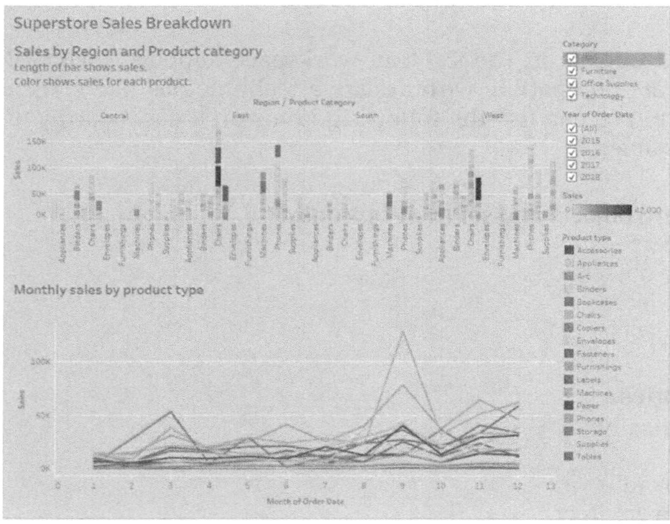

This dashboard is designed to show total sales for each sales region and product type. The line chart at the bottom shows monthly sales by product type. The author of this dashboard wanted to use color to brand the dashboard in the Superstore company's colors of green and grey.

Unfortunately, this dashboard has several features that pose accessibility problems for users, including the company color scheme. The steps that follow show a few ways to make this dashboard more accessible.

Format for accessibility at the dashboard and workbook level

The green text on a grey background does not have a high enough contrast ratio to work for users with visual contrast sensitivity loss. To make this workbook accessible to all users and make the contrast ratio as high as possible, we're going to make the background white and change the text colors on our chart to black.

To update the dashboard shading color, change **Dashboard Shading** in the **Format>Dashboard** menu to **None**.

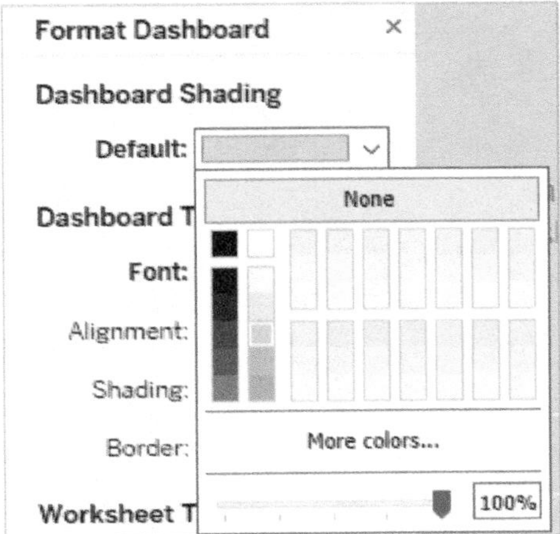

For text formatting changes, we could manually change the formatting on each worksheet. But that will take a lot of time. This dashboard only has two views, but dashboards often contain more.

To update the text on our dashboard to black, select **Format>Workbook** and change **Fonts>All** to **Black**.

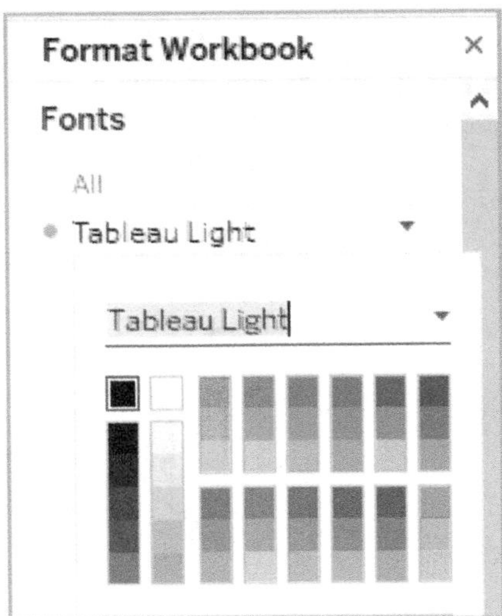

This changes the font color in every sheet of our workbook to black, which is then applied to the views included in the dashboard..

Less accessible – low contrast

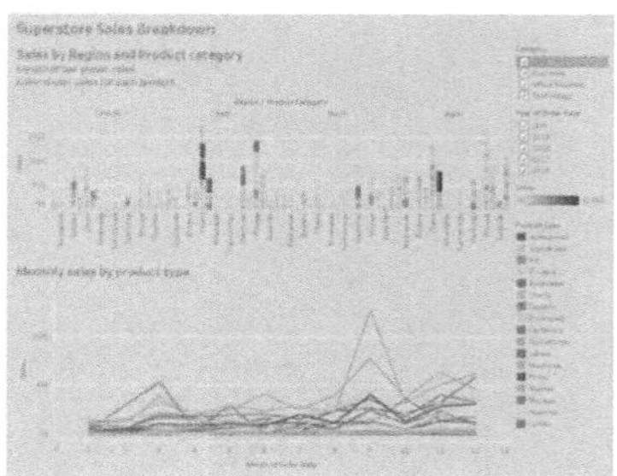

More accessible – higher contrast

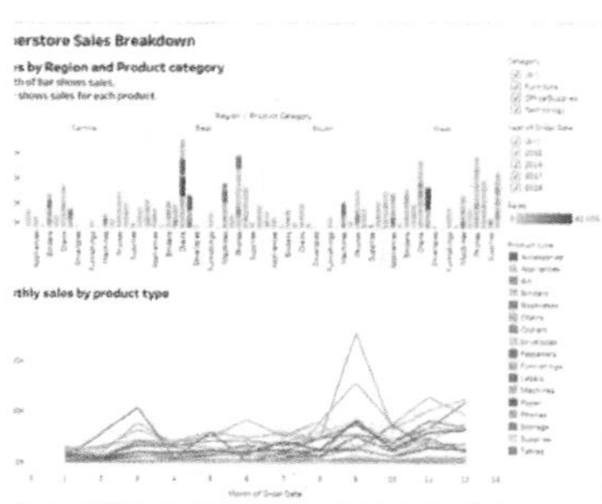

Aggregate and reduce marks

You might have a lot of information that you want to communicate with your dashboard or view. However, a dense view with a lot of marks, like the bar chart at the top of our view, can be difficult to understand using a screen reader or keyboard.

The top view in our dashboard displays over 5,000 marks because each bar in the chart contains the name of each product in that category. If a view uses more than 1,000 marks, it causes the view to be rendered on the server instead of the browser, and server-rendered views are not supported for WCAG conformance. Limit the number of marks to only those that emphasie the most important data points.

To make this view more accessible, make the stacked bar chart into a bar chart by removing the field **Product Name** from **Details** in the **Marks** card. This reduced the number of marks in the view from over 5,000 to 68.

Less accessible – too many marks

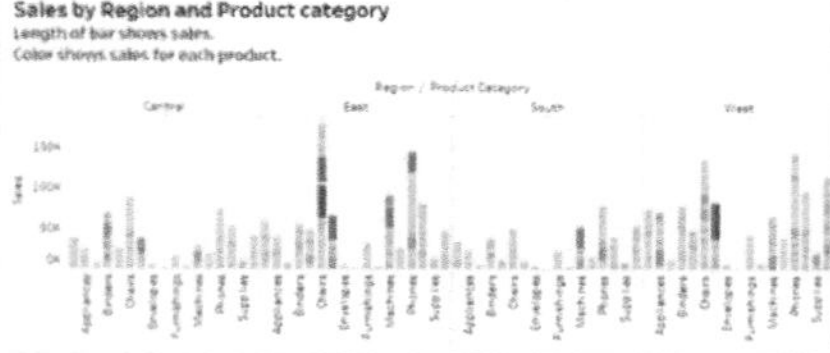

More accessible – aggregated view

Users can also access the **View Data** window (enabled by default) to review the underlying data for the marks or can download the data from that page to an accessible application to view it that way.

To reduce cognitive overload and reduce the numbers of marks in our field even further, we can create groups of related members in a field. To create a group of similar products:

1. Right click on the field and select **Create** > **Group**.

2. In the Create Group dialog box, select several members that you want to group, and then click **Group**.

Here's what the view looked like before grouping and aggregating, compared to after:

Less accessible – too many marks

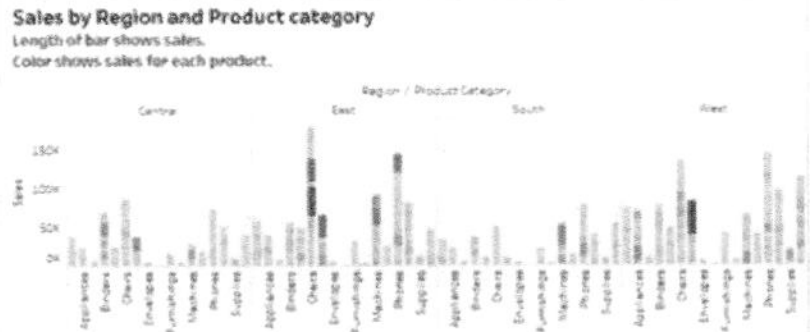

More accessible – aggregated and grouped view

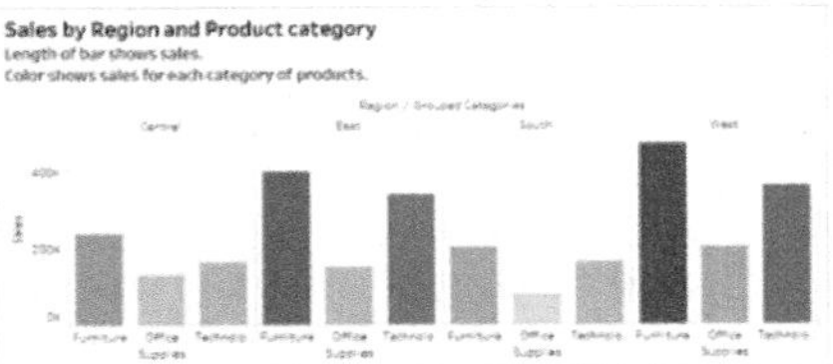

Eliminate redundant information

The aggregated and grouped bar chart reduces cognitive overload for users, but still uses color to convey meaning when color isn't necessary. Since the size of each bar already represents sales numbers, color can be removed from the chart by removing the sales field from Color in the **Marks** card. Removing color also removes the color legend that the screen reader reads.

Less accessible – unnecessary marks

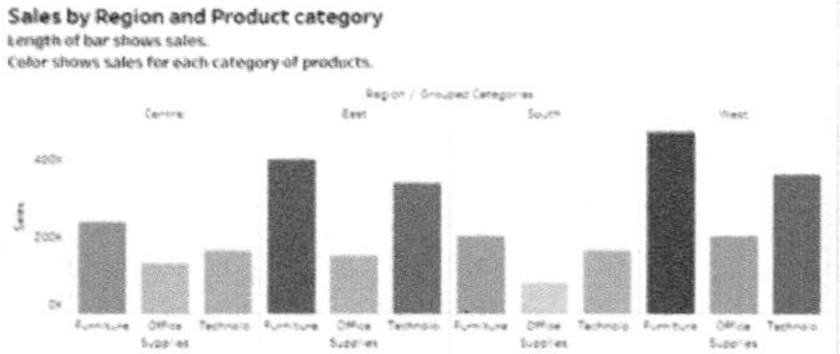

More accessible – unnecessary marks removed

Use color and shape to differentiate marks

The line chart in this dashboard contains marks that are only distinguished by color, which makes it impossible or nearly impossible for people with color-blindness to distinguish marks from one another. The line path provides helpful position information, but the colors do not provide clear distinction between the line marks.

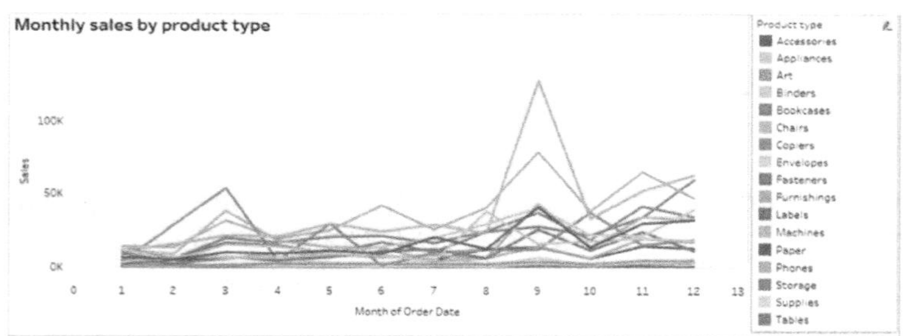

Make this line chart more accessible by applying the **Color Blind** palette and adding shapes to reinforce what is being shown in color.

To apply the Color Blind palette:

1. Select **Color** on the **Marks** card.
2. Select **Color Blind** from the **Color Palette** menu.

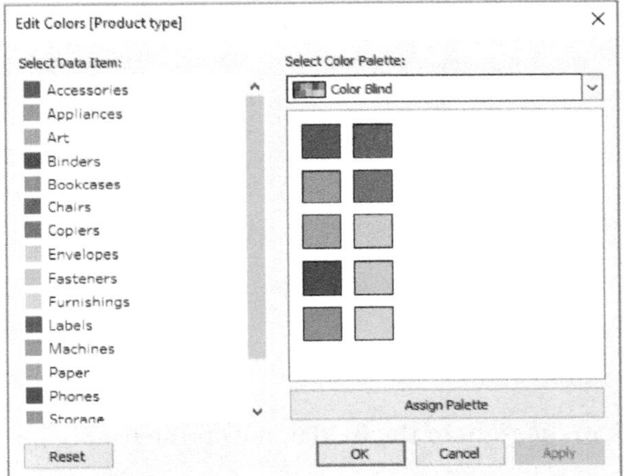

3. Select **Assign Palette** and **Apply** to apply it to the view.

To add shapes in addition to color to your line chart, create a combination chart, or dual axis chart:

1. Control-drag (command-drag on a Mac) the field in the **Rows** shelf to copy it and place it to the right of the first field. This creates two tabs in your Marks card, one for each field in the Rows shelf.

2. On the marks card, select the bottom tab, titled **[Field Name (2)]**. Select **Shape** from the drop down menu in the Marks card.

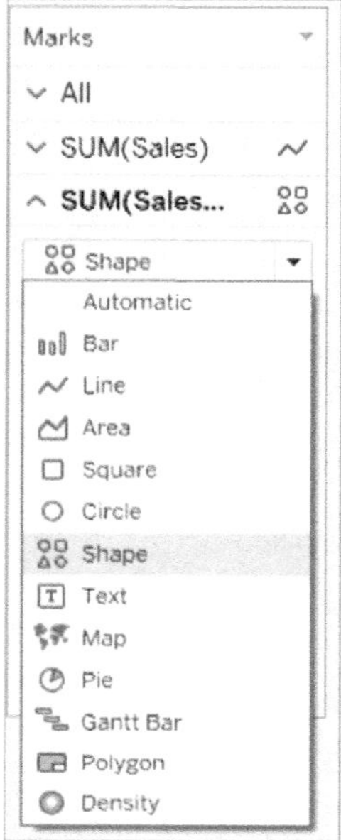

3. Select the Color mark to the right of the field name and select Shape.

4. 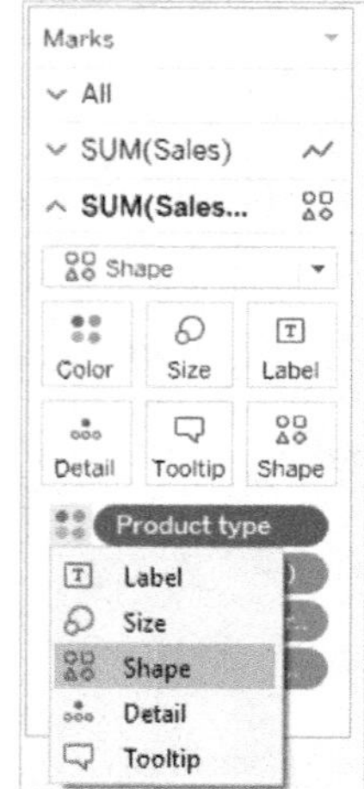

This creates separate shapes for each of the marks in the field. At this point, there are two different charts; one a line chart of colors, another a scatter plot with shapes.

To merge these two charts together into a dual axis chart, in the Rows shelf, select the field on the right and select **Dual Axis**.

Not easily accessible

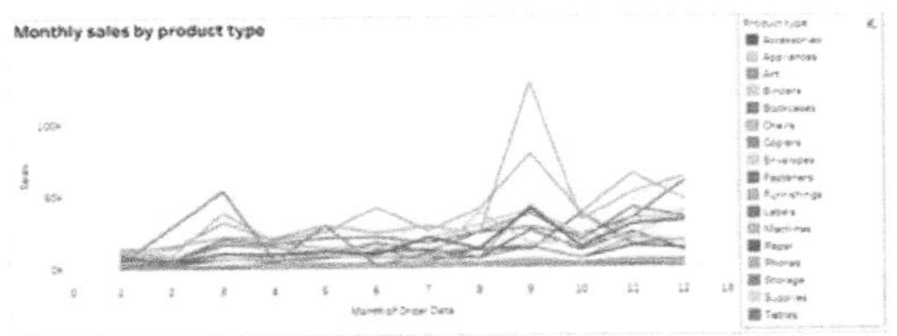

More accessible – Color Blind palette and shapes

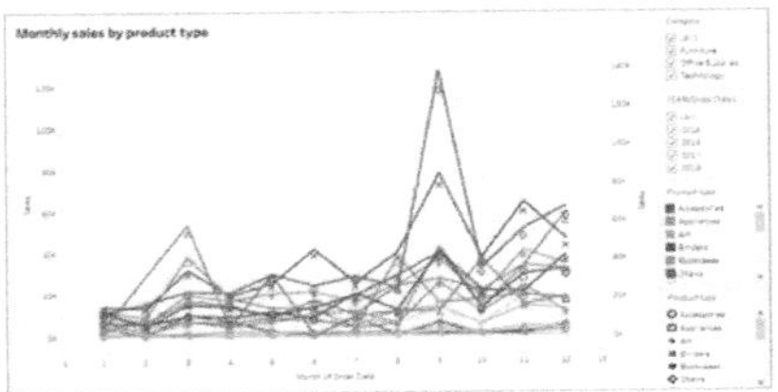

The chart is improved, but the line colors and shapes have started repeating after the 10th mark applied. This makes the view look busy and hard to make sense of, leading to cognitive overload. Let's fix it by adding filters and legends.

Use filters to reduce the number of marks in a view

Using filters helps to focus the number of marks in the view to only what you want users to see.

You can show the following filter modes to allow users to control what data is in the view. The filter modes that Tableau currently supports for WCAG conformance are:

- **Single Value (list)**: a filter with radio buttons. Only one item can be selected at a time. Giving your users single-value filters is a great way to reduce the number of marks in the view.

- **Multiple Values (list)**: a filter with a list of items (with tick boxes) that can be selected at the same time. Multiple-value filters will allow more marks to be shown at the same time.

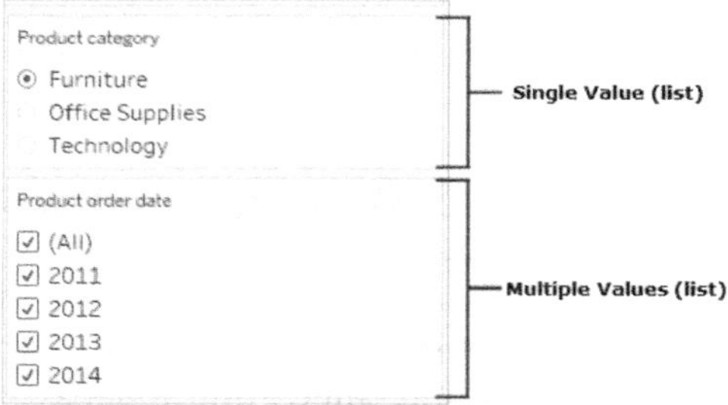

- **Single Value (drop-down)**: a filter with a dropdown list of items. Only one item can be selected at a time. Giving your users single-value filters is a great way to reduce the number of marks in the view.

- **Multiple Values (drop-down)**: a filter with a dropdown list of items that can be selected at the same time. Multiple-value filters will allow more marks to be shown at the same time.

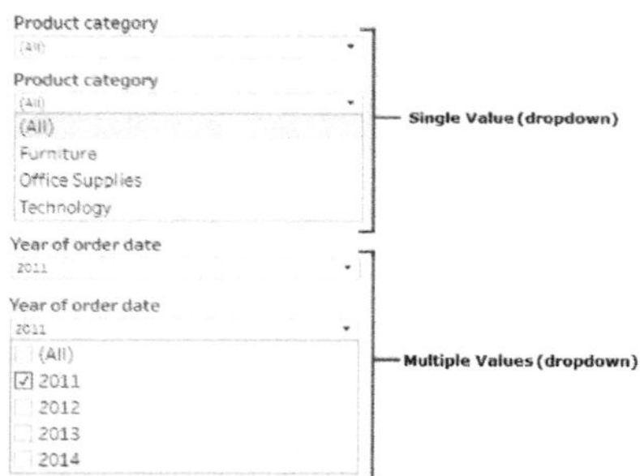

To show a filter, right-click the field you want to use as a filter, and then select **Show Filter**.

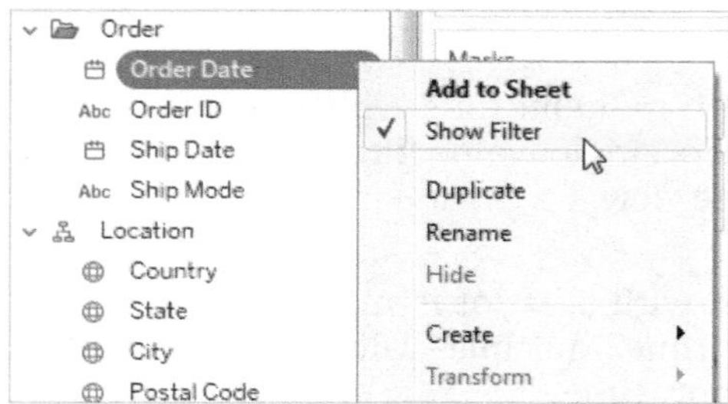

To select the filter mode, in the drop-down menu for a filter, select a **Single Value (list)**, **Single Value (dropdown)**, **Multiple Values (list)**, or **Multiple Values (dropdown)** filter.

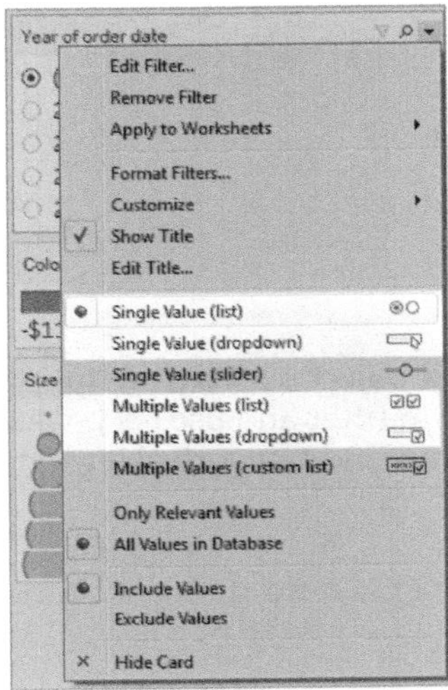

Because the line chart is a Single Value list, we can remove the **All** option from the filter. In the drop-down menu for the filter, select **Customize** and then clear the **Show "All" Value** option.

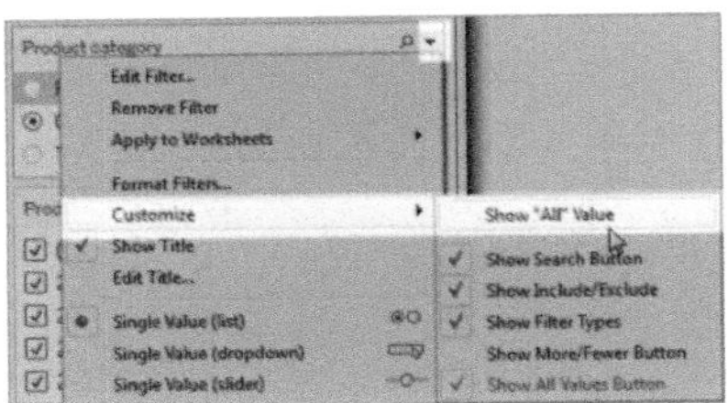

This reduces the level of marks in the view to prevent cognitive overload for dashboard consumers.

Less accessible – too many marks

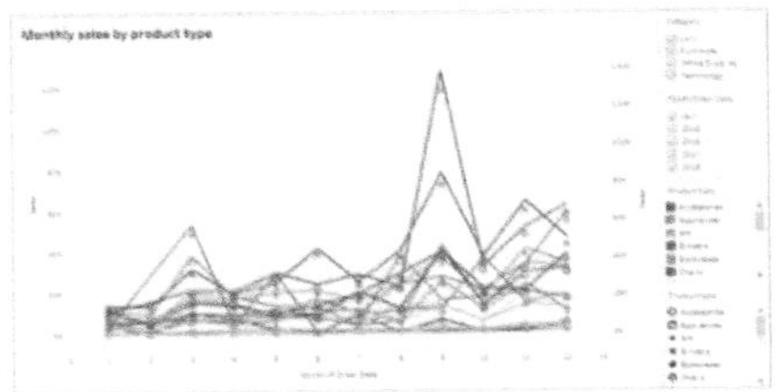

More accessible – less marks in the view

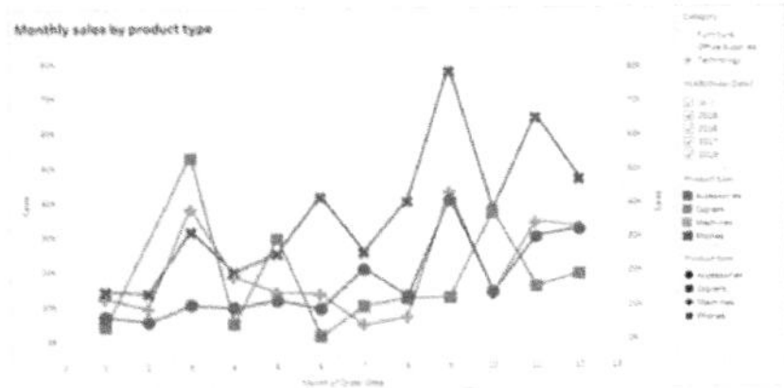

Add captions and legends

To add clarity for our users, we can add a **Text object** with a description of the dashboard and instructions about how to filter and use each view in the dashboard, including how to use the filters and categorical legends that we've added. To add a text object:

1. Grab Text from the Objects menu and drag it onto the dashboard.

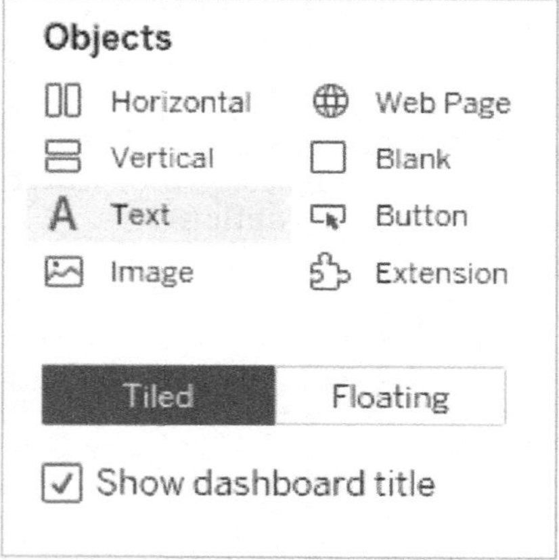

2. Use **Edit Text** window to add text that explains the dashboard's purpose and how to use it.

You can also add chart captions to the dashboard. The default caption text gives a summary of what is shown in the view, but you can add or edit this text to provide better context. To do this, click on a chart in the dashboard and select **Caption** from the **More Options** drop-down menu.

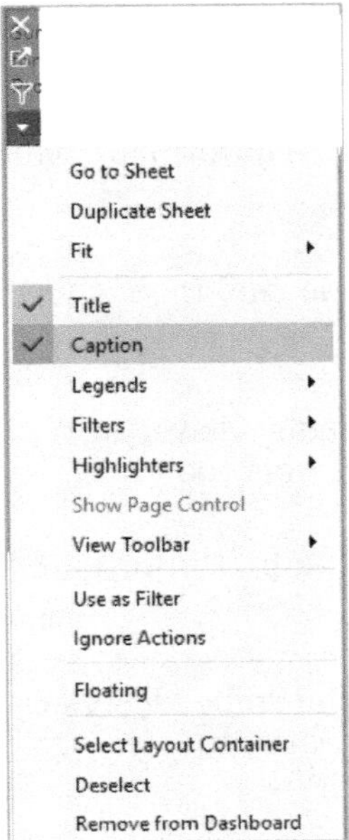

Last, we can update the titles of our legends to reference their associated charts and reduce the amount of redundant text that screen readers consume. To do this, double-click on the legend title, or right-click and select **Edit Title** to add or edit text in the **Edit Filter Title** window.

The result is a dashboard that includes an explanation of the dashboard and chart captions and eliminates redundant text for users.

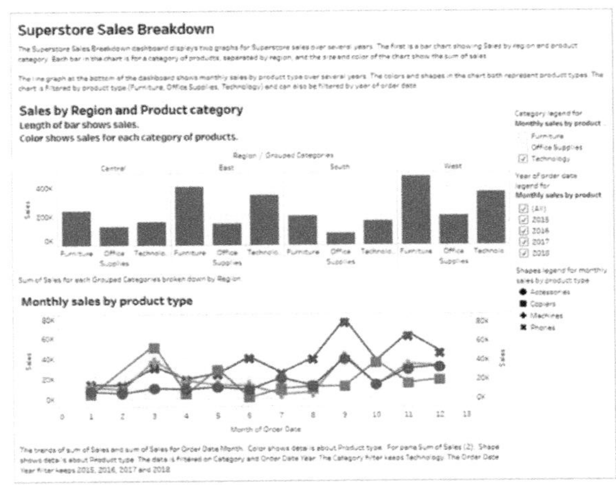

Publish and embed the dashboard

After you create your views, to make them WCAG-conformant, you must:

- Publish views to Tableau Server or Tableau Online, and then embed the view in a WCAG-compliant web page.

- Web editing is not supported in WCAG-conformant views, so Web Edit permissions must be turned off in the published workbook.

- In the embedded views, hide the Custom Views, Subscriptions, and Alerts buttons in the toolbar.

- Make sure users have permissions to access to the embedded views and are able to view the underlying data in the View Data window.

Manage Sheets in Dashboards and Stories

Hiding, showing and navigating to sheets helps you more easily manage workbooks and design dashboards.

Hide and show sheets

To streamline the editing process for large workbooks, hide and show sheets as you work.

What sheets can I hide?

While editing a workbook, you can hide any sheet contained in a dashboard or story. (That includes dashboard sheets in stories.)

Sheets that aren't in a dashboard or story are always visible while editing workbooks. However, you can hide any sheet in workbooks you publish to Tableau Online or Tableau Desktop.

Hide or unhide all sheets

To hide all of a dashboard or story's sheets, right-click (Windows) or Control-click (macOS) the dashboard's tab at the bottom of the screen, and select **Hide All Sheets**. You can later select **Unhide All Sheets** if needed.

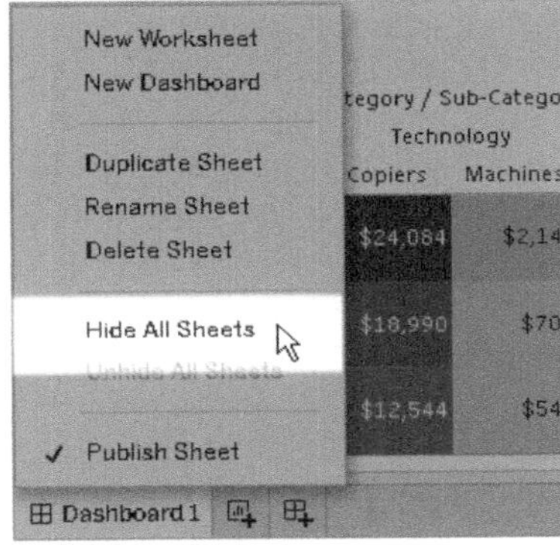

Hide an individual sheet

1. Look for the sheet in the tabs at the bottom of the screen. Or, if you're viewing a dashboard or story, look in the **Sheets** list at left:

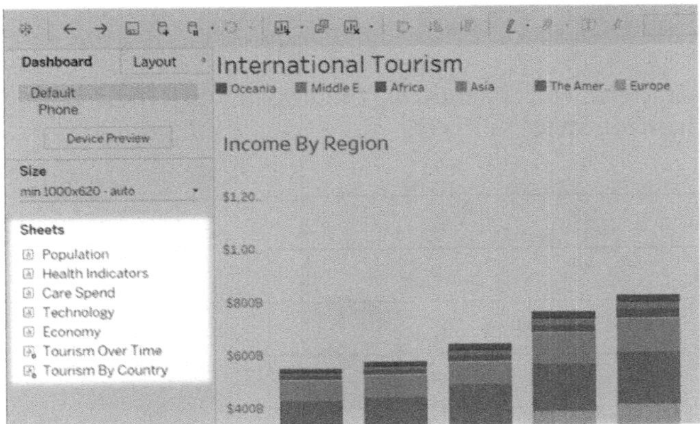

2. Right-click (Windows) or Control-click (macOS) the sheet name, and select **Hide Sheet**.

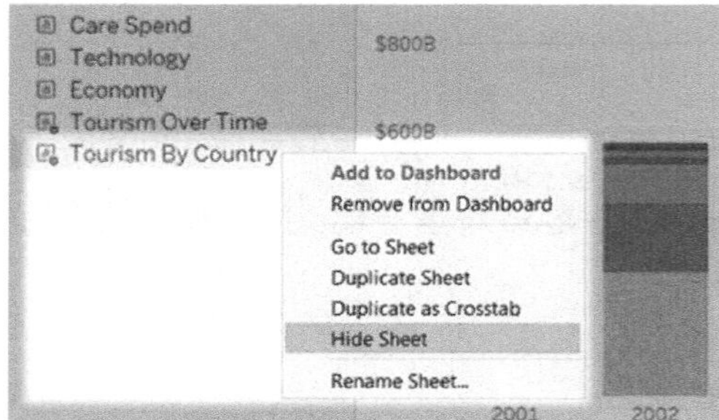

Note: From the sheets list to the left of a dashboard or story, you can hide only sheets used in that particular dashboard or story. You can identify these sheets by the blue tick on the sheet icon.

Unhide an individual sheet

1. At the bottom of the screen, click the tab for the dashboard or story that contains the sheet. You can identify dashboards and stories by grid and book icons, respectively.

Note: If a story has a hidden dashboard that in turn has a hidden sheet, first go to the hidden dashboard from the story, and then to the hidden sheet from the dashboard.

2. In the list at left, right-click (Windows) or Control-click (macOS) the sheet, and clear the **Hide Sheet** tick box.

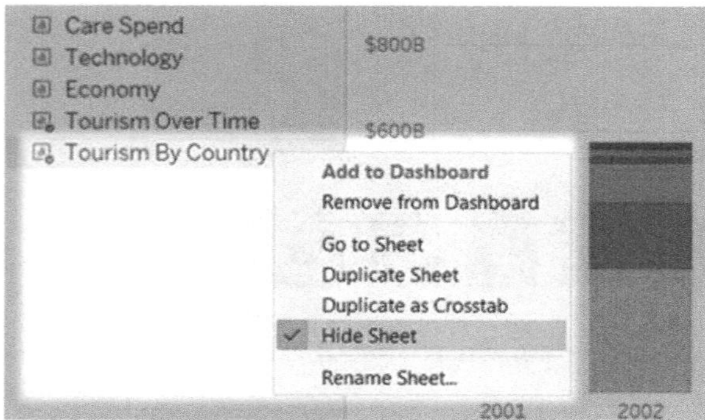

Navigate between sheets, dashboards and stories

Tableau lets you quickly navigate back and forth between sheets and related dashboards and stories, helping you better optimize the design of each.

Go from a dashboard or story to a sheet it contains

Tip: If a sheet is hidden, this technique temporarily shows it so you can get a closer look at it. The sheet is hidden again when you switch to another sheet.

Do either of the following:

- On the dashboard itself, select the item that references the hidden sheet. Then click the drop-down arrow in the top left or right corner, and select **Go to Sheet**.

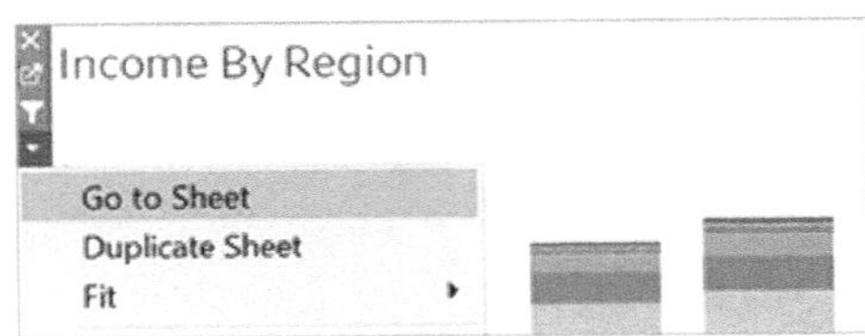

- In the **Sheets** list to the left of the dashboard, click the icon to the right of the sheet name.

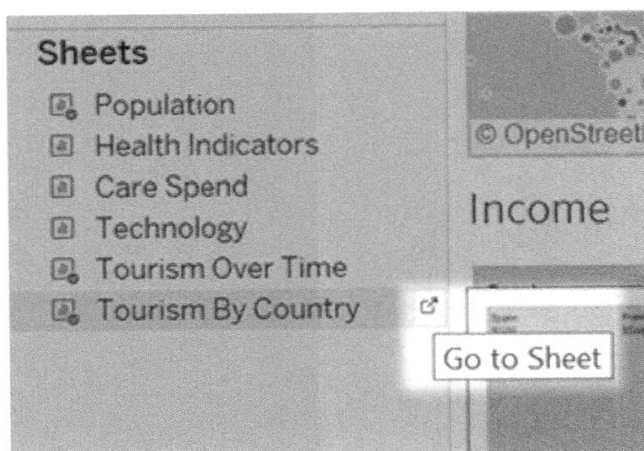

Go from a sheet to related dashboards and stories

To quickly go to dashboards and stories a sheet appears in, right-click the sheet tab and open the **Used in** menu.

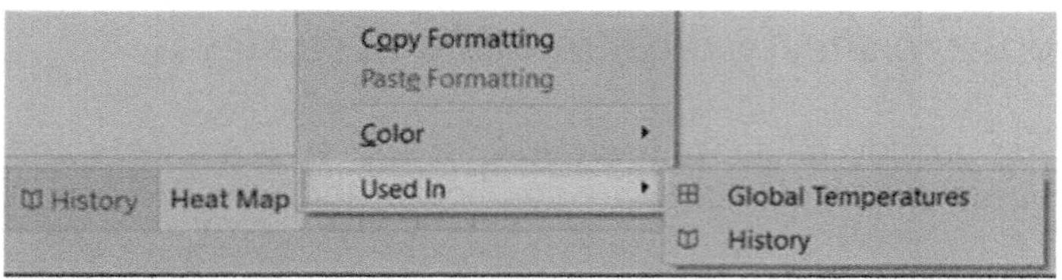
Copy Formatting
Paste Formatting
Color
Used In
History
Heat Map
Global Temperatures
History

Chapter 10
Stories

Stories

In Tableau, a **story** is a sequence of visualizations that work together to convey information. You can create stories to tell a data narrative, provide context, demonstrate how decisions relate to outcomes or to simply make a compelling case.

A story is a sheet, so the methods you use to create, name and manage worksheets and dashboards also apply to stories. At the same time, a story is also a collection of sheets, arranged in a sequence. Each individual sheet in a story is called a **story point**.

When you share a story – for example, by publishing a workbook to Tableau Public, Tableau Server, or Tableau Online – users can interact with the story to reveal new findings or ask new questions of the data.

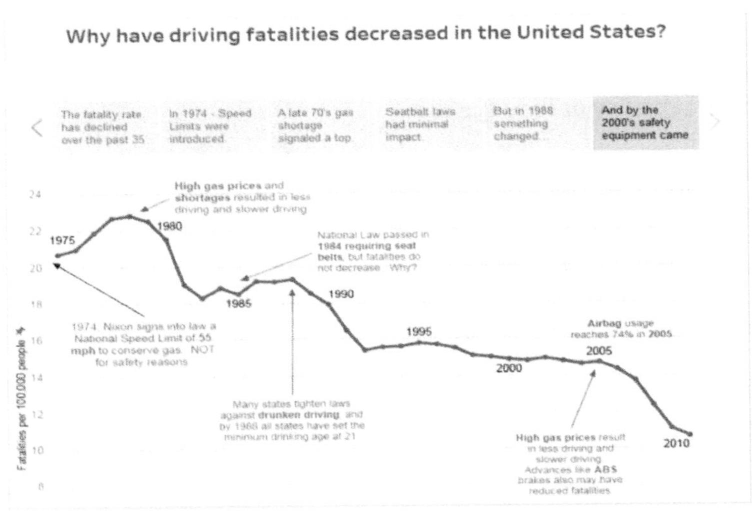

The Story Workspace

As you work on a story, you can use the following controls, elements and features.

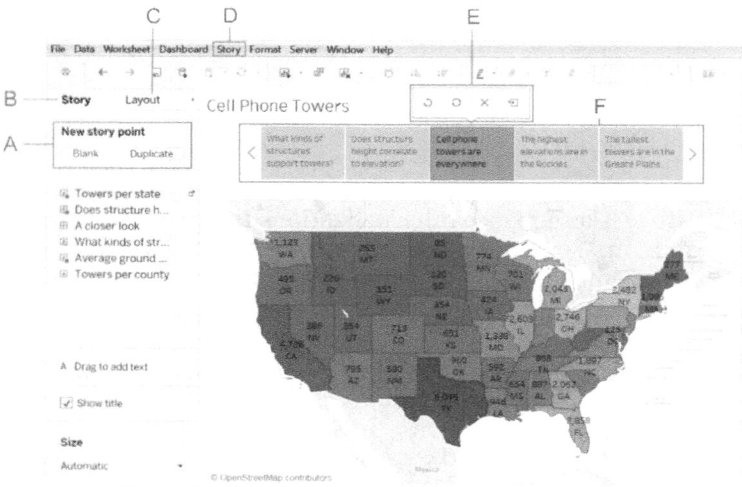

A. Options for adding a new story point: Choose **Blank** to add a new point or **Duplicate** to use the current story point as the starting place for your next point.

B. The Story pane: Use this pane to drag dashboards, sheets and text descriptions to your story sheet. This is also where you set the size of your story and display or hide the title.

C. The Layout pane: This is where you choose your navigator style and display or hide the forward and back arrows.

D. The Story menu: Use this menu in Tableau Desktop to format the story or copy or export the current story point as an image. You can also clear the entire story here or show or hide the navigator and story title.

E. The Story toolbar: This toolbar appears when you mouse-over the navigator area. Use it to revert changes, apply updates to a story point, delete a story point or create a new story point out of the current, customized one.

F. The navigator: The navigator allows you to edit and organize your story points. It's also how your audience will step through your story. To change the style of the navigator, use the Layout pane.

Best Practices for Telling Great Stories

Before you start to build your story, take some time to think about the purpose of your story and what you want your viewers' journey to be. Is it a call to action, is it a simple narrative, or are you presenting a case?

If you're presenting a case, decide whether you want to present data points that lead up to a conclusion at the end, or start with a conclusion then show the supporting data points. The latter approach works well for a busy audience.

Finally, sketching out your story first on paper or a whiteboard can help you quickly identify problems with your sequence.

The seven types of data stories

When you use the story feature, you are building a sequence of points. Each point can contain a view, dashboard, or even just text. Some stories show the same view throughout the story, with text annotations and different filters applied to different points to support the narrative arc.

The following table describes seven different data story approaches you can take and provides an example for each.

Data Story Type	Description
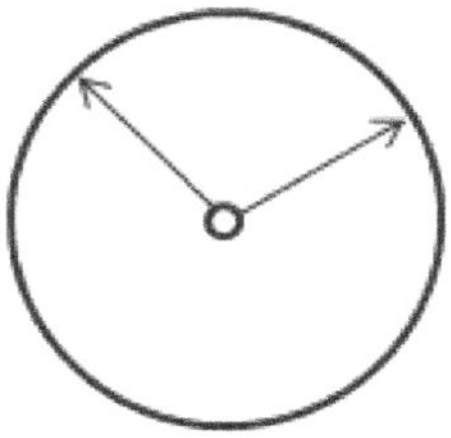 Change Over Time	**What it does**: Uses a chronology to illustrate a trend. **Discussions it starts**: Why did this happen, or why does it keep happening? What can we do prevent or make this happen?
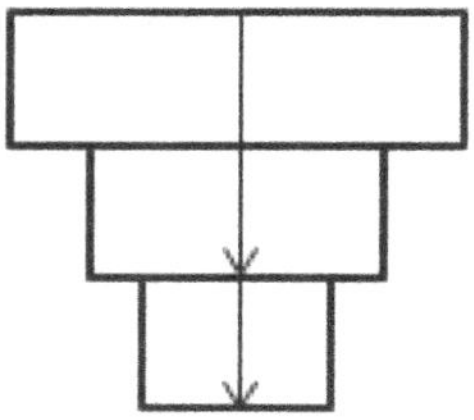 Drill Down	**What it does**: Sets context so that your audience better understands what's going on in a particular category. **Discussions it starts**: Why is this person, place or thing different? How does the performance of this person, place, or thing compare?
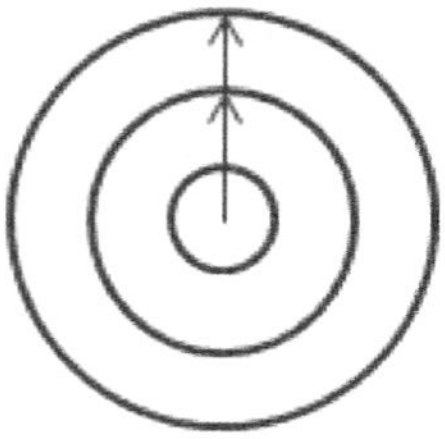 Zoom Out	**What it does**: Describes how something your audience cares about relates to the bigger picture. **Discussion it starts**: How does something you care about compare to the bigger picture? What effect does one area have on the bigger picture?
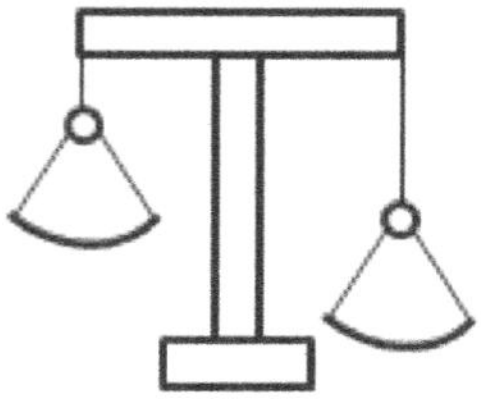 Contrast	**What it does**: Shows how two or more subjects differ. **Discussions it starts**: Why are these items different? How can we make A perform like B? Which area should we focus on and which area is doing fine?

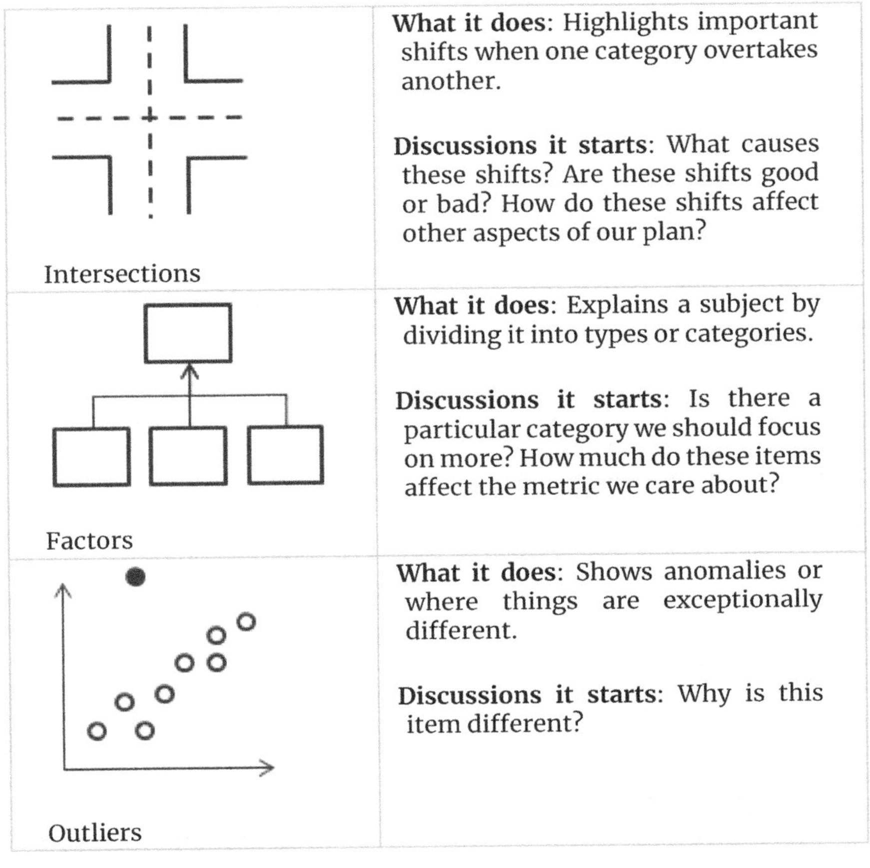

Intersections	**What it does**: Highlights important shifts when one category overtakes another. **Discussions it starts**: What causes these shifts? Are these shifts good or bad? How do these shifts affect other aspects of our plan?
Factors	**What it does**: Explains a subject by dividing it into types or categories. **Discussions it starts**: Is there a particular category we should focus on more? How much do these items affect the metric we care about?
Outliers	**What it does**: Shows anomalies or where things are exceptionally different. **Discussions it starts**: Why is this item different?

Keep it simple

A common error is trying to cram too many views and dashboards into a single story. The result is too many points for your viewers to take in.

The clarity of each story point is also important. Take a step back and consider your story from the perspective of someone who's never seen it. Every element should serve a purpose. If captions, titles, legends, or grid lines aren't necessary, get rid of them!

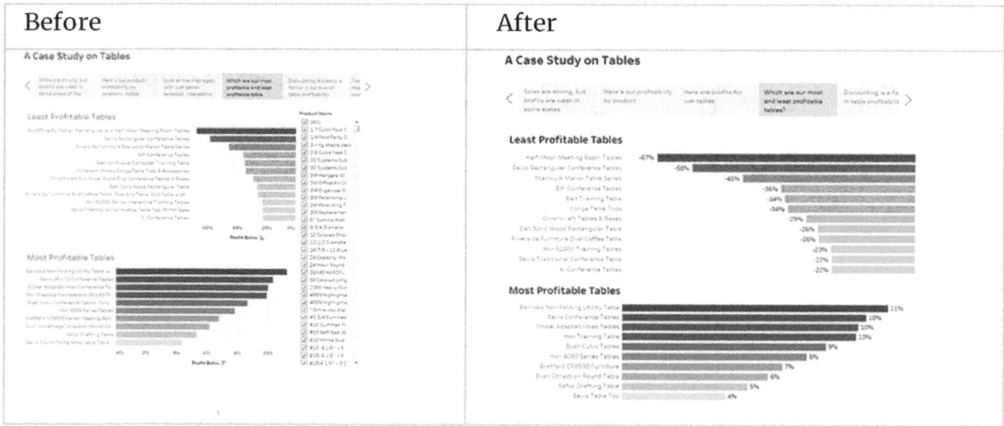

Use 'Fit to' in your dashboards

Dashboards are a common ingredient in Tableau stories. For dashboards that you plan to include in your story, you can use the **Fit to** option under **Size** on the Dashboard pane. It will resize your dashboard so that it's the right size for the story you're creating.

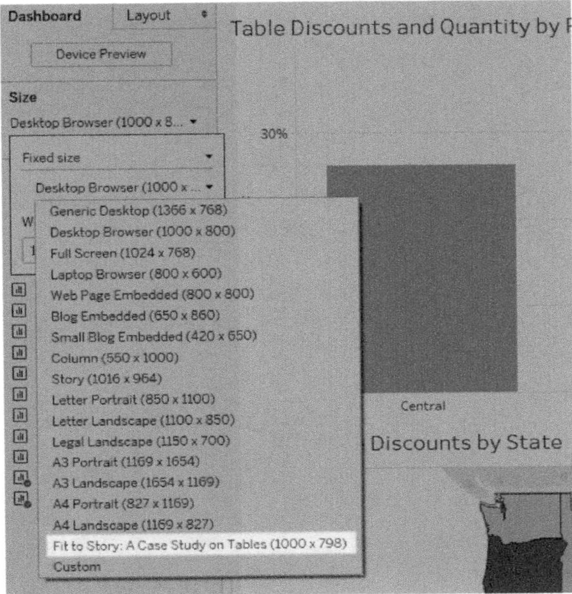

Plan for fast load times

The most wonderful story in the world won't have much impact if it takes too long to load once it's published. People find long waits frustrating.

Filtering is a common culprit for slow load times. Although filters are effective in restricting the amount of data being analyzed, they also impact query performance. For example, **Exclude** filters tend to be slower than **Keep Only** filters. This is because **Exclude** filters load all of the data for a dimension instead of just what you want to keep.

Some of the most critical performance decisions you make as an author begin before you even create your first view or story, in the data preparation stage. Take a moment to familiarize yourself with the data you're working with.

Create a Story

Use stories to make your case more compelling by showing how facts are connected, and how decisions relate to outcomes. You can then publish your story on the web, or present it to an audience.

Each story point can be based on a different view or dashboard, or the entire story can be based on the same visualization seen at different stages, with different filters and annotations.

Create a story point

1. Click the **New Story** tab.

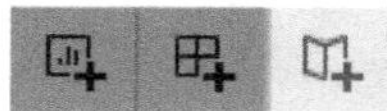

Tableau opens a new story as your starting point:

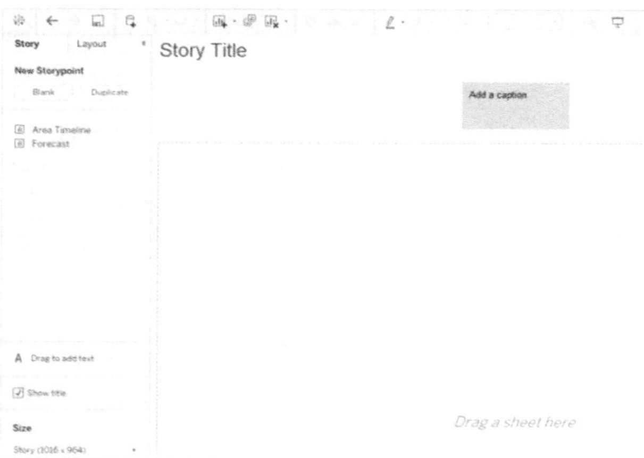

2. In the lower-left corner of the screen, choose a size for your story. Choose from one of the predefined sizes, or set a custom size, in pixels:

Note: Choose the size your story will be viewed at, not the size you're authoring in.

3. By default, your story takes its title from the sheet name. To edit it, right-click the sheet tab, and choose **Rename Sheet**.

If you're using Tableau Desktop, you can also rename a story by double-clicking the title.

4. To start building your story, double-click a sheet on the left to add it to a story point.

In Tableau Desktop, you can also drag sheets into your story point.

When you add a sheet to a story point, that sheet remains connected to the original sheet. If you modify the original sheet, your changes will automatically be reflected on the story points that use it.

If you are using Tableau Server or Tableau Online to author on the web and the original sheet has **Pause Auto Updates** enabled, the story sheet will be blank until auto-updates are resumed.

5. Click **Add a caption** to summarize the story point.

In Tableau Desktop, you can highlight a key takeaway for your viewers by dragging a text object to the story worksheet and typing a comment.

6. To further highlight the main idea of this story point, you can change a filter or sort on a field in the view. Then save your changes by clicking **Update** on the story toolbar above the navigator box:

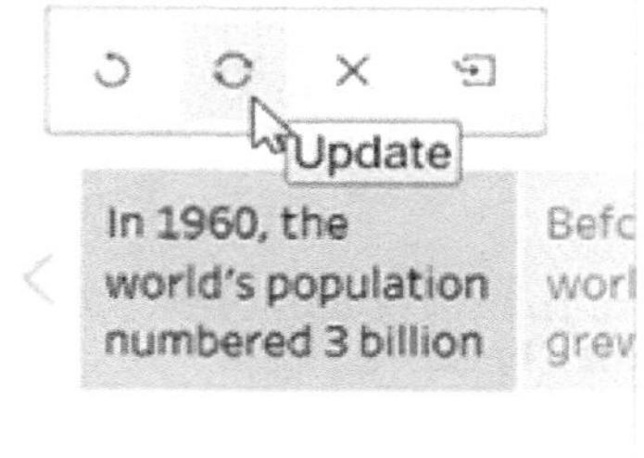

7. Add another story point by doing one of the following:

- Click **Blank** to use a fresh sheet for the next story point.

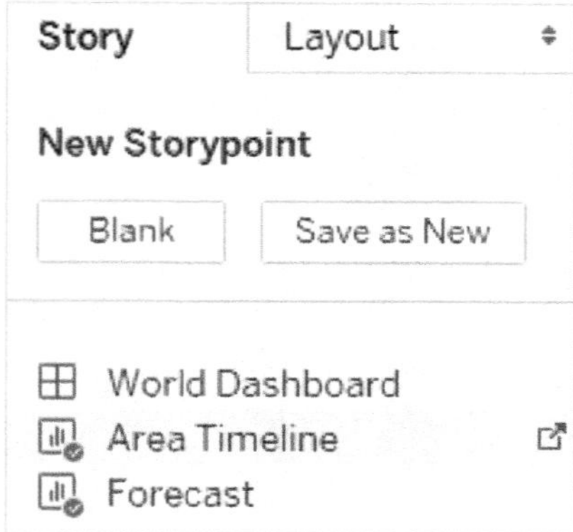

○ Start customizing a story point and click **Save as New** on the toolbar above the navigator box.

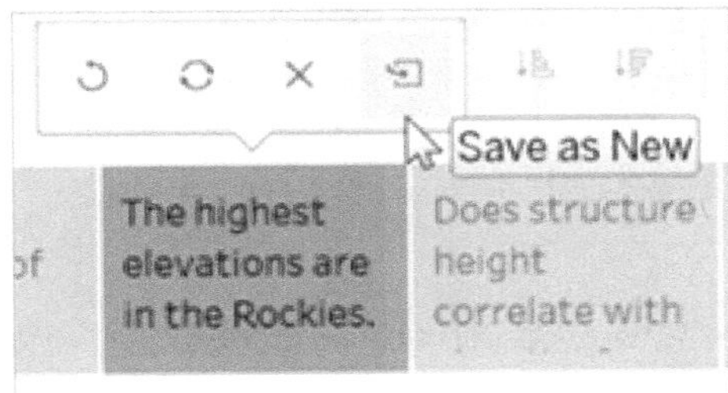

○ Click **Duplicate** to use the current story point as the basis for a new one.

Explore layout options

You can refine the look of your story using the options on the **Layout** tab.

1. Click the **Layout** tab.

2. Choose a navigator style that best suits your story, and show or hide the next and previous arrows.

Format a story

Sometimes the text in one or more of your captions is too long to fit inside the height of the navigator. In this case, you can re-size the captions vertically and horizontally.

1. In the navigator, select a caption.

2. Drag the border left or right to resize the caption horizontally, down to resize vertically, or select a corner and drag diagonally to resize the caption both horizontally and vertically.

All captions in the navigator update to the new size.

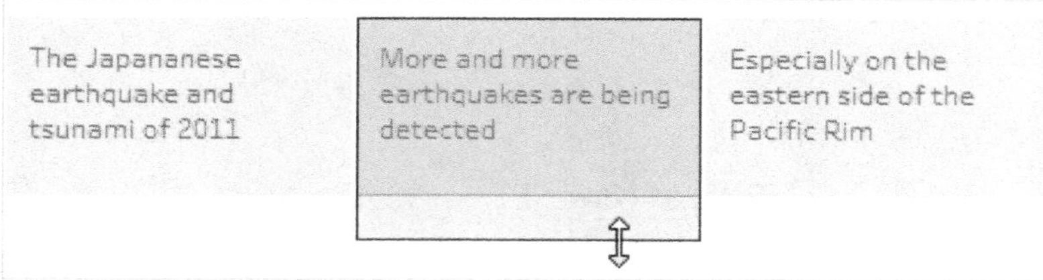

When you resize a caption, you can only select the left, right, or bottom border of the caption.

Fit a dashboard to a story

You can fit a dashboard to the exact size of a story. For example, if your story is exactly 800 by 600 pixels, you can shrink or expand a dashboard to fit inside that space.

Click the **Size** drop-down menu and select the story you want the dashboard to fit inside.

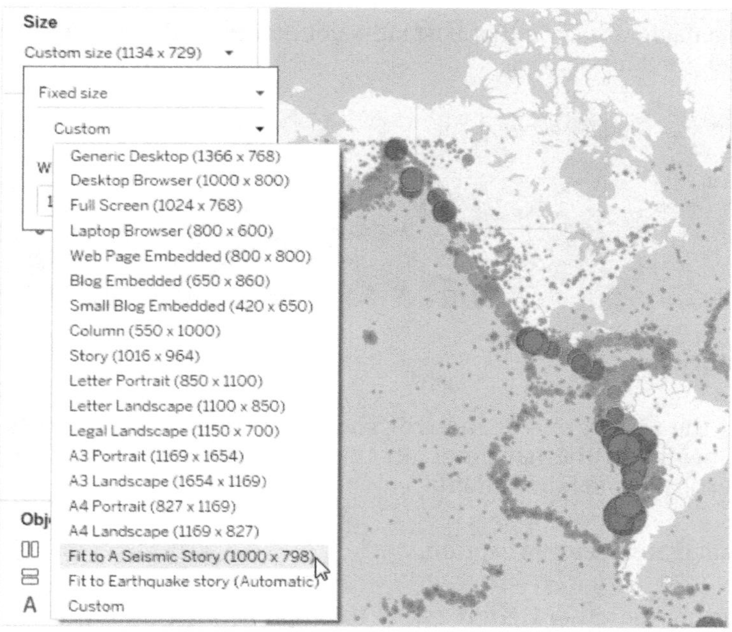

Format a story's shading, title, and text objects (Tableau Desktop only)

To open the **Format Story** pane, select **Format** > **Story**.

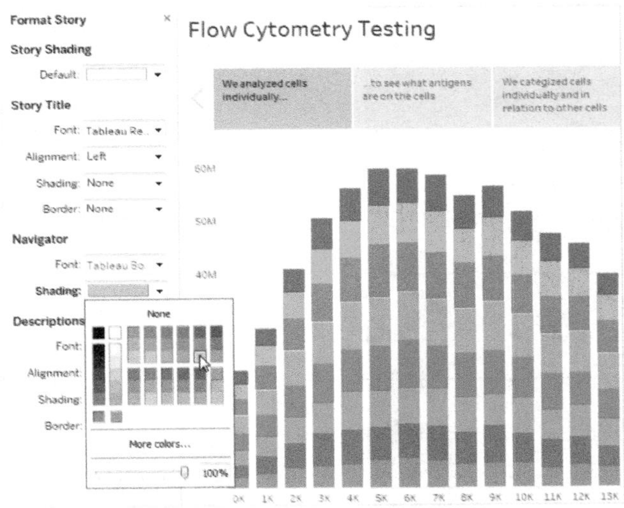

Clear all formatting (Tableau Desktop only)

- To reset a story to its default format settings, click the **Clear** button at the bottom of the **Format Story** pane.

- To clear a single format setting, right-click (Windows) or control-click (macOS) the format setting you want to undo in the **Format Story** pane. Then select **Clear**.

For example, if you want to clear the alignment of the story title, right-click (control-click on Mac) **Alignment** in the **Title** section, and then select **Clear**.

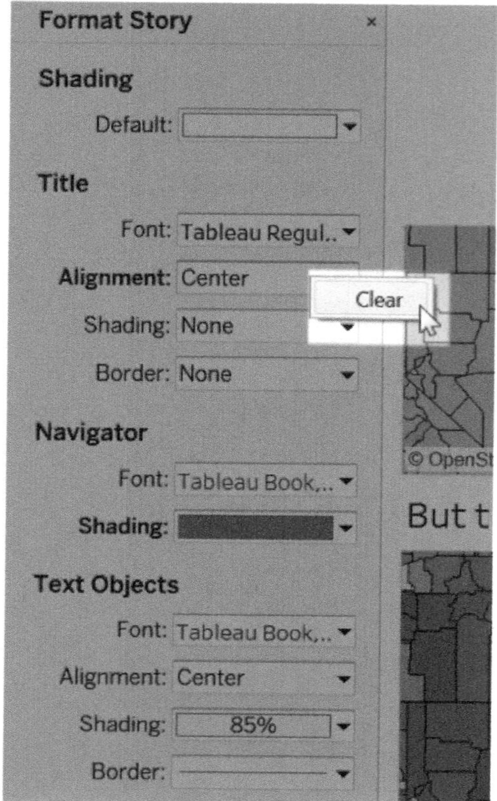

Delete a story point

Click the X in the toolbar above the point's caption:

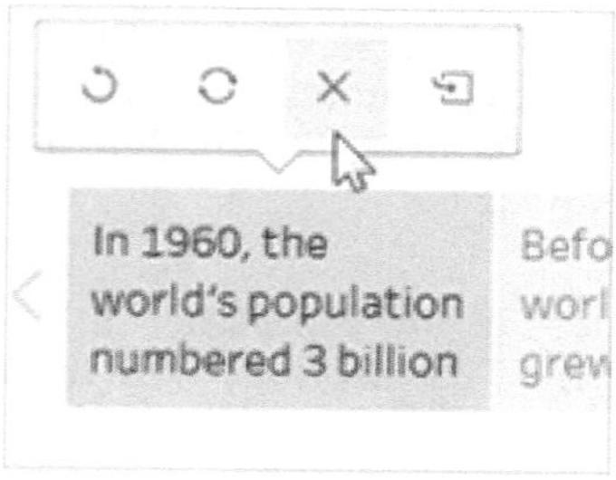

Present your story

1. In Tableau Desktop, click the **Presentation Mode** button on the toolbar. Or, publish the story to Tableau Online or Tableau Server, and click the **Full Screen** button in the upper-right corner of the browser.

2. To step through your story, click the arrow to the right of the story points. Or, in Tableau Desktop, use the arrow keys on your keyboard.

3. To exit Presentation or Full Screen mode, press **Esc**.

Example - A Story That Examines a Trend

The example in this article walks you through building a story about earthquake trends over time.

The story feature in Tableau is a great way to showcase this type of analysis because it has a step-by-step format which lets you move your audience through time.

Rather than showing you how to create all the views and dashboards from scratch, this example starts from an existing workbook. What you'll do is pull the story together. To follow along and access the pre-built views and dashboards, download the following workbook from Tableau Public: An Earthquake Trend Story

Frame the story

A successful story is well-framed, meaning its purpose is clear. In this example, the story's purpose is to answer the following question: Are big earthquakes becoming more common?

There are several approaches you could take but the one used here as an overall approach is Change over Time, because it works especially well for answering questions about trends. As you build the story you'll notice that other data story types, such as Drill Down and Outliers, are blended in to support the overall approach.

Build the story

Create a story worksheet

1. Use Tableau Desktop to open the Earthquake Trend Story workbook that you downloaded.

If you also have Tableau Server or Tableau Online and you want to do your authoring on the web instead of in Tableau Desktop, publish the workbook to your Tableau server, click **Workbooks**, select the workbook, then under **Actions** choose **Edit Workbook**.

Once you open the workbook, you'll see that it has three dashboards. You'll be using those dashboards to build your story. The workbook also has a finished version of the story.

Tip: To see the individual views that are in a dashboard, right-click the dashboard's tab and select **Unhide all Sheets**.

2. Click the **New Story** tab.

Tableau opens a new worksheet as your starting point.

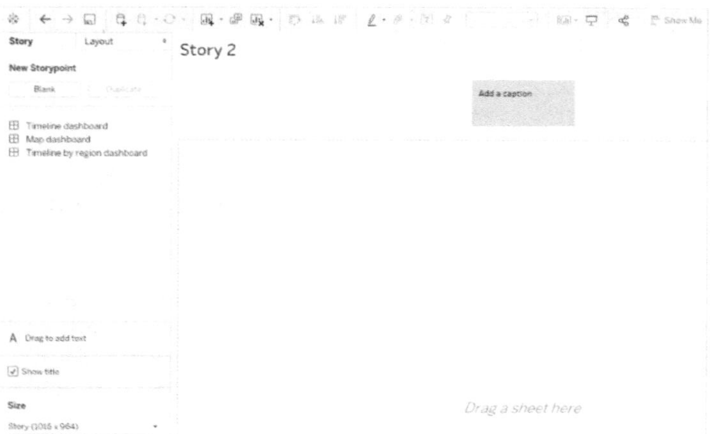

3. Right-click the **Story 2** tab, choose **Rename Sheet**, and type **Earthquake story** as the worksheet name.

State the question

Story titles are in view at all times and they're a handy way to keep your story's purpose in the spotlight. By default, Tableau uses the worksheet name as the story title. In Tableau Desktop you can override that by doing the following:

1. Double-click the title.

2. In the Edit Title dialog box, replace **<Sheet Name>** with the following:

Are big earthquakes on the rise?

3. Click **OK**.

If you're authoring in Tableau Server or Tableau Online, the story tab is the only place where you can change the title.

Start big

To help orient your audience, the first story point you create will show the broadest possible viewpoint – all earthquakes, across the entire planet.

1. On the Story pane, double-click **Map dashboard** to place it on the story sheet. If you're using Tableau Desktop, you can also use drag-and-drop to add views and dashboards to a story sheet.

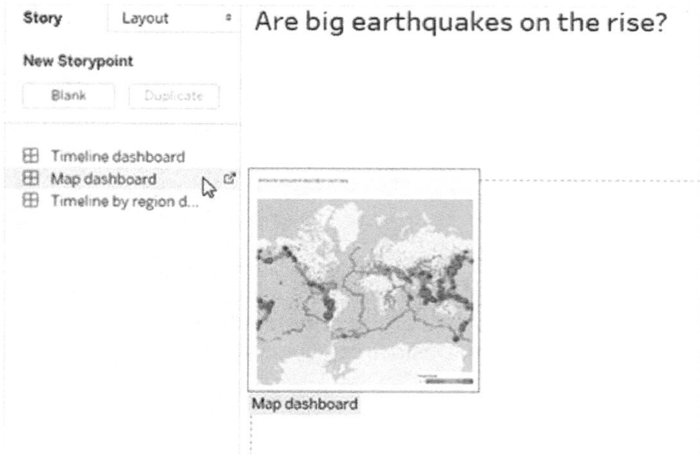

Notice how there's a horizontal scroll bar and the legend isn't fully displayed.

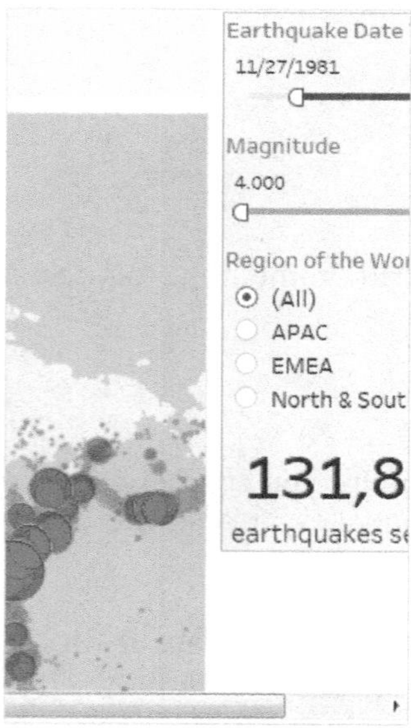

There's a special setting you can use on your dashboards to prevent this from happening.

2. Select **Map dashboard** and under **Size** on the Dashboard pane, select **Fit to Earthquake story**. This setting is designed to make dashboards the perfect size for a story.

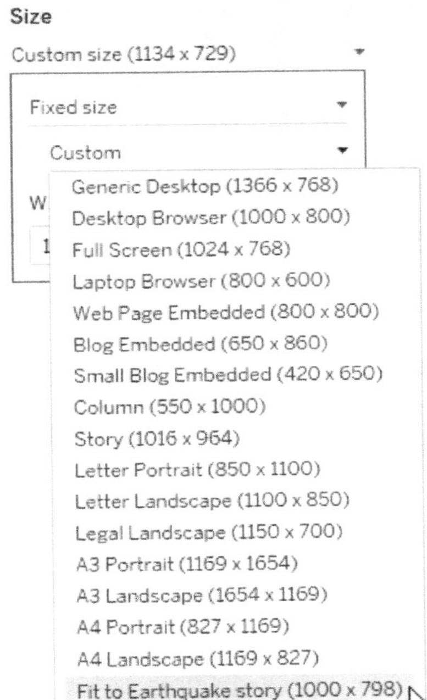

Look at the Earthquake story again. You see that its size has been adjusted and the scroll bars are gone.

3. If you're using Tableau Desktop, add a description for this story point, such as *Exactly 131,834 earthquakes of magnitude 4.0 or greater have been recorded since 1973*.

4. Add caption text by clicking the area that reads **Write the story point description text here**.

5. Click **Update** on the caption to save your changes to the story point.

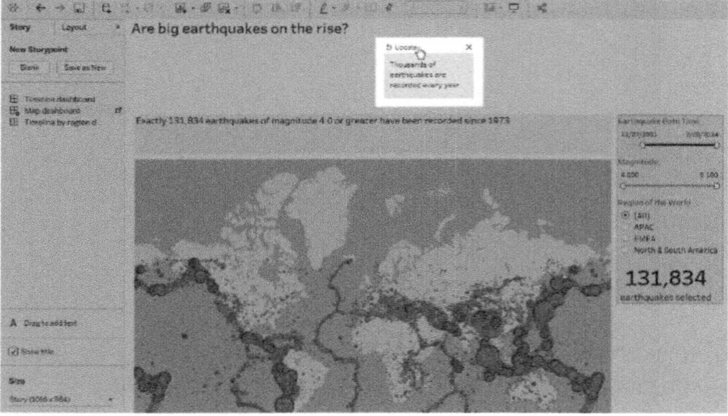

Drill down

Just like the plot of a good novel needs to move the action along, so does a data story. Starting with your next story point, you'll use the drill-down technique in order to narrow down the scope of the story and keep the narrative moving.

1. To use your first story point as a baseline for your next, click **Duplicate** under **New Storypoint** on the left.

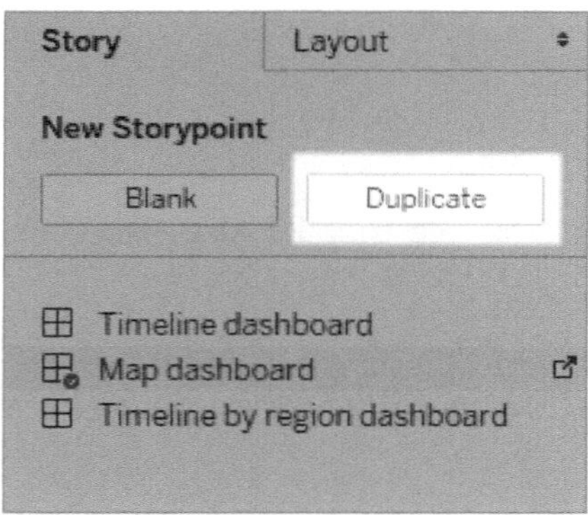

2. Change the **Magnitude** filter to **7.000 – 9.100** so that the map filters out smaller earthquakes. The map pans to show the Pacific '**Ring of Fire**', where the majority of the large earthquakes occurred.

3. Add a caption, such as *About two quakes each year qualify as 'major'*

4. If you're using Tableau Desktop, edit the description to describe what you've done in this story point. For example: *Out of over 130,000 earthquakes since 2004, only 174 were of magnitude 7.0 or greater – about*

two major earthquakes each year. But many people wonder, "Are earthquakes happening more often?"

5. Click **Update** in the story toolbar above the caption to save your changes.

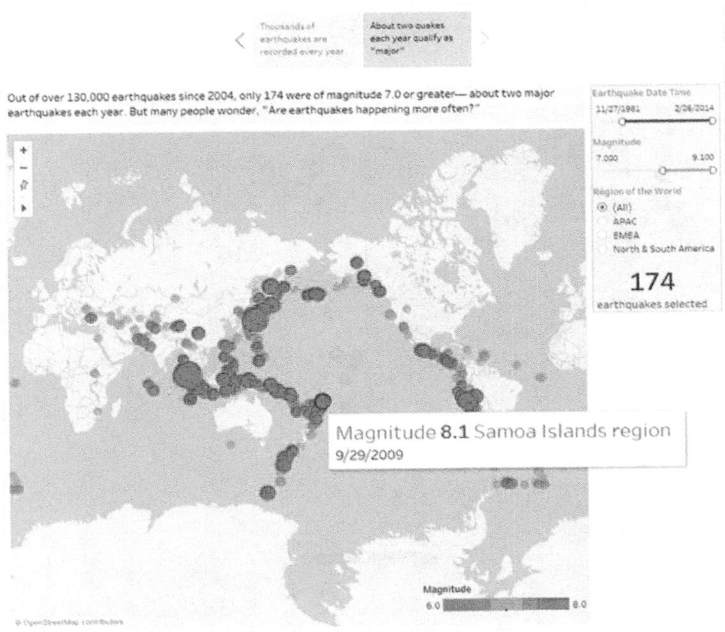

In the next story point, you're going to drill down further, narrowing the story's focus so that a specific type of earthquake – the 'megaquake' – comes into view.

1. Click **Duplicate** in your second story point to use it as the baseline for your third story point.

2. Change the **Magnitude** filter to **8.000 – 9.100** so that the map filters out everything except the megaquakes.

3. Add the caption and description text.

   - Caption: *These megaquakes have drawn a lot of attention*

   - Description (Tableau Desktop only): *Recent megaquakes of magnitude 8.0 and higher have often caused significant damage and loss of life. The undersea megaquakes near Indonesia and Japan also caused tsunamis that have killed many thousands of people.*

4. Click **Update** to save your changes.

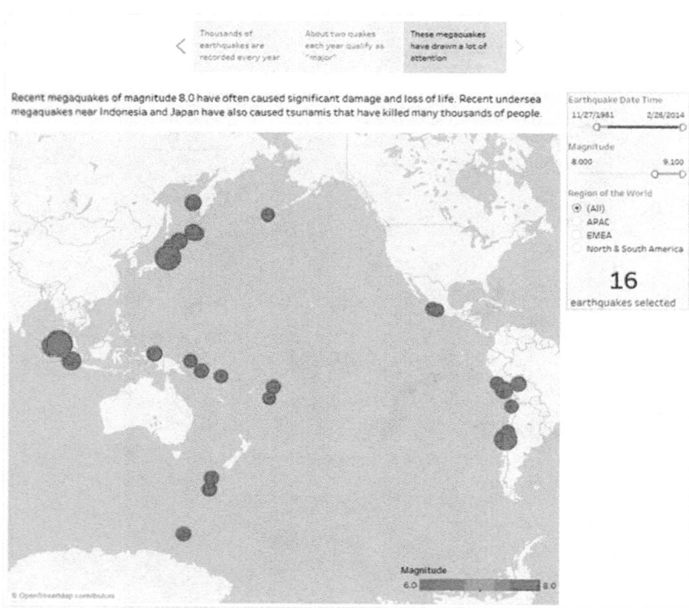

Highlight outliers

In the next two story points, you're going to further engage your audience by examining data points at the far end of the scale: the two most deadly earthquakes in recent history.

1. As you've done before, use **Duplicate** to create a new story point as your starting point.

2. Adjust **Magnitude** to **9.000–9.100** and you'll see just two data points.

3. Select one of the marks, such as the Indian Ocean earthquake and tsunami of 2004 that had a magnitude of 9.1.

4. Use the pan tool on the maps menu to center it in your story point.

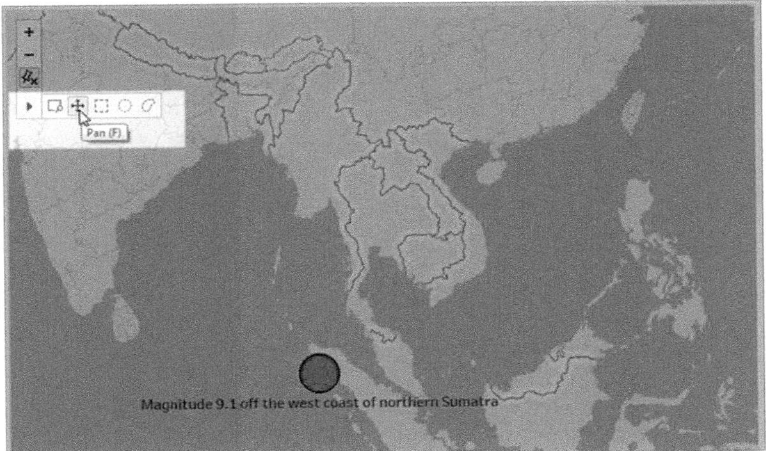

5. Add caption and description text. For example:

○ Caption: *The Indian Ocean earthquake and tsunami of 2004*

○ Description (Tableau Desktop only): *The 2004 Indian Ocean earthquake was an undersea megathrust earthquake that occurred on 26 December 2004. It is the third largest earthquake ever recorded and had the longest duration of faulting ever observed, between 8.3 and 10 minutes.*

6. Click **Update** to save your changes.

7. Repeat the preceding steps for the Japanese earthquake and tsunami of 2011, using the following as caption and description text.

○ Caption: *The Japanese earthquake and tsunami of 2011*

○ Description (Tableau Desktop only): *The 2011 quake off the coast of Tõhoku was a magnitude 9.0 undersea megathrust earthquake. It was the most powerful known earthquake ever to have hit Japan, and the 5th most powerful earthquake ever recorded.*

Notice that you've already created a compelling visual story using just a single dashboard – all by filtering the data and zooming and panning the map.

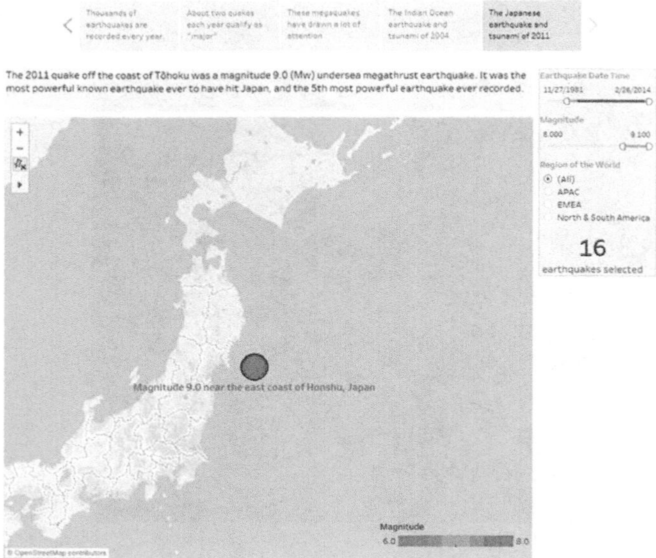

We still haven't answered the key question, however: Are big earthquakes on the rise? The next story points will dig in to that angle.

Show a trend

In the next story point, you'll switch to a line chart (the Timeline dashboard) to show your audience a trend you spotted when you were initially creating views and dashboards.

1. Switch from the story you're building to **Timeline dashboard**.

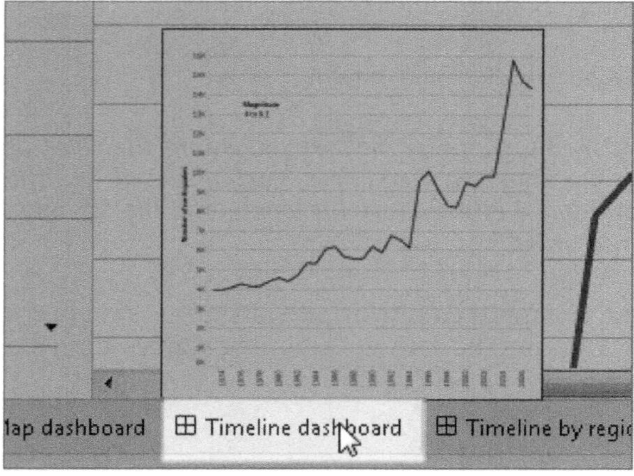

2. On the Timeline dashboard, set size to **Fit to Earthquake story**.

3. Go back to your story and click **Blank** to create a fresh story point.

4. Double-click the **Timeline dashboard** to add it to your story sheet.

More earthquakes are being reported over time since 1973. In fact, it's increased significantly!

5. Add a caption, such as: *More and more earthquakes are being detected*

6. Use **Drag to add text** to add a description of the trend (Tableau Desktop only): *Since 1973, there's been a steady increase in the number of earthquakes recorded. Since 2003, the trend has accelerated.*

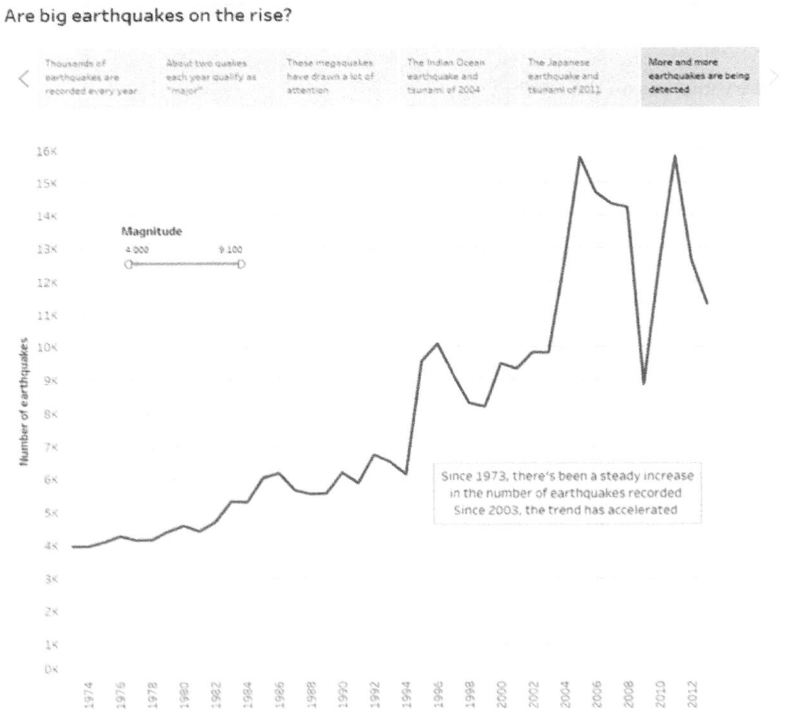

Offer your analysis

From your earlier work in this story with the **Map dashboard** you know that there are regional differences in earthquake frequency. In your next story point, you'll pull in the **Timeline by region dashboard**, which breaks out earthquakes by region, and adds trend lines, which help reduce the variability in the data.

1. Click **Blank** to create a new story sheet.

2. Double-click the **Timeline by region dashboard** to the story sheet. The APAC region clearly stands out.

3. Add a caption then use **Drag to add text** to add a comment that points out the large number of earthquakes in the APAC region.

○ Caption: *Especially on the eastern side of the Pacific Rim*

○ Description (Tableau Desktop only): *A rough categorization of earthquakes into geographic regions (by longitude) shows that the most significant increase in recorded earthquakes has occurred around the Pacific Rim.*

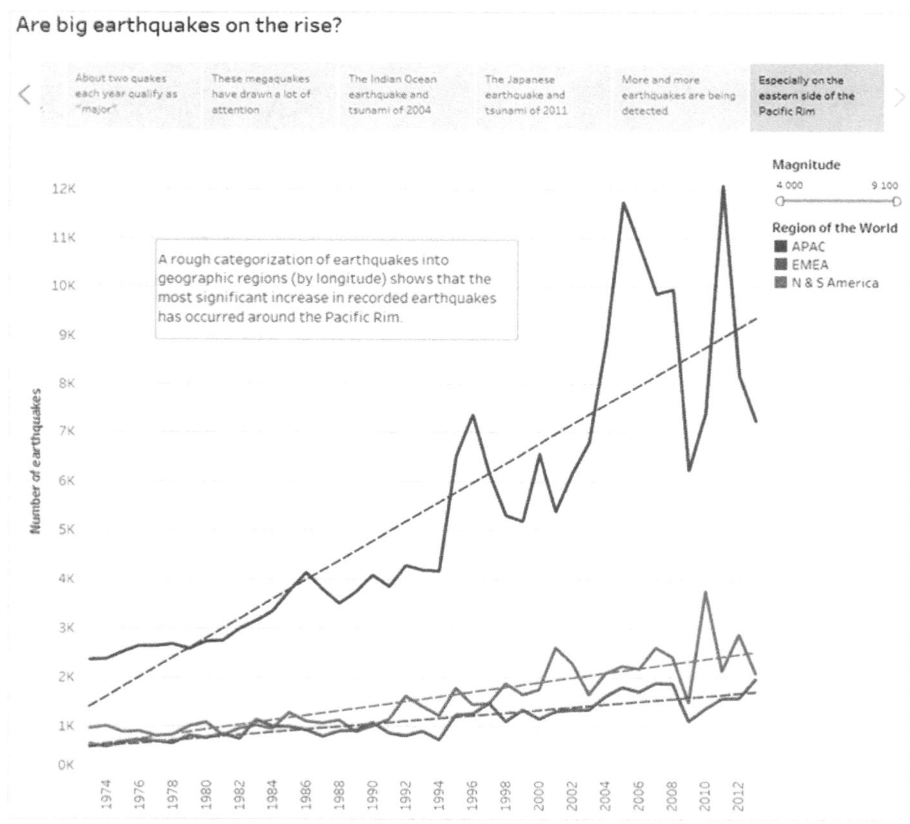

Answer the question

Thus far, your data story has concluded that earthquake frequency in the Pacific Rim has increased since 1973, but your original question was about whether big earthquakes are becoming more frequent.

To answer this question, in your final story point, you'll filter out weaker earthquakes and see what the resulting trend line is.

1. Click **Duplicate** to create a new story sheet.

2. Set the **Magnitude** filter to **5.000–9.100**. Notice how the trend lines have flattened out but there's still a slight increase.

3. Add a caption then use **Drag to add text** to add your answer to the story point.

Caption: *But the trend in big quakes is not as clear*

Description (Tableau Desktop only): *It appears that big earthquakes are increasing slightly. There should be more investigation, however, on whether this trend is real or the result of a small number of exceptionally strong recent earthquakes.*

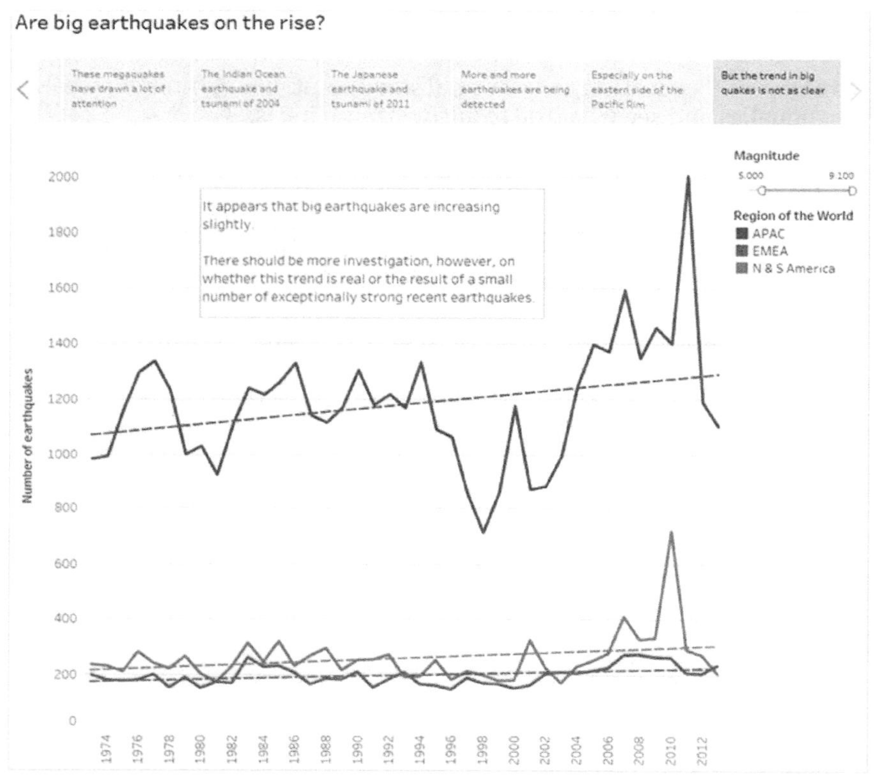

As is often the case with a data story, the story ends with additional questions.

Yes, there's a trend, but it's slight. More big earthquakes (magnitude 5.000 - 9.100) have been reported in recent years, especially in the Asia-Pacific region, but could that be natural variation? That might be a good topic for another story.

Chapter 11
Optimizing Workbook Performance

Optimize Workbook Performance

When we mention *performance*, we mean the speed with which you can work in Tableau. It might mean the speed of data analysis, such as working in Tableau Desktop on a large corporate database that you are accessing remotely. Or, it could refer to the speed of loading views or dashboards that you access on your desktop from Tableau Server.

If you are working with small data volumes, many of the recommendations in this section are optional for you. Your workbook performance is probably as speedy as you expect. But if you work with hundreds of millions of records, designing an efficient workbook is critically important to the speed at which you can work.

Making performance improvements almost always means making trade-offs. For example: Do you sacrifice speed to make sure you have the most current data? Is it important to include *all* the data for analysis, or will a speedier subset do? The bigger and more complicated the data, the longer it takes to interpret and render. But there are things you can do to accelerate the process. Think of fine-tuning your workbook performance as working on a puzzle with multiple pieces. Pick and choose from the topics in this section to find the pieces that solve your particular puzzle.

The topics in this section on performance discuss the big picture and then drill down to specific functionality. It starts with databases, data and extracts, and then focuses on things that affect your data source, your workbooks, your calculations and visualizations.

Know Your Data at the Database Level

Understanding the impact that certain factors in the design of your database have on Tableau performance might give you information you can use to work with your database team to optimize data at the database level.

Enable support for referential integrity

Databases that support referential integrity support the Tableau Assume Referential Integrity feature, which improves the performance of inner joins. Joins cost time and resources to process on the database server.

When you join multiple tables in a data source, Tableau uses functionality that is generally invisible to the user, called *join culling*. Join culling queries only the relevant tables instead of all tables defined in your join. Join culling only occurs where referential integrity is defined between tables.

Make sure database permissions support creating temp tables

Does your database grant users permission to create and drop temporary tables, also known as temp tables, and does the environment have sufficient spool space for the queries being run? Tableau creates temp tables to help improve performance and add functionality. The temp tables temporarily hold information specific to a connection. If the creation of temp tables in the database is restricted, the overall performance of workbooks and views isn't as fast as it could be.

Create indexes for tables

Index the tables in your relational database. To successfully index your data set, identify the fields that you frequently filter on and add them to the index. If you have a field that you use as a context filter often, consider setting it as your primary index. If you are working with Access tables that have more than 200,000 rows of data, consider setting indexes on the tables. You can learn how to do this by searching for "index" in the Access online help. You can officially store 2 GB of data (approximately 1-2 million rows) in an Access database, but it performs poorly well below this limit.

Many database management system (DBMS) environments have management tools that will look at a query and recommend indexes that would help.

Break up your data

You can often improve performance if you partition a large database table into multiple smaller tables. For example, you can create a cluster of Access tables that addresses specific subsets of your data.

Use a database server

If you have a lot of data, you might consider storing it in a database server, such as Oracle, MySQL or Microsoft SQL Server. The Professional Edition of Tableau can connect to these larger database servers.

Test Your Data and Use Extracts

You probably have no control over the hardware, processing power, and disk space that your database runs on. Or how many people access the database at any given time, how many services are running, or how robust the network is. But you can test the *raw performance* of the data before you begin to build a workbook, so that you understand the environment you're working in. And there are things you can do to affect the performance of the workbooks you create, starting with how you choose to connect to your data: the drivers you use, and whether your connection type is *live* or *extract*.

Test as close to the data as possible

A good way to test the raw performance of the data is to install Tableau Desktop on the computer where the data resides and to run some queries. This eliminates external factors such as network bandwidth and latency from performance results, and help you to understand the raw performance of the query in the data source.

Additionally, you can use the *localhost* name for the data instead of the DNS name to help determine if environmental factors such as slow name resolution or proxy servers are slowing performance.

Connect with native database drivers

When you connect to data with native database drivers, you will often experience significantly faster performance than when you connect to the same data with ODBC drivers. When you use native database drivers, make sure that you're using the latest version. Database vendors are always working to improve their drivers.

Work with extracts instead of live data

Depending on your data, you can choose between a live or extract connection on the data source page. A *live* connection is a direct connection to your data. A Tableau data *extract* is a compressed snapshot of data stored locally and loaded into memory as required to render a Tableau visualization. Extracts are designed to use all parts of your computer's memory optimally.

There are several reasons to use an extract, but the main performance-related reason is if your query execution is slow. The extract data format is designed to provide a fast response to analytic queries. In this case, you can think of the extract as a query acceleration cache.

Reduce the amount of data

When you create an extract, use filters to exclude data that you don't need. Also, ask yourself if you need all of the records in a data source, or if you can limit the extract to a representative sample.

Hide unused fields

Hidden fields are not included when you create an extract. Use the **Hide All Unused Fields** option to hide unnecessary fields before you create an extract. This makes the extract smaller, which improves performance.

Optimize extracts

The **Compute Calculations Now** option materializes calculations in your extract, meaning that certain calculations are computed in advance and their values are stored in the extract. Depending on the complexity of the calculations used in your extract, this can potentially speed up future queries.

To materialize calculations, select a data source on the Data menu and then select Extract > Compute Calculations Now.

Use extracts for file-based data

In general it's best practice to import file-based data – text files such as CSV, Microsoft Excel spreadsheets, and Microsoft Access files, as well as statistical files like SPSS, SAS, and R – into Tableau. This makes queries perform much faster and also results in a much smaller file to store the data values.

If your data is a large text or Excel file, using an extract not only improves performance but also makes more functionality available to you. Note that if you connect Tableau to a large text file, you will be prompted to extract the data if Tableau discovers that the file is too large to perform well.

Avoid using custom SQL

In most cases, custom SQL runs slower than queries created by Tableau. Tableau cannot perform query optimizations on custom SQL. But in cases where you must use custom SQL, use an extract so that the query runs only once..

Create Efficient Combined Data Sources

Now that you've made the initial connection to your data, consider how you set up your data source – especially how you combine data – to make it efficient.

If your analysis requires data from different databases, including different workbooks or files, you should consider the impact of relating, joining or blending your data. Combined data sources require more processing power and take more time to execute.

A key factor in efficiency is reducing the amount of data you analyze.

Should I relate, join or blend my data?

The default method of combining tables is with relationships. There are many aspects of relationships that make them efficient and performant. If you need to join or blend instead, make sure you truly do need to use those methods instead of a relationship.

When you consider joining tables or blending tables, think about where the data is coming from, the number of connections and the number of records you have. If the workbook uses multiple tables from the same database, relating or joining the tables can improve performance and filtering control.

Combine tables carefully

Limit data sources to the fewest number of tables possible. In cases where you need access to many tables in a workbook, you may want to create separate data sources tailored to each analytical scenario.

Blending queries the data from both data sources at the level of the linking fields, and then merges the results of both queries together in memory. For this reason, best practice is to avoid data blending on dimensions with many unique values (for example, Order ID, Customer ID or exact date/time).

Design for Performance While You Build a View

You're connected to your data, and you've built your data source. The next step is to begin building a view in Tableau. There are a few things to keep in mind as you build your workbook so that it will perform faster while you're building it, as well as after it is created.

Use the Describe field to get to know your data

Rather than dragging a dimension out onto the rows shelf so that you can eyeball the data – which requires Tableau to render the data as a crosstab, one of the slowest visualization types – use the **Describe field** option. Right-click the field in the **Data** pane to view a description of the data type as reported by the data source, as well as a sample of the dimension member values.

Keep workbooks a reasonable size

The fewer worksheets and data sources in a workbook, the faster it will perform. If you have a big topic to explore and are tempted to put everything into a single monolithic workbook, reconsider. Notice if your workbook starts to slow down with the addition of a new view and additional queries. If the performance starts to suffer as you enlarge the scope of your workbook, think about breaking your workbook into separate files.

Turn off Automatic Updates

When you place a field on a shelf, Tableau generates the view by automatically querying the data. If you are creating a dense data view, the queries might be time-consuming and significantly degrade system performance. In this case, you can turn off queries in Tableau while you build the view. You can then turn queries back on when you are ready to see the result.

Look for warnings

Tableau displays a performance warning dialog box when you attempt to place a large dimension (with many members) on any shelf. The dialog box provides four choices, as shown below. If you choose to add all members, then you might experience a significant degradation in performance.

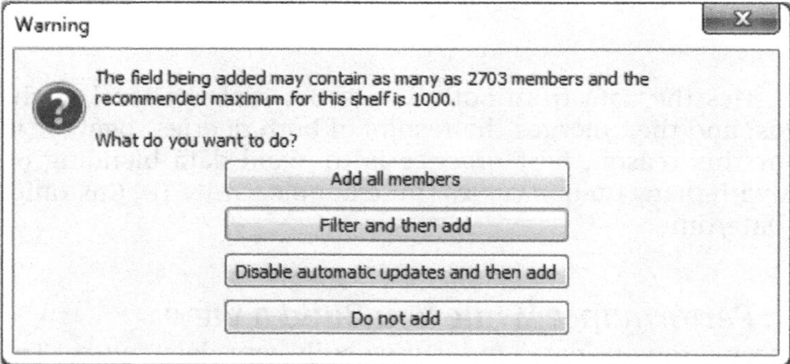

You might also see a warning when you attempt to create too many panes in a table. In this case, Tableau warns you that the requested table "contains more than the recommended maximum number of panes". It is best not to display more than the recommended number of panes, in part because you won't get a useful view.

Chapter 12
Saving And Publishing Your Work

Save Your Work

You can save your work at any time while analyzing or interacting with data in Tableau.

For Tableau Desktop

In Tableau Desktop, there are several ways to save your work:

Automatically save a workbook – Automatically saves the workbook in the same location as the original file. In the event of a crash, a recovered version is available.

Save a workbook – Saves all open worksheets.

Save a packaged workbook – Saves the workbook along with all referenced local file data sources and images into a single file.

Save a bookmark – Saves the current worksheet.

You can share workbooks and bookmarks with your co-workers, provided they can access the relevant data sources that the workbook uses. If your co-workers do not have access to the data sources, you can save a packaged workbook.

Custom fields such as binned measures, calculated fields, groups, and sets are saved with workbooks and bookmarks.

Automatically save a workbook

Tableau Desktop automatically saves your work for you every few minutes – no more losing hours of work if Tableau Desktop closes unexpectedly. This feature is enabled by default, but you can turn it off from the toolbar under **Help >Settings and Performance>Enable Autosave.**

If Tableau crashes, a recovered version of the workbook is automatically created with a .twbr extension and saved in the same location as the original file or in your **My Tableau Repository/Workbooks** folder. New workbooks are saved with the name "Book1" plus a numeric ID. When you reopen Tableau, a recovery dialog box shows a list of the recovered files that you can select and open to continue in your flow.

You can also delete unwanted files from this same dialog box.

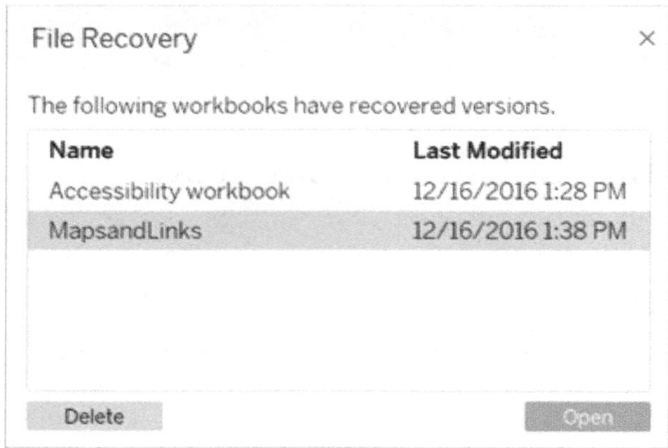

Save a workbook

When you open Tableau Desktop, it automatically creates a new workbook. Workbooks hold the work you create and consist of one or more worksheets. Each worksheet contains a particular view of your data.

To save a Tableau workbook:

Select File > Save.

Specify the workbook file name in the Save As dialog box.

By default, Tableau saves the file with the .twb extension. By default, Tableau saves your workbook in the Workbooks folder in your My Tableau Repository. You can find this repository in your Documents folder. However, you can save Tableau workbooks to any directory you choose.

Tableau file names cannot include any of the following characters: forward slash (/), backslash (\), greater-than sign (>), less-than sign (<), asterisk (*), question mark (?), quotation mark ("), pipe symbol (|), colon (:), or semicolon (;).

To save a copy of a workbook you have open:

Select File > Save As and save the file with a new name.

Save a packaged workbook

Packaged workbooks contain the workbook along with a copy of any local file data sources and background images. The workbook is no longer linked to the original data sources and images. These workbooks are saved with a .twbx file extension. Other users can open the packaged workbook using Tableau Desktop or Tableau Reader, and do not need access to the data sources that the workbook includes.

Save a bookmark

You can save a single worksheet as a Tableau bookmark. When you save the bookmark, Tableau creates a snapshot of the worksheet. Bookmarks can be accessed from any workbook using the Bookmarks menu. When you open a bookmarked worksheet, it adds the worksheet to your workbook in the state that it was in when it was bookmarked. It will never update or change automatically. Bookmarks are convenient when you have worksheets that you use frequently.

To save a Tableau bookmark:

Select **Window** > **Bookmark** > **Create Bookmark**.

Specify the bookmark file name and location in the Create Bookmark dialog box.

Tableau saves the file with a .tbm extension. The default location is the Bookmarks folder in the Tableau Repository. However, you can save bookmarks to any location you choose. Bookmarks that are not stored in the Tableau repository do not appear on the **Bookmark** menu.

You can organize bookmarks into folders in the same way you organize files or documents. This can be useful when you have a large number of bookmarks to manage. For example, you might organize bookmarks based on employee name, product types, or sales results. You can organize bookmarks by creating a new folder, renaming an existing folder, renaming existing bookmark files, and so on.

Delete bookmarks the same way as you would delete any other file on your computer. After you delete a bookmark from the Bookmarks folder in the Tableau Repository, it is removed from the **Bookmarks** menu the next time you start Tableau.

Note: While bookmarks are generally a snapshot of the worksheet and include the data connection, formatting, etc., a bookmark does not include parameter values and the current page setting on the Pages shelf.

For web authoring

When creating, editing, and interacting with views on Tableau Server or Tableau Online, there are a couple of different ways that you can save your work:

Save a workbook - saves a workbook in the project you specify.

Save a copy of a workbook - saves a copy of the workbook in the project you specify.

Save changes as a custom view - saves changes as a custom view, which is related to the original view and updates when the original view is updated.

Save a workbook

When you create a new workbook, or edit an existing workbook on Tableau Server or Tableau Online, you can save your work at any time.

To save a workbook:

In web editing mode, select **File** > **Save**.

Note: If the workbook has never been saved, you must select **File** > **Save As**.

Save a copy of an existing workbook

Sometimes you don't want to overwrite an existing view with your changes. In cases like these, you can save a copy of an existing workbook. When you do this, the existing workbook remains unchanged, and a copy of it is created for you to edit as you wish.

To save a copy of a workbook:

In web editing mode, select File > Save As.

In the Save Workbook dialog box that opens, do the following:

For Name: Enter a name for the workbook.

For Project: Select the project in which you would like to save the workbook.

(Optional) Select Show sheets as tabs to display all worksheets, dashboards, and stories in the workbook as separate tabs.

Click **Save**.

Save changes as a custom view

If you notice you are making the same changes to a view every time you open it, you might want to consider saving the changes as a custom view. This option is not available in web editing mode, but can be accessed when you open a view to interact with it.

A custom view does not change the original, but is related to it. If the original view is updated or republished, the custom view is also updated.

You can also choose whether your custom views are visible to other users (public), or only to you (private).

Packaged Workbooks

Workbooks often reference external resources. For example, workbooks might reference background images or local file data sources such as Excel files, Access files, and Tableau extract files (.hyper or .tde).

When you save a workbook, links to these resources are also saved. The next time you open the workbook, the views are automatically updated with any changes that may have occurred to the data and images. In most cases, you will want to save the workbook in this way. But if you plan to share the workbook with someone who does not have access to the referenced resources or to Tableau Server, you might want to save a packaged workbook instead.

Packaged workbooks contain the workbook along with a copy of any local file data sources and background images. The workbook is no longer linked to the original data sources and images. These workbooks are saved with a .twbx file extension. Other users can open the packaged workbook using Tableau Desktop or Tableau Reader.

Create a .twbx with file-based data sources

Select **File** > **Save As**.

Specify a file name for the packaged workbook in the Save As dialog box.

Select **Tableau Packaged Workbooks** on the **Save as type** drop-down list.

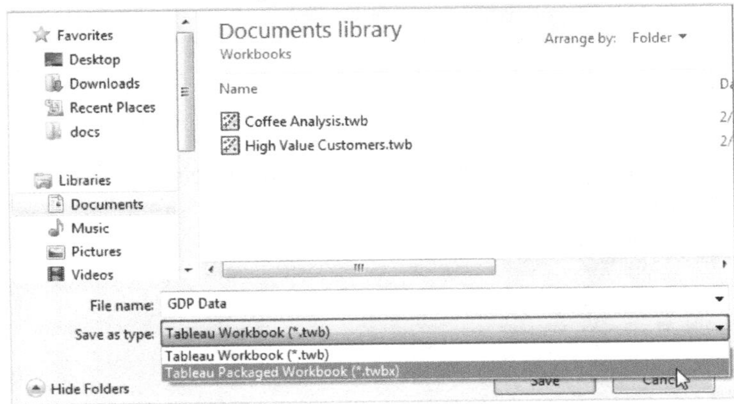

Click **Save**.

The default location is the **Workbooks** folder of the Tableau repository. However, you can save packaged workbooks to any directory you choose.

The following files are included in packaged workbooks:

Background images

Custom geocoding

Custom shapes

Local cube files

Microsoft Access files

Microsoft Excel files

Tableau extract files (.hyper or .tde)

Text files (.csv, .txt, etc.)

Create a .twbx with non-file-based data sources

If the workbook contains connections to enterprise data sources or other non-file-based data sources, such as Microsoft SQL, Oracle, or MySQL, the data must be extracted from the data sources for it to be included in a packaged workbook (.twbx).

In the workbook, right-click the data source in the Data pane and choose **Extract Data**.

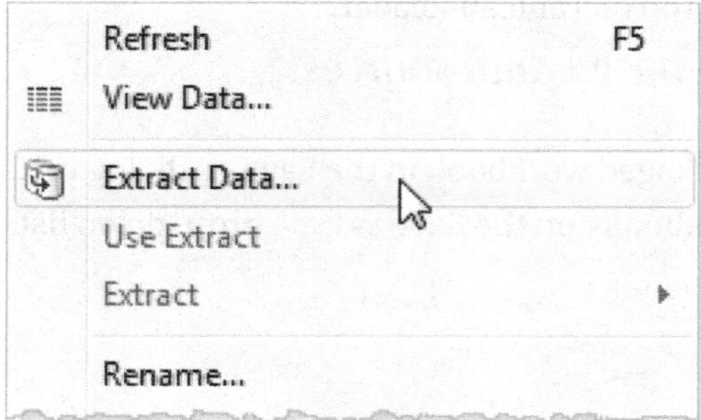

In the Extract Data dialog box, click the Extract button to extract all data from the data source.

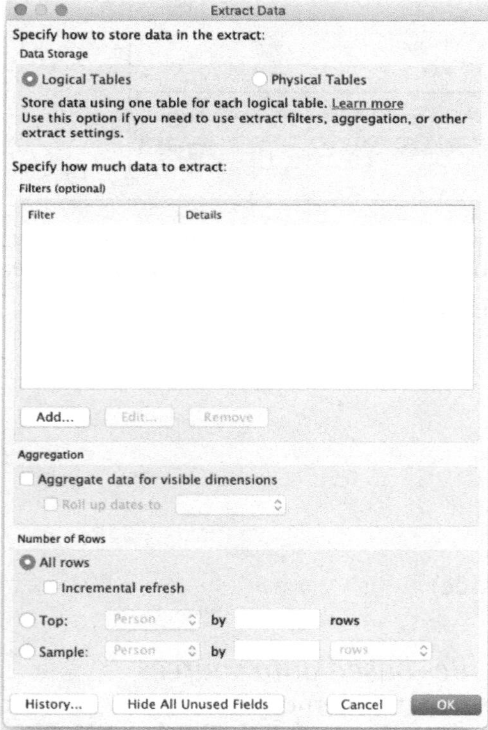

After the extract completes, the data source icon changes to indicate that an extract is active for that data source. Instead of a single cylinder, there are two cylinders connected by an arrow.

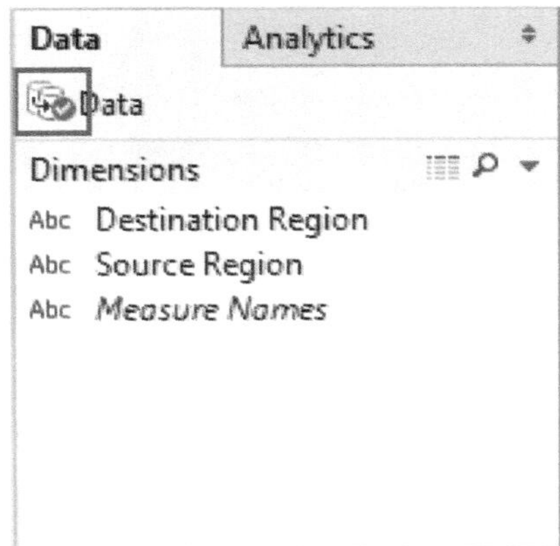

Optional: Repeat the above steps for each data source in the workbook.

Select File > Save As.

From the Save as type drop-down menu, select Tableau Packaged Workbook (*.twbx).

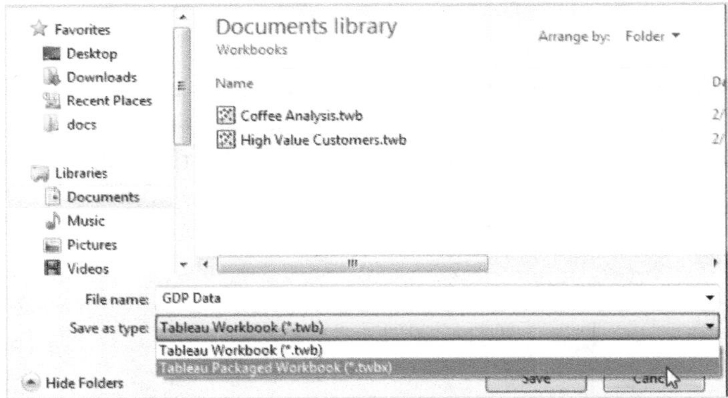

After the extracts have been created for all non-file-based data sources and the packaged workbook has been saved, you can send your workbook.

Create a .twbx with Tableau Server data sources

If the workbook contains connections to a published Tableau Server data source, you must download a local copy of the Tableau Server data source, take an extract of it, and then replace the connection to the local copy for it to be included in a packaged workbook (.twbx).

In the workbook, right-click the published data source in the Data pane, and then select Create Local Copy.

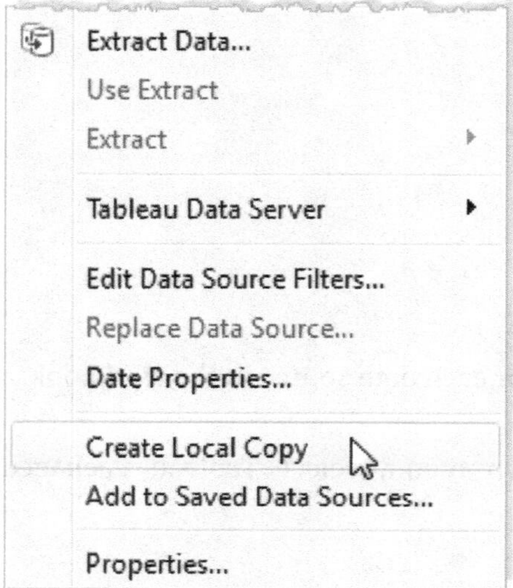

A copy of the published data source is added to the Data pane.

Right-click the local copy, and select Extract Data. **Note:** If the local copy is a published extract you can skip this step.

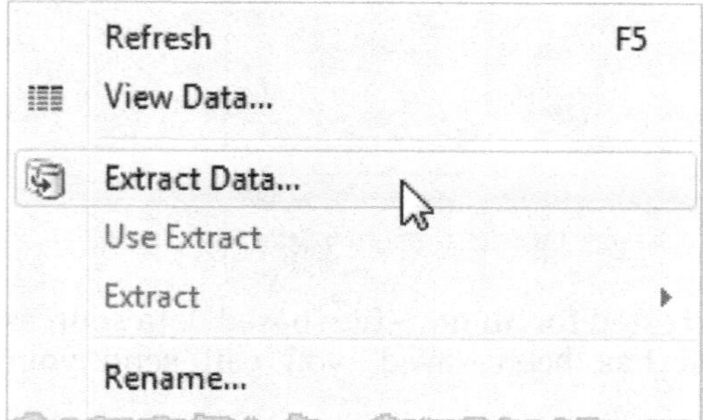

In the Extract Data dialog box, click the Extract button to extract all data from the data source. Creating an extract of the data source allows the person you are sharing the workbook with to have access to a copy of the data source.

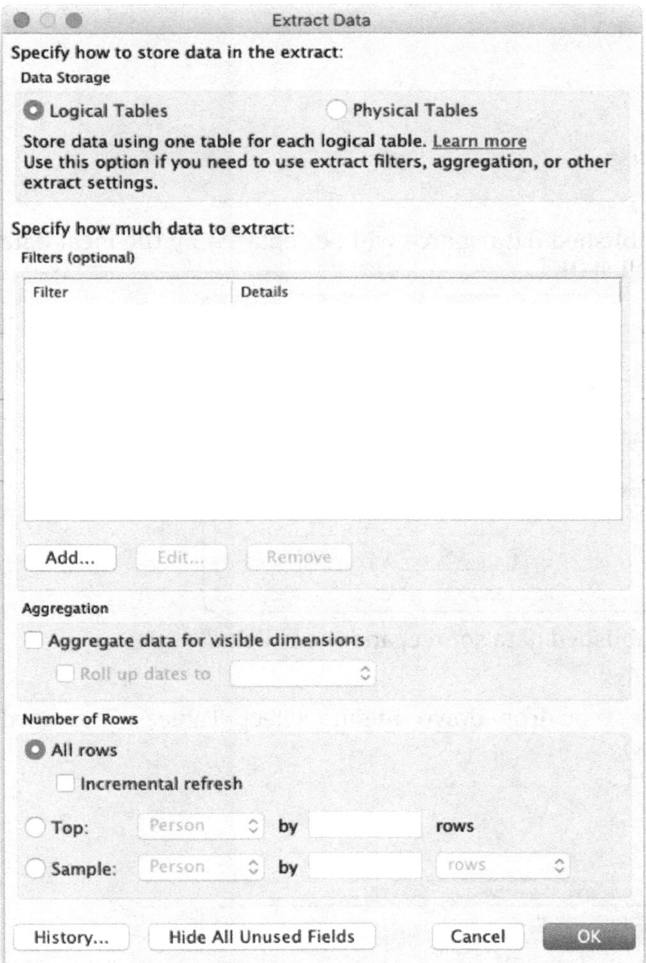

In the Data pane, right-click the published data source, and then select Replace Data Source.

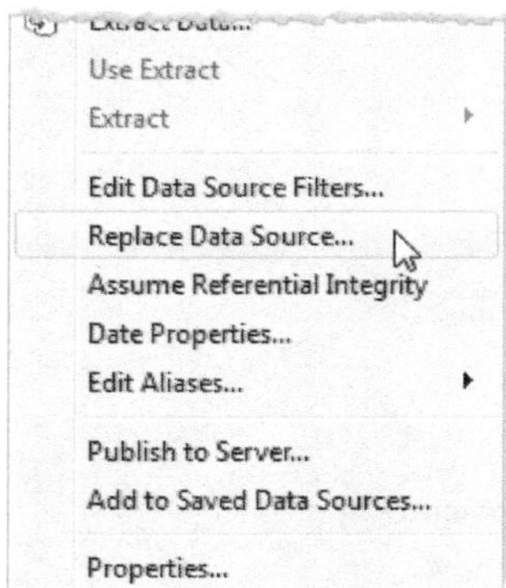

Verify that the published data source will be replaced by the local data source, and then click OK.

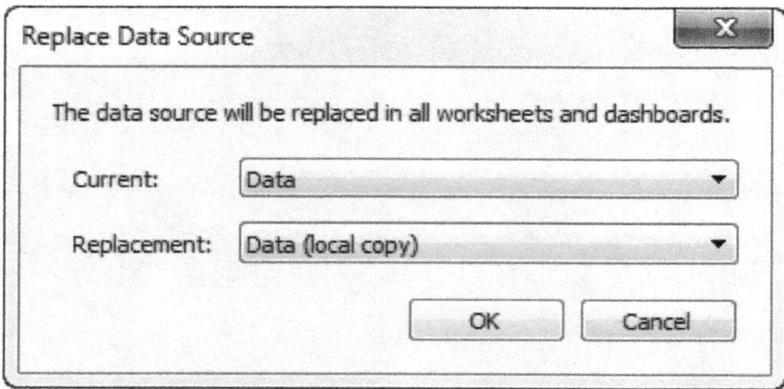

Right-click the published data source, and then click Close.

Select File > Save As.

From the Save as type drop-down menu, select Tableau Packaged Workbook (*.twbx).

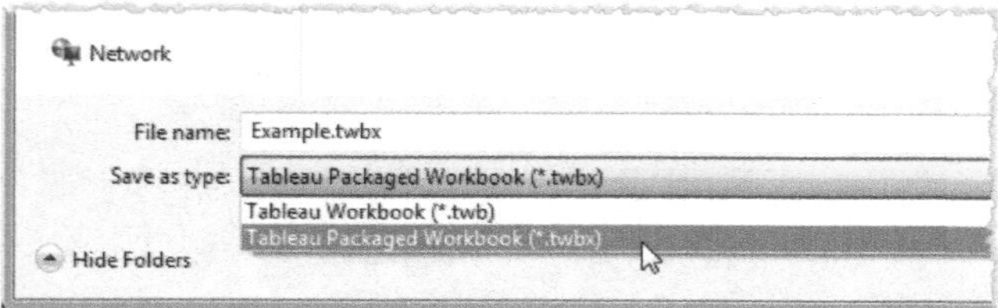

After the local copy and extract of the local copy is created and the packaged workbook saved, you can send your workbook.

Unpackage a .twbx

Packaged workbooks can be unpackaged.

On a Windows or macOS computer, rename the file with a .zip extension (for example, from myfile.twbx to myfile.zip) and then double-click it.

When you unpackage a workbook, you get a regular workbook file (.twb), along with a folder that contains the data sources and images that were packaged with the workbook.

Save Workbooks to Tableau Public

If you want to share your data discoveries with the world outside of your organization, you can save your workbook to Tableau Public, a free cloud service. On Tableau Public, anyone can interact with your views, or download your workbooks or data sources.

Save a workbook

With your workbook open in Tableau Desktop, select Server > Tableau Public > Save to Tableau Public.

Note: This option is available only if you've created a viz that contains at least one field.

Sign in using your Tableau Public account.

If you don't have an account, select the link to create a new one.

Type a name for the workbook and click Save.

When you save a workbook to Tableau Public, the publishing process creates an extract of the data connection.

Tip: The title becomes part of your view's metadata. Use a unique title that will help others find it when they search. (The title shown in the image is a good example of how *not* to name your workbook.)

After the workbook is published, you are redirected to your account on the Tableau Public website

On your profile page on Tableau Public, do any of the following to customize your profile:

Hover the pointer over a viz to get access to actions such as selecting it as your featured viz, or hiding, downloading or deleting it.

Hover the pointer over a viz and then select View to open the viz's home page. There you can select Edit Details to customize metadata such as workbook name and description, add a permalink, and change other settings.

To get a link to share on social media or code to embed in a web page, display a view, and then click Share at the bottom of the view. (You can get links and embed code for other Tableau Public users' views this way, too.)

Revert a Workbook to the Last Saved Version

You can revert a workbook at anytime to undo all of the changes you've made to it since you last saved it.

To revert to the last saved version of a workbook:

In Tableau Desktop, select **File** > **Revert to Saved**, and then select **Revert** in the warning dialog box that opens.

In web authoring mode, select **File** > **Revert**.

The Revert command is only available for workbooks (.twb) that do not have connections to Extract data sources.

Export Views from Tableau Desktop to Another Application

There are several ways to get views and workbooks out of Tableau Desktop and into a presentation, report, or web page.

Copy a view as an image

You can quickly copy an individual view as an image and paste it into another application, such as Microsoft Word or Excel. If you're using Tableau Desktop on macOS, a TIFF (Tagged Image File Format) image is copied to the clipboard. On Windows, a BMP (Bitmap) image is copied.

Select **Worksheet** > **Copy** > **Image**.

In the Copy Image dialog box, select the elements you want to include in the image. If the view contains a legend, under Image Options, select the legend layout.

Click **Copy**.

Open the target application and paste the image from the clipboard.

Export a view as an image file

To create an image file you can reuse, export the view rather than copy it. You can choose BMP, JPEG or PNG format on macOS, with the additional option of EMF on Windows. Note, however, that EMF format substitutes Tableau fonts (Tableau Regular, Tableau Semibold, etc.) with a similar font.

Select **Worksheet** > **Export**> **Image**.

In the Export Image dialog box, select the elements you want to include in the image. If the view contains a legend, under Image Options, select the legend layout.

Click **Save**.

In the Save Image dialog box, specify a file location, name and format. Then click **Save**.

Export as a PowerPoint presentation

When you export a workbook to Microsoft PowerPoint format, selected sheets become static PNG images on separate slides. If you export a story sheet, all story points export as separate slides. Any filters currently applied in Tableau are reflected in the exported presentation.

Tip: To optimize a dashboard for PowerPoint, on the Dashboard tab, choose **Size** > **Fixed Size** > **PowerPoint (1600 x 900)**.

To export a workbook to PowerPoint:

Select File > Export as PowerPoint.

Select the sheets you want to include in the presentation. (Hidden sheets can also be included.)

The exported PowerPoint file reflects the file name of your workbook, and the title slide states the workbook name and the date the file was generated.

Tip: Choose **File** > **Page Setup** to show or hide titles, views, legends and captions for an individual sheet. (These options in the Show section aren't available for dashboards.)

Export to PDF

To create a vector-based file that embeds the Tableau fonts, print to PDF. After customising the layout of page elements using the File > Page Setup dialog, choose File > Print to PDF.

Export Data from Tableau Desktop

You can export the data in a Tableau data source, including all or part of the records from your original data. Alternatively, you can export only the portion of data used to generate the view.

Export data in the data source

After you join tables from one or more connections and make general customizations (for example, create a calculated field, pivot fields, create groups, apply data source or extract filters, etc.) to your Tableau data source, you might want to share or reuse the data in its new form.

Export your data to .csv file

Because the .csv format is one of the most simple structured formats for data, it is supported by a wide range of tools, databases, and programming languages. Exporting your data in the Tableau data source using this format creates an independent data set and can be a convenient and flexible way to share your data with others.

There are two primary ways you can export your data in the data source to a .csv file in Tableau: from the Data Source page and from the view.

From the Data Source page: On the Data Source page, select Data > Export Data to CSV to export all the data in your data source to .csv file.

From the view: On the sheet tab, drag a field to the Columns or Rows shelf, click the View Data icon in the Data pane, and click the Export All button.

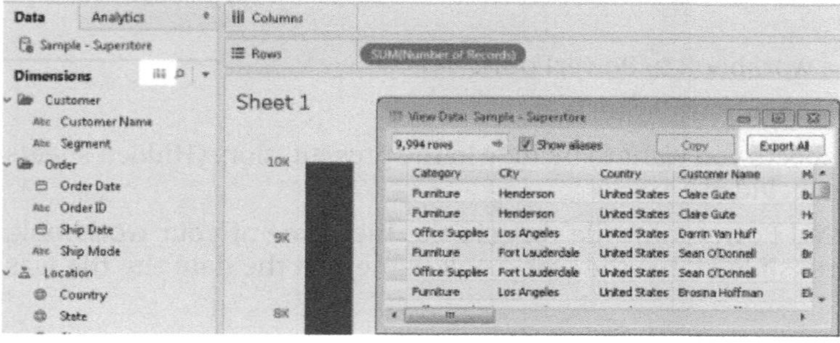

Extract your data

Another way to export all of your data or a subset of your data in the data source is to create an extract (.hyper) file. An extract functions as an independent data set, which you can use to connect directly from Tableau.

Export the data source

After you connect to your data, you can export and save your data source as a Tableau data source (.tds) file. Saving the data source creates a shortcut to your remote data and allows you to avoid having to create a new connection to a specific data set each time.

Export data used in the view

After you create a view, you can also export just the data used to generate that view.

The fields that are exported come from the fields on the shelves of the sheet. However, fields that function as external filters, in other words, the fields that appear only on the Filters shelf, are not included in the export. If you want to include other fields with the exported data without changing the baseline view, you can place those fields on the Detail shelf.

Export data in the view to Microsoft Access or .csv

Export the data that is used to generate the view as an Access database (Windows only) or .csv file (Mac only).

In Tableau Desktop, select Worksheet > Export > Data.

Select a location and type a name for your Access database or .csv file.

Click Save.

If you're on Windows, the Export Data to Access dialog box displays to give you the option to immediately use the new Access database and continue working in Access without interrupting your work flow.

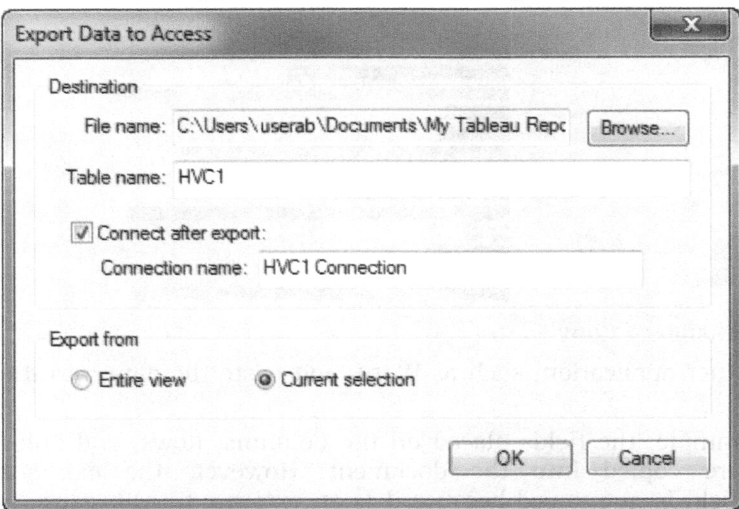

Export crosstab of data in the view to Excel

You can export directly to Excel the data used to generate the view formatted as a crosstab. When you export your view as a crosstab, Tableau automatically opens the Excel application and pastes a crosstab version of the current view into a new Excel workbook.

Although this option provides a direct method for exporting your data to another application, performance of the export can be affected because it is simultaneously copying and formatting the data. If the view you are exporting contains a lot of data, a dialog box opens asking whether you want to export the formatting. In this case, if you choose to exclude the formatting from the export, performance of the export might improve.

In Tableau Desktop: select **Worksheet** > **Export** > **Crosstab to Excel.** If you're using a Mac, this option opens a dialog box where you can save the file. You must then manually open the file in Excel.

In Tableau Server or Tableau Online, open a view or dashboard and select **Download** > **Crosstab.**
Select which sheets from the workbook to export data from.

Copy data in the view to clipboard
Copy the data used to generate the view so that you can paste it into another application.

Create a view.

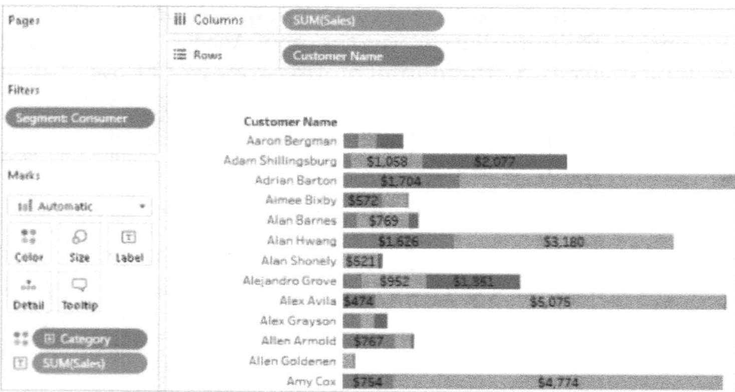

Select **Worksheet** > **Copy** > **Data.**

Open another application, such as Word, and paste the data into the document.

In this example, the fields placed on the Columns, Rows, and Color shelves are copied into the document. However, the **Customer Segment** field is not copied because it is an external filter because it appears only on the Filters shelf.

Category	Customer Name	Sales
Furniture	Aaron Bergman	$391
Furniture	Adam Shillingsburg	$2,077
Furniture	Adrian Barton	$1,280
Furniture	Aimee Bixby	$16
Office Supplies	Aaron Bergman	$274
Office Supplies	Adam Shillingsburg	$1,058

Copy crosstab of data in the view to clipboard

You can copy a crosstab version of a view so that you can paste or transfer the data into another application. The pasted data always appears as a crosstab, even if the initial view of the data in Tableau did not use a crosstab format.

Copying a crosstab is restricted by some general conditions:

You must copy all records in the view. You cannot copy a subset of records.

This option is valid for aggregated views only. It cannot be used on disaggregated views of data because a crosstab is by definition an aggregated view of data. This means the **Aggregate Measures** option on the Analysis menu must be selected in order for copying a crosstab to work properly.

You cannot copy a crosstab if the view contains continuous dimensions such as continuous dates and times.

Other restrictions may apply depending on the data in your view.

After the general conditions are met, copy the crosstab.

Create a view.

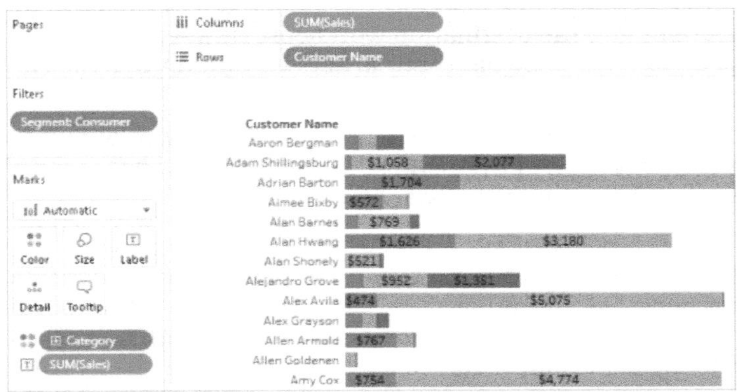

Select **Worksheet > Copy > Crosstab.**

Open another application, such as Excel, and paste the crosstab.

	A	B	C	D	E
1		Category	Category	Category	
2	Customer Name	Furniture	Office Sup	Technology	
3	Aaron Bergman	$391	$274	$222	
4	Adam Shillingsburg	$2,077	$1,058	$120	
5	Adrian Barton	$1,280	$11,489	$1,704	
6	Aimee Bixby	$16	$379	$572	
7	Alan Barnes	$131	$769	$213	

Copying Information Between Workbooks

Individual sheets, dashboards and stories can be copied and pasted between workbooks in Tableau Desktop(although not in web authoring). This feature allows you to easily copy an analysis or port a data source into another workbook. It is also possible to import an entire workbook into your current workbook.

What gets copied or saved with selected sheets

When you copy, save or export selected sheets, the data source or sources that are used on that sheet are also copied. This includes any calculations, parameters, sets, etc. Custom shapes and colors are also included. If the sheet being copied is a dashboard or story, all of the sheets that are used on that dashboard are also copied, whether they are hidden or not.

Custom colors and shapes will be available in the copied or imported sheet but will not be added to your Tableau Repository

How Tableau handles duplicate items

When you paste or import sheets from a different workbook, some items might already exist in the destination workbook, or some items might have the same name in both places. If Tableau encounters an exact duplicate item in the Data pane, such as a calculation, it does not paste or import that item into the destination workbook. However, if an item in the Data pane has the same name but is defined differently, Tableau imports and renames it.

Tableau also pastes or imports sheets and data sources with duplicate names – whether only the name is identical, or their names and contents are identical – and it renames the newer copy.

Copy and paste sheets between workbooks

Copying and pasting sheets is a quick way to combine information from different workbooks or create a new workbook. It is also useful workaround to replace a data source for a single sheet rather than all sheets that use the data source. You can copy one or more sheets from the tabbed sheet view, filmstrip view or sheet sorter view. Use Shift + click or Ctrl + click to select multiple sheets.

To copy and paste a worksheet using the filmstrip view, do the following:

Open a workbook and click the **Filmstrip** button in the status bar.

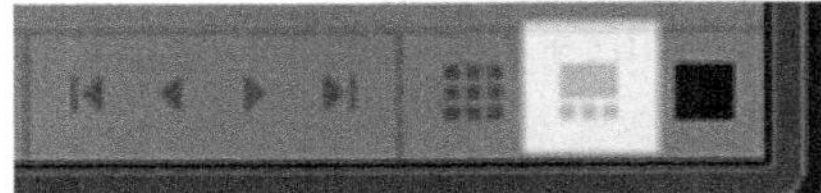

Select the thumbnails of the sheets you want to copy, then right-click (Control-click on Mac) and select **Copy**.

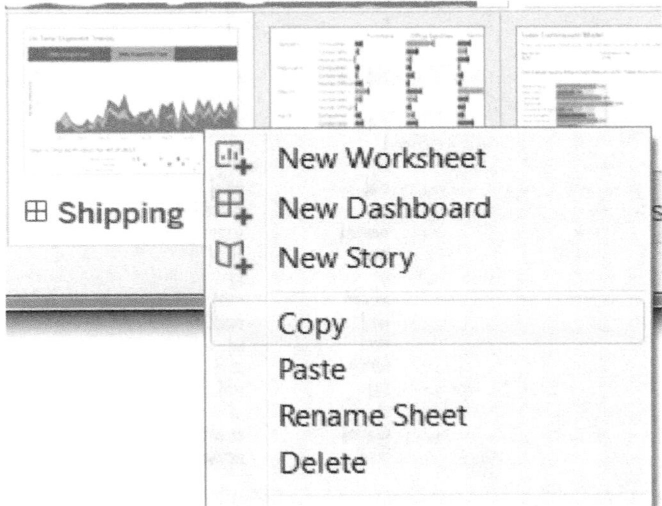

Tableau copies the information in the file format (.twb or .twbx) of the workbook.

Open the destination workbook, or create a new workbook. Right-click (Control-click on Mac) on the tab for any sheet, and select **Paste**.

Pasted sheets are placed after existing worksheets, dashboards, and stories.

Note: The **Paste** option is not available when the active sheet is a story.

Save the changes.

Export and import sheets between workbooks

If you want to extract a subset of information from a larger workbook to maintain as a standalone file, you can export or save selected sheets to a new workbook. You can then import that workbook into an existing one to incorporate its sheets and other objects into the existing workbook.

Open the workbook that contains the sheets you want to export to a new file.

Using the tabbed worksheet, filmstrip view, or sheet sorter view, right-click (Control-click on Mac) the sheet tab or thumbnail view, and then select Export to export a single sheet. Use Shift + click or Ctrl + click to select multiple sheets.

In the Save As dialog box, specify the file format you want to save (.twb or .twbx), select the location for the new workbook file, give it a name, and then click Save.

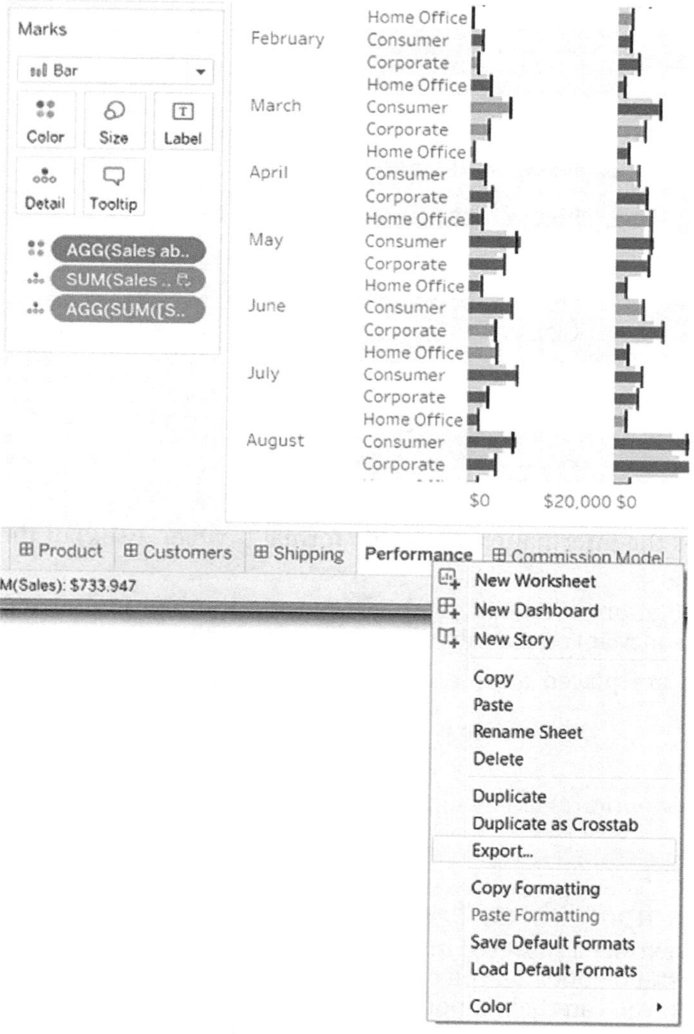

Import an entire Tableau workbook

After you save or export selected sheets to a new workbook (.twb) file, you can import the information into another workbook.

With the existing workbook open, select **File** > **Import Workbook**.

Select the workbook that contains the sheets you saved from another workbook, and click **Open**.

The following image shows the result of importing a workbook that contains a sheet with the same name as a sheet in the existing workbook. Tableau adds a number after the name of the imported sheet.

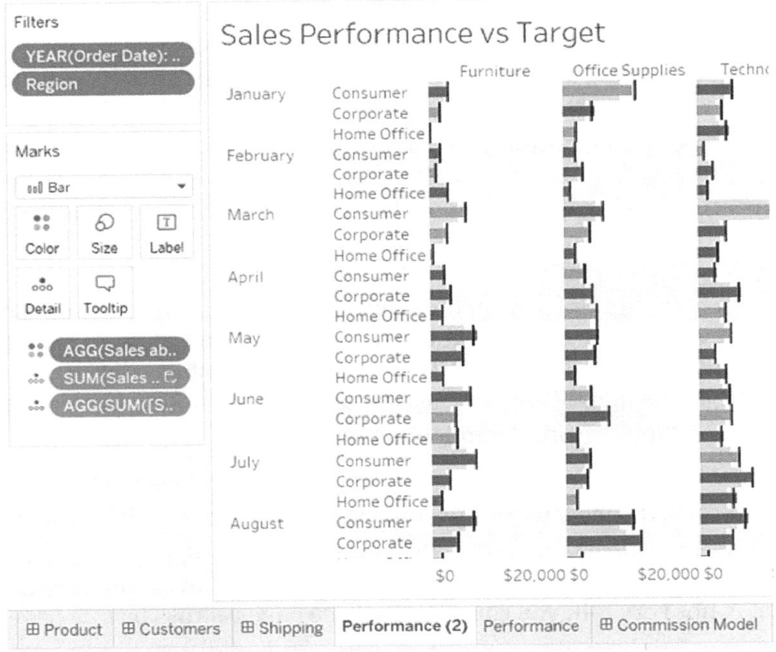

Print Views from Tableau Desktop

Before printing, specify how you want the printed page to look using the Page Setup dialog box. Then print to a printer or PDF.

Set up the page

You can apply different page setup options for each worksheet in a workbook, For example, worksheets can print with titles showing or hidden, with unique page orientation, and more.

To begin, select **File** > **Page Setup**.

General settings (available for individual sheets, not dashboards)

Show - Show or hide the title, view, caption, color legend, shape legend, size legend and map legend.

Headers and Breaks - Control the appearance of these table elements.

Repeat headers and legends on each page – adds table row and column headers at the top of each printed page when a view breaks across several pages.

Break pages on pane boundaries – prevents page breaks in the middle of a table cell.

Pages Shelf - If the view uses the Pages Shelf, specify whether to print the current page or all pages.

Layout settings

Legend Layout - If you include one or more legends, select how you want the legends to appear on the printed page.

Margins - Specify top, bottom, left, and right margins by typing values into the text boxes.

Centring - Optionally, select whether to center the view horizontally or vertically – or both – on the page.

Print Scaling settings

These settings affect only printed documents, not exported images or PDFs. However, the page orientation settings are used as the default when you publish the workbook to Tableau Online or Tableau Server.

Print Scaling - Scale a view to fit within a single page or print across multiple pages. Select from the following options:

Automatic – Scales the view automatically based on the paper size.

Scale to – Scales the view to the specified percentage of its original size.

Fit to – Scales the view to fit within the specified area. Select the number of printed pages across and down. For example, if you have a really wide view that is not very tall, you can specify three pages across by one page down.

Page Orientation - Specify how you want the view oriented on the printed page. Select from the following options:

Use Printer Setting – Use the page orientation that is already specified by the printer.

Portrait – Presents the view so that it is oriented vertically on the printed page.

Landscape – Presents the view so that it is oriented horizontally on the printed page.

The following diagram shows the difference between portrait and landscape page orientations.

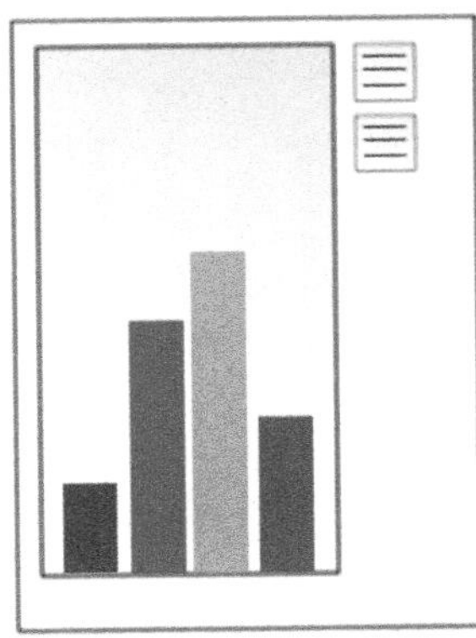
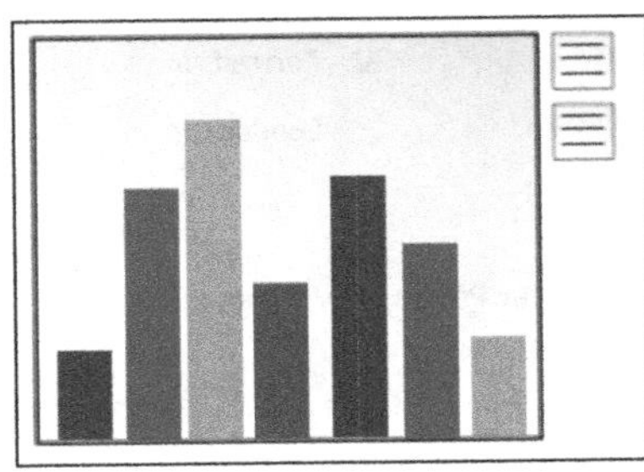

Print a view

After you have configured the Page Setup settings, select File > Print. The following options in the Print dialog box are unique to Tableau.

Show Selections

When this option is selected any selections you've made in the views will be maintained while printing.

Change the Print Range

When you print from a workbook with multiple worksheets, each worksheet represents one or more printed pages, depending on the page setup.

Select from the following print ranges:

Entire Workbook - Prints all the worksheets in the workbook.

Active Sheet - Prints only the sheet currently displayed in the workbook.

Selected Sheets - Prints the selected sheets.

Print to PDF

In Tableau Desktop, you can save views as PDF files rather than printing them as hard copies. You do not need to have Adobe Acrobat installed on your computer.

When you print an individual sheet to PDF, filters in the view are not included. To show filters, create a dashboard containing the sheet and export the dashboard to PDF.

Print to PDF using a Windows computer

Specify page setup options for each sheet in your workbook.

Select File > Print to PDF.

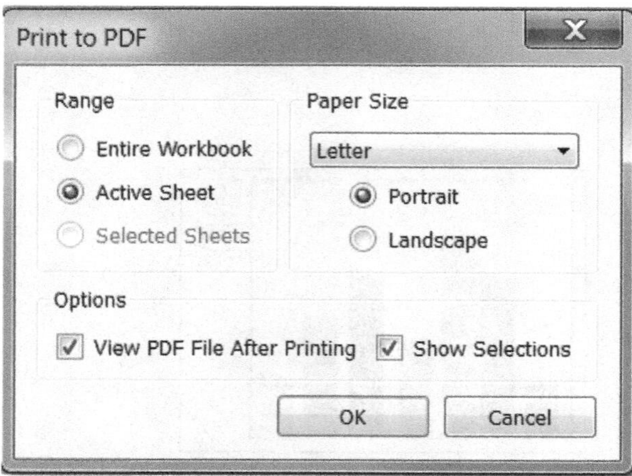

In the Print to PDF dialog box, select the print Range:

Entire Workbook - Publishes all the sheets in the workbook.

Active Sheet - Publishes only the sheet currently displayed in the workbook.

Selected Sheets - Publishes the selected sheets. To select multiple sheets in a Tableau workbook, hold down the Ctrl key as you select sheet tabs along the bottom of the Tableau workbook.

Select a **Paper Size**. If you select Unspecified, the paper size will expand to the necessary size to fit the entire view on a single page.

Select **View PDF File After Printing** if you want to automatically open the PDF after creating it. This option is only available if you have Adobe Acrobat Reader or Adobe Acrobat installed on your computer.

Select whether to **Show Selections**. When this option is selected the selections in the views are maintained in the PDF.

Click **OK** and specify where you want to save the PDF. Then click **Save**.

Print to PDF using a Mac computer

Specify page setup options for each sheet in your workbook.

Select **File** > **Print**.

In the Print dialog box, click **Show Details** to select a print range:

Entire Workbook - Publishes all the sheets in the workbook.

Active Sheet - Publishes only the sheet currently displayed in the workbook.

Selected Sheets - Publishes the selected sheets. To select multiple sheets in a Tableau workbook, hold down the Command key as you select sheet tabs along the bottom of the Tableau workbook.

Click PDF > Save as PDF.

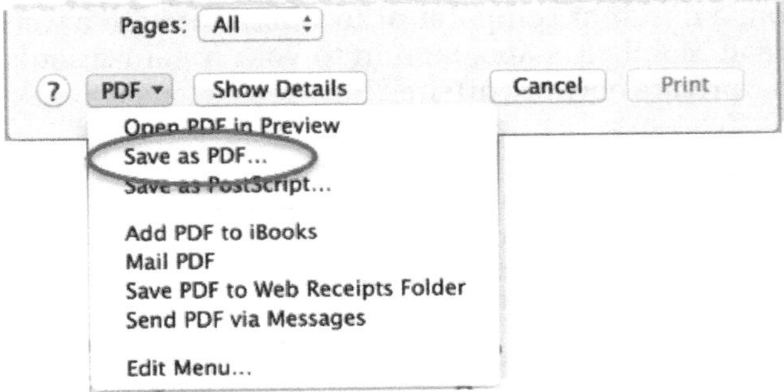

Specify where you want to save the PDF, then click Save.

Publish Data Sources and Workbooks

Suppose you create a view that exposes a new range of questions in the data you're using, and you want to share this analysis with other people using this data. Or maybe you are your team's Data Steward, in charge of building the data models approved for use by analysts, and meeting your organization's requirements for security, compliance, performance and so on.

You can share your work with the rest of your team by publishing it to Tableau Server or Tableau Online. After it's published, you and your team can access it through your web browser or the Tableau mobile app. Publishing data sources can also help you to centralize data management.

Why publish

You can publish data sources and workbooks when you want to widen the audience for your data analysis within your organization. By publishing you can begin to do the following:

Collaborate and share with others

Allow people in your organization to view, interact with, download, subscribe to, share, edit and save published views, even if they do not use Tableau Desktop. Incorporate views into blog posts or websites.

Centralize data and database driver management

Create and publish data models that everyone can use. Centralized data management allows for sharing a single source for your Tableau data. All workbooks connected to the published data reflect updates to it.

In addition, when you publish and connect to data on the server, people connecting to the data from Tableau Desktop do not need to install and maintain database drivers on their own computers.

Support mobility

Access your data from a different computer or location, through a web browser or the Tableau Mobile iOS app. Sign in to your organization's Tableau Server from a private network offsite.

What you can publish

Content types you can publish include:

Data sources: You can publish data sources that others can use to build new workbooks. A data source can contain a direct (or live) connection to your database or an extract you can refresh on a schedule.

Workbooks: Workbooks contain your views, dashboards and stories, and data connection. You can include local resources, such as background images and custom geocoding, if they reside in a location that the server or other Tableau users cannot access.

Who can publish

To publish to Tableau Server or Tableau Online, your server or site administrator must grant you the following capabilities:

A *site role* of **Creator** (formerly Publisher) on the site you're publishing to.

View and **Save** capabilities set to **Allowed** on the project into which you publish.

Summary

Tableau is a powerful and versatile program that you can use to get the most out of the information that your business collects. I hope you've enjoyed learning all about Tableau and that you will soon be on your journey to creating amazing dashboards with great data and analytics insights.

The simple drag-and-drop interface of Tableau allows for anyone with basic data knowledge to create fully interactive dashboards that can be shared with anyone. It is my hope that through this book, we have shown you how you can improve every aspect of your dashboard building.

If you want to take your learning further, do not hesitate to join one of the many groups available online. If you want more practice making amazing dashboards, then you should join the Tableau community-run project, Make over Monday, where a new interesting data set is posted every Monday, and you're invited to make it over. Also be sure to share your dashboards on Tableau Public.

Index

S

T

U

W

Made in the USA
Monee, IL
16 December 2023

49428127R00208